THE NEW INTERNATIONAL COMMENTARY ON THE
NEW TESTAMENT — F. F. Bruce, *General Editor*

COMMENTARY ON THE FIRST EPISTLE TO THE CORINTHIANS

COMMENTARY ON THE FIRST EPISTLE TO THE CORINTHIANS

THE ENGLISH TEXT WITH INTRODUCTION,
EXPOSITION AND NOTES

by

F. W. GROSHEIDE, Th.D.

Professor at the Free University of Amsterdam

WM. B. EERDMANS PUBLISHING COMPANY
GRAND RAPIDS, MICHIGAN

Reprinted, January 1983

ISBN 0-8028-2185

Library of Congress Number 53-8670

PHOTOLITHOPRINTED BY EERDMANS PRINTING COMPANY
GRAND RAPIDS, MICHIGAN, UNITED STATES OF AMERICA

EDITOR'S FOREWORD

It is with special pleasure that I introduce this commentary from the pen of one of my former teachers in the New Testament, Professor Dr. F. W. Grosheide of the Free University of Amsterdam. His readiness to collaborate in the preparation of the new commentary was one of the most encouraging factors in the early development of plans for the *New International Commentary on the New Testament*. And this volume, marked as it is by the reverence, fairness, thoroughness and relevancy characteristic of Dr. Grosheide's work, will prove to be a welcome addition to the exegetical literature devoted to this Epistle.

The General Foreword in the *Commentary on the Gospel of Luke* by Norval Geldenhuys, which was published in America in 1951 as the first completed volume in the new Commentary, has set forth at some length the general character and specifications of the series, and these details need not be repeated here. Due to the distinctiveness of Luke and I Corinthians and of their evaluation in modern times, as well as the individuality of the modern authors, certain differences in treatment appear. But the present work no less than the first published volume achieves the central goal which is to concentrate upon the inspired text and to expound it in a thorough manner.

Since fortunately I Corinthians has almost universally been received as a genuine composition of Paul, and other critical questions have been largely conspicuous by their absence, Dr. Grosheide's Introduction is brief and keeps in view the interests of the general reader. And the Exposition itself proceeds with extraordinary singlemindedness to deal with every minute detail of the text. The author has not chosen to burden his exposition with many references to literature, but those who know the field will readily observe that he writes on the background of a comprehensive knowledge of the modern literature and is taking account of the leading commentaries such as those of Robertson-Plummer and Johannes Weiss.

5

A particularly attractive feature of the interpretation is that, in all of the diversity of the Epistle, a golden thread is discovered which runs throughout and binds the diverse contents into a remarkable unity. The apostolic admonitions are shown to be the result of the application of a single conception of the Christian life to various concrete cases and situations. There is also reflected a recognition on the part of the apostle of the peculiar character of the Corinthian Church. At times, indeed, Paul was concerned with "the weak," whose attitude towards things sacrificed to idols betrayed a failure to grasp the principles of Christian liberty, and again with those whose attitude towards marriage bordered on the ascetic. But the main thrust of the Epistle is directed, according to Dr. Grosheide, against those whose life principles were quite the opposite: the spiritually proud and "puffed-up," who boasted of their "knowledge" and of their "rights." Their temper was expressed in the rule, "All things are lawful unto me," and this declaration of freedom was made the ultimate and only principle of conduct. It is with this fundamental character of the Corinthian Church as a whole in mind that the apostle in various situations teaches that love to God and to one's neighbor must determine when one may exercise his rights and when one must refrain from doing that which in itself is "good." Thus Chapter 9 is not viewed as an isolated defense of Paul's apostleship, but as an appeal to apostolic conduct as an illustration of the principle that one must be prepared to forego one's personal rights when the furtherance of the gospel is at stake. Similarly Chapter 13 is not a parenthetical poem on love, but is introduced as an integral part of Paul's argument in which, while recognizing the divine origin of the charismatic gifts, he is concerned to guard against their overestimation, and to show that their exercise must be restricted by the principle of love towards and consideration for the welfare of the church as well as the salvation of sinners.

Due to the circumstance that a large part of his voluminous writings have been published in the language of his own country, the author is not as well-known in the English-speaking world as he deserves to be. Since 1912 he has been a professor in the theological faculty of the Free University of Amsterdam, and is rounding out a distinguished record of forty years of service there after a period of five years as a pastor. He is the author of several scholarly volumes on the New Testament, including no

6

fewer than six commentaries in the 14-volume learned *Kommentaar op het Nieuwe Testament,* of which he was the initial sponsor. His literary activity includes also scores of articles contributed to encyclopedias, symposiums and journals, including the Evangelical Quarterly. For many years he has been president of the Bible Society of the Netherlands and has participated actively in the preparation of a modern translation of the New Testament which has won wide favor in that country. On the occasion of his 70th birthday several of his former students joined in presenting him with a volume of essays and studies in honor of the occasion, a book published under the title *Arcana Revelata.* In the midst of all his scholarly activity, Dr. Grosheide has found time to be an active churchman and is known especially for his interest in evangelization. The Epistle to the Corinthians serves admirably, therefore, to utilize both the ripe scholarship and the practical sensitivity of this distinguished theologian.

NED B. STONEHOUSE
General Editor

Philadelphia, Pa.
March 1, 1953

Note: Upon the death of Ned B. Stonehouse, November 18, 1962, F. F. Bruce accepted the publishers' invitation to become General Editor of this series of New Testament commentaries begun under the very able and faithful scholarship of Professor Stonehouse.

The Publishers

ABBREVIATIONS

ASV   The American Standard Version (1901)

AV   The Authorized Version (1611)

ERV   The English Revised Version (1881)

KNT   Kommentaar op het Nieuwe Testament (Grosheide and Greijdanus)

LXX   The Septuagint

PThR   The Princeton Theological Review

RSV   The Revisel Standard Version (1946)

TWNT   Theologisches Wörterbuch zum Neuen Testaments (Kittel)

ZNW   Zeitschrift für die neutestamentl. Wissenschaft

The Scripture text used in this commentary is that of the American Standard Version of 1901, and is used by special arrangement with the Division of Christian Education, National Council of Churches of Christ in America. This text is printed in full for the sake of readers who do not read Greek; the expositions arc, however, based upon the Greek text.

CONTENTS

INTRODUCTION

THE FIRST EPISTLE OF PAUL
TO THE CORINTHIANS

INTRODUCTION

It is of importance for the exposition of I Corinthians to note that Corinth was the capital of the Roman province of Achaia to which nearly the whole of Greece and Macedonia belonged. The city was the residence of the governor or proconsul. Acts 18 informs us that during Paul's stay at Corinth the proconsul's name was Gallio, a fact of interest not only for its disclosure concerning the course of Paul's missionary work in that city but also for the dating of the first epistle. An inscription found by scholars at Delphi, though badly mutilated, clearly records a letter of the emperor Claudius granting a series of privileges to the city of Delphi. The name of Gallio, who in those days was proconsul of Achaia, is found in this inscription and a date is also mentioned. Chronologists, by means of complicated computations which need not be reproduced here, have come to the result that Gallio was governor of Achaia in the first part of 52 A. D. Except for a few minor differences nearly all experts accept the theory that Gallio was a governor of Achaia from the spring of 51 to the spring of 52, or from the spring of 52 to the spring of 53 A. D.

Acts 18:12 shows that Paul was compelled to leave Corinth a short time after the arrival of Gallio at Corinth, which must have been in the spring of either 51 or 52 A. D. Considering the many things which happened at Corinth between the time of Paul's departure and the writing of I Corinthians, as is evident from the epistle, we estimate that these events must have taken almost two years. The date of I Corinthians would then be the spring of 53 or 54 A. D.

The epistle itself informs us of the place where it was written. Paul was at Ephesus (16:8) when he wrote our epistle. His intention was to stay there until Pentecost and then to travel through Macedonia to Corinth. The letter was written at Ephesus, in the spring, during Paul's third journey.

Our first epistle to Corinth is strictly speaking not the first one written by Paul to the Corinthians. I Cor. 5:9 speaks of a

13

former letter, part of which was misunderstood. Paul is now trying to overcome this misunderstanding. In the previous epistle Paul had warned against intercourse with public sinners. Now he explains that he did not mean to include all such sinners, but only those who were members of the church. Intercourse with pagans in general is not forbidden.

This issue reveals something of the conditions at Corinth. The city was a seaport and had its peculiar difficulties. People from every part of the great Roman empire, especially seamen and merchants, came together at Corinth. They all, for the greater part Gentiles, brought with them their special sins. Immorality, drunkenness, dissipations were the order of the day. The Christians, who themselves for the greater part were formerly pagans, were unfortunately influenced by all this. There were Jews at Corinth, indeed there must have been a fairly great number of them for they had a synagogue of their own (Acts 18:1-4). An inscription found at Corinth reads: *Synagogue of the Hebrews*. But at Corinth the preaching of Paul to the Jews also had only meagre results (Acts 18:6). Thus Paul was obliged to work especially among the Gentiles, helped by Silas and Timotheus (Acts 18:5). We understand that the demeanor of the Gentiles had a great influence upon the Christians.

The last mentioned fact, we may say, is the principal reason why Paul writes to the Corinthians. The evil found in Corinth was evident particularly in the sphere of conduct. The epistle itself informs us fully on this point. We read that the church had sent an epistle to the apostle containing many questions, chiefly regarding the Christian life (7:1ff). This letter of course also informed Paul of many other happenings at Corinth. Moreover, Stephanas, Fortunatus and Achaicus who brought the Corinthian letter to the apostle had mentioned some other matters (16:17, 18).

But Paul also received information from another source: the household of Chloe (1:11). The last mentioned tidings did not have an official, ecclesiastical character. Nevertheless they helped to give the apostle a complete picture of the conditions at Corinth. The news was not favorable. Sad things were mentioned which, though not always important in the eye of the Corinthians (5:2), were so important to Paul that he treated them even before he answered the questions raised by the Corinthians.

14

The contents of I Corinthians are determined by the communications Paul received and by the questions proposed to him. Paul writes in the first place about the factions. We have explained in the commentary that there were no doctrinal questions at Corinth which gave occasion to the quarrels. There were only small squabbles, in themselves of minor importance. Still this brought discord in the congregation.

It should be noted that about the middle of the nineteenth century the Tübingen School, led by F. C. Baur, found here (and in some other texts, e. g., Gal. 1:11ff.) one of the starting points for its theory. It held that in the early Christian period there was a severe struggle, even a profound antithesis between Peter and Paul, and also between their disciples (so-called "Petrinists" and "Paulinists"). By means of this theory many phenomena of the early Christian period were thought capable of an explanation. Though Baur's viewpoint has few adherents today, it is not without influence. There are still many scholars who assume a sharp contrast between Peter and Paul. This opinion leads among other things to the judgment that the second epistle of Peter, in view of II Peter 3:15, is spurious.

After having spoken of the quarrels Paul treats of the worldly wisdom which was in honor at Corinth and was overestimated by them. The apostle writes of the manner in which he himself fulfilled his office. Not that the Corinthians rejected the apostolic authority (as was done in a later period, according to II Corinthians), but they did not regard it at its true worth (cf. also ch. 9). Paul severely warns the Corinthians against their spiritual pride.

Chapter 5 treats of a serious case of immorality. Chapter 6 disapproves the seeking of justice from pagan judges, after which the apostle warns against lasciviousness. In chapter 7 Paul begins to answer the questions the Corinthians put before him, the first one being the marriage question. Then follows a circumstantial exposition of the different opinions relating to the eating of meat offered to idols, an exposition interrupted by an explanation of the rights and offices of the apostles. More briefly the apostle speaks of holy communion, the *agape* and the headdress of women. A much broader discourse follows concerning spiritual gifts, their signification and use. In this context the apostle writes his famous song of Christian love. Chapter 15 contains

15

the only part of the letter that speaks of a doctrinal difference. There were some at Corinth (but only some) who denied the resurrection of the body. This error gives Paul the opportunity to discuss at length the resurrection of Christ and of the Christians. The last chapter gives business-like communications followed by salutations.

At first sight I Corinthians seems to discuss a series of points without any coherence. However, one main line runs through the whole epistle. The evils at Corinth were lasciviousness, spiritual pride and abuse of Christian liberty in various spheres. The Corinthians took as their starting point the rule that to the Christian all things are permissible; he is free. Paul, on the contrary, expounds the character of Christian freedom. Christian liberty is *exousia* (authority, right). It cannot be the rule for a Christian's behavior, nor does it tell him how he should act. The life of the believer must be ruled by the principle of love. This love, both toward God and toward the neighbor, declares how the Christian's *exousia* is to be used. Paul recognizes the Christian's liberty but he disapproves the manner in which the Corinthians used it.

A few questions require special discussion. More than once the assertion has been made that the Corinthian church was at most to a slight extent an organized one. Officers are not mentioned. Nowhere does Paul appeal to elders or to deacons to help him in his fight against abuses or to take certain measures. That is the reason why some scholars contend that the church at Corinth was in a primitive condition, that there were no elders or deacons, and that there was only a leading of the Holy Spirit. The presence of such a direct, spiritual government is supposed to be clearly demonstrated by the circumstantial discussion of the spiritual gifts, the *charismata*. The German scholar A. von Harnack was the chief exponent of this theory.

Now it is true that church officers are not mentioned in I Corinthians. But that does not prove that there were none. In any case our epistle presupposes a certain organization. The congregation was a closed one according to 5:13 and 14:23. 1:18 also is important in this respect. 12:28 cannot be understood of the local church at Corinth only, for this church at least had no apostles. Rather, the church at Corinth is viewed in

16

terms of the whole of the ecclesiastical organization. We find the same condition in 14:33. The ordinary officers, indeed, are not mentioned, but that is not strange. For although Acts 14:23 expressly speaks of the institution of the offices in the churches of South Galatia, no officers are mentioned in the epistle to these congregations. Generally speaking Paul does not direct himself to the officers to summon them to preach the pure Word of God, to exercise discipline, etc. The reason is that the ordinary ministries had just begun to develop. All or nearly all that was needed was done by the extraordinary ministers. In Paul's later epistles the ordinary ministers come more to the foreground. But all this does not mean that there were no ordinary officers in the first period and that all things were ministered by special gifts of the Holy Spirit.

Finally, we remark that the ordinary ministers do appear in I Corinthians. 12:28 speaks of teachers and not only of apostles and prophets (cf. Acts 13:1). I Corinthians speaks of "helps and governments," which indicate a regular ministry, for the last part of 12:28 must be referring to the government of the church, perhaps to the practice of discipline (cf. chap. 5). Granted that the men who discharged those duties had received special gifts of the Spirit, the offices as such are not in the least bound to these gifts.

We come to the conclusion therefore that the ordinary ministers are indeed not mentioned, but also that a government of the church by spiritual gifts only is not presupposed. And we are justified in asking: If Paul appointed officers in every church he founded, why not at Corinth?

Another point worthy of our special attention is that I Corinthians presupposes everywhere that there was peace at Corinth. No mention is made of persecutions, not even of a hampering or limiting of freedom. Truly the Jews had taken strong action against Paul (Acts 18:12ff.), but they did not do the same against the members of the church. The quiet is a consequence of the situation at Corinth. This great trading center attracted people of every sort, of every religion and from every country. Such a city was bound to have an interest in granting everybody the liberty and the quiet he desired.

COMMENTARY ON FIRST CORINTHIANS

Criticism of I Corinthians has not been severe. The Tübingen school, mentioned earlier, counted I Corinthians among the four main epistles of Paul (Rom., I & II Cor., Gal.). Accepting these four as genuine epistles of Paul, they made this the foundation for their criticism of the others. Only the radicals, who reject all of Paul's letters and deny that he wrote any of them, hold I Corinthians to be spurious. Textual criticism finds no special difficulties in I Corinthians. In the oldest collection of Pauline epistles I Corinthians held the first place, as appears from the canon of Muratori, written about 180 A. D. in which the oldest known list of the books of the New Testament is given. Probably the same conclusion may be derived from the epistle of Clemens Romanus (c. 96 A. D.).

As to the significance of our epistle for the history of New Testament revelation we remark that I Corinthians clearly belongs to the second period. The letter presupposes comprehensive knowledge of the work of Christ, including His return from heaven (15:23f.). The preaching of Christ had come to the great pagan world (15:1f.) and was bearing fruit. The gospel also brings a doctrine of life and that is to be put into practice (11:1f.). At this point the Corinthians were lacking and Paul preaches how the Christian has to live in a godless, pagan world, because he has found salvation in the work of Christ. We noticed earlier that in this Christian life love must be the principle that rules all things. To recapitulate, Paul teaches us that the church is in the world but not of the world.

EXPOSITION

THE FIRST EPISTLE OF PAUL
TO THE CORINTHIANS

CHAPTER I

SALUTATION

1:1-3

1 Paul, called *to be* an apostle of Jesus Christ through the will of God, and Sosthenes our brother,

2 unto the church of God which is at Corinth, *even* them that are sanctified in Christ Jesus, called *to be* saints, with all that call upon the name of our Lord Jesus Christ in every place, their *Lord* and ours:

3 Grace to you and peace from God our Father and the Lord Jesus Christ.

1 The beginning of I Corinthians has the usual form of a Greek epistle. It mentions 1) the name of the writer, 2) that of the addressees, 3) a greeting. But the apostle develops each part of the superscription, thus making it more extensive. *Called to be* is not a literal translation of the Greek. Paul does not speak about what will be, but about what is. Today he is a called apostle. Paul has not appointed himself an apostle, he is called by Christ Jesus, and therefore has authority and can demand obedience (cf. 9:1f., 15:8). Not all the Corinthians took the right attitude towards Paul, and therefore he reminds them in the beginning that his word comes to them as the word of Jesus Christ. *Christ Jesus* may be a possessive genitive, but *apostle* is a verbal noun, and *called* is added. So the genitive is better explained as a subjective genitive. Christ has called and appointed him. One must not forget that the Greek language has one genitive to express several relations, and consequently the distinction between the various genitives is not an absolute one. *Through the will of God* strengthens the authority of the apostle (cf. Gal. 1:1). As in 3:3 Paul ascends from the Mediator to God. When Christ called Paul to the apostleship, He did so because it was God's will. *Through*[1] indicates that Christ not only acted according to the will of God, but that God explicitly expressed His desire to call.

[1] διά, not e.g. κατά.

21

We know nothing definite about Sosthenes. Some think he is one of Chloe's household, (v. 12). We prefer the opinion that Sosthenes is the man referred to in Acts 18:17. *Brother*[2] makes clear that Sosthenes has become a Christian since the facts related in Acts 18. However, the word *brother* alone cannot express the fact that Paul intends to inform the Corinthians of the conversion of Sosthenes. It is difficult to say whether Sosthenes has any part in the composition of the epistle. The precise significance of the names used in the superscriptions to Paul's epistles remains a question. Are they more than a mere salutation from the Christians in Paul's presence? Or is this a way to inform us that not only Paul but Sosthenes as well wrote to the first readers? In this case the first is the more probable. Paul does not mention Sosthenes as a source of his information about the church at Corinth, although he may have been the successor of Crispus as head of the synagogue (Acts 18:17). We do not hear of any work done by Sosthenes for the benefit of the congregation or of his being the apostle's secretary.[3] Paul writes in the first person singular (vs. 4 f.). We assume therefore that Sosthenes was a Corinthian who had left the city long before and that Paul was conveying his greetings to the Corinthians.

2 *Church* is used by Paul of the local congregation as in Gal. 1:2: the churches of Galatia, but also in the sense of the universal church.[4] Here the first usage is clearly intended, whereas 12:28 points to the latter. *Church of God* refers to *through the will of God* (vs. 1). The church has her origin but also her life in the work of God in this world and therefore

---

[2] The Greek has ὁ ἀδελφός, without a pronoun but with the article, implying that Sosthenes is well known to the readers (cf. II Cor. 1:1).

[3] Tertius, who was Paul's secretary when he wrote the epistle to the Romans (Rom. 16:22), is not mentioned in the superscription of that epistle.

[4] The word ἐκκλησία designates the *ecclesia universalis* (Acts 9:31; cf. Mt. 16:18 where the word is used for the first time, considering the actual historical occurrence and not the written record). In Acts 13:1 and other passages it refers to a local church (cf. TWNT, III, p. 508). It is difficult to assume that Paul meant: that part of the *ecclesia universalis* which is at Corinth. τῇ οὔσῃ does not mean: "as far as it is" but rather: "which is" (cf. Rom. 1:7; 13:1; Eph. 1:1; I Thess. 2:14).

Paul has the right and the obligation as an apostle of Christ Jesus to write to the Corinthians. Moreover, the Greek word for "church" is not used exclusively with reference to the Christian church in the N.T. (cf. Acts 19:39). The addition *of God* is consequently not entirely superfluous. This church is characterized by her relation to God. Since the words *of God* stress the unity of the church they may also involve a condemnation of the factions in the Church at Corinth. *Church* is a collective noun which admits *sanctified*, sc. men, as a construction in apposition.

The interpolation *even* corrupts the sense. Better is the RSV: *to those consecrated.* Sanctified, however, cannot be interpreted as "consecrated to God," referring to the believers who separate themselves from the world. This is clear from the word "saints" added to "sanctified" and from Paul's description of the objective condition[5] of the Christians. God has sanctified them. He has liberated them from the unclean world and has put them in a relationship to Himself whereby they might have intercourse with Him (Jn. 17:19; I Thess. 5:23). This sanctification by God is possible only through the work of *Christ Jesus* in whom we are sanctified. The Corinthians are not born saints but they are sanctified by virtue of an act of God in Jesus, the consequences of which last till the present.

Paul writes *called saints,* i.e., the sanctification had not taken place without their knowledge. They were called to this sanctity by the preaching of the gospel (Heb. 1:3) so that they know they are sanctified. Paul the apostle and the Corinthians are what they are by the vocation of God. They heard the call and accepted it. But that vocation comes to them even now, yes again and again, so that they remain called.[6] It is a remarkable fact that Paul asserts the sanctity of the church with such vigor in an epistle in which he unceasingly reproves the readers because of their sins. They are saints in Christ, in spite of all their sins. Thus the epistle is a call to conversion addressed

---

[5] The perfect participle ἡγιασμένοις indicates a condition which has been called into being and which consequently exists. Such a condition can only exist by the grace of God in Jesus Christ (Col. 1:13).

[6] κλητοῖς is an adjective and indicates a permanent condition.

to erring children (cf. Jer. 3:22). The Corinthians are saints, but they live in sin. God does not abandon them but calls them to walk according to their imputed holiness (cf. Eph. 1:4). We are here face to face with a problem which recurs in Scripture and in history over and over again and which we cannot solve. When we call someone holy who is unholy we are guilty of a fallacious representation for we do not use holy both times in the same sense. But there is an imputed and an acquired holiness. Scripture teaches that God justifies the unholy (Rom. 4:5), and it also summons to a holy walk. In that way God wants to convince us of our holiness (I Thess. 4:3 ff.).

The addition *with all that call upon* etc. cannot be an enlargement of the address, as our epistle, unlike the general epistles, is clearly sent to one congregation. To take the expression of Achaia is purely arbitrary. If Achaia were meant this could have been indicated (cf. II Cor. 1:1). Therefore we combine these words with "called *to be* saints." Not only the Corinthians but all who invoke the name of our Lord Jesus Christ, i.e. who confess that He is Lord (12:3, Phil. 2:11), and call upon Him, also confessing that He is God (Acts 2:21; 7:59; 9:19; Rom. 10:12) and who by so doing declare themselves to be Christians, are called to be saints.[7] The Corinthians needed to be reminded of these things for they did not take account of others (12:12f.; 14:36). There is a oneness of all who believe. This oneness may be lost sight of in our quarrels and so we need to be reminded of it.

The last words of vs. 2 are translated in the ARV "in every place, their *Lord* and ours," the word "Lord" being an insertion. As the Greek has the pronouns after *place* it seems better to combine them with that word. Paul stresses the unity of the church. Whatever the place may be where her members live, together they form the one body of Christ.

3 In vs. 3 we find the typically Pauline salutation, which differs from that of the ordinary Greek salutation. Paul's greeting consists of two sentences, the first one in v. 2 in the third person, the second here in the second and first persons. This

---

[7] See Origen's fine exposition in *Comm. Joh.* 6, 59 (38) ed. Brooke, p. 179, where the church is compared with a light that spreads light.

bespeaks a greater degree of intimacy than is expressed in the usual Greek salutation with its use of the third person only.[8]

The Greek word for *grace* is a cognate of the word for greeting.[9] The Christian salutation thus adds depth to the usual Greek greeting. Paul does not just greet the Corinthians but he wishes them grace from God, i. e., the grace in Jesus Christ. Eph. 1:5f. is a good example: "according to the good pleasure of his will, to the praise of the glory of his grace, which he freely bestowed in the Beloved: in whom we have our redemption through his blood, the forgiveness of our trespasses, etc."

This grace manifests itself in *peace,* which is its mature fruit, a peace of soul, a genuine peace since it descends from God (Rom. 8:6; 15:33; 16:20, etc.). Just as the Greek concept of grace is deepened in the Christian usage, so likewise is the Hebrew word for peace when used in salutations. God grants grace and peace because He is a Father to them that call upon Him in Christ. We, the believers, pray to Him as our Father who is in heaven (Matt. 6:9). Grace descends from One who is no longer wrathful, but merciful. *Jesus Christ* is the Mediator of that grace and peace. He is its meritorious cause. Believers may call on Him as their *Lord,* (Jn. 1:17; Eph. 2:14), because He is the victor over sin, the devil and the world (Matt. 28:18; II Tim. 1:16; Heb. 2:14; I Jn. 3:8). The Holy Spirit's work is not mentioned here since Paul only mentions the heavenly gifts, which, descending from God for the sake of Christ, are given to believers. He does not speak of the faith through which the individual obtains these gifts. In other words, not the subjective acquisition but the objective redemption is in the foreground here.

1-3 The distinguishing feature of this salutation is its stress upon the sanctity of the church.

---

[8] E. Lohmeyer, *Probleme paulin. Theol.,* ZNW, 26, 1927, p. 158.
[9] χάρις, grace; χαίρειν, Acts 15:23; 23:26; Jas. 1:1 salutation.

THANKSGIVING

1:4-9

4 I thank my God always concerning you, for the grace
of God which was given you in Christ Jesus;
5 that in every thing ye were enriched in him, in all utterance and all knowledge;
6 even as the testimony of Christ was confirmed in you:
7 so that ye come behind in no gift; waiting for the
revelation of our Lord Jesus Christ;
8 who shall also confirm you unto the end, *that* ye *be*
unreprovable in the day of our Lord Jesus Christ.
9 God is faithful through whom ye were called into the
fellowship of his Son Jesus Christ our Lord.

4 As a rule Paul follows his salutation with a thanksgiving.
These thanksgivings are not all *captationes benevolentiae*: the
apostle does not thank men in order to win their good will. He
does this only in so far as he, before he begins to exhort,
mentions the things which through the grace of God are worthy
of praise in the church. Thus salutations and thanksgivings
point forward to the contents of the epistle.

I thank my God, at the beginning of a sentence indicates that
all blessings that can be enumerated are the gifts of God and
only of Him. Paul emphasizes that everything the Corinthians
possess is grace.[10] At the same time we are granted a look into
the apostle's heart. He is always busy with the churches, and
is concerned with their welfare (II Cor. 11:28). But besides
issuing warnings there is also thankfulness in his heart for all
the good things given by God to the church. To this thankfulness he gives utterance, *thanking always God* in his prayers
(Ps. 141:2; Heb. 13:15).

Always is hyperbolic only to a certain extent. Paul certainly
does not continually pray but his life is a life of prayer and in
his prayers he never forgets the church at Corinth. The apostle
has his citizenship, his commonwealth, in heaven (Phil. 3:20).

---

[10] Note the use of the following words: Χάρις, vs. 3; εὐχαρι-
στῶ, χάριτι, vs. 4; χαρίσματι, vs. 7.

He seeks and sets his mind on things that are above (Col. 3:1). Paul also indicates for whom and for which reason he gives thanks. The cause of his thanksgiving is the *grace of God* given to the Corinthians. Grace in this verse is therefore not a virtue of God but the manifestation thereof.[11] God has made rich through the work of *Christ Jesus,* who merited all grace (1:3), in whom it has its foundation (1:30; II Cor. 5:18, 21; Col. 1:27).[12]

5 *That* has explicative force, i. e., vs. 5 explains the grace God bestowed on the church of Corinth. However, Paul does not describe these benefits in an incoherent series, but he places them in their proper relations to each other. This grace means that the Corinthians are *in every respect enriched in Him,* sc. in Christ (II Cor. 8:7). *Every* and *enriched* speak of the quantity, the second part of the verse mentions the quality of this grace. *Every* is not meant absolutely, as if the sense were "in all possible respects," for the following words *in all utterance and all knowledge* have restrictive force. The meaning of *every* must be: all that is here under discussion; all that you possess. In all that you possess you are enriched, i. e., you have received much. The word "enriched"[13] does not contain a reference to baptism or conversion, for the latter are not mentioned in these verses. Paul indicates that the characteristic feature of the church at Corinth is wealth. The rest of the epistle shows this, especially the words concerning wisdom and spiritual gifts. Christian liberty was another thing the full meaning of which the Corinthians had grasped better than many others. There is nothing small about the congregation at Corinth, but this same grandeur gave also rise to many sins (cf. 4:7). And it is Paul's purpose to preach to the Corinthians that all their wealth has its root in Jesus Christ, in grace (II Cor. 8:9).

---

[11] χάρις here has the same sense as χάρισμα in vs. 7.

[12] ἐν has primarily a local reference. The believers are incorporated in Christ, they live in the sphere that is dominated by Him and participate therefore in the grace acquired by Him. In the second place, ἐν has instrumental force: Christ is the author of this grace.

[13] ἐπλουτίσθητε, passive and aor. This means that God was the author so that Paul is not thinking of the condition existing at this moment but rather of the historical fact.

The second half of the verse describes the character of this wealth. The Corinthians are enriched by God *in all utterance and in all knowledge.* Corinth is a Greek city and Greece is the country of eloquence. *Utterance* is the translation of a Greek word which signifies the word[14] not as it is spoken but as regards its contents. The Corinthians had something to speak about and they could speak about it. The subsequent discussion on wisdom and the proud words: "all things are lawful for me" (6:12) explain this further. But there is not only a word, there is also *knowledge.* They did not speak about things not worth while but had real knowledge. The Greek word[15] has a less intellectual flavor than the English. *Knowledge* as it is used here may be the fruit of intuition, even of a mystic feeling. At least it is not exclusively the result of research or thinking, but is an insight into things (cf. 8:1f.). Ch. 8 describes true knowledge as the result of faith; it is the knowledge of the new man and is related to the knowledge of God Himself. That is why knowledge can be combined with word, *utterance* (cf. 12:8; II Cor. 11:6). Knowledge is related to wisdom but, unlike the latter, it cannot be accompanied by a certain measure of ignorance, neither is it directed toward practical acting as much as wisdom is. Knowledge is not only rest, it is also action (8:2). Both words, *utterance* and *knowledge,* preceded by *all* indicate that Corinth knew of an extensive, elevated discussion on the basis of their insight into spiritual things (II Cor. 8:7). Their richness in Christ consists especially in the ability to speak well about the revelation of God. This is a Christian virtue but the danger is that it degenerates into a boasting of their own theological knowledge. Such a sinful abuse of the gifts of God was found in Corinth (cf. 1:17; 8:1).

6 *Even as* has comparative force:[16] *was confirmed* is put on the same plane with *were enriched.* Both verbs have a quantitative character. Their oneness lies *in Him* (cf. vs. 5). *The testimony of Christ* has received a firm place in, or among, the Corinthians. *The testimony of Christ* is the testimony that deals with Christ (II Tim. 1:8). The Greek word for "to testify"

---
14 λόγος, not ῥῆμα.
15 γνῶσις.
16 καθώς.

does not have the sense of the present English word which may be used as a bearing of testimony to one's own experiences. The book of Acts shows that the testimony of Christ is the objective testifying to the words and deeds of Christ, which the apostles had seen and heard with their own eyes and ears (cf. also Jn. 1:14; I Jn. 1:1f). The testimony of Christ is the preaching of the gospel at Corinth by Paul, which preaching had been accepted by the Corinthians. Consequently they had been enriched in utterance and in knowledge. The testimony of Christ furnished the Corinthians with the things of which they had to speak and which they had to know. The preaching is the source. What the apostle writes here is therefore not in conflict with what he writes in 3:3. There the question is an ethical one since the conduct of the Corinthians is not according to their utterance and knowledge.[17]

7 Vs. 7 gives a conclusion with *so that;*[18] this conclusion goes with vs. 5 as well as vs. 6 since *gift* is a general word. *Gift* indicates the respect in which there is no lack. Paul sometimes uses the word gift in the special sense of the extraordinary gifts of the Holy Spirit, given to the church in her first period (see especially ch. 12-14). However, we may not forget the general sense of the word gift. There is no absolute difference between the two meanings, as the latter is only the special meaning of the former.

In early Christian times people must have seen all the gifts of the Holy Spirit, the special as well as the permanent, as a unity. They were not differentiated, neither had the church as yet experienced that the special gifts were not going to remain. It is therefore better to take the word *gift,* the first time it is used, in its general sense and to consider the special gift as an example of the general gift. It is true, the apostle writes about these special gifts of the Spirit in quite some detail in I Corinthians. But vs. 7 forms the conclusion of a sentence which does not mention those special gifts. Neither do we know whether

---

[17] The difference between the active and the middle of ὑστερεῖν may be noted from Mt. 19:20.

[18] In the koine ὥστε is usually construed with the infinitive. This conclusion, therefore, points to a fact and not to an expected result.

God had already given all the special gifts (cf. "in no gift") enumerated in ch. 12-14 to the church in Corinth.[19] All this pleads for taking the word gift in its general sense here, although at the same time it points forward to the special use, found in the latter part of the epistle. From the fact that the preaching of the Word had had a good reception in the church Paul concludes *that ye come behind in no gift*. Their becoming rich in utterance and knowledge is really also a fruit of this same favorable reception of the gospel preaching.

Waiting for expresses an attendant circumstance. After having heard what the Corinthians are and what they possess, we are now informed as to what they do and what their attitude is. This waiting is not an expectation of an unknown future. Its object is a question of faith. Only those who believe in the Word of God and the witness of the prophets can wait in the sense in which the word is used here. This waiting, therefore, means action on the part of the Corinthians. Their eye looks forward to the end, their life is eschatological (Phil 3:20). This end is the revelation of our Lord Jesus Christ. At the present He is in heaven, but He will come (Col. 3:1-4). His coming will not be like that of a man but it will be a revelation, a removing of the veil, a manifestation of who Jesus is and what He is, a revelation of what hitherto had been believed but not seen (Lk. 17:30; II Thess. 1:7). He will come as *our Lord*. This eschatological moment deserves our attention. Paul will not return to this theme in the following chapters, as he had in I and II Thessalonians. The humiliation of Christ rather than His exaltation seems to be in the foreground in I Corinthians (cf. for example I Cor. 2:2). There were some at Corinth who denied the resurrection of the body (15:12). The situation is, that all the early Christians, the Corinthians included, were looking forward to the return of Christ, but with the latter this longing was not very strong. Their life was directed toward the earth and earthly questions. But by fixing their eyes upon the end they nevertheless excelled the Christians of a later age who live with their eyes directed only toward the earth. Paul has thus prepared us for the coming exposition.

---

[19] Paul does not write: that you do not come behind in any gift.

30

8 The relative pronoun *who* may seem to go with Christ, as He is mentioned last. But the end of vs. 8, *in the day of our Lord Jesus Christ* makes this construction impossible. The word should be taken of ' God, of whom the apostle, after his words in vs. 4: *I thank my God,* is still thinking (cf. vs. 9: God is faithful). Verse 4 has explained what God has done, but God will do more: He will care in the future also. Again we meet the verb *to confirm*. The first time it was used of doctrine, now it is used of life. As to doctrine, everything was right at Corinth, generally speaking. But their life was far from being right. And before Paul comes to his admonitions he places all things in the hands of God. God will confirm and sustain till the end, and since that is so, their life also will be a good life. The work of God continues *to the end*. This can be taken of time as well as of degree. The Greek word for *end*[20] indicates the natural end of something, its top. The result of this confirmation by God will be that the Corinthians will be unreprovable in the last day. There will be no accusations against them (cf. Phil. 1:6, 10; I Thess. 3:13; 5:23). *Unto the end* may be joined either to *will confirm* or to *unreprovable*. The presence of a time clause after *unreprovable* does not form an objection, when the notion of degree, contained in *end,* is emphasized.

The day of the Lord is a common expression in Paul's letters for the return of Christ. Since the Corinthians expect that return, that revelation of Christ, they will be *unreprovable* when He comes, by the saving grace of God. Their waiting can be filled with hope. The rest of the epistle shows that Paul, by putting these things first, does not in the least mean to cultivate a spirit of carelessness.

9 Paul continues his exposition without the use of a conjunction. Nevertheless, the content shows clearly that vs. 9 contains the reason for that which immediately precedes. The question why God will confirm is answered by the statement that He is *faithful,* i. e., He continues His work. The apostle seeks in God the certainty of what he has just said. For it was He who called and therefore He will also continue (cf. Rom. 8:30). The context shows that what is meant here is the audible vocation to salvation, which had come to the Corinthians through

---

[20] τέλος

31

the preaching of the gospel. It is impossible to suppose that Paul would have appealed to something outside the consciousness of the church. Later passages, e.g. 7:17f., will become clear when it is remembered that here the vocation to salvation is meant.

The use of *through* instead of "by" is very remarkable.[21] *Through* is used of the principal cause and is likely to express the thought that the calling of God took place indirectly, i. e., God did not speak from heaven to every Corinthian personally, but He called through the preaching of the gospel. Finally the purpose of the vocation is explained, and here again we must think of later passages (cf. 6:15; 12:12f., 27; and 10:17f.). The Corinthians are called to something very specific, for their calling has brought them in relation with[22] (not into the circle of) His Son, Jesus Christ our Lord (I Jn. 1:3). Note the use of so many names at once. It reveals the glory of the Son and in Him also of the Corinthians who are joined to Him. And this is very important. For how could they walk unholily who stand in a firm relation to the holy Son of God, who chose to be their Mediator and entered into glory[23] (cf. Rom. 8:17; II Thess. 2:14)? The word *fellowship*,[24] therefore, is the clue to the understanding of *unreprovable* in vs. 8. How is it possible that the Corinthians will be unreprovable in the day of Christ? Because they stand in relation to Him and share in the fruits of His work (Col. 3:4).

4-9 There are two distinct parts in this thanksgiving. The first part is a thanksgiving in the proper sense of the word because it deals with things present. The second part is also thanksgiving but it is a giving of thanks for what may be expected in the future and this is done with full assurance. Both parts together anticipate the thoughts which will be developed in the sequel. These opening verses form the basis for subsequent admonitions. Christians can only be admonished successfully after God has made them true Christians. But he who was made a Christian must walk according to his vocation.

---

[21] διά, not ὑπό
[22] κοινωνία, verbal noun.
[23] He is the κύριος, the Lord.
[24] See E. P. Groenewald, κοινωνία *bij Paulus*, Delft 1932.

10 Now I beseech you, brethren, through the name of our
Lord Jesus Christ, that ye all speak the same thing,
and *that* there be no divisions among you; but *that* ye
be perfected together in the same mind and in the same
judgment.

11 For it hath been signified unto me concerning you, my
brethren, by them *that are of the household* of Chloe,
that there are contentions among you.

12. Now this I mean, that each one of you saith. I am of
Paul; and I of Apollos; and I of Cephas; and I of
Christ.

13 Is Christ divided? was Paul crucified for you? or were
ye baptized into the name of Paul?

14 I thank God that I baptized none of you, save Crispus
and Gaius;

15 lest any man should say that ye were baptized into my
name.

16 And I baptized also the household of Stephanas; besides,
I know not whether I baptized any other.

17 For Christ sent me not to baptize, but to preach the
gospel: not in wisdom of words, lest the cross of Christ
should be made void.

10 The Greek word, which is translated *beseech*[25] has a
consoling and a warning sense. In vs. 10 the warning sense
is most prominent as the context shows. The words: *the name
of our Lord Jesus Christ* are not to be explained in the same way
as "our Lord Jesus Christ" without any additions. *Name* implies naming. The name of Jesus Christ is uttered and in that
way, not merely through Christ, but through the utterance of
His name the apostle exhorts. The use of "through" can thus
be explained (Rom. 12:1). By uttering the name of the Lord
Jesus Christ Paul recalls to the mind of the Corinthians the
sufferings and the glory of the Mediator and the fruits thereof
for the children of God (cf. "fellowship" vs. 9). The apostle's

---

[25] παρακαλεῖν.

33

exhortation is a very earnest one. He admonishes the Corinthians to place themselves before the face of the Lord. This does not surprise us when we consider the seriousness of their sin. Paul exhorts them that they must *speak*[26] *the same*, i.e. assert the same (10:29; Gal. 3:17). If all Corinthians *speak the same* they will be unanimous and think the same. There must be unity in the Church instead of divisions. *That there be* is a cautious expression. The divisions do exist but Paul leaves undecided whether he means that they should no longer be or that they should not arise. The proof for their existence is still to come. The apostle uses caution throughout this whole passage. This is not for lack of information but partly because he wishes to deal prudently with the Corinthians, partly also because he is reproving the division itself rather than its cause.

Division, the Greek word[27] means "fissure," "rent," (Matt. 9:16), secondarily "discussion," "difference of opinion." In the N.T. the word does not *per se* have a bad meaning but it may simply be "difference of opinion" (Jn. 7:43; 9:16; 10:19). But difference of opinion easily leads to sin and division, as was the case at Corinth. *Mind*[28] is the intellect in its judging faculty, *judgment*[29] stands for the expressed opinion, the conviction. The Corinthians must be *perfected together*[30] through their opinion and its expression. Vs. 10 pronounces a very decisive verdict. However, Paul does not want to banish all diversity from the church, as is clear from the following verses where such diversity is not opposed (cf. 3:6ff.), but only an unbrotherly attitude. Diversity may not become pride or a looking down on someone whom one does not happen to follow. The way toward this

---

[26] The Greek λέγειν may be translated not only with "to speak" but also with "to mean" and "to assert" (cf. Bauer, Wörterbuch N.T., s.v.).

[27] σχίσμα.

[28] νοῦς.

[29] γνώμη

[30] Note the perfect κατηρτισμένα. Paul does not only urge that the evil be corrected but he implies that the improved condition must continue. The latter will be the case if the Corinthians by the continued action of their mind will always judge in the same manner and if, as a consequence, their conviction concerning specific things expresses itself concretely in the same manner.

true unity is not indicated since it is supposed that unity will prevail when discord is opposed and left behind. There is a unity in Christ (cf. vs. 13), and in the Spirit (12:4f.). That unity is bound to manifest itself.

11   Paul now gives the grounds for his exhortations. A friendly *my brethren* shows the apostle's benevolence to the Corinthians. He mentions explicitly the source of his information so that the Corinthians cannot contest its correctness. We have no other information concerning *Chloe* or her *household*. Chloe, "the fair" or "the blond," is a surname of the goddess Demeter and Chloe may have been a liberated slave. *The household* is to be understood as the *familia*, that is the slaves. Chloe may have been the head of a business, as Lydia was at Philippi (cf. Acts 16:14). Paul did not receive his information from Chloe herself. Her slaves must have come to Ephesus, called on Paul and informed him of the conditions at Corinth. The words *it has been signified unto me concerning you* suppose that Paul at first did not believe conditions were so bad at Corinth, but that, upon questioning the slaves of Chloe, he could only conclude that there were contentions in the church.

Contentions[31] are not the same as divisions, schisms (vs. 10). The term shows that there was sin at Corinth, that the difference led to quarrels, because everyone held his own opinion as the only right one and detested the views of others. *Among you* passes a judgment on the quarreling brethren, but implies nevertheless that the church had not yet broken up since it met at the same place.

12   *This I mean,*[32] the apostle explains his foregoing words in order to persuade his readers. *Each one of you* indicates that everyone had chosen position:[33] The whole church was divided in that everyone had his own standpoint and condemned that of the other. The four slogans occupy the same place in the verse and are therefore to be explained in the same manner. These

---

[31] ἔρις
[32] Λέγω δὲ τοῦτο. On λέγω cf. note 26. τοῦτο often refers to the preceding; here, however, clearly to the following.
[33] Although the literal meaning of the Greek words might be that everyone used all four of the slogans, Paul implies that each used only one.

35

slogans have raised a great number of difficulties and have led to many interpretations, which will be reviewed only briefly. How is it possible that Christ receives the same place as Paul, Apollos and Cephas? Some scholars suppose that another name was originally written by Paul, e.g. Crispus or Chrestus. But those men also were not the equals of Paul, Cephas and Apollos. Other scholars have guessed that a scribe wrote in the margin: "I of Christ," as a personal confession, and that his successor put it in the text, an unlikely supposition especially since the fourth name is of quite another character than the former.

In this connection the influence of F. C. Baur and the Tübingen school has been considerable. Following the principles of Hegel he saw in our verse a key to the understanding of primitive Christianity. Judaism was the thesis and found its support in Peter and Christ. Paul and Apollos were the men of the Gentile Christians, the antithesis. Out of the dispute the unity of the catholic church must arise. This interpretation, however, cannot be the right one. There are four groups, not two, four slogans, and not two. To deduce a difference between Peter and Paul from Gal. 2:11ff., as is done by Baur, is not permissible. Gal. 2:11ff. forms an exception since on the whole there is great unanimity between Peter and Paul. Peter, and not Paul, was the first one to preach to the Gentiles. Silas and Mark are found in the company of Peter as well as in that of Paul. At the council of the Apostles, Acts 15, Peter and Paul follow the same line of thinking. There is no fundamental difference in the preaching or in the epistles of both.

Today there are few that are completely loyal to Baur's views, but his interpretations still have some influence in so far as also today many scholars claim to find in our epistle the opinion of different parties. Apollos is said to be the man of wisdom. The Judaistic teachers, mentioned in II Corinthians, are held to be the followers of Peter, and so on.

Those who claimed to be adherents of Christ offer the greatest difficulty. Not seldom are they interpreted as spiritualists, antinomians, in any case anti-Judaists. But there is no ground for this interpretation. We cannot appeal to II Cor. 10:7 for such an opinion, since in I Cor. 1:12 the apostle condemns the slogan "I am of Christ," whereas in II Cor. 10:7 he says: "so also we are," i. e., he declares that he belongs to Christ. Paul does not say in I Cor. 1 that the members of the church with their slogans adhered to a definite doctrine, i. e., a false doctrine. The apostle does not combat a false doctrine in I Corinthians. One might think of 15:12 but it should at least be remembered that neither the opinion of the *some* mentioned there, nor the denial of the resurrection of the dead is linked with the parties of I Cor. 1. The tone in I Corinthians is quite different from that in Galatians or in II Cor. 10-13, where Paul opposes the Judaizers. The one thing we find here is that each Corinthian has his slogan. No other difference is mentioned but these slogans. All are exhorted to unity. Nobody is right. And when in the following chapters Paul reprimands several sins it is not one group but the whole church which is reprimanded. Therefore we conclude that there was no essential or doctrinal difference between the four groups.

Paul denies that he himself, or Apollos, or Peter, have been guilty of recruiting adherents. On the contrary, it was the Corinthians who began to make distinctions and name themselves after persons. We do not know of any difference between Paul and Apollos. Neither was there any essential difference between Paul and Peter. As has been said already, the event mentioned in Gal. 2:19f is not a symptom but an incident. We must bear in mind that the church of Corinth was a large one. Paul had preached there. After him came Apollos to whose preaching some preferred to listen, while others claimed that Paul's preaching was superior to that of his successor. These groups named themselves after Apollos and Paul respectively. Once this had become a custom a third group, aiming higher still, chose Peter for its champion. The reason why Peter was selected is not clear, although we do know that the Corinthian church was striving for ever higher things (cf. 4:6). Christ, being still higher than Peter, was abased by some Christians to be the leader of a party which was named after Him. Corinth, therefore, boasted in men in the full sense of that word. It lined itself up with one person and detested the other, and such without any reason. Paul does not choose sides and ignores even the "Paul-party." All of them are wrong for trivial things may not form an occasion for dissension. He who wants to boast must boast in the Lord (vs. 31). This interpretation fits the context for now vs. 13 follows 12 quite logically and it also becomes clear why Paul does not oppose false doctrine. The sin rebuked was one of quarrelsomeness, a common evil in Greek democracies and here transferred to the church.

Cephas, as written by Paul, must be Peter (cf. Jn. 1:42). This name is used here because Paul prefers to use official names. Paul designates the Roman provinces by their Latin names and calls himself by his Roman name Paulus, not Saul.

13 This verse contains a rebuke. Paul does not speak of the quarrels and their results but simply shows the absurdity of this discord. It is an old question whether the words *is divided* should be taken in the interrogative or in the affirmative sense. Against the translation: "Christ is divided!" speaks vs. 12, where "Christ" refers to the person of Christ, whereas in vs. 13 it would have to mean His body, the Church. Another possible translation: "Christ is assigned" (to one of the parties), i.e. Christ belongs to a party, could be taken ironically only. The meaning would then be: You, Corinthians, have given Christ to a part of the congregation by your sin. This comes very close to an interrogative sentence. The translation: "Is Christ divided?" or: "assigned"[34] is therefore to be preferred, also with a view to the questions which follow. The rendering "assigned" is favored by the context. One group of the Corinthian church had made Christ's name its proper mark of distinction and had deprived, in so doing, others of Christ, a very sinful trait of character. The apostle thus points to the greatest sin of the Corinthians (cf. 3:23) since Christ is of the whole church.

To name oneself after Paul is equally sinful.[35] To the question *Was Paul crucified for you?* the answer can only be negative. It was permissible to name oneself after Christ who was cruci-

---

[34] μερίζω means both "to divide" (I Cor. 7:24) and "to assign" (I Cor. 7:17).

[35] The preceding question did not have an interrogative particle since it did not require one. By using μή here Paul indicates that he expects a negative answer. This implies that to name oneself after Christ is something uncommon which again corroborates our earlier view that there is a gradation in the sins of the Corinthians.

fied for the church. They only sinned in depriving others of Christ. To name oneself after Paul was not permissible but constituted an offense to Christ. The strong word *crucified* indicates how far Paul stands beneath Christ. To be baptized into the name of someone means to be brought into the most intimate relation with this person's revelation (cf. Mt. 28:19). *Name* presupposes that the name is expressed. That is why Paul, after speaking of the cross which he puts in the center of Christ's work, now speaks of baptism. Not Paul's name but the name of Christ had been used at the baptism of the Corinthians (cf. Acts 2:38; 8:16; 10:48; 19:5).

14-15 Paul speaks of baptism because at its administration the name of Christ is expressly mentioned, thus showing to whom the believers belong and for whom they may call themselves (Acts 10:48). But since people often tend to look more at the administrator than at the king who authorizes him, Paul also might have been given a special place at Corinth if he had baptized many in that church. The Corinthians might then have forgotten whose name it was that had been used at their baptism. This is now impossible. And Paul may appeal to this fact because it was not just accidental that he did not baptize but it was according to his commission. Consequently, nobody can say that he was baptized in the name of Paul.[36]

16 The fact that Paul does not mention Stephanas and his house until now will be understood when it is remembered that the house of Stephanas is the first fruits of Achaia (16:15). Evidently Stephanas' baptism belongs to a period preceding that of the great work at Corinth (cf. Acts 18:5ff). Initially Paul had the later period in mind. It may also be that Stephanas did not live in Corinth for Paul does not write "Corinth" in 16:15 but "Achaia." *Besides* is to be taken with *I know* and the following sentence. Paul uses care: he may have baptized somebody else, but he does not recall. Vs. 17 shows that, whether he had baptized anyone else or no, the main thing is that Paul did not come to baptize but to preach the gospel.

17 *For,* vs. 17, does not give the ground for the immediately preceding verse only, but for the whole argument to the effect

---

[36] ἵνα εἴπῃ not final: "lest", but consecutive: "so that not".

that Paul had baptized only a few. Not only is he grateful for that fact but also that no one can rightfully accuse him of forsaking his vocation. The following references explain Paul's conduct: Acts 9:15, 20; 22:15; 26:16ff.; Gal. 1:15. On the other side Jn. 4:2; Acts 10:48 are enlightening. Paul does not disregard baptism, on the contrary, he thinks it necessary. But as everybody has his own vocation Paul's vocation is to preach the gospel in the full sense of the word. We may suppose that the apostle's assistants instructed the converts more exactly and that they also baptized (cf. Acts 8:35; 18:26). Missionary preaching has demands of its own and it was for that preaching that Paul had received from God all the necessary gifts. He had to use those gifts and fulfil the task God had committed to him. (Rom. 15:19ff). Others could build where he had laid the foundations (3:10).

Wisdom of words is a very remarkable expression.[37] As "word" is meant here as the word with its content, the concept "wisdom" does not fit it. From this peculiar combination it must follow that the Corinthians were not content with words or with speech, but that they connected a special wisdom with their words, or speech, thus making their word a sort of wisdom. *Wisdom* lacks the article in the Greek. This shows that Paul does not speak about his own words or addresses, nor about his preaching of the gospel, but about a preaching which was in use at Corinth, although it very definitely was a preaching of the cross of Christ (cf. the end of the verse). *Wisdom of words,* therefore, must have been a slogan of the Corinthians and indicates at the same time that Paul has come to a new subject: wisdom. The expression does not mean: "wisdom consisting in words" as if Paul had said that he rejected the tendency in the church to use nothing but words only and to sacrifice everything to the form. "Wisdom" in this context always implies content, either in the good or in the evil sense of the word, as is also borne out by 2:5 (faith should not consist in wisdom). Neither does the expression mean a preaching with wisdom, i. e., a taking account of all the circumstances. *Words* after *wisdom* would then be superfluous. What is prohibited is the transformation of *words* into *wisdom.*

---

[37] σοφία λόγου. λόγος means "word", "speech". σοφία is that virtue which leads to a wise, sensible conduct.

When Paul preaches the gospel he does not use worldly wisdom (2:1). *Words* is therefore the governing concept. Just as there is a wisdom of the world and a wisdom of God, vs. 20,21, so does the word have its *wisdom*. The word, i. e., the preaching had a presentation all of its own at Corinth, not so much regarding the form as the content. The context teaches that Paul with *wisdom* means the wisdom of the world, and, secondly, that the contents of the preaching is Paul's exclusive interest. He himself does not present his message in a persuasive form (2:4). Our conclusion from these various data is that the Corinthian wisdom with which they adorned the preaching of the word must have been a specially persuasive form, which approached the wisdom of the world and was harmful to the contents of the gospel (cf. also 2:1 where wisdom is put after word). We may think here of the various phrases of Greek philosophers, of the time honored expressions of men of the world, which were regarded as wisdom. All those forms harmed the gospel since they captured the attention of the hearers and thus the gospel of the cross did not come to its full rights. The Corinthians had not come to the point where they no longer believed in the atoning work of Christ, but they nevertheless attached themselves in such a measure to the wisdom of the world that Paul is constrained to speak of a *making void* of the *cross of Christ*. The apostle does not say that the Corinthians had made void the cross of Christ, nor does he associate his warning with one of the "parties" of vs. 12. He simply states that he has not preached the gospel to the Corinthians with such wisdom as they desired, lest the cross of Christ should *be made void*. Thus Paul proceeds to his new subject: the cross of Christ.

10-17 Paul's argument, which leads him from the disputes to the subject of baptism and from there to the preaching in wisdom of words, shows that he does not consider the quarrels of very great importance. It is true, he begins his letter with a consideration of them and later on he returns to the same subject. But it is also true that he shows much more interest in the questions concerning baptism and the preaching of the gospel. The quarrels alarmed the apostle and troubled him especially because their cause was such a trivial one. The chief thing is that the Corinthians broke up the unity of the church for no good reason whatever. That is why Paul puts this ethical point first in this letter which is ethical in character. He does this also because the Corin-

41

thians did not see the greatness of their sin. Furthermore, 3:21 implies that Paul considered the practice of the Corinthians of naming themselves after certain persons a part of wisdom of the world. These quarrels, therefore, could well form a motive for writing about worldly wisdom. Basically, however, the point concerning wisdom is of far greater importance than that of the quarrels themselves.

DIVINE AND WORLDLY WISDOM

1:18-31

18 For the word of the cross is to them that perish foolishness; but unto us who are saved it is the power of God.

19 For it is written, I will destroy the wisdom of the wise, and the discernment of the discerning will I bring to naught.

20 Where is the wise? where is the scribe? where is the disputer of this world? hath not God made foolish the wisdom of the world?

21 For seeing that in the wisdom of God the world through its wisdom knew not God, it was God's good pleasure through the foolishness of the preaching to save them that believe.

22 Seeing that Jews ask for signs, and Greeks seek after wisdom:

23 but we preach Christ crucified, unto Jews a stumblingblock, and unto Gentiles foolishness;

24 but unto them that are called, both Jews and Greeks, Christ the power of God, and the wisdom of God.

25 Because the foolishness of God is wiser than men; and the weakness of God is stronger than men.

26 For behold your calling, brethren, that not many wise after the flesh, not many mighty, not many noble, *are called*:

27 but God chose the foolish things of the world, that he might put to shame them that are wise; and God chose the weak things of the world, that he might put to shame the things that are strong;

28 and the base things of the world, and the things that are despised, did God choose, *yea* and the things that are not, that he might bring to nought the things that are:

29 that no flesh should glory before God.

30 But of him are ye in Christ Jesus, who was made unto us wisdom from God, and righteousness and sanctification, and redemption:

31 that, according as it is written, He that glorifieth, let him glory in the Lord.

18 In this verse the apostle begins to speak about the *word*. This indicates once more that the word is the main subject treated by Paul and that "wisdom" is a determinative of "word." Paul speaks of *the word of the cross*, i. e., the preaching which deals with the cross of Christ. This is remarkable for the apostle usually puts the resurrection in the center, but here he starts with the cross. The same is done in Galatians where we have a detailed exposition of the significance of Christ's death, especially in Gal. 5:11, where the best reading has: "the stumblingblock of the cross" (cf. Phil. 3:18). It appears that there was in the Greek world a view which could not recognize a Saviour who died on the cross. Paul starts with that fact. Certainly, in the eyes of the world the cross is folly. The Corinthians have not come to the point that they reject the cross. But danger threatens. He who attacks the character of the preaching, whether it be with respect to form or to content, will easily arrive at the place of those who reject the cross. Earlier the apostle had indicated that it is possible to deprive oneself of the fruits of the cross through faulty preaching. He now goes beyond that and states the reason for writing as he did. The preaching of the cross always has results. Some call this preaching folly; they are those who perish. The use of the present participle[38] implies that they will not just perish in the future but that they are on the way to perdition at this very moment (cf. II Cor. 4:3). And the Corinthians, who are still on the other side, run the danger that they may some time belong to that other group which really exists. Paul does not write that certain persons are going to perdition because they regard the preaching of the cross as folly, but he states that these people actually do so in fact. For God has commanded men to preach the cross of Christ as the only way of salvation (2:2) and those who despise this only way will suffer the consequences. On the other hand, the preaching of the cross is salvation to them who are being saved (pres. part.). To them it is a *power of God* (Rom. 1:16). Only God can save from a world in sin (1:8, 9). To this end He gives the preaching of the cross. He who has experience

---

[38] ἀπολλυμένοις. The dative has a subjective coloring. As such it means: "as those who are perishing think". But it also has an objective force: "to the perishing it is indeed a folly." The same remark can be made concerning the dative σωζομένοις (cf. also Ἰουδαίοις, ἔθνεσιν, κλητοῖς in vss. 23, 24).

44

of its power is on the way to salvation and cannot abandon that
way since he is kept through that power. To consider the preaching of the cross *foolishness* implies an element of rest, since it
adheres to a judgment once consciously and intentionally expressed. Those who judge so are going to perdition and may not
know it, but the power is always working and is always experienced. He who goes to eternal life has made the right choice.

Us is to be taken of Paul and the Corinthians. The Corinthians
belong to the group of the saved in spite of everything that Paul
finds fault with. The thought has now returned to the thanksgiving of vs. 4. To the Corinthians the preaching of the cross is
power of God. The living God reveals Himself in it. Again,
therefore, the apostle warns against dangers. There are some
traces of evil, but this evil has not yet come to full fruition.

19 Paul quotes Is. 29:14 literally according to the Septuagint.[39] There are men who boast of their wisdom and understanding, but God will stultify their wisdom and understanding
because they are human and ungodly (Job 5:12; Ps. 33:10; Is.
19:3). True wisdom is obtained from God alone. All other'
wisdom[40] is opposed to God and is not tolerated by Him. With
for it is written Paul declares that in the Old Testament already
God judged human wisdom, so that this opposition between the
wisdom of God and the wisdom of man is an old one. Paul is
here warning the Corinthians, who believed in the Holy Scriptures, against the world and he does so by appealing to those
Scriptures. Thus God Himself speaks in the world. He will
thwart all wisdom of man.

20 In connection with this quotation Paul asks some rhetorical
questions. *Where is the wise man?* The non-expressed answer
should be: He does not exist, for he is overpowered by God and
put to shame. The implication is not that there are no longer
any more worldly-wise men. The meaning is rather that where
the cross is preached human wisdom can no longer stand. Paul

---

[39] Only κρύψω is replaced by ἀθετήσω. It is difficult to say for
what reason. The Hebrew text has תסתתר: will conceal himself.
Paul may have followed another version or reading. By using the
first person the LXX indicates that it is God who destroys the
worldly wisdom.

[40] σοφία designates practical insight, σύνεσις refers to understanding, both with their implied results.

knows that the Corinthians will come to repentance through his questions. They need not answer these questions for they themselves know that worldly wisdom cannot be compared with divine wisdom. The first question is taken from Is. 19:12, the second one from a related passage, Is. 33:18. If both had been taken from the same passage we might think that the apostle had quoted a little more than was strictly necessary for his argument. As it is now the question arises why the apostle puts the *scribe* alongside of the wise man, while the context does not seem to call for that at all. The answer is that human wisdom may refer to Holy Writ. Knowledge of the Scriptures does not help if it is not accompanied by a believing submission to the word of the cross, the wisdom of God. When men defend their own wisdom with Scripture they also evidence this eloquent wisdom, a wisdom of words (cf. 4:6: "Not go beyond the things which are written"; 10:1-13).

The first word translated *world* denotes in the Greek the world as it exists in time, age,[41] the world not in rest, but in motion. It is almost: the spirit of the time. The *disputer*[42] *of this world,* the debater of this age, is the man who examines accurately and who disputes thereafter. This is a typically Jewish phenomenon. There have always been people who think that they are ready with everything when they understand their own time which they deem important above all. This is not the apostle's opinion. Human wisdom does not reach to the divine wisdom. Scripture teaches what the nature of the divine action is: *God makes foolish the wisdom of the world.* The Corinthians are convinced of that, as the apostle knows (Is. 44:25; Rom. 1:22). The second word *world* (kosmos) is the world at rest. What the apostle has really in mind here is the cross of Christ (cf. vs. 21). God entered into the world with its false presumption of wisdom and introduced something which goes counter to the wisdom of this world and condemns it, shows it up as foolishness in bringing about what the wisdom of the world was unable to accomplish. Christ was crucified and brought salvation to all who believe. This work of Christ demonstrates that the wisdom of the world is not wisdom

---

[41] The Greek has αἰών, the second word for "world" is κόσμος: the well ordered universe.

[42] Greek: συζητητής, a word used only here in the N.T. Its meaning is clear from the context and from the verb συζητεῖν.

at all, because it does not reckon with God (Jas. 2:15), neither does it accomplish anything.

21 Vs. 21 establishes proof for vs. 20. It begins with *for seeing* (RSV: *for since*[43]). Paul is absolutely sure that the Corinthians will agree with his argument. The world faces the wisdom of God, which here is not the wisdom revealed by God in His creation but His wisdom in the salvation of sinners by the cross of Christ, and the world affirms the existence of God without however seeing anything divine in the cross.

The explanation of the relation between the casual clause and the principal sentence is difficult. It would seem impossible that the sin of the world should be the motive for God's decree. The solution lies in the use of the Greek word[44] which is often employed of the decree of God, but may also have another meaning. Here it means the execution of God's decree in history. From the human point of view the world's ignorance comes first, God's work second, a work then represented as an omnipotent action of God ultimately based on His decree. God works out His decree of salvation, although the world considers it foolishness. God wrought foolishness because the world did not give up its wisdom (cf. Jn. 1:46; 7:47f.; Acts 4:27; I Cor. 2:8 and also vs. 14, which in recapitulation names the deepest reason why the wisdom of God is called folly). The words *wisdom* and *foolishness*, it should be noted, are used alternately of God and of the world. The first wisdom was, as Paul indicates, the wisdom of God, the second, as is also evident, is human wisdom. With "foolishness" there is no such indication but the context proves that it is foolishness according to the mind of man. The *foolishness of the preaching* represents the content of the preaching which God has commanded. The world calls Christ's work folly because He died on the cross. Paul preaches that it pleases God to work salvation in a way that is contrary to the ways of the world, because it is divine and it thus accomplishes an end which the world does not attain. The world condemns the preaching of the cross and yet only that folly which stirs up the wisdom of man can save. Believers are those who accept the divine preaching and abode by it. Faith, like the cross, is contrary to the world, since it belongs to

---

[43] Greek: ἐπειδὴ γάρ, in reality a double causal conjunction.
[44] εὐδόκησεν.

COMMENTARY ON FIRST CORINTHIANS

the folly of the world not to subject itself to God. Faith beholds wisdom where knowledge (cf. vs. 21) sees foolishness only. Vs. 21 has given a sufficient answer to the last question of verse 20. God's good pleasure makes foolish the wisdom of the world. The world does not get beyond the negative: a not knowing of God. Those *who believe,* on the contrary, find salvation.

22 This verse is also a causal clause.[45] The whole of vss. 22-24 furnishes the ground for vs. 21, in both of its parts. First it is demonstrated why the world with its wisdom did not recognize God in His wisdom, after which vss. 22 and 23 argue that God through the foolishness of the preaching saves believers. The apostle divides the world into Jews and Greeks, the two groups with which he himself and the Corinthians also had to deal. His intention is not to distinguish between people who had received the divine revelation and those who had not, but rather to point out the similarity between Jews and Greeks in their attitude toward the cross. Both are equally guilty before God. Paul strikingly speaks here only of the wisdom of the Greeks. The reason will be that the apostle in the preceding verses had the Corinthians concretely in mind, and they were Greeks. In this verse he refers to the Jews not because he wants to write about them but because he wants to show that he is not too bold when he speaks of the whole world (cf. Rom. 3:9f.).

The Jews *asked signs* from Jesus, i. e., they decided themselves in which way He had to show them His power. The Jews were only willing to submit if God would do something which was unusual in their eyes. They did know divine revelation but required that God should reveal Himself in a way which fitted their opinions concerning revelation. Thus they renounced the work of Christ in whom God was revealing His majesty and power. Christ's resurrection after His death upon the cross is such a revelation of God's majesty. (Mt. 12:38f.; 21:23; Jn. 2:18; 4:48; Rom. 1:4). The ideal of the Greeks is wisdom. This must be taken here as philosophy[46] and may include rhetoric. It leaves no place for the wisdom of God.

---

[45] Vs. 22 begins with ἐπειδή; so does vs. 21. Because we read καὶ before Ἰουδαῖοι and before Ἕλληνες and δὲ after ἡμεῖς, the clause with ἡμεῖς could not very well be the principal sentence.
[46] σοφία—φιλοσοφία.

48

23 This wisdom of God Paul and his helpers *preach* publicly in the world, at God's command and in God's way. The essence of this preaching is Christ crucified. Such a crucified Messiah is contrary to everything people expect. It should be remembered that the sound of the word "cross" was worse to Jewish and Greek ears than "noose" sounds to us.[47] A Christ on the cross is a *stumblingblock* to Jews, i. e., it is something that leads them to sin. They do not believe in a crucified Messiah (Mt. 27:42; Rom. 9:32).

To Gentiles Christ is folly because they have a wisdom of their own which leads them to reject the true Messiah. To preach such a Messiah is an honor for Paul, it is his vocation. The congregation should subject itself to this preaching, without making high demands or desiring eloquent wisdom (vs. 17), lest they deprive themselves of the bliss of the cross of Christ.

24 Paul knows of other people as well: them, *that are called.* The call to salvation occupies a rather important place in I Corinthians (cf. 1:2, 24, 26; 7:20). It is here connected on the one side with "them that believe," by which words it is further explained; on the other side it is related to "preaching" which points to yet another aspect. The power of the preaching is that it calls to faith (Rom. 1:16). God Himself calls through it and He calls definite persons, either Jews or Greeks, who are at this point one. To them that are called and believe, the crucified Christ is the power of God and the wisdom of God. This wisdom, which, as we observed, the world thinks foolishness, is nevertheless true wisdom because it saves sinners. The preceding word "power" means that God exercises power by it. The quiet of death prevails in the world with its wisdom. Just think what life is like in the world of the Greeks, despite their ethics. God, however, exercises power unto salvation through Christ crucified. The life of God's children is quite different from that of the sons of the world. There is a wisdom of God which works and saves in Christ. The world, because it despises this wisdom, lies under judgment.

---

[47] Cicero, pro Rabir, 16: nomen ipsum crucis absit non mode a corpore civium Romanorum, sed etiam a cogitatione, oculis, auribus. In Verrem, 5, 165: crux, crudelissimum taeterrimumque supplicium.

25 Vs. 25 indicates the grounds for the last words of vs. 24. Christ died on the cross and nevertheless He is the power and the wisdom of God. *The foolishness*[48] *of God* is that work of God which the world considers foolish: the work of God in Christ. What the world considers foolish and feeble, namely the death of Christ, is salvation for believers. It saves whereas the world cannot save. That is why the foolishness of God *is wiser than man.* These words denote man in all his knowledge and power. God's revelation, which by men is thought foolish and weak, is *stronger* than the strongest work of man.

26 Verse 26 contains the application of the foregoing to the church of Corinth. *Brethren* points to something new. As Paul approaches his final theses he begins to write truths that are universally valid.[49] *Calling* is a noun of action: "You see in what manner you are called." According to vs. 27 this is a calling to salvation (cf. "called," vs. 24). Vs. 26, and, strictly speaking, all the rest of this chapter, contain the reason for the preceding, inasmuch as Paul, who first wrote that Christ is the wisdom and the power of God and that the folly of God is wiser than man, is now proving all this by reminding his readers who they are according to worldly standards and who they are in Christ Jesus. God's calling is such that He chooses the foolish things of the world in order to put to shame the wise by giving Christ to the chosen ones to be their wisdom, etc. (vs. 30). The fact that Paul demonstrates this truth with the example of the Corinthians shows at the same time that his words may be applied to all who are called. This wisdom and power of God work always and everywhere. Paul does not say that the Corinthians are no longer the foolishness of the world, for that they remain. But they are also elect of God and that reveals their true character (Cf. Phil. 3:20). Christians are in the world but not of the world.

After the flesh: flesh is here not meant expressly as sinful flesh, though it should not be forgotten that "the flesh" is *de facto* always sinful. The context does not permit one, however, to limit the word to material appearance, since "wise" could not then be an attribute of it. The word "flesh" refers to the whole

---

[48] Greek: τὸ μωρὸν τοῦ Θεοῦ.

[49] Βλέπετε, indicative or imperative. Here it is indicative because of γάρ. The sentence is an affirmative one.

outward appearance, both material and spiritual. Paul writes *after the flesh*, because the believers have flesh and will keep it. The apostle does not say what they are in the eyes of the world but what they are and were in themselves, apart from their calling. *Noble* appears side by side with wise and *mighty*, which are explained in the foregoing verses. A noble birth is often the first thing that leads to power, at times also to wisdom. *Not many*: many members of the congregation may have been slaves or freed men.

27 *But* implies that Paul's preceding statement about the church, which, at first sight, might not seem honorable, need not cause any disturbance. On the contrary, even men of this sort are elected by God. Thus God elected Israel, the least of all nations (Deut. 7:7). Thus Christ called publicans and sinners. *Foolish things* are here qualified by *of the world,* i. e. what the world considers foolish.[50]

Chose: we need not determine whether Paul is speaking here about the counsel of God or about His work in history. For the Corinthians and all Christians with them are the object of God's work, which takes place according to His decree and which they recognize as God's work. (Jas. 2:5). *Chose,* or "elected," implies that the calling has a solid basis and that it also has results. Paul is explaining here that the work of God is contrary to that of the world. God chose for Himself[51] what was despised by the world and He did so to *put to shame them that are wise,* i. e., to show that an other, higher, divine wisdom exists which truly makes wise. God, who gives the final decision, puts the world to shame by showing that it is mistaken even though it considers itself wise. The same thing holds true of *the weak*. It is God's power which makes truly *strong,* so strong that what is strong in the world cannot challenge it. Facing the disdainful attitude of the world the church may be comforted to know that God Himself has called and elected her. Therein the church bears the

---

[50] The neuter τὰ μωρά is significant. It is distinguished from the masculine τοὺς σοφούς used both here and in the preceding verse. This neuter serves to emphasize the quality of those whom God chooses. That they are human beings is of secondary importance here. Τὰ μωρά (vs. 25 τὸ μωρόν) implies that there are many cases
[51] ἐξελέξατο is middle.

character of the crucified Christ (Is. 42:1f.; Mt. 21:42; I Pet. 2:6f.).

28 The word *noble,* introduced in vs. 26, is now elaborated upon. To this some other elements, not mentioned before, are added. In other words, the apostle sums up a series of qualities which are found in the members of the congregation and from which it appears that God made something of what was considered nothing. This is to demonstrate that all the glory must be rendered to the Lord.

Base is the opposite of noble (vs. 26).[52] It means: "of low birth," with reference to slaves; secondarily it denotes inferiority. The latter meaning, which is here intended, is expanded in the word "despised."[53] *The things that are not* are the things that have no real existence. These words summarize the opinion which the world holds with respect to church members. They simply do not count. *The things that are* are those things and persons that have authority in the world. They will all be destroyed by God and *brought to nought,* that is, reduced to a condition quite contrary to what they think of themselves and are thought to be in the world.

29 This work of God has a special purpose. The Corinthians gloried in men (cf. 1:12ff; also 3:21; 4:7 and II Cor. 10:17). Their boasting of men had led them to extol worldly wisdom which is also of man. Over against that Paul has placed the wisdom of God and the power of God, which are of quite a different character from human wisdom and power. By bringing the latter to nought God has shown that all glory must be brought to Him. By placing *that no flesh should glory* at the end Paul gives it added stress. The position of the negative *no* which in the Greek is placed before *should glory* causes the words *all flesh*[54] to retain their full strength. These words are indeed very strong but they nevertheless suit the context for in it the apostle has argued, on the one hand, that God has put the world to shame in its imaginary wisdom and, on the other, that the church is nothing of herself but has received everything from God. Since

---

[52] The Greek text has εὐγενής vs. 26, ἀγενής, vs. 28.

[53] Greek: ἐξουθενημένα, perfect participle, used not only to denote quality (when considered as an adjective) but also to indicate that that which once is despised will continue to be despised.

[54] Greek: ὅπως μὴ καυχήσηται πᾶσα σάρξ.

there are no other categories, the expression "all flesh" is appropriate, as indicating all of mankind according to its earthly existence (cf. "flesh," vs. 26). This flesh, standing before God, will not boast (Eph. 2:9). That is what God wanted to accomplish in order that He might reveal His power.

30   In vs. 29 the apostle arrived at a general statement, dealing with both believers and unbelievers. Vs. 30, on the contrary, has only believers in view and it elucidates with respect to them what was said in the preceding verse. The Church, also belonging to "all flesh," should not boast either, since it has received all its favors from God, owing to the work of Christ. Vs. 30 must not be taken to mean that the Corinthians owe their origin to God but they are here told to consider that they, at every moment of their life, are what they are through the power of God. And such they are in Christ Jesus for He was made all that the Christians are today. The Christians are therefore occupying a place of their own in the midst of all flesh. But that place they have only if they are closely united with Christ. Believers are not strong or wise of themselves, for their own would again be a wisdom of the world. They are joined to Christ who is their wisdom. So the words: *in Christ Jesus* are the main thing. This brings us again to vs. 24, the difference being that the apostle in vs. 30 does not speak of the cross of Christ but of the fruits of His work, as is implied in *was made,* which points to the work of Christ as revealing Himself in this way[55] in history. In connection with this Paul writes *unto us . . . from God.* These words, which go with "wisdom" must be taken as well with the other words of the verse. The use of *ye* and *us* indicates that Paul's word concerns all Christians and that he is speaking of what Christ has done for all believers. We also see here that Paul has been using the term "wisdom" quite appropriately inasmuch as Christ, in whose work the divine wisdom reveals itself, is our *wisdom from God* so that we know God through Him (Jn. 17:3; Col. 2:3). The wisdom of God is also making wise. However, Paul does not onesidedly limit the work of Christ. Christ is more than our wisdom, He is also our *righteousness* and *sanctification* and *redemption.* We may have here a standing expression from Paul's preaching. Such a view finds support in the fact that the

---

[55] ἐγενήθη is aorist.

53

apostle, while reverting to the term "wisdom" in chapter 2, does not mention righteousness and sanctification. But in any case, Christ is our all. What we are and have we are and have received from God through Christ. United to Christ we are righteous and holy, since all those blessings are founded in His work. *Righteousness* is followed by *sanctification,* i. e. there is justification once and for all but a continuous sanctification. *Redemption,* often used of the liberation of slaves through the payment of a ransom, indicates in what way Christ delivers us (Eph. 1:7), namely by His sacrifice, His death on the cross. In surrendering Himself He brings us knowledge, righteousness and holiness.

31 *That,* i. e. that it be. Already in vs. 29 Paul stated that all boasting is excluded. After vs. 30 has elaborated this point it is even more clear that we may glory only in the Lord. Whenever the Corinthians boast, they should do so in Christ and in perpetual union with Him.[56] Christians are allowed to glory for they are rich. However, they have received their riches from Christ, who redeemed them and therefore they ought to glory in Him as witnesses of His work. It should be noted that the quotation from Jer. 9:29 speaks of a boasting in God, which is here applied to Christ as is done often in the N. T. Its significance here is that God does this work through Christ (cf. vs. 30: *of Him in Christ Jesus*).

18-31 Paul describes to us the work of God as well as the condition of the Corinthian church. God's work is of quite another character than the work of the world. And that is exactly the reason why God is able to redeem a lost generation (cf. Rom. 8:3). This is what the Corinthians had to learn to understand since they were inclined toward the wisdom of the world, a wisdom of words. The apostle leads them to reflect upon the work of God in Christ Jesus. Let that, and not any wisdom of the world, be the Corinthians' expectation. In the eyes of the world they are accounted as nothing; and that world, which scorns the cross as foolishness, is on the way to eternal misery. Let them therefore look unto Christ, the power of God and the wisdom of God.

---

[56] ἐν κυρίῳ, in the sphere of the Lord Jesus Christ.

It strikes us that Paul does not refer to the parties and factions but addresses himself to the whole congregation. This is due to the fact that the formation of factions is a work of worldly wisdom in itself so that everyone needs to hear what Paul says. The apostle has thus lifted the question of the divisions to a higher plane.

CHAPTER II

FALSE AND TRUE WISDOM

2:1-16

1 And I, brethren, when I came unto you, came not with excellency of speech or of wisdom, proclaiming to you the testimony of God.

2 For I determined not to know anything among you, save Jesus Christ, and him crucified.

3 And I was with you in weakness, and in fear, and in much trembling.

4 And my speech and my preaching were not in the persuasive words of wisdom, but in demonstration of the Spirit and of power:

5 that your faith should not stand in the wisdom of men, but in the power of God.

6 We speak wisdom, however, among them that are fullgrown: yet a wisdom not of this world, nor of the rulers of this world, who are coming to nought:

7 but we speak God's wisdom in a mystery, *even* the *wisdom* that hath been hidden, which God foreordained before the world unto our glory:

8 which none of the rulers of this world hath known: for had they known it, they would not have crucified the Lord of glory:

9 but as it is written,
Things which eye saw not, and ear heard not,
And which entered not into the heart of man,
Whatsoever things God prepared for them that love him.

10 But unto us God revealed *them* through the Spirit: for the Spirit searcheth all things, yea, the deep things of God.

11 For who among men knoweth the things of a man, save the spirit of the man, which is in him? even so the things of God none knoweth, save the Spirit of God.

12 But we received not the spirit of the world, but the spirit which is from God; that we might know the things that were freely given to us of God.

13 Which things also we speak, not in words which man's wisdom teacheth; but which the Spirit teacheth; combining spiritual things with spiritual *words*.

14 Now the natural man receiveth not the things of the Spirit of God: for they are foolishness unto him; and he cannot know them, because they are spiritually judged.

15 But he that is spiritual judgeth all things, and he himself is judged of no man.

16 For who hath known the mind of the Lord, that he should instruct him? But we have the mind of Christ.

1 In 1:31 the apostle concluded by claiming all glory for God. Chapter 2 continues in the same trend to the extent that Paul begins by stating that his preaching in Corinth had been absolutely subject to the will of God and performed in His power only. Such preaching, it is further stated, can only be accepted through the working of the Holy Spirit. *And I;* the conjunction *and* takes up the main thought, mentioned in 1:18-25. *When I came* refers to the time of Paul's arrival at Corinth.[1] The Corinthians ought to remember that things had happened as the apostle relates. And if they did, their conduct was already partly condemned. The apostle's words characterize his preaching at the time of his first arrival at Corinth as well as his preaching in general.[2] With *brethren* Paul marks the beginning of a new part of his letter. *With excellency* is to be taken with *I came* as well as with *proclaiming,* because of the close connection between "came" and "proclaiming."

Not with excellency of speech or of wisdom: these words are not intended to deny that Paul could have come because he considered himself such a great orator, but they state simply that he did not come to proclaim the gospel with great oratorical talent. *Speech* and *wisdom* are coordinate in this verse. In 1:17 we have *wisdom of words*, in vs. 18 *word* alone, vs. 20: *wisdom* alone, in 2:4 we find *speech* first, and then *wisdom*. It appears necessary, therefore, to distinguish first between "word" or "speech" and "wisdom." The former term denotes the preaching, the latter represents the contents of the preaching. This could then be either

---

[1] The aorist participle ἐλθών precedes the aorist indicative ἦλθον. It must be translated: "when I came".

[2] ἦλθον (aorist); καταγγέλλων (present). This indicates the purpose of Paul's coming to Corinth but also what he kept doing wherever he went.

57

the cross of Christ, or the wisdom of the world (cf. II Cor. 1:12). The "word" may have a wisdom of its own (cf. 1:17), a wisdom which does not belong to it and therefore a worldly wisdom, yea the "word" may have such worldly wisdom as its only contents (2:4). In this verse *word* (speech, preaching) and *wisdom* are coordinate, and Paul states that he did not preach with excellency in either (II Cor. 11:16).

Excellency[3] denotes a rising out above something. Since Paul does not mention the standard of comparison we do well to take it as rising out above the ordinary measure. The term *excellency of speech* would thus become clear. The word, or the preaching, is only a means: it is the content which counts. When the preaching itself is stressed to such a degree that it obscures its own contents there is a case of excellency of speech. About the same thought lies in "wisdom of words" (1:17). But what of *excellency of wisdom*? Paul uses "wisdom" always of content, never of the manner of preaching (1:24, 30). We must bear in mind that wisdom in the end always implies an evaluation of the contents of the preaching. Christ crucified is its contents, which is part of true wisdom. Paul denies ever having set forth his preaching as wisdom in any but a seemly manner. It is one's duty and task to call the crucified Christ wisdom (1:30), but not in such a manner that his hearers would be mainly impressed by the fact that He is wisdom. That would be a making void of the preaching, against which 1:17 issues a warning. The true preaching of Christ has His saving work for its center (1:21). In our verse Paul does not yet use the term "preaching of Christ" but the context shows that this is meant. Verse 1 uses a different expression in order to bring to the fore another side of Christ's work: Paul preaches *the testimony of God*. From Acts 1:8 we learn in what sense this word *testimony*[4] must be taken. The giving of a testimony is not a relating of things believed and experienced by oneself. The apostles are witnesses because they attended the things Jesus did and spoke and because they are called to preach them (cf. I Jn. 1:1f.). The *testimony of God* is therefore the testimony which God gives and which has God as its contents.[5] Paul holds a mandate from God and he speaks of

---

[3] Greek: ὑπεροχή.
[4] Greek: μαρτύριον.
[5] The genitive Θεοῦ is both subjective and objective.

no one else but God. God has revealed Himself and the center of this revelation is the work of Christ. To speak of God is to speak of Christ. Here is a complete surrender to God and a giving up of all that is human. All this is expressed in the contrast between *I* at the beginning and *God* at the end of the verse.

2 Vs. 2 gives the reason of what Paul wrote in vs. 1. The reason is that Paul had not come to a decision or judgment, to know anything at Corinth, besides Jesus Christ.[6] The answer to the question whether Paul had ever preached anything but Jesus Christ must of course be negative. It is not that the apostle did not resolve to preach Jesus Christ until he came to Corinth. The meaning is rather that Paul, under the impression of his misfortune at Athens (cf. Acts 17), had formed for himself anew a clear idea of his task when going to Corinth. As he was reflecting upon his duty he had found none other to preach but *Jesus Christ and Him crucified*, regardless of the outcome. Paul did not set himself to a consideration of what he was to preach now, but he simply states that after considering everything he had come to the conclusion that he had to go on preaching Christ.[7] Hence *among you* cannot mean that Paul chose a special manner of preaching for the Corinthians, but it indicates that what he did at Corinth he did everywhere else and the Corinthians should know that (cf. 14:33).

To know does not speak of the preaching itself, but of its contents, of that which lies behind the preaching. "To know" here means: to accept as true for oneself and consequently to bring to others. That is the reason why the object of the verb is not "the testimony" but *Jesus Christ,* for thereby is indicated that knowledge of Christ also involves an accepting of Him. *Save:*[8] Jesus Christ is included in "anything," which precedes. The use of the full name of Jesus Christ implies that Paul has in view the whole work of our Saviour, on earth as well as in heaven. The name "Lord" is omitted because the reference is here to the cross.

---

[6] The Greek has ἔκρινα (aorist), stating a fact which has come to its conclusion when Paul arrived at Corinth.

[7] Paul does not write: ἔκρινα οὐκ εἰδέναι, but οὐκ ἔκρινά τι εἰδέναι.

[8] The Greek εἰ μή may be followed by something which is included in the preceding negation or by something not previously referred to. The context argues in favor of the first possibility.

The apostle does not omit the cross even though he knows that it is a stumblingblock unto the Jews and foolishness unto the Greeks (1:23; cf. Gal. 6:14) Had Paul been a preacher of worldly wisdom he would not have spoken about the cross, but his preaching would then have lost its power (1:17).

3 With another *And I* at the beginning of the verse (cf. vs. 1) the apostle takes up a new subject, shifting from his preaching to his person. In II Cor. 4:7ff. Paul argues that the gospel preacher is but a weak human being in every respect, to be compared with an earthen vessel containing a treasure. This truth is borne out not only by the outward circumstances but also by personal shortcomings of which the apostle speaks in our verse. The fear he mentions is not a fear of men or of misfortune. It is a fear for a possible failure to perform the great work to which he had been called. A feeling of weakness, of not being equal to the task he had to perform at Corinth, manifested itself in *fear* for what might happen to him and in a *trembling* under the burden of his work.⁹ The reference is here not to the apostle's outward acts (cf. v. 4) but rather to his inward condition. The apostle's work had not been done in his own strength (II Cor. 12:10), not with excellency of speech or of wisdom, but in humbleness (cf. Acts 18:9, where fear must have been the occasion). Although Paul in his letters and in the account of his activities in Acts never makes the impression of being a weak man, he often speaks about his weakness (4:10, II Cor. 11:30; 12:5, 9; Gal. 4:13). The special mention made of it here is probably due to the fact that there was so much haughtiness in the Corinthian church; also that the apostle had not had much fruit either in Athens or during his first period in Corinth. *I was* does not refer to his initial coming to Corinth only, but to the whole of his work in that city.¹⁰ The Corinthians no doubt had not noticed that Paul was in this state of mind while abiding in their midst. Such a relation can arise only after a repeated calling to Christ. They, who themselves are so haughty, are now informed that Paul performed his work without any spirit of self-sufficiency.

---

⁹ Since ἀσθένεια is coordinate with φόβος and τρόμος (cf. Eph. 6:5; Phil. 2:12), and all three are joined with ἐγενόμην, ἀσθένεια cannot be taken of an actual bodily weakness but must indicate a sense of weakness which determines one's conduct.

¹⁰ ἐγενόμην is aorist to be sure, but πρός indicates a relation.

4 After having spoken of his person Paul now returns to his preaching. He distinguishes between his *speech* and his *preaching*. The former probably concerns the contents, the latter the public proclamation of the gospel to all men.[11] His aim is to show that he did not use any illicit means with respect to either contents or form as the Corinthians had desired him to do (cf. 1:17; 2:1). *Wisdom* here has clearly the connotation of worldly wisdom. The apostle rejects a preaching in worldly words of worldly wisdom. Paul has no objection to *persuading words,* on the contrary he uses them himself, but he objects to persuading words dictated by worldly wisdom.[12] Since "wisdom" in this context refers to content, it must stand for words containing worldly wisdom, i. e. words used as such in the pagan world of that time. It is an established fact that the Greeks during the first century would use that sort of stereotyped forms. But Paul, refusing to use words that were inspired by worldly wisdom, goes on to say that his words had rather been *in demonstration of the Spirit and of power.* This does not mean that Paul in his preaching displayed spirit and power, but rather that the Holy Spirit and the power of God (1:18, 24) manifested themselves in his preaching. And in doing so they demonstrated thereby the truth of Paul's preaching. Several other N. T. references bear out the fact that the preaching of the gospel was accompanied by a special working of the Holy Spirit: Mk. 16:17, 18; Lk. 10:19; Acts 28:3-6, and especially Heb. 2:4. (cf. Rom. 15:19; I Cor. 1:6; 4:20; I Thess. 1:5). Paul has in mind the miracles of God which demonstrated the truth of the proclamation of the gospel. No doubt the many particular gifts of the Spirit, the so-called charismata, which were found in the church of Corinth, are meant in

---

[11] Greek: ὁ λόγος μου καὶ τὸ κήρυγμά μου.

[12] The various readings of vs. 4 are worthy of note. ℵ A B C D present the reading πειθοῖς σοφίας λόγοις. A universal acceptance of this reading might have been expected, if it were not for the word πειθός which is not otherwise known as an adjective (see Bauer, s.v. et al.). Many expositors follow a different and later reading. The ancient Fathers, on the other hand, offer no objection to the word πειθός. There are also other words of the same type. There is therefore no sufficient ground for rejecting the reading πειθοῖς.

this verse (See chs. 12 and 14; also II Cor. 12:12).[13] The world, according to the apostle, has its own wisdom, characterized by certain words. With its wisdom the world may persuade the people but it will accomplish nothing. With Paul it is different: when he preaches the testimony of God, God comes from heaven and works miracles. Yea, the very existence of the Gentile church itself is a manifestation of the power of God.

5 Vs. 5 states the reason why Paul refused to use words of human wisdom, or, more accurately, it indicates the goal of *the demonstration of the Spirit and of power* and consequently the goal of all that precedes, i. e., the work of God through Paul's ministry. *Faith* refers here to the act of believing, since the content of faith is not mentioned in this context. To *stand in* means "to rest upon." If Paul had preached human wisdom and if the Corinthians had become Christians on that basis then human wisdom would have been the ground of their faith. But instead God had given wonders from heaven and that had worked faith in their hearts. This had not happened without the preaching, inasmuch as the signs cannot be separated from the preaching. Christ, the center of the preaching, is the *power of God* and for that reason the preaching itself is also *power* (1:18,24). In other words: the one power of God, revealing itself chiefly in Christ and accompanying the preaching of Christ is the ground for the act of faith of the Corinthians. It is the power of the Spirit that changes the sinner (cf. vs. 14, 15) so that he recognizes the power of God in Christ. Thus Paul gives us a description of the goal of all proclamation of the gospel. And he rejects especially a type of preaching which, according to 1:17, was desired at Corinth.

6 In vs. 6 Paul continues to state that in spite of all that he wrote he does *speak wisdom*. Here the riddle is solved and two sorts of wisdom are plainly distinguished. The use of the plural (*we speak*) implies that what follows concerns not only Paul

---

[13] ἐν ἀποδείξει indicates the manner of revelation. The absence of the article before πνεύματος and δυνάμεως shows that the reference is not to one particular expression of power. Since δυνάμεως lacks the article, it was also omitted before πνεύματος. Of course πνεῦμα and δύναμις are not of the same order. The Holy Spirit is the source of this power. That is demonstrated by vs. 5 where δυνάμει occurs with Θεοῦ.

himself but also all preachers. *Among them that are fullgrown*
The word translated "fullgrown" means: having reached its end,
its zenith. It is here used of Christians who are perfect Christians
(Heb. 5:14). The truth that absolute perfection is not found on
earth is not now under discussion. The reason why Paul uses
this word here is not that he would recognize many kinds of
Christians, some more and others less initiated. That would
conflict with the whole tenor of this letter. The distinction is
rather between those in the Corinthian church who valued highly
the wisdom of the world and despised the preaching of the apostle
and those who had freed themselves of the world and recognized
Paul's preaching as true wisdom. The latter are those who are
fullgrown. *Among them that are fullgrown* must be closely
connected with "wisdom." True wisdom is regarded as such by
the fullgrown.[14] They who have broken with the world now see
Paul's preaching as wisdom because there is no connection
between what the apostle and his helpers proclaim and the world.
Neither is there such a connection with the *rulers of this world,*
i. e., with those who determine the character of this world. The
word "rulers" must not be taken of magistrates only since Paul
has in mind all those who set the pattern of this world, including
the rulers in the sphere of science and art. Of all of them it holds
true that they *are coming to nought.*[15] The answer to the question why this is so lies in the victory which Christ, who is the
wisdom of God (1:30), has gained (15:24f.). However, that is
not the point the apostle is stressing here as he speaks of his
missionary work.

7 *But* introduces the positive side again. At the same time
there is a strong negative emphasis as well: (1) the wrong standpoint of the Corinthians is condemned and (2) the mighty character of the divine wisdom can hardly be expressed in positive
terms only.

Paul has been giving us a more detailed exposition of the
wisdom of this world than in chapter 1. He now proceeds to do

---

[14] The Greek has ἐν τοῖς τελείοις, i.e. in the eyes of those who
are fully grown.

[15] The present participle καταργούμενοι reminds us of the present
participle in 1:18. The rulers of the world are coming to nought.

the same with regard to the divine wisdom.[16] The fact that *in a mystery* precedes *that hath been hidden* demonstrates that the two phrases are not to be taken together but must be regarded as two determining clauses with "wisdom." *In a mystery* indicates the way in which wisdom manifests itself: Its form is one of mystery. *Mystery,* in Paul's usage, refers to things long hidden but now revealed (Eph. 3:3; Col. 1:26). *Hidden* does not mean "totally unknown," but "not yet existing." The words *mystery* and *hidden* are particularly fitting since "wisdom" in this context materially refers to Christ and His work (1:24, 30). The use of "mystery" also points out that Christ, our wisdom, surpasses our human understanding (cf. 15:15; Eph. 5:32). The meaning of "hidden" is not: which is still hidden, but: which was hidden, as is evident from the position of the word itself (after "mystery") and from vs. 10: *but unto us God revealed them.* Paul is using such a full expression in order that he, as afterwards appears, may convince the Corinthians that they are in the possession of very great benefits. They should not complain that they have to give up worldly wisdom, for God's direction causes them to enjoy something never revealed before, real wisdom, rich in content. That this is the sense of Paul's words can be gathered from what follows. The time in which Christ, the wisdom of God, came to this earth and did His work is present even now. This wisdom is a saving one (1:18, 21). Paul ascends to the decree of God: *foreordained before the worlds* (cf. Mt. 13:35). *Before the worlds* stands in opposition to *of this world,* vs. 8. The rulers who reject Christ belong to this present age, but God was working before all worlds.[17] With God the wisdom which was hidden, i. e., the work of Christ, stood firm even before time began. That gives the Corinthians solidity and certainty because it shows that the work of Christ, i. e., the wisdom of God, was from all eternity included in God's decree. Its revelation was not something accidental and hence it must open the eyes of the Corinthians to the great benefits they received in experiencing this revelation. This is also implied in *unto our glory.* The glory of the believers is an essential part of God's decree. Not only did God fix His wisdom, He also ordained that this wisdom would bring glory to us who

---

[16] Θεοῦ σοφίαν lacks articles, and so means: "divine wisdom", not "the wisdom of God".

[17] Greek αἰών, i.e. the world as it exists in time; age.

are Christians. The rulers of the world, on the contrary, will perish. The very fact that God determined the work of Christ from all eternity, connected with this work such consequences, and caused it to come to pass in time is the reason why it can be called wisdom of God. In 1:18, 21 the apostle spoke of salvation, now he comes to its final goal: *glory* just as he also descends to its deepest source: the decree of God.

8 *Which,* a relative pronoun coordinate with "which" in vs. 7, and hence not to be taken with "glory" but with "wisdom." Paul reverts to the negative (cf. vs. 6), and he does so in a relative clause which is still depending on the adversative *but* of vs. 7, which, in turn introduced a contrast with verse 6. The first reason for this arrangement of subject matter may be the apostle's desire to speak in this context about the cross of Christ and to do so in connection with the rulers of this world. The second reason is his intention to write of the deliberate deeds of the rulers in order thus to furnish evidence for the strong statement in vs. 6. Moreover, since many at Corinth were enticed by worldly wisdom it was necessary for them to realize even negatively how much the possession of only worldly wisdom would cost them.

None of the rulers: the use of this strong expression does not deny the existence of a Nicodemus and a Joseph of Arimathea. It simply implies that all that is high and exalted among the Jews as well as the Gentiles in this world is in opposition to Jesus. What the Jews did in cooperation with Pilate is the manifestation of the spirit of this age over against Christ. Those who crucified Christ are the representatives of the rulers of this world, i. e., they are the powers who determine the character of this world. *None* does not refer to individuals but to the group. The apostles in Jerusalem expressed the same thought (Acts 4:27). The idea of knowing in this verse includes the idea of acknowledging, as is often the case. It designates an intentional spiritual act which forms the foundation for the whole behavior. That spiritual act is the main thing as is evident from the fact that Paul does not write: they crucified the Lord of glory for they did not acknowledge him, but on the contrary: they did not acknowledge Him as appeared from their crucifying Him.

Jesus is called *the Lord of glory,* even though Paul speaks about Christ in His humiliation. Before His ascension Christ already had glory but that glory did not shine forth. The rulers ought to have seen this glory, and they could have if they had believed, for if one believes he esteems as wisdom that which seems to be foolishness (1:21; 2:14; Jn. 5:24, 38; 6:29, 36). During his life on earth Christ was acknowledged as Saviour by them that believed (Mt. 16:16). To condemn Him to the ignominy of a cross is evidence of unbelief and of a not acknowledging the wisdom of God who revealed Himself in Christ's glory. Paul's emphasis on the glory of Christ must be seen in the light of vs. 7: *unto our glory*. That glory is the great goal toward which Christ leads us and He is able to do so because He possesses glory himself (II Cor. 3:18; Phil. 3:20f).

9 *But as it is written* is an abridged clause. The whole of verse 9 is an anacolouthon for *but unto us God revealed* in verse 10 cannot be construed as the apodosis of vs. 9a. We might paraphrase: But in contrast with what the rulers of this age did, the words of Scripture were fulfilled where it is written etc. This quotation is consequently not introduced in order to prove some of the foregoing statements. It is not a matter of proof for Paul but one of similarity: hence the word *as*. Things that were true in former times appear to be true in Paul's time. The passage quoted demonstrates the unity of the work of God and points to the great glory of believers.

The exact O. T. reference of these words was unknown to the early church fathers as it is to us. Some have thought that Paul is quoting from the apocrypha but others have denied that.[18] The well known fact that Paul is often very free in quoting the Old Testament, so that he joins different texts together, makes it possible that a number of texts were here combined into a hymn and that this hymn is now quoted by the apostle (cf. I Tim. 3:16). The view that Paul quotes the Old Testament, using passages like Is. 64:4, LXX (64:3 in the Hebrew) for the first and the last part of the quotation and Is. 65:17 for the middle, remains the most plausible one. The question whether this quotation does justice to the original meaning of the passages is irrelevant, because it is introduced with *as* and not with *because*. Paul had been speaking of the wisdom of God in Christ which the

---

[18] For a fuller discussion see e.g. A. Resch, *Agrapha*, 1906, pp. 25f; 110 f.

world did not acknowledge. Of this wisdom he says that no eye hath seen it, etc. The salvation God gives in Christ surpasses all thoughts of men. Sense organs and mind combined are not able to come to the knowledge of the wisdom of God, revealed in Christ. The apostle has in view the fullness of bliss which Christ has acquired, as appears from the word "glory" (vs. 7). But not only that final bliss is at stake but all the wisdom of God, revealed in Christ Jesus. As the first and second part of the verse imply the greatness of this blessedness, the third part indicates those for whom it is destined.

Whatsoever implies that all that God does is great. *For them that love Him* suits the context. For the words quoted consider God's wisdom from our viewpoint, point out our duty with respect to it and the condition under which we may rely upon it. We who are sinners are permitted to love God! *Prepared* implies that all these benefits descend from God, since He prepared them in His counsel so that they are ready to be revealed (vs. 7, cf. 1:30, *of Him*). If the love of God dwells in our hearts then the benefits are ours and are revealed to us. The teaching of vss. 14ff. is that we cannot come to that love of God of ourselves (cf. I Jn. 4:10, 19). All things come from God.

As verse 8 elaborated upon vs. 6b, so verse 9 contains an explanation of *in a mystery* in vs. 7. Verse 10 is to develop the thought contained in *hidden* (vs. 7).

10 In this verse Paul states, this time without quotation, what God has given to believers (*unto us*). To a certain extent we have here a transition, since the apostle does not refer to wisdom any more but speaks of the mature and, in this connection, of the way in which this work of God prepared beforehand had become known in the world. *For* introduces the reason why the apostle could say that things were as they were written. *Revealed* relates the historic fact that God showed to believers the things which the rulers did not see, namely that Christ is the wisdom of God, through which revelation Christ could be recognized as such (cf. Mt. 16:17). Not only Christ Himself comes from God but also the recognition of Him. A mystery must be revealed, it is a revelation which can be made only *through the Spirit*. The Spirit, in this context (cf. vs. 11), is the Spirit of God, the Holy Ghost. Nevertheless it is important that Paul does not write "through the Spirit of God" but "through the Spirit," lest we should think that here the self-consciousness, or personality of God are meant. But that is out of question. The Spirit is the Person of the Holy Ghost. Furthermore, we must bear in mind that Paul bases his whole argument on the threefold sense of the word "spirit." It is used of the Spirit of God, of the sanctified spirit of the believer and of the highest organ of man. The fact that "spirit" is not used in that threefold sense today might cause us to miss the point of Paul's argument to a great extent. Since to the apostle the three are to a certain extent one, he can argue the way he does; hence the use of *for*.

Through,[19] not: by, because God is subject of *revealed*. God works through His Spirit on earth. Before stating the manner of this operation the apostle wants us to know that we cannot recognize Christ as the wisdom of God of ourselves but only when the Spirit reveals it to us. That is the implication of the second part of vs. 10. The Spirit *searches all things,* therefore (cf. *for*) God reveals through the Spirit. The work of the Spirit is here spoken of in general. The Spirit penetrates into all things and searches them. Not because there are certain things which the Spirit would not know but because the very work of the Spirit is to search (cf. Jn. 5:17). There is nothing but action, always present, never past. God's omniscience is here especially predicated of the Spirit. He even searches *the deep things of God*: nothing is excluded from His searching. The depths of God are the same as "the things of God" in vs. 11. This shows that the deep things of God are God Himself in His infinitude. God is endless, eternal, omnipresent, inscrutable (Job 15:8: Ps. 139:17, 18; 147:5; Is. 40:13; Jer. 23:18; Rom. 11:34). Versc 16 shows that this is Paul's train of thought. To these depths of God the plan of salvation in Christ Jesus also belongs as Rom. 11:33 bears out. Likewise the context makes clear that the reference is not to some abstract inscrutability of God but to the concrete work of salvation. This points us to the benefits of believers inasmuch as God, through the Spirit, has revealed unto us His wisdom, Christ Jesus (cf. 12:3). To believers the cross is not a stumblingblock or foolishness. Christ is to them the wisdom and power of God (vs. 14). When Christ came to earth His own

---

[19] διά, not ὑπέρ.

people did not receive Him, but to all who received Him He gave power to become children of God (Jn. 1:11, 12).

11 Verse 11 introduces another causal clause which must serve as a clarification of the statement made in vs. 10 concerning the Spirit searching the deep things of God. There are two elements: a rhetorical question which implies a negative answer, followed by a clause introduced by *even so*. The positive notion of the second clause agrees with the positive idea of the rhetorical question.

Who among you, a very general expression. The same can be said of *the things of man*. These words include everybody, wherever in the world and whenever he may have lived, and all things concerning man, even the deepest motives of his soul. *Save* has the sense of "but."[20] *The spirit of the man, which is in him* stands for the person of man, his ego, his self-consciousness, because this phrase is again general, and is applicable to everyone. The spirit of man refers to that which dwells in every man (Prov. 20:27). That spirit is in man and in the way of self-examination man can know things of which no outsider at any time can be aware. *Which is in him* has therefore an important function in the sentence. The addition of these words makes it impossible to consider the relation which the Spirit of God sustains to God as comparable to that which the spirit of man sustains to man, so that the Spirit of God would thus be interpreted in terms of God's person or self-consciousness. Not only verse 10 but verse 11 also militates against such an interpretation because of the emphasis on the words *which is in him*. In other words, the relation of the human spirit to man is expressed in a way which differs from the relation of the divine Spirit to God. The point of comparison is that a spirit can know something which anybody else or anything else cannot know. In order to explain at least to a certain extent how it is possible that the Spirit of God knows the deep things of God Paul mentions what the human spirit is capable of doing. The Spirit of God, the Holy Spirit, is with God and is Himself God (cf. Gal. 4:6). He therefore knows the deep things of God. This interpretation is also demanded by vs. 12, because in that verse it is impossible to take the words

---

[20] εἰ μή has an inclusive and an exceptive use; here it is exceptive: τὸ πνεῦμα τοῦ ἀνθρώπου τὸ ἐν αὐτῷ is not comprehended under ἀνθρώπων.

the Spirit which is from God of the self-consciousness of God. The *Spirit of God* in this context is always the Person of the Holy Ghost, as usually in the Pauline epistles (Rom. 8:9, 14; I Cor. 3:16; 6:11).

Verse 10 spoke of the Spirit's searching activity, thus indicating a fullness of action. To this is added the idea of result in the word *knows* (vs. 11), which differs in meaning from the identical English word at the beginning of the verse, as it includes recognition (cf. vs. 8).[21] The searching goes on, certainly, but not because it would not yet be finished (cf. Rom. 8:27: *searches, knows,* side by side).

12 Vs. 11 was but a link in the chain of the argument, serving to demonstrate the reason for the words *through the Spirit* (vs. 10). Now Paul returns to the main point: God did reveal it to us through the Spirit because we received the Spirit. The words: *we received not the spirit of the world* do not imply that such a spirit of the world exists. Neither is this spirit to be identified with the devil, for the thought that the believers had received the devil would never occur to anyone. Paul simply wants to set forth the Christian's privilege, not only positively but negatively as well, in connection with the trend of the argument. All that is meant is: we received the Spirit, not a spirit of this world (cf. Rom. 8:15). Nor does Eph. 2:2 imply the existence of a spirit of this world, because there the devil is meant, which is not the case in our verse. Here we have again the antithesis between what is from the world and what comes from God (cf. 1:20, 21, 27, 28). Thus it is made clear that the Spirit whom we have received has no connection with the world. The order of words sets forth very clearly what the privileges of believers are. When the apostle speaks of *the Spirit which is from God* he designates the Spirit as the self-existent One. The Spirit proceeded from God and came to believers. That is more than was said in verse 11. The reference is here to Pentecost (cf. Gal. 4:6). What is meant is not the perpetual indwelling of the Spirit in the congregation but the historical fact of His coming (cf. Gal. 3:5).[22] *We received the Spirit* once *that we should know* always the gifts of God. Our spirit, changed by the

---

[21] The Greek has οἶδεν at the beginning of vs. 11 and ἔγνωκεν in the last sentence. RSV: "knows" and "comprehends".

[22] Because the apostle uses the aorist ἐλάβομεν.

Spirit of God, knows (cf. vs. 15). The apostle does not enumerate all the various purposes of the Spirit's coming as a comparison with Rom. 8:25 bears out. In our context he speaks of the intellectual gifts of the Spirit. *Freely given,* bestowed (RSV), are the gifts of God's grace. This has reference to the benefits acquired by Christ (1:30). The Spirit grants us knowledge of those gifts, i. e., we possess them not only but we can discern them.

Paul has herewith returned to 1:21ff., where he emphasized that the world, by not knowing Christ, stands against the believers. We, the believers, know now that it is through the gift of the Spirit that we may know Christ as the power and the wisdom of God.

13 Consequent upon knowledge is *speaking;* there is a close connection between the two. On the one hand, this speaking is something new and not just a natural consequence from the words *revealed unto us* in vs. 10, but on the other hand we should not forget that at the head of this pericope we read: *we speak wisdom* (vs. 6). The apostolic activity, referred to in vs. 6, is further enlarged upon in vs. 13. But that is not all, since the apostle clearly has in view speaking as it is the task of every Christian. The Christian, distinguished from the world by the Spirit, speaks, as often as he does speak, of the grace of God. All the following verbs are in the present tense and thus point to what the Christian once endowed with the Spirit always does.

The reference to *words* is not surprising in the light of the preceding (1:17; 2:1, 4) in which there was frequent mention of words. The character of the words used by Christians are now positively described as words taught by the Spirit and not by any wisdom of man.[23] *Spirit,* the Holy Spirit again. In drawing up another antithesis, as in verse 12, the apostle does not want to infer that human wisdom does teach words, although we know from the preceding that that is actually the case. The apostle's intention is rather to set forth, first antithetically and then also thetically, the manner in which believers speak. Their words also are from the Spirit. The importance of this lies in the fact

---

[23] The Greek διδακτοῖς is a verbal adjective with the sense of a perfect participle: when someone speaks in words "that can be learned" those words have actually been learned. διδακτός, therefore, has developed into an adjective construed with the genitive. The expression means: not in words taught by human wisdom.

that these words are not neutral but have a definite content, a special color, and lead the thoughts in a certain direction. This must be understood of the certainty we have that words, which are used to speak of the things revealed by God, are in harmony with that revelation and themselves are given by the Spirit. How to explain this is taught in the following words. The word *spiritual* which Paul uses here always has the sense: connected with, or inspired by, the Holy Spirit. The word is used of all the members of the church, not only of those endowed with special gifts (charismata). *Spiritual* are all Christians because they have received the Holy Spirit. Spiritual things, spiritual words, are things or words stamped by the Spirit.

Combining, or better: comparing[24] (cf. II Cor. 10:12). The believers speak in words taught by the Spirit, which is evident also herein that they compare etc. So the comparing is added to the speaking, of which it is a further definition. *Spiritual* indicates the character of the contents. Paul intends to speak of the work of believers through which they in their speaking, in words taught by the Spirit, compare spiritual things with other spiritual things in order to come to a more definite conception and to penetrate more deeply into them. The comparing precedes the speaking. Thus the apostle calls attention to the spiritual task of believers. With full consciousness and ardent love they are engaged in the things which are of the Spirit of God and their speaking gives testimony thereof. The life of the believers has a character of its own, it is quite different from that of unbelievers. A glance at 3:1 shows us that Paul is picturing the ideal in our verse. Not as if he would imply that the Corinthians do not belong to the spiritual category. To hold that would be contrary to vs. 16b (cf. vs. 12). The Corinthians are not yet perfect but they are nevertheless spiritual in Christ.

---

[24] The RSV translates: interpreting spiritual truth to those who possess the spirit. A footnote suggests the following: *comparing spiritual things with spiritual*. This translation must, in our opinion, be preferred. Reasons: a) the first meaning of συγϰρίνω is "to compare" (see: Moulton and Milligan s.v.) b) πνευματιϰοῖς lacks the article. c) Paul speaks here of the contents of the words and of the way in which they are spoken, not of the people to whom they are spoken (cf. vs. 14, 15).

14   *Natural* is that which belongs to nature.[25] A natural man is a man who has an unchanged nature, i. e., unconverted. Natural is the opposite of spiritual (cf. Jude 19: "sensual," RSV: "worldly people"[26]), not having the Spirit. There is no reference here to an antithesis between soul and body but to one between the unconverted and the converted life. A natural man is a man who only lives but who has not received the Holy Spirit. Such a man does not *receive,* i. e., acknowledge, recognize or understand *the things of the Spirit* (Jn. 8:47; Jas. 1:21). The believer is entirely under the influence of the Spirit, the natural man is so utterly destitute of the Spirit's working that he cannot even see the things of the Spirit and consequently cannot speak of them. The contrast is an absolute and a general one (Jn. 14:17; Rom. 8:5f). Verse 14 no longer deals with the speaking of which vs. 13 made mention, as is clear also from the absence of any reference to speaking in vs. 15. Verses 14 and 15 give a general characterization. They have in view hearing, speaking, acting and even thinking. Paul reaches back to 1:18, for certainly, one of "the things of the Spirit" which the natural man does not receive is the word of the cross. The apostle's statements concerning the cross (1:18) and Christ (1:24) are here given in a more general form. All the works of the Spirit are considered *foolishness* by natural wisdom so that it does not acknowledge them. The words: *he cannot know them* are still stronger, since they do not merely refer to what the natural man attempts but what is objectively true about him; they refer to his condition. The natural man is closed to the workings of the Spirit in the same way that the cross of Christ is foolishness to him (1:18). *Know* is one of the elements implied in acknowledging: this knowing must precede the act of acknowledgment. Why this is so is stated in the last part of the verse. Things spiritual can only be searched and judged spiritually, i. e., through the illumination of the Holy Spirit. *To judge* is here to compare, to combine, to know the one thing after the other.[27] The cause of the inability

---

[25] ψυχικός is he who only has ψυχή and no πνεῦμα which is born again by the Holy Spirit.

[26] The Greek has ψυχικός, the same 'word as in I Cor. 2:14.

[27] Greek ἀνακρίνειν is defined by Thayer's Lexicon: "looking through a series of objects or particulars to distinguish or search after".

of the natural man is not traced back to God's decree but is said to be due to the character of the work of the Spirit. Thus the benefits of believers and the misery of unbelievers are clearly set forth. This the Corinthians with their "wisdom" should understand at once.

15 The contrast with vs. 14, expressed in vs. 15, links it with the thought of vs. 12 and 13. The contents of these verses is not repeated or elaborated upon but something new is added. Perhaps the occasion for this addition is to be found in the verb "to judge," since of the natural man it was said that his inability to judge spiritually prevented him from receiving the things of the Spirit. The spiritual man, on the contrary, is able to judge in the right way. That a spiritual judging is in view here is not said in so many words but is nevertheless apparent from the fact that the acting subject is the spiritual man himself who will act spiritually. *All things,* with emphasis. Not as if the spiritual man would have to state his opinion about everything. The implication is rather that he is able and permitted to judge. The spiritual man is not limited in his judging: everything he desires to judge he may judge. Precisely because the Spirit searches all things (vs. 10) the spiritual man, who received the Spirit (vs. 12), can judge also.

And *he* himself *cannot be judged* by anyone, which is another privilege of those who are in possession of the Spirit. Of course *all things* has its self-evident limits: the depths of God, the work of God in the believers, etc., are excluded. From the foregoing also follows that *no man,* i. e., nobody, must be understood in the first place of the unbeliever, the natural man. The latter, though he may imagine many things, is nevertheless far removed from the spiritual man, since he esteems the cross of Christ foolishness. He cannot know, or judge, spiritually.

16 The quotation is from Is. 40:13. The word *mind,* which is not found in the context, is here used because it was in the Greek text of Is. 40. It introduces for the first time an anthropomorphic expression with reference to God and follows quite properly after the use of "to judge," which implies an activity of the discriminating mind. Perhaps Paul chose this quotation precisely because of the use of the word "mind" in it.

The spiritual man, who received the Spirit, is thereby enabled to judge or not to judge. For of the Spirit, who is God, it is true

74

that nobody knows His mind to *instruct Him*. This Spirit works in the spiritual man. No natural man can understand, or even judge, the work of God in the spiritual man.

The last words of the verse show how God works in those who are spiritual. *The mind of the Lord* is unsearchable, as members of Christ we participate through Him in the mind of God. We have *the mind of Christ*, and consequently also the mind of the Lord, for Christ is the Lord and much of what the Old Testament says of the Lord Jehovah must be applied to Christ (cf. 3:23; 11:3; Rom. 8:5f., 14f.) All this can of course be said of the perfect, the fully grown spiritual man, in connection with the blessings of Pentecost.

1-16 The answer to the question of whom Paul writes all these things must be: of all believers (cf. 1:18-31). It is true, Paul sometimes thinks especially of the gospel preachers (1:23), but he links their preaching with the blessings of all. It is the privilege of all believers which leads the apostle to the subject of preaching. Of chapter 2 one can say at best the reverse: In vss. 1-7 Paul speaks of the preaching of the gospel to believers in order in vs. 8 to make a gradual transition to all believers. Verse 12 cannot be meant of the preachers only; moreover vs. 13 does not refer to the apostolic proclamation but to the speaking of all who believe.

In the light of this evaluation the aim of this whole pericope is apparent. Paul points out the great blessings of those who possess the preaching of the divine wisdom, either as preachers or as hearers. He sets forth what is the cause of those benefits and how they distinguish those who possess them from those who do not possess them. The apostle sings a hymn of praise to the wisdom of God, given to the believers by the Holy Spirit.

CHAPTER III

GOD, HIS SERVANTS AND HIS CONGREGATION

3:1-17

1 And I, brethren, could not speak unto you as unto spiritual, but as unto carnal, as unto babes in Christ.

2 I fed you with milk, not with meat; for ye were not yet able *to bear it*: nay, not even now are ye able;

3 for ye are yet carnal: for whereas there is among you jealousy and strife, are ye not carnal, and do ye not walk after the manner of men?

4 For when one saith, I am of Paul; and another, I am of Apollos; are ye not men?

5 What then is Apollos? and what is Paul? Ministers through whom ye believed; and each as the Lord gave to him.

6 I planted, Apollos watered: but God gave the increase.

7 So then neither is he that planteth anything, neither he that watereth; but God that giveth the increase.

8 Now he that planteth and he that watereth are one: but each shall receive his own reward according to his own labor.

9 For we are God's fellow-workers: ye are God's husbandry, God's building.

10 According to the grace of God which was given unto me, as a wise masterbuilder I laid a foundation; and another buildeth thereon. But each man take heed how he buildeth thereon.

11 For other foundation can no man lay than that which is laid, which is Jesus Christ.

12 But if any man buildeth on the foundation gold, silver, costly stones, wood, hay, stubble;

13 each man's work shall be made manifest: for the day shall declare it, because it is revealed in fire; and the fire itself shall prove each man's work of what sort it is.

14 If any man's work shall abide which he built thereon, he shall receive a reward.

15 If any man's work shall be burned, he shall suffer loss: but he himself shall be saved; yet so as through fire.

16 Know ye not that ye are a temple of God, and *that* the
Spirit of God dwelleth in you?

17 If any man destroyeth the temple of God, him shall
God destroy; for the temple of God is holy, and such
are ye.

1 The opening words: *And I* remind us of 2:1 and 3. There
is more than just formal similarity, for, as previously, the apostle
again leaves his argument in order to return to the facts. But
there is a difference too: 2:1 forms a link in the argument which
began at 1:18. In chapter 2 Paul continues to speak about the
contrast between divine and human wisdom and the things pertaining to them. When he refers to concrete facts (2:1, 3), it is
only to record that his own attitude with regard to the twofold
wisdom had been such that it agreed with the thoughts which he
is now expounding. In 3:1, however, Paul relates facts which
are so loosely connected with the discussion of wisdom that the
logical sequence of the argument must first be established. What
is more, Paul not only ceases to speak about the wisdom of God
and that of the world, but he reverts to facts preceding the discussion of wisdom, facts which appeared to be settled, since the
apostle had disapproved of them and had afterwards (1:17. 18)
continued to speak about an entirely unrelated question which
was prompted by an antithesis in 1:17b.

Our exposition of chapter 1 sought to establish that the discussion of foolishness and wisdom did not stand in any relation to
the divisions at Corinth and that the standpoint which Paul condemned there could not be identified with any one of the parties.
The question now arises: can we maintain this position when
faced with the fact that the apostle at the end of his argument
reverts to the subject of the parties. Does that not demonstrate
that these divisions do relate to the attitude concerning the
wisdom of this world?

The main reason that we feel justified in maintaining our exegesis of chapter 1 is that such an alleged relationship between the
divisions and the matter of worldly wisdom is not borne out by
chapter 3 itself. The end of chapter 2 clearly forms a conclusion,
thus marking the end of the argument. And in 3:1 Paul does not
take up any elements of the preceding discussion but he rather
considers the effect his writing may have with the Corinthians.
Their own conduct and the apostle's conduct during his stay with

them might strike them as being quite out of harmony with that which the apostle had written in his letter concerning the life of a believer. This consideration might even lead them to doubt whether they themselves were true believers since the words of vss. 15 and 16 did not agree with their conduct.

It is that point which Paul takes up now. He considers an objection which could arise in the hearts of his readers. Having written concerning the objective glory the church has in Christ, he now points out that conditions at Corinth do not agree with the believers' state in Christ, as described in 2:12. This is done in the words of 3:1, 2, which in turn lead up to vs. 3: *for ye are yet carnal,* a strong accusation for which the mentioning of the parties must serve and does serve as evidence. Paul does not deal with these divisions anew; they just are an example furnishing proof. This proof leads to the verdict of vs. 6f., a verdict which needs further clarification. It remains true therefore that 1:18-2:16 does not have any connection with the parties, neither does it cast any light upon them.

Vs. 1 begins with *and I* (cf. 2:1). There is a slight contrast with the foregoing. The use of the singular indicates that Paul no longer speaks of all Christians and that he is now coming to concrete facts. *Brethren* indicates that the apostle touches on a new subject, concerning the Corinthians personally, for which subject he asks the special attention of his readers. Let them not resent it when he says certain things not agreeable to them for he seeks their true profit. In our verse the apostle does not have in view the point of time of his arrival in Corinth, as in 2:1, but rather the whole period of his labors there. Although he preached a long time in their midst he could not yet speak to the Corinthians as *to spiritual.* This does not imply that they are not spiritual but refers to their present condition. That condition is such that he cannot speak to them as unto fully spiritual but only as *unto carnal,*[1] *as unto babes in Christ. Carnal,* i. e., not spiritual. They are babes in the sphere in which Christ rules, not fully grown in the realm of the good. They are not yet more advanced upon the

---

[1] The Greek has two different words: σάρκινος (vs. 1), and the more usual σαρκικός (vs. 3). The difference between the two is not great. The connotation of the first word is: "of flesh", of the second: "ruled by the (sinful) flesh". Paul may have used this word in an attempt to avoid a stronger term at this point.

way to salvation than when Paul was at Corinth (cf. Heb. 5: 12f.).

2 Verse 2 explains verse 1. Because the Corinthians were babes in Christ Paul *fed* them *with milk and not with meat.* They were not able to stand any other food but milk when Paul was with them. And today it is as it was then. There had been no improvement. *Milk* cannot be understood as a symbol of a type of preaching which does not place Christ in the center nor proclaim Him as the wisdom of God. For in the preceding chapters Paul did not thus preach nor did he do so at any other time (2:2). The difference between *milk* and *meat* must be sought in something else. In 2:14, 15 Paul described the contrast between the natural and the spiritual man and in 3:1 he speaks of those who are spiritual. From this we may conclude that *milk* is approximately the same as the preaching to those who are natural, i. e., a preaching with contents identical with other preaching but aimed especially at calling souls to surrender themselves to God; in other words: missionary preaching. Since the Corinthians were not natural but carnal, babes, too much inclined to worldly wisdom, they must be called to the right knowledge of the Lord.

Meat is the symbol of a preaching to convinced Christians in which it is possible to unfold the full richness, the magnificence of the gospel. A foundation for this interpretation is given in vs. 3, where it is stated that what was absent in Corinth was not knowledge but fruits of conversion. We may say therefore that the Corinthians were *babes in Christ* through their own fault and that was the reason why they were not able to receive the fullness of the preaching.

With: *nay, not even now are ye able* Paul leads us from the past to the present. Not even now, i. e., after a period in which many things happened, such as the preaching of Apollos at Corinth, the receipt of Paul's first letter (5:9), and, at any rate, the regular preaching of the gospel. Keeping in mind Paul's general usage (Rom. 8:7, I Cor. 10:13), we may supply a verb from the context after *ye were not able,* a verb like "to eat" or "to bear." This reproach is a strong one. According to Paul the Corinthians are not yet fully grown, they are hardly spiritual, but babes at the most. Their inability to receive meat is argued with: *for ye are yet carnal,* vs. 3.

3 *Carnal* means here: under the dominion of sinful flesh (cf. vs. 1, with note). The Corinthians did not suffer themselves to be fed by the spirit of God (Rom. 8:14f.) but were ruled by the sinful flesh, as is shown by their works enumerated in vs. 4 (cf. Jas. 3:14, 15).

Here arises the question, which presents itself often during the exposition of I Corinthians, as to how to square these reproaches of Paul with the praise at the beginning of the epistle. The answer must be that no doubt the thanksgiving in ch. 1 is sincere, but that it is nevertheless limited to a certain sphere. For example, Paul does not praise the conduct of the Corinthians very highly and in 1:8 the word "unreprovable" seems to point to a certain deficiency. But even so there is no contradiction between 3:3 and 1:4f.

The designation "carnal" is justified as Paul points in a rhetorical question to their *jealousy and strife*. Here again no mention is made of doctrinal differences. The sin of the Corinthians was jealousy and strife, which are also found side by side in Gal. 5:20, where the apostle writes about the works of the flesh. The Corinthians did not bear with one another but opposed each other because of trifles and futilities. To call this a *walking after the manner of men* is to a certain extent a smoothing over of the situation, a speaking at least in the same vein as in 3:1. But even so we must consider that: "after the manner of men" means: according to the standard of someone who is no more than a man, i. e., one who is natural and not spiritual. The cause of their quarrelling is that they attribute to men what belongs properly to God. Again we must bear in mind that the apostle does not contend that they are unchanged men (*natural*), but that they live as those who are unchanged. They do not walk according to the Spirit.

4 As vs. 3b demonstrates the correctness of Paul's *you are carnal*, vs. 4 shows that the words: *after the manner of men* are well founded. Paul does not revert to these quarrels in order to dwell upon them as such, but only to quote them as an example. In this light it is not strange that only Paul and Apollos are mentioned. Neither is: *one saith . . . and another* in conflict with: "each one of you" (1:12). In mentioning some of the groups Paul shows the condition of the whole congregation. Of course, this example only has the force of an argument after what preceded in 1:12f. The Corinthians did not mind those quarrels but Paul pointed out the evil of them and consequently he may use them now to prove that they are carnal. *Men* at the end of the verse must be taken here as the identical word in vs. 3: unchanged men. Again Paul uses a rhetorical question, a device which contains less sharpness than a positive statement and which suits the cautious type of argument used here and throughout the epistle.

5 In vs. 5 the apostle examines what Apollos and he himself really are. However important the work of these men may be, their work is not the real work. And the Corinthians, in quarreling about that work, betray a carnal disposition.[2] *Ministers* is not used here in its technical sense but designates the men God uses for the work in His kingdom, although such men often will be ministers in a technical sense as well. Those men are but means, they are not the workers in the full sense of the word. *Through whom ye believed,* i. e., came to belief, with special reference to the missionary work in Corinth. *Each*[3] *as the Lord gave to him*: Paul concedes that there is some difference between his work and that of Apollos. But this does not give the Corinthians a right to make this difference an occasion for quarrelling, since it is God Himself who assigned to each one of His ministers a special task (cf. Rom. 12:6). There is a calling from God and God who calls is One.

There is a transition in this verse. The carnality of the Corinthians is no longer spoken of and the names of Paul and Apollos will form the occasion for treating the relation which God sustains to His ministers and to the church. The Corinthians did not correctly understand that relation.

6 Vs. 6 describes in a figure of speech the special task of Paul and that of Apollos. This figure of speech implies two things: a) that those tasks are closely related to one another for which reason they may be at best distinguished but not separated; b) that neither the work of Paul nor that of Apollos had brought the full reality. Paul *planted,* he founded the congregation, *Apollos watered,* i. e., he took care of the spiritual growth, *but God gave*

---

[2] The double τί inquires into the significance rather than the persons of Paul and Apollos.

[3] ἑκάστῳ stands for ἕκαστος ὡς αὐτῷ.

81

the increase, i. e., He maintained its life and made it grow.[4] By thus ascending to God, Paul has reached what is last and highest (cf. vs. 23). The blessing proceeds from God, hence it is carnal to hold the work of men to be the real thing and to quarrel about it. Moreover, did not the very fact that one Corinthian gave preference to Paul and another to Apollos show that neither of the two was everything?

7 Vs. 7 is almost a proverb. It implies that God is doing[5] the real work. *So then* introduces a conclusion, i. e., "from the foregoing we must conclude that." That this is Paul's intention appears from the fact that he mentions the name of God and in so doing applies the proverb concretely. No name is necessary with the first part of the proverb, since it states that *neither he that planteth, nor he that watereth* is anything. This is the same thought expressed in 1:31: there must not be any glorying except in the Lord.

8 In vs. 8 the figure of speech is used in a different way. *He that planteth and he that watereth* are both on the same side, precisely because they do not do the real work. They belong together and do not measure up to the principal thing. They will *receive* their *reward,* i. e., they are but servants (vs. 5). The apostle does not deny that he and Apollos are supposed to do what they do (cf. 9:6, also Lk. 17:10). The idea of reward is only introduced to demonstrate the subordinate position of him that plants and of him that waters. He who does the real work is the leader, who does not receive any reward but gives it to His subordinates. That same thought lies in *each* and in the twice repeated *own.* Everybody receives the reward he deserves. There is someone else who evaluates the work of each and determines what each one ought to receive.

9 Vs. 9 implies that the other in view is God Himself. The sense of *fellow-workers* is ambiguous. It may refer to men who cooperate with God or to men who cooperate in the service of God. The context decides in favor of the latter of the two mean-

---

[4] It is of some importance to note the difference in the tenses between the Greek verb forms ἐφύτεσα, ἐπότισεν (aorist) and ηὔξανεν (imperfect). The activities of planting and watering come to an end but the giving of increase is a continued action.

[5] φυτεύων, ποτίζων, αὐξάνων, all present participles.

ings. The use of *for*, with its causal meaning, can be explained only if this verse implies that both Paul and Apollos stand in the same relation to God by whom the work is really done.

The second part of vs. 9 is plain and clear but deserves some special attention in connection with the ensuing argument. Paul's use of two unconnected figures ("husbandry" and "building") may be due to the fact that both are well known from the Old Testament (Jer. 11:10; 18:9; Ezek. 36:9; cf. Deut. 20:5, 6). The former of the two refers back to the preceding figure, the latter anticipates the immediately following. Besides a transition is made from the servants of God to the congregation. The words *ye are* give to this transition not only a very personal character but they also make the congregation realize its dignity, a thought which continues in vs. 16 and which in our verse serves to demonstrate how serious it is for the Corinthians to live in sinful carnality.

Ye are God's husbandry, or better: you are God's field (RSV). These words honor and extol the congregation. God is pleased to regard the church as His field. This word, in distinction from the word "building" which implies the thought of a slowly rising edifice in which stone is joined to stone, refers to a cultivated piece of land which is now awaiting the blessing of God. The idea of a building is that each stone is given its proper place so that a beautiful and harmonious whole arises: the house of God (I Peter 2:4, 5). Even though God makes use of men for His service, He nevertheless is the Artificer; He gives the increase.

Speaking of the sins of the congregation, of which he gave a concrete example, the apostle has nevertheless at the same time given us a beautiful exposition of the relation which the congregation sustains to God and to His ministers. This is in keeping with the general character of Paul's epistles. The congregation must look upon the ministers as means only.

10   In vs. 10 Paul develops the figure of a building. There is first a virtual repetition of a thought expressed in the preceding. It is God who does all things and what Paul does he does as a minister. To be such a minister of God is — and this is a new thought — a work of *grace*. *According to the grace of God* enlarges upon the idea expressed in "gave" (vs. 5, cf. "given," vs. 10). The fullness of expression: *According to the grace of God, which was given unto me*, which must be on a par with *God gave* *the increase,* must serve to prevent the Corinthians from saying that there is some reason to attribute a special place to Paul. The apostle has implied more than once that he is *allowed* to work through the grace of God (cf. 15:10). Thereby he gives us an estimate of his own work.

These opening words make it possible for him to continue without difficulty: *as a wise masterbuilder,* i. e., one who knows his profession. Such a man knows which foundation should be laid and how best to do it. Paul's ability is received from God and he thus informs the Corinthians in order that they might know that their *foundation* is a good one.[6] This concerns not the individual members of the congregation but the congregation as a whole, of which Paul writes *I laid a foundation.* This foundation does not refer to the first fruits of the congregation (cf. vs. 11) but to Jesus Christ. To lay the foundation is to preach Christ (2:2). However, the absence of the article before *foundation* indicates that Paul does not yet speak of that. The contrast is here between foundation and building. Both elements of this figure, the foundation and the building, are going to be developed further, which again is a common feature of the apostle's way of writing. *Another buildeth thereon* marks the contrast between Paul himself, who is the founder, and all the others, who are the builders: a contrast between the initial missionary work and the consequent work of edification by others. Although vs. 12 makes mention of a wrong type of building the word *another* is not to be taken as a sort of reproach. On the contrary a foundation only makes sense if someone builds on it, and that is what Paul hoped would happen. Most likely the apostle does not refer to concrete happenings such as the quarrels. The words *another* and *each man* are too impersonal for that. Their vagueness is perhaps due to a desire on Paul's part to spare the Corinthians since he primarily has them in mind with these words. After all, the apostles and their helpers do little more than laying the foundation. They leave the work of building to the congregation itself. The Corinthians were actually engaged in building but in a way which the apostle felt obliged to condemn (see ch. 2; also 4:6f.). Paul is not content with what the Corinthians have done themselves. They must take care not to build with what is nothing but

---

[6] The aorist ἔθηκα refers to the first foundation of the congregation.

wood, hay, stubble. The indefiniteness of *"another"* is sufficiently explained in this light. *Buildeth* in the present tense also speaks of a continuous process of building, i. e., on the part of the Corinthians. *Each man,* i. e., each of the builders in the congregation. There is an ever present need *to take heed* (present tense). Every builder must be aware that he will have to give an account to God. To labor well in the church of God means to labor consciously.

11   Vs. 11, beginning with *for,* contains the reason for what was said in vs. 10. The foundation is good and so no builder can ever blame the defects of the building on the foundation. *Can* implies that the good foundation of the church at Corinth has once been laid and cannot be altered or replaced by another. It should be kept in mind that Paul is not interested in discussing the various foundations which can be laid. His argument is rather that if anyone would want to build a less solid building on this good foundation which has once been laid by the apostle's care, the fault for a possible collapse of the building will lie not with the foundation but with the builder.

Separately the apostle affirms that this unalterable foundation which was once laid is Jesus Christ (cf. Eph. 2:20, where apostles and prophets are called the foundation and Jesus Christ the chief cornerstone; also I Peter 2:4f.) In calling the anointed Saviour the foundation the apostle returns to 1:30 where he expresses the same idea in other words. Some see a difference in meaning in the word "foundation" as it is used in vs. 10 and vs. 11 respectively. They hold that vs. 10 uses it of the preaching, vs. 11 of Jesus Christ Himself. But it should be borne in mind that the preaching of Jesus Christ brings Jesus Christ Himself. Through the preaching of Paul that Jesus is the foundation, Christ becomes the foundation of the church.

12   The builders may build in different ways. The apostle here abandons the original figure and gives us one which is made up of two elements. Of course no house is ever built of *gold, silver,* or *precious stones.* The obvious explanation of the enumeration of these materials lies in the fact that it constitutes a list of decreasing values and increasing inflammability. The subsequent words show that this is the point in view. Paul is not concerned with the question what the best possible building material would be, for in that respect wood would far exceed gold.

If the laying of the foundation refers to the preaching, then the construction work must also refer to the preaching. The objection which has been raised against this exegesis in connection with vs. 9, namely, that the result of the building is an edifice identified with the congregation, loses its strength in the light of the consideration that just as Paul's preaching makes Christ the foundation of the church, so also the building on that foundation has the church as its result. To say that gold, silver, etc., *constitute* the building is to conclude more from the figure than is permissible. Paul does not say that these materials constitute the building but that they are put on the foundation. The main thing in these verses is not the growing edifice but the purifying judgment.

13 The words *each man's work,* i. e., the work of everyone separately, imply that everyone will have to account for his own work. *Shall be made clear*: the implication is that now net all things are clear. The work of builders is not always evaluated correctly in their own times. This the church has to consider, lest she regard most highly that which is esteemed as such in the eyes of men. She will have to put to the test everything which is being offered to see whether it agrees with the character of the foundation. But more especially they who teach must bear in mind that their work will come to light, *for the day shall declare it.* The causal connection lies in the fact that being *made manifest* is the result of the *declaring,* which is an intentional action exposing the nature of a thing. *The day* is the judgment day (Rom. 2:5, 16 etc.). On the day of the Lord every man will be rewarded according to his works (cf. 4:5, II Thess. 1:8). In our context the apostle speaks of the coming of Christ in connection with *take heed* (vs. 10) in order that he might restrain them from every evil work.

It is revealed: the subject is not "work," in which case this phrase would express the same thought as the immediately following one. Hence "day" must be the subject. *The day reveals itself in fire* (cf. Mal. 4:1; also Heb. 3:19). *Fire* is used figuratively (Mt. 3:11) as a figure of the cleansing judgment which punishes evil (*shall be burned*). If *day* is the subject of *is revealed* the subsequent sentence is an independent clause and has no connection with *because*, as is also evident from the construction of the sentence. *Shall prove* is to be placed on one line with *shall declare.* The decision comes on the day of the Lord. The Greek

86

word translated by *to prove*[7] bears the sense of bringing to light
of the good by means of testing in the expectation that something
good will be found in the thing tested. But it must be kept in
mind that Paul does not imply that something good will be found
in every instance, a thought definitely excluded by the reference
to wood, hay and stubble which will be burnt completely.

14, 15 These verses mention both possibilities. *If any man's
work shall abide,* i. e., if it is built of gold, silver, precious stones
and can endure the fire. When it appears in the Lord's day that
a teacher built on the right foundation he will be rewarded. This
reward is mainly that by the grace of God the work *abides* (cf.
9:18). The subject of *shall receive,* therefore, is both the teacher
and his work. This is a necessary observation since in vs. 15 the
apostle writes: *he himself shall be saved;* there the teacher alone
is subject.

The thought of vs. 14 is contrasted with that of vs. 15: if
combustible material is placed on the foundation, in other words,
if preaching has been wrong, then the material will be *burned*
by the fire of judgment. This preaching will have no remaining
fruit and thus the teacher is punished in his work. Nevertheless,
it is possible that the teacher will be *saved* (cf. II Jn. 8). From
the context it appears that this must be taken of eternal salvation
since the reference is here to the day of judgment and the destiny
of one individual (cf. Jn. 5:29; Rom. 2:7f.; II Thess. 1:8). The
teachers who build badly may be believers. They build on the
good foundation without having the intention of destroying the
work of God, and although they are guilty by reason of the lack
of permanency of their work, their state before God may be
secure. Here again Paul assumes that there are teachers at
Corinth who lead the church in the wrong direction. His words
contain a consolation for those who feared they might perish
because they had not built in the right way.

Yet so: this expression shows that the word *fire,* used at the
end of this clause, does not refer to the fire mentioned in vs. 13.
As through fire is a new figure, perhaps occasioned by the previous reference to fire. The word here does not stand for the
fire of the judgment but implies that evil teachers will narrowly
be saved, just as something that passes through the fire hardly

---

[7] δοκιμάζειν.

escapes destruction (cf. Am. 4:11; Zech. 3:2). The doctrine oi purgatory is not taught here, since the apostle has in view works rather than persons, works built by teachers on the good foundation. Vs. 15 does not speak of all men in general but of teachers only. Paul moreover assigns this purification to the Lord's day, not before.

16 The question of vs. 16 is not directly connected with the immediately preceding context but goes back to vs. 9, *God's building*. In vss. 10ff. Paul has elaborated this point by speaking of the foundation of that building and of the manner in which the work of construction may be furthered or hampered. Our verse continues the thought of vs. 9 in a manner which is more closely connected with the original meaning of vs. 9 than the vss. 10ff were. Vs. 9b spoke of the excellence of the church. That point Paul now takes up but he combines this with the ideas expressed in vss. 10ff. This furnishes added proof for the contention that it was Paul's definite intention to write about the way in which the congregation at Corinth had been ministered to. It also points anew to the fact that the reference here is to teachers living in the Corinthian church itself.

This pericope is much more personal than the preceding one (*Know ye not, ye, in you*). *Know ye not*: a rhetorical question, because Paul says something self-evident but nevertheless forgotten by the Corinthians. The calling to mind of a self-evident fact must awaken them, especially since Paul calls the church not only a building of God (vs. 9) but even a *temple*[8] *of God*. Paul has in mind here the temple of old Israel, as is shown by the second part of the verse. God dwelt in the midst of His people by means of the miraculous cloud (Lev. 2:11f). In the new dispensation, after the day of Pentecost, God dwells among His people through the Holy Spirit. That is true of each church individually, it is also true of the church universal, even as the Holy Spirit dwells in the whole congregation and in each of its members (Rom. 8:9). This fact, mentioned before in 2:12, is referred to again in order to demonstrate the excellence of the church. Her glory it is to be a temple of the Holy Spirit (Eph.

---

[8] Greek: ναός, i.e. not the whole temple complex with its courts, but only the building, the house (holy place, holy of holies).

2:22). That is her state before God albeit many of her members are carnal.

17 *If any man destroyeth the temple of God,* i. e., damages, profanes it. Here again the reference is to sins which occurred within the Corinthian church, for the second part of the verse shows that Paul is speaking of things which concern the members of the congregation. This is not just an abstract exposition.

To destroy is to inflict much evil upon the church; to go counter to the character of the church as a temple of God. Destroying the church is the same as building with bad material. Preaching false doctrine destroys the church. It is true, however, that Paul speaks more clearly here than in vss. 10ff. of doing damage to the existing congregation. It should be noted that Paul does not write as if some one has already destroyed the church; hence the words: *if any man* (cf. vs. 12). But the danger is there; there are Corinthians who do not act properly and they are now warned by the apostle. If they are on the wrong path they will be punished. It is not stated wherein this destruction exists. This would indicate that there are bad principles at work in Corinth but that the error had not proceeded very far. There is not any heresy or conscious departure form the right way. Therefore a simple reminder may open the eyes of the congregation and of its teachers. As in vs. 12 the standard for judging the material was said to be its fitness for the foundation, so here the readers are admonished to treat the temple of God as a holy thing because it is *holy.* In the last clause of vs. 17 the Apostle once again emphatically sets forth the holiness of the church. He does so in order to demonstrate its excellence anew. Pointing out the church's holiness does not conflict with reproving her many sins (see 1:2). In 3:17 Paul speaks of the objective holiness of the church in Christ. The church is the dwelling place of the Holy Spirit, the temple of God. She is therefore not holy through the actions of her members. Nevertheless those members do form the temple of God (*such are ye[9]*).

How God is going to *destroy* is not indicated. It is clear that the judgment of God is meant. This may refer to *suffering loss* (vs. 15) but also to the eternal punishment.

---

[9] Greek: οἵτινές ἐστε ὑμεῖς. It is better to take οἵτινες of ναός which is a collective noun, than of ἅγιος in the singular.

89

1-17 The main thought in this pericope is stated at the beginning: the carnality of the Corinthians. But, as often in Paul's epistles, the subsequent discussions have a significance of their own. Paul describes the condition of the church under three figures. The church is a field, cultivated by men and blessed by God; a building resting on the foundation Christ Jesus; a temple in which God dwells. We are therefore shown the glory of the church in spite of her sins and the carnality of her members. In the day of the Lord all things will be clear. Paul gives us the history of the church in a nutshell. There are two sides: That which God works in His church, and the trespasses of unworthy men.

SUMMARY

3:18-23

18 Let no man deceive himself. If any man thinketh that he is wise among you in this world, let him become a fool, that he may become wise.

19 For the wisdom of this world is foolishness with God. For it is written, He that taketh the wise in their craftiness:

20 and again, The Lord knoweth the reasonings of the wise, that they are vain.

21 Wherefore let no one glory in men. For all things are yours;

22 whether Paul, or Apollos, or Cephas, or the world, or life, or death, or things present, or things to come; all are yours:

23 and ye are Christ's and Christ is God's.

18 This section has a character of its own. There is, on the one hand, no connection with verses 16 and 17, but, on the other hand, this pericope calls to mind many things treated in the preceding, such as the wisdom of the world, the glorying and the disputes (at least the names of those used by quarreling persons). The end of this section is a doxology (vs. 22, 23). Paul, therefore, in this small pericope, reiterates all the things spoken of in the preceding chapters, summing them up in one clause: *Ye are Christ's and Christ is God's.*

The Corinthians were too much in love with the wisdom of the world. They did not see that they dishonored God by their quarreling and were thus likely to *deceive* themselves. Paul warns the Corinthians in connection with all the subjects thus far treated, but, as appears from the subsequent words, they are especially warned not to esteem worldly wisdom to be the right wisdom. The apostle's intent is to insist on self-examination.

The next clause begins with: *if any man* (cf. vs. 12, 14, 15, 17). Its implication is again to signalize a real danger without stating that the threatened evil has become reality. *In this world* belongs, according to some, with what precedes, according to

91

others with what follows, or it belongs with both. It should be noted that there must be contrast between *among you* and *in this world*. The Corinthians do not see this antithesis since to them there is no absolute difference between the church of Christ and this world. If this is so then *"in this world"* does not go with *"wise,"* nor with *"to become a fool,"* but it is rather the center of the clause and this clause states that there are some at Corinth who think they have arrived at a wisdom which has value in the church as well as in the world. That, according to Paul, is a self-delusion, a fancy, and so he uses *thinketh* and *in this world* in one clause. According to the Corinthians it was possible to be a member of the congregation and to be wise in the world at the same time. If anybody is of that opinion *let him become a fool.* He that knows himself to be a fool, devoid of true wisdom, is on the way to true wisdom as described in 1:24, 30.

19 In vs. 19 we find the reason for Paul's statement in vs. 18. This thought has been developed fully in chapter 2. There Paul argued that the wisdom of God reveals itself above all in the saving cross of Christ. If the world thinks this cross to be foolishness, as it actually does, then it must follow that the wisdom of the world is *foolishness with God* (2:19, 20, 27).[10] It is remarkable that Paul in this verse offers evidence for this thesis, even though he had given abundant evidence for it in chapter 2. Then as well as now an appeal to Scripture was made (cf. 2:19). The reason for this lies in the fact that Paul in our pericope arrives at very important conclusions. This causes us to see that not only one but several passages in the Old Testament bear out that God considers the wisdom of the world to be foolishness. *For* the Scriptures show that God does not suffer the wisdom of the world to go its own way, but that He interferes with the execution of its plans, i. e., He disapproves of that wisdom. The same Scriptures also teach that God *taketh the wise in their craftiness.* The first quotation is from Job 5:12, 13. It is not an exact quotation but approaches the idea of a summary of the words in Job. The words quoted are by Eliphaz. Though true in themselves they are given a wrong application by him. The apostle does not speak about that application but he uses the words which Eliphaz spoke about God and those words are true. *To take,* i. e.,

---

[10] "With", Greek: παρά "after the meaning of" (Rom. 12:16).

to catch, to seize.[11] The idea is that while the wise in their craftiness seem to attain to something, or even to many things, God comes from heaven and seizes them and their work is stopped.

20 *And again* introduces a second quotation (cf. Rom. 15: 10, 11, 12; Heb. 1:5; 2:13, etc.). There is an abundance of proof texts. Paul now quotes Ps. 94:11 with a remarkable modification. Paul writes: *of the wise,* the Hebrew has *of man.*[12] The question, whether by means of this alteration this text was not made into a proof text, is not without basis. The answer must be that Paul's alteration is closely linked with the course of his argument. The wise of this world are people as such, unchanged people. Paul contrasts believers with the wise of this world not only, but also with people in general (1:19f.; 2:6f.; 3:3, 4). "Wise people" and "people in general" are thus interchangeable since both terms denote those who have not yet seen that Jesus Christ is the wisdom of God. *Wise* refers to the wisdom of *men,* which is opposed to the wisdom of God. The word "man" implies that these same people are unchanged. Hence it is possible, in speaking of *reasonings,* to substitute "wise" for "man," inasmuch as reasonings lead us to the supposed wisdom of natural man.

Lord, in this quotation refers to God. *To know* when used of God denotes full knowledge, acknowledgment. *Vain,* without any result. The two quotations are thus seen to supplement each other. In the first the wise are already engaged in the execution of their plans when God interferes. In the second God knows before that the plans of the wise will come to naught.

21 *Wherefore*[13] introduces the following sentence as a consequence drawn from the preceding. This type of argument is only possible because Paul is here recapitulating all he has written before. Vs. 21 can thus be regarded as a negative parallel to 1:31. As Paul pointed out: the Corinthians named themselves after men. Those who do this are the same who have loved too much the

---

[11] Greek δράσσομαι; δράξ, the open hand.

[12] Greek τῶν σοφῶν, LXX (Ps. 94:11) τῶν ἀνθρώπων ; Hebr. אדם

[13] Greek: ὥστε with imperative. ὥστε is either an adverb or a coordinate conjunction.

wisdom of this world. Since that worldly wisdom will perish, this particular form of worldly wisdom, the naming of oneself after men, must also perish. Going one step further this part of Paul's argument may also shed more light on the transition of 1:17 to 1:18, which has been difficult to understand. For now it appears that not just one party, e. g., the Apollos party was condemned for its love of worldly wisdom but that Paul rather condemns every form of glorying in men as worldly wisdom and as destined to perish. The stringency of this conclusion becomes greater yet when it is remembered that Paul has demonstrated that the apostles and their helpers are servants only and that the church receives its growth from God (3:7). The admonition, *let no one glory in* men, is therefore, not at all alien to the statement that the reasonings of the wise are vain in the eyes of God.

The next clause, introduced by *for* is quite different in character from the clause with *wherefore*. This is due in part to the fact that the *wherefore*-clause forms a conclusion not only of the immediately preceding words but of the whole argument. The second reason is that Paul, after treating of the divine, the objective side which existed apart from the Corinthians, now comes to the subjective, the personal privileges of believers, which formed another reason not to glorify in men. This idea was anticipated in 3:9. 16 where Paul writes of the privileges of the Church. This thought is now brought to its zenith which makes it possible for Paul to end, not with an admonition to the congregation, but with a hymn sung to its glory: *all things are yours.* Vs. 22 compels us to take these words in their broadest sense. All things are in the possession of the church. That is why the Corinthians must not choose certain things, e. g., certain teachers, for all things are theirs. Besides, the Christian does not boast of his riches in any other way than to praise the Lord, who has given so many blessings in Christ Jesus (1:4f).

22 In vs. 22 Paul is summing up, choosing out of the riches of the church that which possesses special interest for the Corinthians and demonstrates at the same time the greatness of their richness. *Paul, Apollos, Cephas,* they all are the property of the congregation inasmuch as God puts His servants at the disposal of the church (cf. 4:1f.). At Corinth they were choosing one of these men and rejected the others. That is foolishness, it is wisdom of the world, for God gave them all. *World, life, death, things present*[14] or *things to come* are the great powers that govern the life of man and before which he feels his smallness and dependence. That is why the richness of the congregation could never be described more ably than by the statement that all these things are theirs.

23 Vs. 23 offers the ground for the hymn of vs. 22. This ground lies in the fact that the church is *of Christ and Christ is of God*.[15] The Greek shows that the church is the property of Christ in another sense than all that richness is the property of the church. How the church is the property of Christ Paul indicates more than once in I Corinthians. Christ is the one body of which all are members (1:12, cf. Eph. 1:22, 23). Christ is the Victor, to whom all things belong (15:27). All authority has been given to Him (Mt. 28:18). If the church is of Christ, she shares His glory. In Him she is rich, in Him she possesses all things: the servants, sent by Him; the world; life and death. The present and the future are of Him for He rules history (15:24f.). Paul does not touch upon the comfort which is implied in all this for the church, as he does in Rom. 8:31f. The principal thing here is that he who is the property of Christ shares His power and His glory. It is true that Paul does not say this in so many words. But *"ye are Christ's"* only makes sense if it includes all of the above. Especially chapter 15 entitles us to this interpretation.

The last words are *Christ is God's*. The apostle uses the name which designates the Saviour according to His office. Jesus Christ did His work by mandate of the Father. He received glory as a reward from the Father and He makes the church share in this reward. The idea of subjection on the part of Christ the Mediator to the Father (Jn. 14:28; 20:17) receives further explanation in 11:3 and 15:23f. In our verse it serves to point out the firmness of the church's possession, as the latter is founded in the work of Christ with God.

---

[14] Greek: ἐνεστῶτα, i.e. what is present.

[15] The Greek has δέ twice, which implies a slight contrast. There is also a change in the case of the personal pronoun. Instead of Χριστὸς ὑμῶν Paul writes ὑμεῖς Χριστοῦ.

COMMENTARY ON FIRST CORINTHIANS

With *"God's"* we are back at vs. 19, *with God,* which implied that only that will continue to exist which exists with God. This genitive also indicates that the church is not of this world but is loosed from the earth and all worldly wisdom, and that it stands in direct relation to God.

18-23 This pericope, which, as was indicated above, forms a summary is nevertheless not the final conclusion as appears from the close connection between chapter 4 and the latter part of chapter 3. It may be compared to a mountaintop since the glory of the church of God is at no place painted as beautifully as here. Against this background the sins of the Corinthians appear in their blackest colors. They appear as anomaly, as foolishness. How is it possible that a church, so richly favored, should be in disorder because her members call themselves after men!

CHAPTER IV

LET NOBODY JUDGE IN PRIDE

4:1-13

1 Let a man so account of us, as of ministers of Christ, and stewards of the mysteries of God.

2 Here, moreover, it is required in stewards, that a man be found faithful.

3 But with me it is a very small thing that I should be judged of you, or of man's judgment: yea, I judge not mine own self.

4 For I know nothing against myself; yet am I not hereby justified; but he that judgeth me is the Lord.

5 Wherefore judge nothing before the time, until the Lord come, who will both bring to light the hidden things of darkness, and make manifest the counsels of the hearts; and then shall each man have his praise from God.

6 Now these things, brethren, I have in a figure transferred to myself and Apollos for your sakes; that in us ye might learn not *to go* beyond the things which' are written; that no one of you be puffed up for the one against the other.

7 For who maketh thee to differ? and what hast thou that thou didst not receive? but if thou didst receive it, why dost thou glory as if thou hadst not received it?

8 Already are ye filled, already are ye become rich, ye have come to reign without us: yea and I would that ye did reign, that we also might reign with you.

9 For, I think, God hath set forth us the apostles last of all, as men doomed to death: for we are made a spectacle unto the world, both to angels and men.

10 We are fools for Christ's sake, but ye are wise in Christ; we are weak but ye are strong; ye have glory, but we have dishonor.

11 Even unto this present hour we both hunger, and thirst, and are naked, and are buffeted, and have no certain dwelling place;

12 and we toil, working with our hands: being reviled, we bless; being persecuted, we endure;

97

13 being defamed, we entreat; we are made as the filth of
the world, the offscouring of all things, even until now.

1 At first it seems strange that Paul after his concluding
hymn of praise returns to the subject under discussion. But upon
second thought we observe that there is but a loose connection
between 4:1-13 and the preceding pericope, the latter being the
occasion rather than the foundation for 4:1-13. When speaking
about the teachers in their relation to God and to the congregation, Paul had done so with special reference to the Corinthian
custom of naming one's self after men. But the subject of the
relation of the teachers to the church needed some further
elucidation and that is why the apostle, after having touched upon
this subject once, continues the discussion. The Corinthians
needed this, for they did not sufficiently appreciate the apostles
of Jesus Christ. Naming themselves after Apollos they dishonored Paul. Besides, Paul uses this wrong attitude with regard
to the apostles as a starting point for the discussion of pride and
presumption in general. On that subject, which because of its
importance is mentioned more than once in the following chapters, Paul had not yet written. We now learn that the quarrels
in Corinth and the slogans were connected with spiritual pride
also.

So must be taken to mean: things being as we have demonstrated.[1] Let people consider us ministers of Christ in the way
which we have demonstrated, i. e., negatively, let them not look
on us as men in whom they can boast. *A man;* here, as often:
anybody. *Account* implies a reasoning activity of the mind.
Paul assumes that the Corinthians will give special attention to
his exposition of the position of ministers and that they will
consider the minister's calling. They must then come to the
conclusion that all those ministers are servants of Christ. *As*
must be understood in the light of the Corinthian situation. The
Corinthians knew on the one hand that Paul and Apollos were
preachers of the gospel, on the other hand they knew that Christ

---

[1] οὕτως is the first word of the sentence. It cannot correlate with
ὡ but it has a backward reference to διάκονοι Θεοῦ (3:5, 21) who
are included in πάντα.

98

is working on earth through His ministers.[2] The conclusion must be that these preachers are servants of Christ. If the church is Christ's she will receive all those who are sent by Christ as Christ's emissaries and refrain from extolling them as men. A *steward* was often a slave who cared for the goods of his master. Therefore Paul puts *steward* next to minister. The apostles distribute *the mysteries of God*. "Mystery" in the epistles of Paul indicates a thing hidden in former times but revealed now, in the new dispensation, and initiated by Christ (cf. especially Eph. 3:4f.). "Mystery" is a formal word, the content of which is supplied by the context. Our present context shows that Paul is strongly emphasizing the formal aspect of the word, implying all that God has revealed in Jesus Christ, the treasures of His grace. (Mt. 13:11, 52). The work of Christ stands in the center. The principal thing which the apostles may distribute is the message of the coming of the promised Messiah and the completion of His work.

2 The second verse is a sort of parenthesis, vs. 3 being linked to vs. 1. The meaning of *here* is not "here on earth," but under the present circumstances. The intention of vs. 2 is to prevent anybody from saying that it apparently is not necessary to judge Paul and his associates. Vs. 4 is to show that that opinion is erroneous. It begins by saying that office-bearers, however much they may be above a wrong kind of judgment on the part of the congregation, nevertheless have to answer certain requirements. *Required* is a strong term. The requirement is *faithful*ness, which is the main virtue of office-bearers. A steward is expected to act faithfully, without interruption, and with the sacrifice of his own interests. This is also demanded of the stewards of God. *A man* refers to every steward and *found* makes clear that this faithfulness must be of such a nature that it comes to light. Faithfulness is a formal concept. God makes known what must be done and the stewards have to perform that faithfully.

3 The ones who are to judge the actions of the ministers are not the Corinthians, as they themselves seemed to believe (cf. 9:3). The sin of judging the ministers of Christ without love is

---

[2] ὑπηρέτης, a general word denoting any kind of servant.

a very general sin indeed. Paul knows that he is being judged[3] at Corinth (cf. vs. 5; 9:3). The words *a very small thing* do not mean that Paul does not mind the judging, for this would conflict with what he writes in 8:13; 9:19f. (cf. also II Cor. 4:2; 5:11). It is rather the objective value of the judgment of the Corinthians which Paul has in view. The question whether they condemn or exonerate him is of no significance for his actual condemnation or exoneration.

The next few words reading literally "by any human day,"[4] have not been correctly translated in the ASV by *of man's judgment.* The RSV has: *by any human court.* In 3:13 the day referred to is the judgment day. On the analogy of the meaning there the "human day" must be the day on which men judge. The apostle has in mind that, since no human judgment is decisive for him, he no longer judges himself any more for that would be just another of these human judgments. Paul does not speak here about what we call self-criticism. His epistles show that he is not opposed to such self-criticism (cf. 9:15f.; 15:9). In our verse the apostle rather writes about the decisive judgment which will justify or condemn a person on account of his works. The use of the first person here indicates that the apostle does not speak of other people but only of himself (cf. 2:11).

4 *For I know nothing against myself,* or, with the more preferable RSV translation: I am not aware of anything against myself. The literal meaning of this difficult expression is: I am not conscious of anything[5] with regard to myself, i. e., there is no question of any evil. This not being conscious of any evil thing is the reason why Paul does not judge himself. The apostle does not know enough about himself to be able to judge himself. The words: *yet I am not hereby justified,* however, seem to demand a reference to something evil in the immediately preceding context and so the question must be considered whether that would not be the sense of the first words of our verse after all. The answer

---

[3] The Greek word ἀνακρίνειν implies a consideration of the pro and con.

[4] Greek: ὑπὸ ἀνθρωπίνης ἡμέρας.

[5] Greek: οὐδὲν γὰρ ἐμαυτῷ σύνοιδα.

100

is that Paul acts according to the rule: *in dubiis pro reo*. Not knowing himself well enough he could and probably would come to a justification of himself. But in so doing he might overlook some evil, especially some defects in his ministerial work (for that is what Paul is speaking of, not of his person, as e. g., in Rom. 7), which render him guilty in God's sight. That is why Paul's statement about a lack of knowledge of self can be followed by the words: *yet I am not thereby justified. Hereby* [6] i. e., under these circumstances. The judgment belongs to God. The use of the perfect tense should be noted: I am justified, and not ; I shall be justified in the future. In other words, if the apostle had been justified because he was not conscious (of any evil) then he would now be in the permanent condition of righteousness. *But he that judgeth me is the Lord*, follows logically. The Lord, i. e., Christ Jesus (cf. Jn. 5:22; Acts 10:42) is not the one who condemns but the one who has the right to judge and judges regularly the work of Paul. The apostle is resigned to that.[7]

5 *Wherefore* introduces a conclusion. The form of this clause is elliptical. Strictly speaking Paul writes that the Corinthians ought not to pass any judgment until *the Lord*, i. e., Christ, *comes*. But according to the context the meaning is that only the Lord can judge and that He will judge at the moment of His return. That this is the implication is shown by the second part of the verse. In paraphrase we may say: Therefore, do not judge in any case. The judging will be done when the time comes, and that time will have come when Christ will return. Paul means to say three things: a) he forbids judging; b) he speaks of the time of judgment; c) he speaks of the coming of Christ. *To judge* must be explained from its context . . . The apostle does not forbid every form of judging, such as, e. g., proving (I Thess. 5:21), but he does forbid the judging of teachers on the part of those not called to do so. *Until* etc. : the time of the Lord's return is fixed by God but people on earth do not know that time (I Thess. 5:2). The relative clause states what Christ is going to do when He returns. *The hidden things of darkness*, i. e., the

---

[6] Greek: ἐν τούτῳ.

[7] A present participle with an article (ὁ ἀνακρίνων) designates a person who is used to do something.

things which were particularly hidden, because darkness covered them (Rom. 2:16).

Jesus will illumine that darkness, He will reveal the hidden things (I Tim. 2:10). Hidden are also the *counsels of the heart.* These counsels are still more hidden because they are hidden by their very nature. But when Christ comes He will show that He knows them and He will reveal them. So we see that Christ is competent to judge and also able to do so. The first thing required in judging a case is to take cognizance of it. No man is able to do so but Christ is (cf. 2:11).[8] *And then,* i. e., when Christ judges in the manner indicated. The apostle does not deal with the frightful character of the judgment but with the correctness of God's judging (II Cor. 10:18). When Christ has judged and the sentence has been pronounced *then each man shall have his praise from God.* That concerns in the first place the teachers. They will have their judgment, not from men, whose sentence has no value, but from God Himself, who portions out reward and punishment in the right way. This reward is of course always the fruit of grace as is evident from 3:5f.

6 In vs. 6 Paul begins a new subject, which is nevertheless closely related to the preceding. To *transfer in a figure*[9] is to give to something the form, or the shape, of something else. The persons who have received another form are Paul and Apollos (cf. vs. 1, and vs. 3, etc.). *These things* are the things treated in vss. 1-5, with the greatest emphasis on the command not to judge. Paul implies that while speaking of himself and of Apollos he had others in view. If the congregation understands that it is forbidden to judge Paul and Apollos, she will more easily concede that all judging is forbidden. Paul and Apollos themselves belong to the others, but more particularly are meant the teachers, or even all the members of the church (cf. the end of the verse). Paul, therefore, in commanding the Corinthians to treat the apostles in the right way, i. e., especially not to judge them, indicates simultaneously how they have to treat all Chris-

---

[8] Chapter 6 shows that Paul does not forbid judging the government. The apostle is here dealing with the pride of the church which thought that it could judge its teachers.

[9] Greek μετασχηματίζω: "to give an other σχῆμα", form.

tians. Having come to this point the apostle writes that they must not be *puffed up for the one against the other*, the implication being that the attitude of the Corinthians with respect to the apostles was one of pride. Is it not true that incompetent and premature judging may be the consequence of pride. Paul does not judge himself. His only desire is to be a faithful servant of Christ. The Corinthians' relation to God and to one another should be of a similar nature.

For your sakes: it was for the sake of the church that Paul spoke about her attitude to the preachers. *That*: introducing a final clause. This clause is a remarkable one. We would expect Paul to say: that ye might know in general how to conduct yourselves with respect to the apostles and their assistants. Instead Paul writes: *that in us ye might learn not to go beyond the things which are written.* With these words the question of the attitude to the ministers is raised to a higher plane. These words must be a sort of quotation, or, in any case, a standing expression.[10] *Which are written* refers, as everywhere else, to what is written in the Old Testatment. *Beyond* speaks of exceeding a limit, and *not* implies that it is forbidden to do what is expressed in the words. The whole expression must have been a part of the preaching, either of Paul, or of Apollos, or of somebody else, a preaching well known to the Corinthians, so that Paul could assume the words to be clear. A further explanation is given by 10:6 and 11, where we read that the history of the Old Testament has a great value for the church of the new dispensation. In that chapter the apostle admonishes the Corinthians with the words and types of the Old Testament. In this light we must explain 4:6. Paul writes that they ought not to go beyond what is written in the Old Testament. The admonitions of the Old Testament still apply to them, they should subject themselves to the words of God spoken in the old dispensation. Although we do not find any traces of an attitude of disobedience on the part of the Corinthians toward the commandments written in the Old Testament, yet the fact is remarkable that Paul quotes and argues very sparingly from the Old Testament. It seems as if

---

[10] The Greek has a substantival clause τὸ μὴ ὑπὲρ ἃ γέγραπται.

that is not useful to him in this epistle. Besides, the epistle bears out that the Corinthians were very easygoing in their conduct. That is, according to our opinion, the ground for taking the words: *not to go beyond*, etc., as a necessary admonition not to deviate from the precepts of the Old Testament, especially the ethical ones among them. These words are a summary of the ethical teaching of Paul. And the reason why these words are given in this context is stated in the final clause which follows, introduced with: *that*.

The last thing Paul has to teach the Corinthians about himself and Apollos is *that no one of you be puffed up for the one against the other*. They are not allowed to be haughty against the one in order to favor another. After the Corinthians have first learnt how to conduct themselves with regard to the ministers, they are now taught by those ministers how to use this teaching, i. e., how to live with one another. For in their mutual intercourse they commit the same sin as in their conduct with regard to the ministers. Moreover, Paul points out that underlying the quarrels regarding the office-bearers lies the sin of being puffed up. The real evil of those quarrels is thus laid bare.

That in us ye might learn, etc., another purpose clause, to show that the Old Testament already warns against the sin now committed by the Corinthians. If they exalt themselves above the Old Testament the consequence will be that they will not hear the warning against pride. Anyone who boasts against the commandments of God, revealed in the Scriptures, must come to a spirit of pride against the brothers. Let him learn from the example of Paul and Apollos to submit to the Scriptures. But the reverse is also true: in exhorting the Corinthians to act properly toward Paul and his helpers the apostle warns against pride in general and he uses this opportunity to warn also against another sin, already reproved, namely the sin of holding in contempt the Old Testament. This he could do so much more readily since the Old Testament also warns against boasting. The merit of the latter interpretation is that it refrains from placing an undue emphasis on the contemptuous attitude toward the Old Testament, an evil only mentioned in passing and discussed no further. Finally it should be remembered that Paul could write

104

all this only because he himself and Apollos were subject to the Old Testament.

7 Vs. 7, introduced with *For*, states the reason why the Corinthians were forbidden to be puffed up. Here we have one of those cases in which a purpose clause is followed by a causal clause but the latter does not actually agree with the scope of the purpose clause. The first purpose clause of vs. 6 is preceded by a clause of a formal character, and is itself also formal in nature. The material reason for the second purpose clause is now stated in vs. 7. *Who maketh thee to differ*: a rhetorical question. The implication is that no one distinguishes the Corinthians above others. The use of the singular pronoun (*thee*) is due to the widespread character of the sin of pride. The sin of being puffed up proceeded from the many blessings which the Corinthian congregation had received (cf. 1:4f., where especially intellectual gifts are mentioned). In chapters 12-14 Paul speaks about the many spiritual blessings. But all those things had to be acknowledged as coming from God (cf. 1:30). If everything the Corinthians possessed was received they should not boast; moreover, their life should be in harmony with the grace received (cf. also Rom. 2:17f.). The three questions of vs. 7 must make the Corinthians feel how unbecoming it is to judge in pride.

8 The stronger verdict of vs. 8 is again in the plural. These statements for which the questions form the preparation are positive and ironical.

Already implies that the Corinthians suppose that they are in a condition which they might at best attain only at a later time. Their triumph is premature, not only because they have been Christians for a short time, but also because they think they possess that which is given only at the end of the course. *Filled* points to a feeling of sufficiency, of satiety, of not wanting anything. Such a feeling is a fertile soil for pride. Paul uses ironical, not to say sarcastic, language here. He expresses the sentiment of the Corinthians. They think that they are rich and that they have become rich by their own effort.[11] The richness referred to is in the first place one of spiritual gifts (cf. 1:7).

---

[11] πλουτέω: "to become rich"; ἐπλουτήσατε: "you became rich"; 1:5 ἐπλουτίσθητε, "you were made rich".

The second half of the verse bears a character somewhat different from that of the first. For the words: *ye have come to reign* are joined to: *without us.* Not only did the Corinthians think that they had arrived at their position by their own exertion but at the same time they had cut off the connection with the apostles who preached the gospel to them. In so doing they forgot the gospel itself. *Reigning* is not the thing commended by the gospel but it is rather a walking after men. This reigning also leads to judging. A criticism is implied in these words of Paul. *Yea and I would that ye did reign*: in other words, if it were only true that they did reign! But it is not true, as Paul states ironically with the words: *that we might also reign with you.* Paul implies that he is not nearly ready to reign. If the Corinthians know a way that leads to such a position of honor they are invited to inform the apostle about it.

9 Vs. 9 states the reason for Paul's ironical words. The reason why he would like to know the way to power is that the existing situation is a sad one. It is remarkable that the apostle does not just write about the condition in which he himself and other preachers of the gospel find themselves, but that he prefaces his words with: *I think,* implying that this is his own opinion only. Nevertheless Paul indicates that the condition of the preachers is what it is because God has made it so: *God hath set forth us,* i. e., God has given to the apostles a place which is perspicuous to all. This in itself bears implications with regard to the Corinthians. *Us the apostles* refers to Paul and to all who are his fellow apostles, the latter word taken in its broader sense of all the preachers of the gospel. *Last of all*: God gave to the apostles the lowest place.[12] *As men doomed to death*: it seems as if the apostles were condemned to death. That is why they can be said to have received the lowest place. They are continually in danger and misery, much more so than others, for that is the consequence of their vocation (cf. vs. 11-13; Rom. 8:36; II Cor. 11:23-30). The apostles are far removed from a reigning position to which

---

[12] ἐσχάτους may be used attributively as well as predicatively since attributive clauses sometimes lack the article in the koine. But since Paul's words here do not refer exclusively to the apostles which were called last we take it predicatively. "Doomed to death" is also part of the predicate. ὡς expresses a comparison.

the Corinthians, according to their own opinion, had already come (vs. 8). The clause with *for* stands on one line with *doomed to death* and contains the reason for the statement: *last of all*. The apostles *are made a spectacle* because everybody looks at them since there is something peculiar about them. This refers to the customs of antiquity in which many people delighted in the suffering of slaves, criminals and conquered people. *World, angels and men* hold the apostles in contempt. "World" in this context is used of the whole of God's creation. Through their suffering the apostles stand in the center of the world. To this world belong angels and men.[13] We find much evidence in Scripture to the effect that the angels are informed about man's life on earth (11:10, Gal. 3:19; Heb. 1:14). But the Bible does not explain how the angels enter into life on earth. It is possible that we, as men, cannot understand or even circumscribe that particular way. Nevertheless the fact is revealed to us. The angels behold with astonishment the sufferings of the apostles. Finally: *men, i. e.,* not only believers but men in general. Indeed, Christians, both in ancient and more recent times, have received public attention because of their suffering and their heroism.

10 In vs. 10 the apostle explains what gave him the right to say: *we are made a spectacle*. The way in which he does this is that he first writes what the apostles actually are, after which he goes on to say ironically what the Corinthians are in his own opinion. In this way he discloses to the church her sins. This last mentioned element is lacking in vss. 11-13 where the apostle paints in dark colors the difficulties of the apostolic ministry, at the same time indicating with a few strokes how the apostles were able in spite of all to accomplish their task with joy.

The contrast *we-ye* is the first thing to be noted. *Fools for Christ's sake* is explained in 1:18f. and Phil. 3:8. Because the apostles are followers of Christ they are fools in the eyes of the world for the world does not know Christ (2:8, I Jn. 3:1). To be fools in the eyes of the world is part of the suffering of the apostles, for it brings them the disdain of the world. After having stated with respect to himself how the world sees him, the apostle

---

[13] That is the reason why κόσμος has the article, whereas ἄγγελοι and ἄνθρωποι lack it.

now writes concerning the Corinthians as to how they see themselves. Since neither of the two opinions is in accordance with the truth they can be put side by side. God's opinion is a different one. *In Christ* is, as everywhere in Paul's epistles, in communion with Christ, in the sphere of Christ, i. e., through Christ and where He is reigning. In that sphere the Corinthians are *wise,* they have risen to great heights, as the apostle says mockingly (II Cor. 11 :19). It is true, the Corinthians are wise in Christ but they undo this privilege by boasting in it as if they had not received it. Consequently their wisdom becomes a wisdom of the world, in comparison with which Paul can call himself a fool. The apostles are *weak* in the eyes of the world, (2 :3) but the Corinthians think themselves *strong* (II Cor. 13 :9), e. g. in the sphere of wisdom, in view of the charismata.

In the last words of this verse the apostle not only states what he himself is in the eyes of the world and what the Corinthians are in his opinion, but also what they actually are in their conduct. This change is due to a change in meaning in the adjectives used. The words : fool, wise, weak and strong mention a person's quality, but to have glory or dishonor (the Greek has adjectives[14]) does not refer to a quality but rather states how someone is regarded by others. The Corinthians *have glory*: the world speaks honorably of the church which thinks she is entitled to such honor. Paul and his co-laborers are despised by the same world.

11, 12, 13 These verses depict the sufferings of the apostles. The goal of this enumeration is not to inform those who do not know what the task of the apostles involves, but rather to show how far removed the apostles and the teachers of the church are from reigning. In this way Paul warns the Corinthians against their pride and summons them to imitate him (vs. 16).

The first point is that the apostle's sufferings continue until that very day, yea, that they have gone on and are going on all the time he accomplishes his apostolic ministry. *Unto this present hour* is in contrast with *already* (vs. 8). The repeated *"and"* compels one to give attention to every single word. All those sufferings are to be endured at the same moment. *To hunger, to*

---

[14] ἔνδοξος, ἄτιμος.

thirst, to be naked speak of a want of food, drink, and clothing. These verbs cannot be taken in an absolute sense; obviously no one can live without food, etc. (cf. Phil. 4:11f.). *To buffet,* i. e., to strike with the fist, to maltreat, calls to mind Paul's experiences when the people assaulted him and the government kept aloof (Acts 14:19; 17:5, etc.). *No certain dwelling* refers to Paul's wanderings when he was obliged to depart (cf. Mt. 8:20; 10:24). *To toil* means to labor, as is explained by the following words: *with our own hands* (9:15). Paul is willing to work but it is a difficult thing to work and to preach also. The apostle has to work while other preachers can rest. We must consider here that the Greek despised all manual labor. Paul, however, does not experience his labor as dishonor but as an aggravation of his task. *Our own hands*: the apostle has to provide for his own support.

From this point on the apostle also refers to the reaction of himself and others to their suffering in order that he might thus glorify the grace of God. But his words also have significance in this immediate context. For the Corinthians gloried in virtues they supposed they possessed. Paul's attitude is quite a different one. He continues to keep his head erect even though he is oppressed. There is an admonition implied in these words.

Reviling is matched by the apostle with *blessing,* i. e., he dispenses a blessing in general by preaching the gospel (I Pet. 3:9).[15] In spite of persecution the preachers endure, i. e., they do not stop bringing the gospel to such impious persecutors. The apostles stand in evil repute in the world, nevertheless they comfort and admonish.

Finally, there is a summarizing expression which shows that Paul is in no respect near the position of dignity to which the Corinthians thought they had attained. *Filth* is the dirt, scraped together after cleaning has taken place. The apostle knows that they are thought to be the most despicable thing in the world. The world does not recognize them as belonging to the world. *Offscouring* is what is wiped off from an object when it is cleaned all round. No one loves the apostles. They are like dirt which

---

[15] The participles are all present participles. There is a continuation.

is wiped off and thrown away. *Even until now,* cf. even until this present hour, vs. 11. The apostles' evil case continues and consequently there is no question of having dominion.

1-13 It cannot be denied that Paul deals with a variety of subjects in this pericope. But two things stand out clearly and both are very important in this correspondence between Paul and the Corinthians. First, Paul writes of the relation which office-bearers sustain to their Sender and to the people, within the church as well as without. Second, Paul deals with the principal sin of the Corinthians: their spiritual pride, and its consequence: a feeling of emancipation, even from the law of God.

MATTER OF FACT COMMUNICATIONS

4:14-21

14 I write not these things to shame you, but to admonish you as my beloved children.

15 For though ye have ten thousand tutors in Christ, yet *have ye* not many fathers; for in Christ Jesus I begat you through the gospel.

16 I beseech you therefore, be ye imitators of me.

17 For this cause have I sent unto you Timothy, who is my beloved and faithful child in the Lord, who shall put you in remembrance of my ways which are in Christ, even as I teach everywhere in every church.

18 Now some are puffed up, as though I were not coming to you.

19 But I will come to you shortly, if the Lord will; and I will know, not the word of them that are puffed up, but the power.

20 For the kingdom of God is not in word, but in power.

21 What will ye? shall I come unto you with a rod, or in love and a spirit of gentleness?

14 Again Paul surprises us more or less (cf. 4:1). There is a close relation with the preceding pericope, as is expressed in *these things*. But the apostle also treats matters not connected with vss. 6-13. He is giving communication such as we find at the end of most of his epistles. Perhaps the solution of the difficulty is as follows. In chapter 5 Paul discusses an altogether new subject. It may be that that is the reason why he inserts a few matter of fact communications at this point, the more so because the apostle concludes the discussion of the various subjects by referring to the chief sin of the Corinthians, their pride. This becomes thus the foundation for the following exposition.

Not to shame you, but to admonish you. Paul does not intend to cause bitterness, he wants to admonish; hence the words: *my beloved children. These things* refers to the preceding words of irony with regard to the Corinthians. Since these words had been

111

sharp Paul now assures them of his good intentions. Pride is always difficult to reprove. The proud person cannot easily take rebuke from another since he looks down on others. Therefore Paul writes *beloved children*. The same words are used of Timothy in vs. 17.

15, 16 These verses contain the reason why Paul spoke as he did. Perhaps the Corinthian church had *ten thousand tutors*. The apostle does not say that the church had as many teachers as that, but he only mentions the possibility. The Greek word *tutor* often designates a slave who had to teach the children of his master and to conduct them to and from school. Those tutors were usually severe men. But that is not what Paul has in mind; he only wishes to emphasize that he alone is the *father* of the church. He founded it by the preaching of the gospel. Just as a child may have many teachers but only one father, so Paul also occupies a special position at Corinth. The addition *in Christ* shows that Paul does not intend to speak evil of tutors. They are willing to be led by Christ (cf. vs. 10) but they cannot have the place Paul himself holds. The reason for this statement, which in itself was already given as a reason, is found in: *For in Christ Jesus*, etc. In the original the pronouns *I* and *you* are put side by side, which lends them special emphasis. Paul is obliged to speak about himself. But he is not moved by pride, as is evident from the fact that he mentions himself only in the last words of the verse in the Greek text. The most important expression is: *in Christ Jesus*. He created the possibility of founding a church by giving Himself unto death and by conquering death. He saved poor sinners and He sent His ministers to preach the gospel of salvation and He blesses their work. Paul makes clear that the begetting of the church rests in Christ. It is all from Him. As the means of this begetting Paul uses the *gospel* which has Christ for its content (2:2; 15:1f.). That means is not of Paul himself but of Christ. It is the Word of God which awakened the Corinthians. Thus Paul is able to speak about his own work and at the same time to give all the honor to Christ in order that the church may perceive her glory and the firm foundation on which she rests (cf. 1:30, 32; 4:1).

I beseech you[16] is used because the grounds for the admonition have just been given, so that "to beseech" links up with "to admonish" in vs. 14. In vs. 16 Paul sums up his previous warnings with a few mild words. Paul's summons to the Corinthians to be followers of his seems to be ill fitting in a context which warns against pride and conceit. However, we should not forget that Paul, as an apostle, besides preaching the Christian faith, also has to show its significance for the life of every day. Moreover, Paul has called himself a father of the Corinthians and a father may expect that his example be followed. It is self-evident that Paul thinks especially of the things mentioned in vss. 9-13: the experiences of the gospel preachers. To think of what follows in chapter 5 is rendered impossible by *"these things"* (vs. 14). Paul's intention is that the Corinthians should follow the entire practice of the apostolic ministry.

17 *For this cause,* literally: precisely for this. It is a strong expression serving to indicate that Timothy is sent for the very purpose of summoning the church to imitate Paul (cf. *who shall put you in remembrance,* etc.). *I sent* does not mean that Paul at this very time is sending Timothy to Corinth as the carrier of this epistle. Timothy was well known at Corinth, yet he is not mentioned in the epistle either at the beginning or at the end, as is done in II Cor. 1:1. The supposition that Paul would not convey Timothy's greetings because Timothy himself was to go to Corinth loses its point in the light of 16:10: *if Timothy come.* Apparently Timothy is on his way to Corinth and is no longer with Paul. Paul is unable to say where his helper is now nor when he will be at Corinth. But the apostle expects the letter to arrive there before Timothy himself arrives.[17] Apparently the apostle had sent Timothy earlier when unfavorable tidings reached him. After the arrival of the Corinthian emissaries (16:17) it had become necessary to write an epistle as well, which should reach Corinth as soon as possible and which would be there at least before Timothy's arrival. Acts 19:22 mentions a journey of Timothy to Macedonia. We may suppose that Timothy had

---

[16] Greek: παρακαλῶ, this verb is not as strong as "to beseech". Here it means "to admonish".

[17] Neither is ἔπεμψα an epistolary aorist but rather one of the historical fact.

orders to travel to Corinth also or that he had received such orders later from Paul. The epistle is sent by sea and will be at Corinth before the arrival of Timothy who travelled by land. Paul calls Timothy his *beloved and faithful child in the Lord*. By means of, and on the basis of the work of Christ (cf. vs. 10 and 15), Timothy is united to Paul as a son (see: 16:10, Phil. 2:20). And Paul does not only love him, but he praises his faithfulness also. This is important after what was said in 4:2. After first speaking of the relation between himself and Timothy Paul refers to Timothy's ministerial work. Thus he makes clear that it does not make any difference who comes, Timothy or the apostle himself. The task which Timothy will have to perform agrees fully with vs. 16: he will have to admonish the Corinthians that they ought to imitate the example given by Paul. *Put in remembrance*: Paul had lived in Corinth and every one had seen his conduct. *My ways* is a Semitic expression signifying a person's conduct (Ps. 37:23; Is. 57: 18; Jer. 17:10; Ezek. 33:8). Just as in vs. 15, Paul adds: *which are in Christ* in order to show that his conduct is ruled by Christ and only in so far as it is can it be an example for others.

The following words show Paul's prudence. The Corinthians who had received so many rebukes from the apostle should not think that he speaks only to them in this manner. The ways of which Timothy was to put them in remembrance agree with what the apostle teaches everywhere. Everywhere he admonishes to follow his example (cf. 14:33).[18] *I teach*: these words, used with reference to Paul's conduct, show that doctrine and life always go together. Paul lives as a Christian but he also preaches that everyone else should live thus. Timothy will also have to preach in the same way.

18 The apostle deals again with the conduct of the Corinthians, and now mentions one specific sin. Their general sin of being puffed up had now shown itself concretely with reference to Timothy's journey to Corinth (Acts 19:22). There were Corinthians who asserted that Paul had sent Timothy because he

---

[18] The Greek does not have ἆς but καθώς, i.e. Timothy has to teach the Corinthians what Paul teaches everywhere, namely, that they have to imitate his conduct.

dared not come himself. This same sort of sin is found at Corinth afterwards (II Cor. 10:10). And Paul feared that when Timothy arrived at Corinth some would say that Paul himself would rather not come. The fact that Paul wrote a letter instead of coming himself could also be interpreted in a wrong way.

This sin must now be unmasked in order that it may not reveal itself later in a worse form. Fortunately only *some*, not all the members of the congregation, are guilty. We may assume that Paul has in view those members who called themselves after Apollos, Peter or Christ. *I were not coming to you* mentions a fact; *as though*[19] calls that fact in question. Against the opinion of some that he might not come the apostle writes that he is coming. The sin of pride is also evident in the contention of some that Paul was not going to come, for thus they scoffed at the apostle and extolled themselves.

19 That is why Paul writes forcefully: *I will come to you shortly*. Paul does not fear. There is but one restriction for him: *if the Lord will;* it is possible that God will call the apostle to go to another city (Acts 16:6f.). At this moment he could not abandon Ephesus (Acts 19:22). This is not inconsistent with *shortly* for Paul, most likely, felt that he had to finish a certain task, or he had received a revelation of Christ. *And I will know,* i. e., I will take cognizance of, and at the same time recognize, the significance of those who are puffed up. To know has a special sense here as in Mt. 7:23; Jn. 1:10; I Cor. 8:3; Gal. 4:9. *Word* and *power* are contrasted. Those who were puffed up had words, they could speak and boast that Paul was not coming. But where is their *power*, i. e., in this context, not the power to perform miracles but the power of a genuine Christian life? Paul will ask for their works at his arrival and he assumes that he will not find many works. This contrast between word and power reminds us of the contrast between wisdom of words (1:17) and of power (1:24), between excellency of speech (2:1) and of power (2:4). Those passages shed sufficient light on our verse. Those who are too fond of worldly wisdom can be expected to become puffed up easily so that they would think that Paul would not come to Corinth. Some people at Corinth did not speak the word of the

---

[19] As though, ὡς, *e mente Pauli.*

Lord that exercises power (Heb. 4:12), but rather words of men which were idle and vain of themselves (Mt. 12:36; I Cor. 2:13).

20 Be this as it may, Paul states anew very clearly why he ought not to give attention to words but to works. The nature of the *kingdom of God* requires that of him. With this the Corinthians should agree. Paul uses the term "kingdom of God," as the gospels also do, in a double sense. There is an objective sense: the realm or the dominion of God, and a subjective one: the citizenship in the kingdom. Here the expression has objective meaning. Because the kingdom of God reveals itself as power (2:4) the true citizens of that kingdom in their life will stress not words but power. The kingdom of God comes in and through them (Lk. 17:21). That is also the ground of Paul's mention of the kingdom of God. He is able to show thereby why he had the right to reject words and to require power, which means to condemn pride.

21 This is an application directed to the whole church. It is necessary for, although there were only some who charged that Paul was not going to come, the whole congregation was guilty of the sin of being puffed up. After Paul has informed the former category that he is coming, at least if the Lord will, he now has a few words for everyone concerning his proposed coming. The way in which he will come will depend on the attitude of the church. *What will ye? With*[20] *a rod,* i. e., to chastise? The second possibility is expressed without any figurative language. The question may be asked whether Paul should not come *in love and in a spirit of gentleness* under every circumstance. As to *gentleness*, it may refer to kindness, meekness. The word *love,* however, must be understood in a special sense. It is not love in general but the utterance, or the expression of love (cf. II Cor. 8:24) as the Greek word may be taken. Moreover, the absence of articles in the Greek enables us to think not of the general Christian virtues of love and meekness but of a special manifestation of them. In other words, Paul always possessed love but he might

---

[20] Greek: ἐν, indicating the manner of Paul's coming.

come in such a way that the Corinthians would think that he did not have any love.

14-21 In this pericope Paul changes the subject several times. It is a part of a regular letter in that Paul takes the liberty of treating different points. In it he sets forth the nature of his admonitions: the fact that his heart is filled with love does not mean that he will not admonish sharply.

CHAPTER V

OUTRAGEOUS FORNICATION

5:1-13

1 It is actually reported that there is fornication among you, and such fornication as is not even among the Gentiles, that one *of you* hath his father's wife.

2 And ye are puffed up, and did not rather mourn, that he that had done this deed might be taken away from among you.

3 For I verily, being absent in body but present in spirit, have already as though I were present judged him that hath so wrought this thing,

4 in the name of the Lord Jesus, ye being gathered together, and my spirit, with the power of our Lord Jesus.

5 to deliver such a one unto Satan for the destruction of the flesh, that the spirit may be saved in the day of the Lord Jesus.

6 Your glorying is not good. Know ye not that a little leaven leaveneth the whole lump?

7 Purge out the old leaven, that ye may be a new lump, even as ye are unleavened. For our passover also hath been sacrificed, *even* Christ:

8 wherefore, let us keep the feast, not with old leaven, neither with the leaven of malice and wickedness, but with the unleavened bread of sincerity and truth.

9 I wrote unto you in my epistle not to have company with fornicators;

10 not at all *meaning* with the fornicators of this world, or with the covetous and extortioners, or with idolaters; for must ye needs go out of the world:

11 but as it is, I wrote unto you not to keep company, if any man that is named a brother be a fornicator, or covetous, or an idolator, or a reviler, or a drunkard, or an extortioner; with such a one no, not to eat.

12 For what have I to do with judging them that are without? Do ye judge them that are within?

13 But them that are without God judgeth. Put away the wicked man from among yourselves.

1 With chapter 5 Paul begins the treatment of some Corinthian abuses concerning which the Corinthians had not even written him. That was also the case with the disputes, which in turn formed the occasion for writing about various things not always closely connected with them. This accounts for many brief, special expositions. From now on Paul abandons that method. Chapters 5 and 6 deal with a case of fornication and with the evil of going to court before a pagan judge. With those two subjects everything in these chapters is closely connected.

Actually, i. e., generally speaking,[1] a word which may belong to either *is reported* or to "fornication." The former possibility is to be preferred, both because "actually" is an adverb and because of its place in the text. The sense is then: there is a general report that there is *fornication among you.* The case is well known. The word "general" must not be taken of extent in the first place but of inclusiveness. There is no exception to it: whenever the church of Corinth is spoken of people think of that case of fornication. The present *is reported* implies that the rumor was being spread until the very day of the writing of Paul's letter. This may also mean that this sin still continued. *Among you* is to be taken with *is reported.* "Among you there is a rumor of fornication." Anyone at Corinth who spoke of the church in that city mentioned the fornication among the Christians. This explains why the apostle in vs. 2 writes: *and ye are puffed up.* Their pride had not diminished even though everybody at Corinth was acquainted with their trespasses. *Fornication*[2] is the most general word for all kinds of sins against the seventh commandment. *Even* speaks of the greatness of the fornication; there is an extremely severe case of it at Corinth. Paul means to say that there is fornication in general in the church, but that one case surpasses the others (cf. also vs. 11; 6:12f.). This particular sin was so serious that it did not even occur among the gentiles. We know that at this particular period among the heathen the sin of fornication was not considered serious (cf. Rom. 1) but for someone to live with the wife of his father, i. e., his step-

---

[1] Greek: ὅλως
[2] Greek: πορνεία

119

COMMENTARY ON FIRST CORINTHIANS

mother, was outrageous. (cf. Gen. 35:22; 49:4; I Chron. 5:1; II Sam. 16:22; 20:3).

That is dependent on *such*. First Paul characterizes the sin and then he states what sin he had in mind. *One of you*: no name is mentioned, since Paul directs himself here not in the first place to the sinner but to the congregation which tolerates such a sin in its midst. *Hath* refers to a longer time, not just to one trespass but to a life in sin.

2 *And ye*: even ye, boastful Corinthians. Paul attempts to awaken the Corinthians. For they continue to be *puffed up,* they go on in their sin of pride. Not that they actually boast of the sin committed but they still do not understand that there is not any ground for boasting. The sin of pride had dazzled them so that they did not see things as they really were. There is never any reason for pride and certainly there was not at Corinth.

Did not rather mourn: you have not even begun to feel sorrowful, since you think everything is all right. The clause introduced by *that* indicates what ought to have the result of a necessary sadness. They ought to have expelled the sinner from the congregation. It is of importance to notice the duty of the congregation according to Paul (cf. vs. 13), namely to banish the obstinate sinner. Paul asks for an action on the part of the church and gives the directive to such an action. The church would have to declare that this man no longer belonged to their circle. The apostle does not set forth the way in which the church had to perform this act. We may assume that the congregation knew how to do it. In any case, the church is the temple of God (3:17) and as such she has to remain holy. Therefore an action of banishment is not an action of pride or of hard-heartedness. The honor of God and the holiness of the church are at stake. Paul does not ask that the sinner be admonished. A church living in such pride is not yet able to admonish but has to expunge her own sins first. *He that hath done that* is again a very general, but nevertheless in this context, a very clear statement. Paul does not speak about the sinner but in the first place about his sin.

3 Vs. 3 sets forth what Paul has done himself, a certain thing that the church ought to have done something also. Or, in other words: the church should have done something of her own accord

120

a long time ago. The church did not yet know what Paul had done, but she is now informed of it and this must prompt her to action, namely to the expulsion of the sinner. It is our opinion that Paul does not speak of any real action on his part but of something he did in the spirit (cf. vs. 4), at the most of a declaration which he made, according to which the church would have to act. Paul does not only pray for the churches, he also works along with them (Acts 20:18f.; II Cor. 11:28). It is therefore according to Paul's custom that he should do something after hearing of the sin committed at Corinth, even though he was absent. Bodily he was absent, but in the spirit he was at Corinth. *As though I were present*: in connection with the preceding words which mention a spiritual presence we translate: *because I am present*. The first "present" touches upon Paul's right to act, the second sets forth how he acts. *Judged him*: Paul has taken a resolution the consequences of which are seen in the present.[3] "I judged him" is the principal verb. What Paul has done is not a delivering over to Satan, but the passing of a judgment, *already*, a long time ago. Because Paul does not speak of an action but of a judgment there is no question here of divine judgment as in the case of Ananias and Sapphira. The only thing the apostle states is what he in the spirit has done with the sinner, and he does so in order to teach the church what his view of this sinner is. The main action has to come from the church and must result in an excommunication. Paul's action, therefore, regards the sinner; the action which the church was obligated to take regards her purity. In harmony with his apostolic office Paul cares for both the sinner and the congregation.

As though I were present implies that Paul does not only maintain his right, but also that he has given his judgment in the presence of the church and of the sinner. That is why the apostle did not conceal this judgment but divulged it to the Corinthians. The latter should have understood that the apostle could only have acted in this way. *So*: the sin has been committed in a special way (cf. vs. 1). *Hath so wrought*: the sin has come to its full fruition.

---

[3] Greek: κέκρινα is perf.

4-5 It is very difficult to give a satisfactory explanation of the connection of the words. The words: *in the name of the Lord Jesus* (A) may be combined with: *ye being gathered together with my spirit* (I), and the words: *with the power of our Lord Jesus* (B) with: *to deliver such a one unto Satan* (II). This may be considered combination (a). Other possible combinations are (b) A and B combined with I; (c) A and B combined with II; but also (d) A combined with II and B with I. Combinations (b) and (c), although grammatically quite possible are not very likely because we would then be required to hold that Paul in a sentence such as this would have combined two adverbial clauses with the one verb and none with the other. Moreover, against (c) tells the order of the words. The decision between (a) and (d) is a difficult one however. It might on the one hand be argued that each adverbial clause is best joined to the following verb. On the other hand, *"with the power of our Lord Jesus"* is more naturally linked with: *"being gathered together"* and likewise *"in the name of the Lord Jesus* goes best with the principal verb *to deliver*. This last consideration appears to us to be the decisive one, and thus we choose in favor of (d) as being the best combination.

Ye being gathered[4] *together and my spirit with the power of our Lord Jesus*: these words speak of three who, though belonging together, are nevertheless not each other's equals as appears from the use of *and* and *with* respectively. *My spirit*: Paul is thinking of a meeting held at Corinth, where he could be present in spirit only. This meeting could have been a real one. What Paul implies is that the Corinthian church ought to have called to mind the spirit of Paul, in asking herself what the apostle would have done in these circumstances. This also explains the words: *I . . . judged him as though I were present*. Paul states what he has done in the spirit. The Corinthians should have called a meeting, but since they omitted doing that, Paul is obliged to state his own judgment, a judgment to which the Corinthians should have come by themselves.

With the power of our Lord Jesus: Since *"with"* expresses not only mere presence but also cooperation, the presence of this power

---

[4] συνάγομαι, deponent middle. Paul does not speak of a bringing together but of a coming together.

is a different one from that of the Corinthians and of Paul. Where Paul meets with the church there is the power of Jesus Christ, i. e., the power of Him who suffered and died for our sins and was glorified thereafter (Mt. 18:20; 28:20). Just because He is present measures can be taken so that the meeting does not proceed on its own authority but delivers the sinner in the name of Jesus. Where the name of the Lord is named, His glory is brought to mind.[5]

To deliver such a one unto Satan: to abandon him to the devil so that he may do with the sinner as he desires. This is defined further by the words: *for the destruction of the flesh,* where a definite purpose for the delivering unto Satan is stated. Satan is here viewed as being subject to God who ultimately determines what Satan will be permitted to do and who will also take care that all this will add to His own glory.

In vs. 3 we had a distinction between body and spirit, here is one between flesh and spirit. This compels us to take flesh in the sense of "sinful flesh." The deliverance unto Satan aims at the destruction of the sinner's sinful nature. The objection that the devil never destroys sin but rather cherishes it (Mt. 12:26) must be met with the consideration that Paul does not say, that Satan must destroy sin but rather that the deliverance unto Satan must have the destruction of sin as a result (cf. II Cor. 12:7). It should, moreover, be remembered that a great sin was here the cause of this abandonment so that the abandonment was also a judgment. Paul hoped that its consequence would mean the end of "sinful flesh," although this remained to be seen. This man may be lost for the church, but if his flesh is destroyed, his spirit will appear to be sanctified, at the time when Christ comes to judge, in the full sense of the word and he may enter into eternal life. *Be saved*: this salvation is accomplished but it is also hoped for (cf. I Tim. 1:20, then Prov. 23:14; II Cor. 13:10). This interpretation does not involve a contradiction between the act of delivering and that of putting away (vs. 13), since the former forms the spiritual background of the latter. Paul, being an apostle, is able to deliver unto Satan, but the congregation can go no further

---

[5] See: F. W. Grosheide: Kommentaar op het N.T., I, on Mt. 28:19; V, on Acts 3:16.

than an exclusion. Yet this banishment from the church to the congregation is equal to an exclusion from the kingdom of God. It is a deliverance to Satan so far as a congregation may do that (Mt. 18:17, 18; cf. 8:12; 21:31, 32). The church is obliged to do this, although the sinner may be saved. Its measure may be means in the hands of God to save the sinner.

6   Vs. 6 shows anew that Paul in the first place thinks of the congregation as a whole. The fact that there is a *glorying* at Corinth *is not good*. This the Corinthians did not understand and yet they ought to understand it not only because any kind of glorying is wrong but also because the apostle had convicted them of such a great sin. They must admit that the apostle was right. Paul uses a well known figure: a little lump of *leaven leaveneth* all the flour. Its exact reference is less clear. Is the sinner compared with the leaven and does Paul imply that the presence of this incestuous person makes the whole congregation unclean? Against this speaks the fact that the affair of the sinner has come to a provisional end (vs. 5) and is not mentioned again until vs. 13. It is better, therefore, to take *leaven* of the immediately preceding *glorying*. This glorying must then be taken in the concrete sense in which it occurs in this sentence, i. e., a wrong sort of glorying which at the same time tolerates immorality. The church had received many privileges from God (1:4f.) but she glories in a wrong way and consequently that glorying is like a leaven which spoils the whole congregation. Here again we meet with spiritual pride as the main vice of the Corinthian church.

Know ye not: these words, with their implied answer: "of course we do," serve to teach the Corinthians that due to their pride all the glory of the church was at stake. Thus the apostle, starting with one concrete sin, ends at the church's sinful attitude in general.

7   The admonition of vs. 7 refers to the ceremonies which the ancient Israelites had to perform before eating the Passover. Israel had to eat unleavened bread for seven days and was to remove all leaven from its houses on the first day. This eating of unleavened bread was done in remembrance of the exodus from Egypt. But before the exodus God gave a commandment to remove all leaven, which was a figure of the liberation from the

124

sins of Egypt (Ex. 12:6, 15, 39; 13:6; 23:15; 34:18; Dt. 16:3).
That Paul has this last thought in view appears from the use of
"old," i. e., that which is no longer new, or fresh. Among the
Corinthians there are still many remnants of their former pagan
period, working as a leaven and corrupting their Christian life.
All that ought to be removed, so much the more since there is a
sin within the congregation that should have been an occasion of
deep humiliation. In vs. 6 "little leaven" referred to a wrong type
of glorying, in vs. 7, where "little" is lacking, *old leaven* can refer
to sins in general which still remained of an earlier period. If
the Corinthians remove that *old leaven* they will be a *new lump.*[6]
Their structure ought to be quite different from what it was
before, the pagan leaven and the evil glorying now being removed.

The clause with *"even as"* states what the Corinthians are,
objectively considered. They are without leaven since some One
else removed it, namely Christ, when He redeemed them from
their sins. Their obligation to live accordingly is so much greater
and their sin, which breaks up the normal relations, is so much
worse. In the first part of the verse the figure implies that the
Corinthians themselves are not the lump so that they are able to
remove the leaven. But in the second part of vs. 7 they themselves are the leaven and yet they are also thought to be able to
do something with the leaven, i. e., with themselves. In the third
part they are the lump of dough in the hands of another who
removed the leaven from them, or, perhaps, took care that the
leaven would not be in them. In spite of this diversity the picture
is quite clear. Equally clear is Paul's intention to emphasize with
"even as" that the Corinthians are able to remove the old leaven
because Christ has redeemed them. They ought to remove it and
they are able to, for they are clean (Rom. 6:3f.). The sentence
with *"for"* emphasizes that still more. In an expansion of the
original figure the Corinthians are now compared to the people
for whom the *passover* was *sacrificed.* Israel ate the unleavened

---

[6] φύραμα in the proper sense of the word means sponge, i.e. flour
with leaven, but Paul uses it here of the lump of flour without
leaven. He does so because the Israelites only took flour along
from Egypt. What they prepared on their journey had no leaven
and was of quite a different structure from what they used in Egypt.

125

bread after the passover. Christ, the true paschal Lamb, after once having given Himself for His people enables His people to eat unleavened bread perpetually, or, to be *unleavened*. Perhaps the reference to Christ's sacrifice caused the apostle to alter his figure. Christ is Priest and Sacrifice, He gives Himself as a passover Lamb. When Christ is considered as a sacrifice believers may be the unleavened bread, but when He is considered as a priest then they are the people who eat the bread and remove the leaven. Here again, however, the thought is clear: Christ gave Himself to propitiate for sins. His sacrifice has been made and all that had to be done is done. Believers are therefore delivered from sins, objectively, and they are called, subjectively, to remove all remaining sins.

8   Vs. 8 is a conclusion. Because Christ gave Himself for our sins we are obliged to *keep the feast*, i. e., the feast of unleavened bread (cf. vs. 7). *Old leaven*, to be understood in the sense of vs. 7, fits the thought of keeping feast. Christ's sacrifice compels and enables one to live as a true Christian. The feast must be kept but that must be done in a special way. They must *keep the feast* by leaving aside all iniquity, by parting with all sin even as the ancient Israelites did with their leaven.

Neither with the leaven of malice and wickedness: an expansion of thought by way of naming some special sins. Strictly speaking these words must be taken of actions not included in "old leaven" (cf. *neither*), but in this context that cannot be the meaning. The apostle circumscribes the idea of leaven in two ways: chronologically and qualitatively. There is a moral laxity at Corinth which is designated by Paul in more general terms[7] but the apostle warns especially against a wrong attitude toward one's fellow man. Perhaps he also wanted to declare that the boasting of the Corinthians was nothing but *malice* and *wickedness*. Of course the words *neither . . . wickedness* are to be understood parenthetically, since *but with the unleavened bread*, etc., is to be combined with *keep the feast*.

---

[7] G. Heine, *Synonymik d. Neutest. Griechisch,* 1898, p. 106: πονηρία est nequitia eius, qui alteri etiam sine suo commodo, nocere gaudet; κακία est vitium, quo alter alteri nil boni conferre potest.

Sincerity refers to the condition of the mind: there must be purity, harmony between the thought, the intention and the act. The subsequent virtue is of a more intellectual nature, but it shows at the same time how this purity manifests itself. We must remain faithful to the *truth,* that is in reality to the preaching of Paul. He who lives thus, looking at the real passover Lamb, Christ, keeps the feast in the right way.

The question has often been asked whether Paul wrote this way because it was about the time of Passover. However, the data for an exact answer are lacking. We must not forget that the figure used by Paul is a very obvious one, because it is borrowed from a well known portion of the Scriptures.

9 It might seem as if the apostle begins an entirely different subject. This is only seemingly so. There is a connection with the foregoing, for the command given in vs. 13 is founded on two grounds: the one expounded in vss. 1-8, the other in vss. 9-12.

I wrote[8] *in my epistle*: Paul had sent an earlier letter to the Corinthians, and they knew its contents very well. We do not possess the smallest remnant of that letter but know only of its existence. That former letter contained the warning not to have any *company with fornicators,* i. e., to have no regular association with them. *Fornicators*:[9] the Greek is a general term including all kinds of fornication. The apostle must have taken it here of public sins so that the church might know those with whom it was not supposed to associate. This public sin was characteristic of the church at Corinth In an earlier letter he had to treat this sin and it still had not disappeared. Corinth was notorious for its immorality and not even the church was free of it.

10 The words of verse 10 also had a place in the lost epistle. But perhaps not literally, or at least not as clearly as they are given in this verse. Otherwise it is hard to understand how misunderstanding could have arisen. At any rate, Paul had to give a

---

[8] ἔγραψα may be an epistolary aorist. It would then mean that in the epistle he is now writing Paul had already inserted a warning as the one given in vs. 9. But one looks in vain for such an admonition in I Corinthians. Besides, the words "in my epistle" would then be superfluous. These considerations compel us to take the verb as an historical aorist.

[9] πόρνος.

new clarification, beginning with: *not at all meaning,*[10] i. e., not
in all circumstances, not without exception. *This world* (cf.
1:18) has a special meaning. It implies that the church is already
separated by a wide gulf from the fornicators who belong to this
world because there is no connection between the church and the
world. When believers do mix with the sinners of the world,
their association with them is quite different from their association with fellow members of the congregation. Against that
sort of association the apostle does not object. Having mentioned
the fornicators before, Paul enumerates other serious sins in order
to justify his conclusion. *Covetous* men are not content with a
moderate profit. *Extortioners* are people who take what is not
due to them. Such people are found in every city of commerce,
and generally speaking they strike the keynote in the world.
There are many of them at Corinth. The congregation was sur-
rounded by *idolaters,* and if it were to avoid their company it
would be impossible to live. The Corinthians understood that
readily. By naming these sinners along with fornicators Paul
taught the Corinthians what their attitude toward fornicators
should be. If every association with fornicators were forbidden
the Corinthians would have no other choice than to *go out of the
world.* The apostle knew that the whole church would be convinced that this was impossible (cf. Jn. 17:15). Paul appeals to
that conviction in order to show that it is impossible to avoid all
association with fornicators and also in order to prove that the
interpretation which he now gives of his earlier words is the
right one.

11 *But as it is,* i. e., at this moment. *I wrote,*[11] refers to what
Paul is writing at this moment and is equivalent to our: I write.
The apostle repeats what he wrote in vs. 9, i. e., he sets forth
again the words of his earlier letter and he gives an explanation
in the following clause. We may conclude from this that the
warning in the first epistle had been understood wrongly. That
warning had been written for the church and had the conditions
of the church in mind. But the Corinthian church had acted as

---

[10] οὐ πάντως, vs. 1 ὅλως πάντως has in view all possibilities, concerns the whole.

[11] ἔγραψα is an epistolary aorist.

if the church belonged to the world. That is why Paul repeats his
utterance in a positive form. We have here a very important
question. God gives His commandments to His people. Those
commandments must be fulfilled by all men but God gives the
power to do so to His people only. The kingdom of God is not of
this world nor can the laws of that kingdom be carried out in
worldly associations (cf. Dt. 14:21; 15:3; 23:19, 20; Heb.
12:20-21.) The Corinthian Church had transformed a specific
injunction, evidently given to the congregation alone, into a
general precept. The question arises whether a close association
with the fornicators of the world would not be much more dan-
gerous than such an association with sinners who, be it outwardly
(cf. *named*), belong to the congregation. Paul does not consider
the question from this point of view. Two things are here at
stake: 1) the sanctity of the church and 2) the salvation of the
sinner. The church, in treating public sinners like all other men,
is desecrated; the sinner is not called to conversion. For that
reason the church is obligated to break off all intercourse with the
fornicators in the church (cf. vs. 12).

If any man that is named a brother is to be connected as a
conditional clause with *not to keep company*. And *with such a
one not to eat* is coordinate with *not to keep company*. Paul is
here explaining the case in which all intercourse is forbidden.[12]
Named: the man has the name of a brother, he is a member of
the congregation but in reality he is a public sinner. The apostle
enumerates a list of very frequent sins, without following a
definite order. The absence of the sin of murder is remarkable but
perhaps Paul is mentioning things which are considered sinful
by the church and not by the world. The reference to idolaters, a
term which must here be taken in a literal sense of people who
still clung to their idols, points definitely in that direction. In a
church like the Corinthian, where ecclesiastical discipline was not
at all or only loosely exercised, such sinners were found and there
was intercourse with them. To insist on the breaking off of such
intercourse is at the same time to insist on the exercise of discipline (Mt. 18:17). *Not to eat* implies that not keeping company

---

12 ἐάν τις ἀδελφὸς ὀνομαζόμενος ἦ κτλ., i.e. as often as the case
arises.

together is stronger than not eating together. The former speaks of regular intercourse which includes eating together, the latter refers to having a meal together, not including regular intercourse. In a time in which hotels were not numerous private hospitality was indispensable, and thus eating together could most easily occur (cf. Acts 10:6; 21:16; II Jn. 10).

The question why Paul reminds the Corinthians here of his earlier letter and straightens out misunderstanding must still be answered. It is because the church tolerated this incestuous man in its midst and acted thus against what Paul had written. Love is one of the main things in the life of the church. The sinner is to be excluded from every evidence of love in the church in order that he may see his sins and be converted.

12 Vs. 12 contains the ground whereby the apostle clarifies that what he wrote in vs. 11 was the true meaning of his earlier letter. This clarification agrees with the rule which Paul always observes. The apostle has no communion with those who are outside the church. The meaning is not that Paul does not have contact with persons who are not Christians — Paul is a missionary. But the apostle writes here about judging. He judges only the members of the church because he summons them to convert themselves (cf. vs. 3f). This judging may end in a banishment from the church. Again Paul appeals to the congregation, this time by reminding her of her task and of her present condition.[13] *Ye*. i e., the members of the church. This suggests that the church did judge and that it did exercise discipline. But Paul says that it does not judge in the right way because it did not judge the incestuous person.

13 Vs. 13 performs a double task. First it states that, although neither Paul nor the church are able to judge those who are without, the latter are nevertheless not altogether without judgment. It is God Himself who will judge them in the day of the Lord (cf. Rom. 2:5; Heb. 13:14; I Pet. 4:17). To the church God gives the grace of exercising discipline which serves to warn sinners. They that are without lack that grace so that they come at once before the judgment of God, not having any benefit at all.

---

[13] οὐχί expects an affirmative answer.

The second matter is that the church, according to her vocation, must be willing to *put away the wicked man from among* herself. She is obligated to perform her task of judging (cf. also Dt. 3:6; 17:7; 19:19; 22:24; 24:7 (LXX 24:9), where the law speaks of a grave sin and of its punishment). It was God's will that His people should be a holy people in whose midst public sins should not occur. In Israel God required capital punishment of gross sinners so that the demand for banishment from the church under the new dispensation does not amaze us. The Corinthians were obligated to assent and so to perceive their task.

1-13 The purpose of this whole chapter is to disclose the grave sin of the church. It is the church more than the sinner which is spoken of. The church is guilty and has to correct herself and do what is required.

CHAPTER VI

FORBIDDEN LAWSUITS

6:1-11

1 Dare any one of you, having a matter against his neighbor, go to law before the unrighteous, and not before the saints?

2 Or know ye not that the saints shall judge the world? and if the world is judged by you, are ye unworthy to judge the smallest matters?

3 Know ye not that we shall judge angels? how much more, things that pertain to this life?

4 If then ye have to judge things pertaining to this life, do ye set them to judge who are of no account in the church?

5 I say this to move you to shame. What, cannot there be *found* among you one wise man who shall be able to decide between his brethren,

6 but brother goeth to law with brother, and that before unbelievers?

7 Nay, already it is altogether a defect in you, that ye have lawsuits one with another. Why not rather take wrong? why not rather be defrauded?

8 Nay, but ye yourselves do wrong, and defraud, and that *your* brethren.

9 Or know ye not that the unrighteous shall not inherit the kingdom of God? Be not deceived: neither fornicators, nor idolaters, nor adulterers, nor effeminate, nor abusers of themselves with men,

10 nor thieves, nor drunkards, nor revilers, nor extortioners, shall inherit the kingdom of God.

11 And such were some of you: but ye were washed, but ye were sanctified, but ye were justified in the name of the Lord Jesus Christ, and in the Spirit of our God.

1 This pericope also treats a question about which the Corinthians had not written Paul. Again the apostle does not state who his informant was. In 1:12 this was done possibly because in that case Paul could not expect that the Corinthians would

assent to the correctness of his information. Paul's information
was well founded. The Corinthians, though Christians, brought
their judicial cases before pagan judges. Paul sets forth the great
difference between such pagan judges and the members of the
Christian church. *Dare any of you* implies a venture. It should
at once make the Corinthians aware of their sin. They did not see
that there was a moral defect in their life. *Anybody of you*: nobody ought to have done this. *Having a matter*: i. e., if he has a
matter. Paul first mentions a case in which two members of the
congregation have difficulty with each other, in vs. 7, however,
he goes beyond specific cases. *Go to law,* in order to have their
case adjudicated. Paul calls the pagan judges *unrighteous* since
they are not members of the church, who are the *saints*. Generally speaking Paul's opinion of pagan magistrates is favorable
(see Rom. 13). The Greek word for "unrighteous"[1] is used only
thrice in the epistles of Paul. In Rom. 3:5 the word means: not
doing right, but in I Cor. 6:9 it indicates sinners, transgressors of
the law. In our verse the apostle says that the Corinthians are
seeking justice with men who, because they do not keep the law
of God, cannot judge righteously. "Unrighteous," in contrast
with "holy in Christ," means: not righteous before God and
therefore not truly righteous. Here again the human wisdom of
the Corinthians is foolishness. We might think of the evil of
bribery which was not uncommon among Greek judges. But this
cannot have been the main thing for else the Christians would
not have gone to the pagan law courts. The ground of Paul's
warning is the thought that a pagan judge cannot decide in a
case between Christians since he is not acquainted with the things
of the kingdom of God (2:8). Paul, therefore, does not condemn
any individual judge but the whole class of them together. *And
not before the saints* implies that the seeking of justice as such is
not forbidden. To deduce from vs. 1 that any going to court is
forbidden to Christians is unwarranted. In a Christian country
jurisprudence is a blessing from God if it reckons with the laws
given by the Lord. From vs. 5 we learn that Corinth did not yet
possess any Christian judges. For *saints* cf. 1:2. We might
expect "righteous" but this is perhaps avoided by Paul because

---

[1] ἄδικος.

133

COMMENTARY ON FIRST CORINTHIANS

the congregation cannot handle its own cases. Moreover, the term "righteous" does not appear in either of the Corinthian epistles. The reason is that in these epistles the relation to God is not treated by Paul but rather the moral purity of the church.

2 The question in vs. 2 serves to lead the church to an insight into the greatness of its fault. She who in the matter of judging possesses such glory has completely forgotten that glory. Paul appeals to a known but nevertheless neglected fact. The statement refers to the objective benefits which not only this but all congregations share, as is clear from the use of the third person. *World* has a double sense here: it indicates the well ordered universe but designates at the same time the sinful world to which the pagan judges belong. The church ought to remember her own glory but should also realize that she turns the existing order of things upside down. *Shall judge*: that will happen in the day of days. That is part of the church's glory, now present in principle only but to be realized fully in the future.

The second part of vs. 2 has as a protasis a conditional clause, as apodosis a question. That question is rhetorical and mitigates somewhat the statement which might have been an outright negative one: then you are not unworthy. *And if;* if it is so as it really is. To *judge* is to share the royal glory of Christ, a prerogative which awaits the believers[2] (cf. Mt. 19:28; Lk. 22:30; Jn. 5:24-29; Rev. 3:21; 20:4). *Unworthy*: it is an absurdity that you who will enjoy so much glory in the future could not be judges in the present. *Smallest matters*:[3] there were questions at Corinth about trivialities and they were submitted to the judgment of pagans! The answer Paul expects to this question is negative especially after he has reminded the church of her judicial dignity. Thus it appears how the Corinthians are trampling on their own glory and at the same time dishonor God

---

[2] ASV and RSV read "by you", the Greek, however, has ἐν ὑμῖν, "in your midst" (cf. Heb. 12:1, where those who are glorified are the lookers on in whose presence the believers on earth are running their race. In I Cor. 6:2 those who are glorified, i.e. acquitted by Christ are the spectators in whose midst Christ on the day of days judges the world and who therefore share that judgment.

[3] Greek κριτηρίων ἐλαχίστων, i.e. of courts which have to treat the smaller matters.

134

who bestowed such glory upon them. The apostle directs himself
to the whole church; there is not just one sinner (any of you,
vs. 1.) but all are guilty.

3 He mentions *angels,* which proves that *"world"* in vs. 2
must have meant the earth. Paul does not place the angels above
the world perhaps they are not even thought as being outside of
the world. It is obviously his intention to mention something
that is exalted above *the things that pertain to this life,* something
which is above the human horizon. The church may not every
day reflect upon the fact that it will judge angels. These must
be the good angels for Paul always means them when he speaks
of angels without qualification. Other places in Scripture teach
us likewise that there will be a judgment of angels (II Pet. 2:4;
Jude 6, Rev. 20:10). Believers will participate in that judgment.
That implies that they are above the angels, they will have been
acquitted already and participate in the judgment of the angels.
Things that pertain to this life: this shows that the Christians
went to pagan courts about trifles. Paul's question is abbreviated.
In full it would read: Are we who will once judge angels not
worthy and able to be judges about the trifles of the life of every
day?

4 Vs. 4 may be a question as well as a positive statement.[4]
ASV and RSV take it as a question: When you have a case *do
you set them to judge, who are of no account in the church?* You
do not. Why, then, do you go to pagan judges who have much
less insight in your affairs than they who are of no account in
your midst? We personally prefer to take this statement as a
positive one: *set them to judge,* etc. The clause then receives an
ironical meaning. The grounds for this interpretation are as
follows. Vs. 5 shows that the Corinthians had not thought of the
possibility of judging their own lawsuits. Furthermore, vs. 5
implies that Paul is in favor of a board of arbitration possibly
because there were no Christian judges to be had. Under those
conditions Paul could not *ask:* do you set etc. On the other hand,
there is place for an ironical admonition. Then we feel the absurdity of the whole situation, because then the church is sum-
moned to do what she cannot do, namely institute law courts

---

[4] In the first case καθίζετε is imperative, in the second indicative.

135

which is properly the work of the government. And yet the church, which is able to institute courts of law and which is not permitted to go to pagan courts, would have to do this. The absurdity arises from the evil fact that there are lawsuits in the Corinthian church.[5] Paul virtually says: I show you a way to yield to your evil desires of citing each other to court. That evil desire deserves no other expression, but that expression itself you cannot use.

Who are of no account: this cannot refer to the pagan judges because the latter were not held in contempt; on the contrary, the members of the church went to them. Besides, the church cannot appoint pagan judges and to summon her to do so, even though it be done in an ironical sense, would be an impossibility. The reference is rather to those who were of no account in the church, and this in turn furnishes a new argument in favor of understanding this statement in an ironical sense. Vs. 5: *I say this to move you to shame* can also be explained more easily after an ironical clause than after a rhetorical question.[6]

5 The Greek word[7] that is translated by *to move you to shame* is better rendered by "exhortation." Paul explains that his ironical admonition intended to lay bare existing evil. In paraphrase, the consequence of your doing would be that you would be obligated to set church members who are of no account as judges in your law courts. If you cannot do this you should realize that you are going in the wrong direction.

The following sentence is again a shortened one. It requires the addition: that you go to pagan judges. Paul's question must have overwhelmed the Corinthians who thought that they were so wise. And yet, their foolishness again had appeared. They might be well versed in worldly wisdom but in the practice of Christian life they were lagging behind so far that they did not

---

[5] The subjunctive mood of ἐὰν ἔχητε speaks of something that could happen but should not happen.

[6] If this sentence is a question and if ἐξουθενημένους is taken of the members of the church, then καθίζετε must be translated by *would you set?* But this is an almost impossible translation of an indicative. Οὖν also suits better in a positive sentence than in a question.

[7] ἐντροπή.

even think of the possibility of finding within their own circles a wise man who might handle their judicial disputes.[8] Paul condemns every form of going to court before a pagan judge on the part of brethren. On the other hand, it should not be forgotten that there were no Christian judges as yet, and that a private person could do no more than act as arbiter. We cannot, therefore, say that Paul condemns all legal proceedings. It is a remarkable fact that Paul proceeds step by step. In this verse he places himself on the standpoint that there are disputes in the congregation (cf. 1:12), and they ought to be solved by arbitration. But in the words: *shall be able* it is already hinted that this is not the ideal. The use of "brother" two times in vs. 6 points in the same direction, for it emphasizes the intimate connection between arbiter and defendants as over against the great difference between pagans and Christians.[9]

6 Vs. 6 is also taken by some as a question, by others as a positive statement. If this is a question it is a continuation of v. 5. A question like that would make no sense after what Paul asked in vs. 1. It is better to take it as a positive statement, beginning with *but*. It then contains a contrast and states what the Corinthians did do. Vs. 8, another positive statement introduced with *but* furnishes an additional argument in favor of this interpretation.

Vs. 6 introduces to a certain extent a new element. It teaches that Paul does not merely treat the seeking of justice before pagan judges as such, but that he treats it as an expression of an evil attitude of mind. In vs. 12 Paul discusses the point of right.[10] In our verse it is already made clear that the Corinthians as a consequence of their being puffed up did not see their faults and considered a thing that was actually a sin a matter of Christian

---

[8] The Greek word διαχρῖναι implies an amicable settlement by means of arbitration.

[9] ἀνὰ μέσον τοῦ ἀδελφοῦ is perhaps an abridged expression for ...τοῦ ἀδελφοῦ καὶ τοῦ πλησίου αὐτοῦ (cf. Sir. 25:18). It is also possible to explain ἀδελφός as a collective, the singular being used for the plural (cf. also Alford ad loc.). αὐτοῦ, the arbiter or the man who would go to a pagan judge. The difference is of no importance although the second possibility is most probable.

[10] ἐξουσία.

liberty. To have difficulties among brethren is absurd, says Paul, not having in view any concrete facts but only the disposition of mind. How is it possible that a Christian would go to court with someone whom he loves as a brother? That is only possible if there is no love to the brethren. Especially if one goes to a pagan judge.

7 Vs. 7 provides a confirmation and extension of vs. 5. *Nay,* introduces a conclusion from *"brother with brother."* *Already* implies that behind going to court before gentiles there lies a *defect.* And *"altogether"* (cf. 5:1) implies a complete disapproval of this sort of litigation. *Defect,* properly "defeat,"[11] is a remarkable word in this context. It does not brand lawsuits as sinful, but it states that the boasting Corinthians, who lived in a flush of victory, were actually defeated. This defeat is shown in their conducting lawsuits against one another. There ought to be a mutual tie of brotherhood but there is disunity and of such a nature that the judges had to interfere. The apostle here sets forth what ought to have been the attitude of the church and what it must be in the present.

The question (*why not,* etc.) is again a rhetorical one. The apostle does not expect an answer but it is his intention to indicate another possibility. In choosing this form Paul indicates that the suffering of injustice is *commanded.* Justice may be sought but only in the way vs. 5 outlines. It is still better, however, to suffer the wrong caused by brethren. Here Paul sets forth the right attitude of a Christian. The reason why suffering wrong must not be demanded in all circumstances is not stated. Probably because this would lead him into the sphere of social life in the stricter sense of that word. According to 7:32 we can say that justice may be sought when one's whole life's existence is at stake. But again, this is not the principal consideration. For Paul seeks the solution in quite a different direction: brother may not do injustice to brother (cf. vs. 8). In the church of the Lord we must be humble and follow the example of Christ, we must not reign but rather serve (Mt. 20:25ff.; Jn. 13:13ff.; I Thess. 3: 17ff.; 5:5). But at Corinth there was pride and a seeking of one's own rights. In other passages in I Corinthians as well Paul

---

[11] ἥττημα.

indicates what is the most desirable thing without giving any strict command (cf. 7:1). Not as if the apostle would be content with a minimum, or as if he would preach a higher and a lower code of ethics. But Paul on the one hand reckons with the difficulties earthly life presents to the Christian, therein remaining true to the rule that one cannot leave the world (5:10); and on the other hand, he does his best to eliminate those difficulties (vs. 8; 7:6ff, 40). Those conflicts should not be the main thing: the citizenship of the Christian is in heaven (Phil. 3:20f.; Col. 3:1f.; I Thess. 1:9f). Paul wants to demonstrate above all that not the external things, such as the seeking of justice in this specific instance, must be thought to be of the highest value, but rather a life according to the law of love, which includes the doing of no injustice.

8 Vs. 8 issues a direct rebuke against what is sin in every case, a wrong attitude of the heart, which was also the cause of the blameworthy practices found in the congregation. Things were wrong in the hearts of the Corinthians, they did not even consider the possibility of suffering injustice.

The question arises why Paul did not begin with a warning against doing wrong in order to show thus that one of the evil consequences thereof is the seeking of justice before the gentiles. Our answer must be that the Corinthians did not recognize going to court before unbelievers as a sin, they considered that an ordinary procedure. It was therefore necessary for Paul to point out its sinfulness. That doing wrong is sinful everybody will soon admit. Secondly, it appears that they went to the judges for trifling reasons, which could have been tolerated (vs. 7). Paul cannot choose sides by saying this one is right and that one is wrong. These are trifles only in which both parties are guilty. So Paul has to be satisfied with a general statement. The words: *ye do wrong and defraud* are enough. It is shocking to transgress the commandment of love against someone who is a member of the same congregation. *Ye yourselves* implies that even the congregation, of whom something else was to be expected, is guilty and also that the sin is a general one in the church.

9, 10 Vs. 9 is even more general, in speaking of the *unrighteous* by which word the gentiles are meant (vs. 1). Vs. 9 is not directed to the Corinthians only but it does remind them of their evil, by telling them that they, however holy, commit the sin which is typical of the unrighteous. And the latter are stricken by an awful judgment: they *will not inherit the kingdom of God,* i. e., they will not be citizens of that kingdom and will not receive the benefits of its citizens. The kingdom is here the future kingdom in all its glory (*shall not inherit*). This word preaches to the Corinthians what will happen to them if they remain in their sins. He who thinks of himself as a king (4:8) runs the risk of standing outside the kingdom of God. *Be not deceived* does not occur only in the Pauline epistles (I Cor. 6:9; 15:33; Gal. 6:3, also Js. 1:16). It may have been a technical term with which the apostles charged men not to participate in the sins of the gentiles. In this context: do not continue to deceive yourselves by walking in the ways of the pagans. You think you are kings but run the risk of not entering the kingdom of God at all (Mt. 8:12).

There now follows an enumeration of sins which will place those who commit them outside the kingdom. Paul does not imply that the Corinthians are guilty of all these sins (cf. v. 11), but he wants to show that by their trespasses they have joined the company of the unrighteous. Paul enumerates the typical sins of the pagans (cf. Rom. 1:28f.). The general "unrighteous" is herein defined. A special order in this enumeration does not appear. *Fornicators*: this includes all trespasses of the seventh commandment. *Effeminate men* and *abusers of themselves with men* designate passive and active homosexuals respectively.

Thieves is a general word for thief, *covetous* refers to people who are always after the property of another even though they may not actually steal. *Extortioners* expresses violence. All such sinners are outside the kingdom of God. And the Corinthians might by their trespasses place themselves in that same line of sinners. Not as if they have done this already, but the apostle writes this in order to point out the danger in which they live.

11 Vs. 11 is another evidence of the remarkable fact that, although the church be full of sins, she remains nevertheless the church of Christ. There are many other passages in I Corinthians bearing out this same truth but this particular one is very explicit. There may be a difference between the members as to their individual involvement in the sins just mentioned; when it comes to the benefits of grace they all share alike.

Such were some, i. e., there were people who belong to the church now but who were great sinners in former times, trespassing in a way which even gentiles of high moral character condemned. How great was that change in their life! Paul recalls their former sins in order that they might see that they were reverting to their former life by going to court before pagan judges, by their doing wrong and by their defrauding. They may not have gone all the way but certainly the greater part of it.

There now follows a description of the congregation as it really is. *But,* he exclaims, *ye are* different today. The Corinthians are *washed* :[12] the primary reference appears to be to baptism after conversion. Back of that baptism lies objective grace. *Ye were sanctified* :[13] sanctification is mentioned first in this context which deals with the sanctity of life. Ye are sanctified and are therefore saints (cf. vs. 1). Back of sanctification lies justification: *ye were justified* by an act of God and so you are righteous. The fact that they desired to be baptized rests upon the fact of their being justified by God. Implied in the apostle's words is the thought that a Christian's condition here on earth does not yet agree with his state before God. Nevertheless all benefits of grace are firmly secured in Christ.

The words: *in the name of the Lord,* etc., may belong to the three preceding verbs or to *sanctified* and *justified* only. The twice repeated *but* pleads for the first possibility.

In the name of the Lord Jesus Christ and in the Spirit of our Lord. In has primarily a local reference here: in the sphere of: in the domain where the Lord and the Spirit rule. *Name* refers to the name as revelation, but always with the name being pronounced. It is known that this happened at baptism (cf. 1:13, 15). Whether there was a fixed formula of baptism at the time Paul wrote to the Corinthians is not known. If there was such a formula we may suppose that it was not yet a trinitarian one but one having only the name of Christ expressed (Acts 2:38; 8:16;

---

[12] ἀπελούσασθε, middle aorist: you allowed yourselves to be washed. This action proceeded from the Corinthians, they desired to be baptized and received baptism (Acts 22:16).

[13] The following aorists are passive.

141

10:48; 19:5; Rom. 6:3; Gal. 3:27). Those converted were baptized in this manner: the name of the Lord Jesus Christ, i. e., of the anointed Saviour, who is now in glory, was pronounced and the person baptized entered into the most intimate relationship with Him. In indicating the sphere the word "in" also states the ground: where the Lord rules He gives His benefits to rely upon. The work of our Saviour is the effectual cause of our sanctification and our justification. God sanctifies and justifies on the ground of the work of Christ, i. e., in His name, His revelation (I Jn. 2:12). That work is being preached and therefore there is sanctification through His revelation.

In the Spirit of our God: more than once the Scriptures teach us that the real baptism is not a baptism with water but one with the Holy Spirit (Mt. 3:11; Jn. 1:33). *In* again denotes the sphere of activity and the ground. It is not the Holy Spirit who baptizes but yet baptism is administered where and because He works. The work of the Spirit brings one into connection with the work of Christ who is the One Who justifies and sanctifies as the God-given Mediator (Rom. 8:2, 9, 11, 14, 15; I Cor. 2:12f.; II Cor. 1:22, etc.). The Spirit is called *the Spirit of our God*, i. e., the working in the hearts of the believers which brings them into connection with Christ, or, in other words, the working of the Spirit, comes from the same God who sent His Son. The objective ground of God's work in the believers is thus circumstantially described (cf. Tit. 3:3-7).

1-11 Paul shows that the evil at Corinth was a serious one since its immediate cause was something that should not occur in a church of Christ. The challenging power of Paul's argument is very great. Throughout he urges his readers to strive to be what they are! They are not allowed to abuse their Christian liberty. They should not boast but be humble and meek. The Corinthians should learn not to place those things highest which are not the most important.

FORNICATION

12 All things are lawful for me; but not all things are expedient. All things are lawful for me; but I will not be brought under the power of any.

13 Meats for the belly, and the belly for meats: but God shall bring to nought both it and them. But the body is not for fornication, but for the Lord; and the Lord for the body:

14 and God both raised the Lord, and will raise up us through his power.

15 Know ye not that your bodies are members of Christ? shall I then take away the members of Christ, and make them members of a harlot? God forbid.

16 Know ye not that he that is joined to a harlot is one body? for, The twain, saith he, shall become one flesh.

17 But he that is joined unto the Lord is one spirit.

18 Flee fornication. Every sin that a man doeth is without the body; but he that committeth fornication sinneth against his own body.

19 Or know ye not that your body is a temple of the Holy Spirit which is in you, which we have from God? and ye are not your own;

20 for ye were bought with a price: glorify therefore God in your body.

12 The following passage treats the subject of fornication. But it does more: it treats this specific point in connection with a general one. Paul begins by positing a general principle, a rule of life, observed in Corinth, and then he descends to a specific sin. This he probably does because the sin of fornication is connected with that general rule. Again it is remarkable that the Corinthians do not see this as a sin; they have not thought it necessary to ask the apostle questions about it.

All things are lawful: this must have been a well known saying. It is found twice in this immediate context and also in 10:23 (without: "for me"). Besides, the word *right* (exousia) is found ten times in I Corinthians, eighteen times in all the other

143

epistles and there sometimes in a slightly modified sense.[14] *Are lawful*: are allowed. You may do all things. Paul speaks here of Christian liberty, as the entire epistle emphasizes, not so much as what a person can do as what he may do. The issue is one of one's attitude in life. That which may be done, the apostle implies, need not to be done under every circumstance. The words: *all things are lawful for me,* must, as we feel compelled to assume, be taken as an expression of Paul's own opinion. The words which follow mention certain strictures to be true, but they do not nullify the former statement, since they belong to a different sphere. The reason why these limitations do not do away with the truth of the initial proverb is that the latter only states what a person may do, not what he must do. Paul may well have used this slogan himself, in any case he did not think it to be an incorrect summary of his own preaching on morality. Does not Paul in other places also teach us that the Christian is free to do all things (I Cor. 9:19; Gal. 5:1)? The proverbial saying is here limited by two qualifications, differing from each other but yet showing that these words cannot be taken as the main principle of action. This would seem to indicate that the Corinthians had made abuse of a rule which was not incorrect in itself. Other statements in I Corinthians point in the same direction. Paul acknowledges Christian liberty but makes clear that the question whether or not to use it in a certain case does not depend on the liberty itself but on the circumstances outside of it (see I Cor. 8:9; cf. also Gal. 5:13; I Peter 2:16). Human action demands a positive rule of conduct. It is not sufficient to know what one is permitted to do in general; we will have to know what we must do in every concrete case. When Christian liberty is elevated to the status of a governing principle, the danger is great that things which are forbidden under all circumstances are thought to be permissible. Our pericope gives an example of this wrong attitude. The Corinthians were lax in their morality. Liberty became dissoluteness.

---

[14] ἐξουσία: observe also three times in this context ἐξουσιάζω "to bring under the power of someone" (6:12; 7:4) — three times in I Corinthians, not at all in any other Pauline epistle. ἔξεστιν, "it is allowed", only in I Corinthians (II Cor. 12:4 ἐξόν).

That *all things* cannot be taken in an absolute sense, so that idolatry, murder, etc., would be included, is of course self-evident. It is clear from this epistle that especially in matters such as fornication, quarreling, and in the attitudes taken within the congregation, frontiers were being moved. It should therefore never be forgotten that it is the Christian standing under the command of his Lord who says: *all things are lawful to me.* If the Christian is free to do all things, he is not by the same token free to sin. Because the Christian bows before his God he will under no circumstance do what is in itself forbidden to him.

"All things are lawful to me" is limited in the first place by: *Not all things are expedient.* That means that we should not only ask whether a certain action is permitted but also what its consequences are. After considering that we will have to decide whether to act or not. One and the same thing may be lawful but not expedient. We might have expected that Paul would have told the Corinthians that if they would count fornication among the lawful things they were infringing the holy law of God. But, just as in the preceding pericope, Paul puts such a statement off until the end. The Corinthians started with "All things are lawful" and they consequently looked upon fornication as being quite ordinary. Hence it was impossible for Paul to remind them simply of the commandment: thou shalt not commit adultery. The Corinthians were sure to answer that they did not commit adultery. Far from using a utilitarian principle when he writes: *all things are not expedient* the apostle simply uses these words in the expectation that the Corinthians will admit their correctness so that the way will then be open to go on from there.

I, for my part, *will not be brought under the power of anybody,*[15] says the apostle. Paul draws up a contrast between himself and the Corinthians (cf. 4:7f.; 6:7). The latter thought they were free and competent to do all things but in reality they were slaves, yea they had come under the power of sin (cf. Jn. 8·34; Rom. 6:16, 20). They forgot that although all things belong to believers, the believers themselves belong to Christ so that they

---

[15] Paul makes use of the various meanings of the words that are cognate with ἔξεστιν. ἐξουσιασθήσομαι is obviously used in the sense of "power" — the apostle stresses the idea of δύνασθαι rather than that of lawfulness.

must be subject to Him (cf. 3:23). By becoming slaves to certain things, slaves to sin, they have lost their Christian liberty. Paul speaks here in terms of his own self in order that he might not discourage the Corinthians. By stating what he himself will not do, he reminds the Corinthians of what they have done (cf. 4:6). This loss of liberty reaches much farther than was the case with the first limitation. This second limitation implies that the Christian no doubt is competent to do all things but that he must remain in control and be subject to God only and not to anything or anybody else (cf. 3:23; 6:20; 7:23; 9:21).[16] The Christian is competent to do all things, not only with respect to the so-called adiaphora, because he shares the power of Christ unto whom is given all authority (Mt. 28:18). The mistake of the Corinthians was that they thought they were able to determine their conduct by means of this rule. They forgot that to possess the right to do all things is not the same as doing all things.

13 Paul now deals with the question of *meats*. This is the only place in I Corinthians where this point is treated. Chapter 8 and 9 discuss the eating of meat sacrificed to idols. Paul does not exhort his readers to do or to omit doing certain things in the matter of food. It seems best, therefore, to assume that he in speaking of food is using a figure or an example. The discussion of the relation between *meats* and the *belly* must serve to clarify the relation between *fornication and the body*.

Meats: food in the broadest sense of the word, everything that can be eaten. *Belly*: the digestive organs. There is a certain connection between *meats* and the *belly*, they are of the same order, and *God shall bring to nought*, i. e., destroy, *both*. They have no importance for the kingdom of God but are of a lower order and are not meant to stay. Thus Paul shows where and how the rule that all things are lawful may be applied. The intestines have no other function than to digest the food, and yet even here the limitations of vs. 12 must be observed, so that, e. g., drunkenness is excluded (cf. vs. 10), for in such a case wine has power over a person. Otherwise, however, in matters of food the Chris-

---

16 ὑπό τινος, neuter, not masculine, because there is no mention made of persons; moreover, the expression is quite general.

tian is free (cf. 10:25) just because meats and the belly will be brought to nought.

Vs. 13b mentions a case in which the Corinthians used the rule: "all things are lawful" in the wrong way. It was wrong to apply that rule to two things which were not correlated. If Paul's argument here is to the point, we must assume that the Corinthians had actually defended fornication under appeal to this slogan. Again it is striking that the apostle does not condemn the Corinthians for using this rule wrongly by appealing to God's commandment: thou shalt not commit adultery. We reiterate that such an argument would not have made any impression on the Corinthians because they would have called intercourse with a harlot fornication but not adultery.

Speaking about the body, i. e., the body as an organism, it must be distinguished from the belly since it belongs to the very nature of man and will not be brought to nought but to glory (15:35f.). That body, therefore, must be *for the Lord,* i. e., for the exalted Saviour and dedicated to Him. The remark that, according to 10:31, eating and drinking must also be done to the glory of God, has no bearing on this question. For 10:31 speaks of the way in which and the goal with which we eat and drink and act. In the case of the belly and the meats it is implied that the belly may determine which meats shall be eaten; it is also implied that the meats shall go to the belly, so that there is no need to distinguish. A person may act according to his liberty in these matters. But if someone might think that it is the goal of the body to yield it to a harlot, he forgets that the body has another destination, namely to be *for the Lord,* i. e., to glorify Christ. Belly and food are of the same nature, but the Lord is far exalted above the body. The title "the Lord" implies dominion and demands adoration. Yet the Lord is willing to be "for the body," He is willing to protect it. He arose from the dead in order to raise our body also and to lead it to glory (cf. v. 14; Rom. 8:11). How to use such a body cannot be determined by the rule: all things are lawful.

14 He now mentions the close union between Christ and the body and the glory the body derives from that union. That which the Lord is for the body serves to make us realize that in this

147

respect there cannot be any question of fornication or of the rule: all things are lawful. The two things Paul mentions (*and* . . . *and*) can never be separated from each other. It is, moreover, a thought very common to Paul's epistles that what happens to Christ also happens to them who believe in Him (Rom. 6:4f.; 8:11; I Cor. 15:20, etc.). *God raised the Lord,* writes Paul, following one way of expressing this truth, the other being that the Lord arose. The former mode of expression implies that God accepted Christ's sacrifice, deeming it satisfactory, and that He led Christ to glory (Acts 2:36). This passage states that God will *raise up us,* whereas 15:44 speaks of a raising up of our bodies. This difference becomes clear if we keep in mind that in this context the word "body" is used with reference to man's essence so that if that body is raised up man himself is raised. Even so Christ arises as His body returns to life. At the parousia belly and food will perish but the bodies, that is, *we* will arise. Secondly: the word "Lord" designates the risen and glorified Christ. In like manner it is stated that when God has raised us up, *we* are again as complete men. In both cases, therefore, the object of the resurrection is that which will be after the resurrection. Our resurrection is the fruit of the *power* of Christ (15:23). God raises us up through the work of Christ (Rom. 6:5; II Cor. 4:14). The dignity of the body is great. It is not destined to perish but to come to glory.

15 Again Paul appeals to something with which his readers are very well acquainted. The church knew that the bodies of the believers are *members of Christ.* This presents the case from a different angle. Not only is the body's destination to serve the Lord of glory; the body is also a member of the Saviour who was sent by God. 12:27 states this more fully. The church is the body of Christ, and so the members of the church are members of Christ (Rom. 12:5; Eph. 5:30). The coherence is indeed most intimate, it is one life which rules both Christ and those who are His. The fact that in 12:27 *you* is used while in our verse *your bodies* are said to be the members of Christ can be explained from the context (cf. vs. 14). If the bodies are so closely united with Christ, they are to be used in accordance with that union. It is inconsistent with the glory of a body which is linked to Christ to make it a *member of a harlot*. The original does not say: shall I take the members of Christ away from Him, but literally: shall I, having lifted up[17] the members of Christ, make them members of a harlot? This again, expresses the thought, which is common to the whole epistle, that the Corinthians, in spite of their great sins, remain the holy church of Christ. *Members of a harlot*: because of the organic coherence not Christ but the harlot determines the character of the members. Vss. 16 and 17 explain further how a sinner becomes a member of a harlot. But first Paul writes a strong negation: *God forbid*[18] knowing that he can reckon on the agreement of his readers.

16 The expression: *members of a harlot* was not too strong. *Or know ye not*: this second question, although on the same level with the preceding, is nevertheless slightly different in that it states the ground of the preceding verse. *Joined*[19] (Greek: present participle) need not imply a continuous intercourse with the harlot. The use of the definite article before "harlot" in the Greek is indicative of the species so that *joined* must refer to what is true under all circumstances: as often as a person has intercourse with a harlot, he becomes one flesh with her. A union like that is not broken off, it is always existing. But there have been people, and they must have been in Corinth also, who argued that intercourse with an unchaste woman did not matter, just because she in any case lives unchastely. There is no union effected in such a case. In order to contradict that opinion Paul appeals to the Scriptures, especially to the word that God Himself instituted physical communion between men and women, where it also appears that such a communion, no matter how it is realized, causes a man and a woman to be one flesh. *Saith* has no subject, but it is natural to take God or the Scriptures in which He reveals Himself as the subject. The words of Gen. 2:26 which are probably quoted here are either of Adam or of Moses. If of Adam, they were spoken by him before the fall in his quality of a prophet of God. If of Moses they are still a word of God. *The twain*: the two who are joined. The answer to the question

---

[17] ἄρας.
[18] μὴ γένοιτο, that must not be!
[19] κολλώμενος.

149

whether the words quoted can be used as an argument for the oneness of body must be sought in the peculiar relation between flesh and body which is of such a nature that the oneness of flesh must have as its consequence the oneness of body, since "body" is "flesh" viewed as an organism; it consists of "flesh." Thus the quotation actually proves the point.

17 The situation, called into being by the sin of fornication, is now contrasted with that which exists for the members of the church. The apostle refers to the glory of the church and anew he shows the Corinthians how great their sin of fornication is and how necessary it is to hate this sin (cf. the beginning of vs. 18: *flee fornication*). Vs. 17 becomes clear only when at the end of the verse *"with Him"* is added. Those words may be supplied from *unto the Lord*. It was furthermore in the interest of parallelism that Paul should write "one spirit" as he had written "one body." But in this case "the twain" could not be used since the Lord and the members of the church are too much different in kind. Hence Paul chose the same construction as in vs. 16 in which verse it was clear enough from the preceding words *"members of a harlot"* that "with her" had to be supplied. In vs. 17 we may, on the analogy of that, add the words "with Him."

Vs. 17 reminds us of II Cor. 3:17. Combining the two texts we receive an insight into their meaning. The words: *The Lord is that Spirit* may not be taken as referring exclusively to the Holy Spirit. The spirit mentioned there must first be explained figuratively: the Lord is the spirit of the new dispensation, its moving power. But in the new dispensation our Savior works through the Holy Spirit for *God sent forth the Spirit of His Son into our hearts, crying, Abba, Father* (Gal. 4:6; cf. Rom. 8:11). Therefore it is possible to identify the Lord not only with the Father but also with the Spirit. In vs. 17 spirit stands over against body and is superior to body (cf. ch. 15: a spiritual or celestial body in contrast to a terrestrial body, which all men possess). When two people have carnal communion they become one body. The union with Christ brings about something of a higher order, namely *one spirit*. But such a union can be effected only by the work of the Holy Spirit (Rom. 8:9f.). The word "spirit," though used figuratively, has consequently some reference

150

to the Holy Spirit (cf. also vs. 19). The main thing is that *the last Adam became a life giving Spirit* (15:45). He who is joined to Him becomes one spirit with Him. Such a spiritual union with Christ is exclusive of a carnal union with a whore.

18 Vs. 18 draws the conclusion from everything Paul had written in this context: *flee fornication*. The use of the present tense here indicates that the Christian must always be fleeing fornication (cf. I Thess. 4:3). *Fornication*, not adultery but unchastity of every kind. Although Paul has given many arguments for his admonition he adds another one. Still his appeal is not simply to the commandment of God, nor is his argument of a purely moral character. *Every sin that man doeth, is without the body*: the apostle means all sin except fornication. It might be objected that sins like suicide, drunkenness and so on are surely not without the body. Yet it is fornication alone which has no other purpose but the satisfaction of the lusts of the body. An unchaste person does not care what becomes of the harlot. In a case of suicide the pleasure of the body is not sought. As to intemperance, it arises mostly in sociable company. In the case of insobriety it is not the act of eating and drinking but the excess of eating and drinking which is sinful. In the case of fornication, however, the action in itself, the carnal communion, is sinful. Food comes from without to the body, the sexual appetite arises in the body and has it as its only domain. Thus Paul is able to write that fornication is a sin against the body. The words: *without the body* must mean therefore: having their purpose without the body. A fornicator aims solely at the satisfaction of his own body and he disregards the essential purpose of the human body.

19 This verse sets forth what the body is and what its purpose is. First the Corinthians are asked if they do not know that their bodies *are a temple of the Holy Spirit*. Thus the holiness of the congregation is maintained. *Or* is used to introduce a completely new thought which must also serve to keep from fornication, a thought which is again expressed in the form of a question. *Your body*: Paul's words regard the body of every believer, but also the bodies of all the believers together. In vs. 15 *your bodies* implies that the individual bodies are members of Christ but *your body* implies that the whole of the bodies is a temple of

151

Holy Spirit. The singular noun "temple" goes with the singular noun "body." Thus it is also made clear that each one individually has to refrain from fornication. The Greek word used here for "temple" designates the house of the temple, i. e., the holy and the most holy place. The Holy Spirit dwells in the church as a whole, but in such a manner that each believer is the temple of the Spirit also as regards his body. The thought that the church has received the Holy Spirit is a common one with Paul. Not the outpouring of the Spirit on Pentecost (Gal. 4:6), but the fact that the church has received the Spirit and possesses the Spirit as an abiding possession is prominent with Paul (Rom. 8:15; I Cor. 2:13; I Thess. 4:8). The latter is also meant in *which ye have from God*, in which words is expressed the divine origin of the Spirit and also His abiding presence. Because the Spirit has come and abides every believer can be a temple of the Spirit. Since "flee fornication" preceded no further conclusion is necessary. Paul's final statement is a general one: *and ye are not your own*. Chaste living is a part of that. *Not your own*: a temple does not have its goal in itself, nor does it have a dignity of its own. The temple is holy because God will dwell in it and because it belongs to Him (Mt. 23:17, 21). This brings us back to 3:21, where an entirely different discourse was also concluded with: *ye are Christ's*. That imposes obligations and demands subjection to the law of God. Believers may not live as they choose, for of themselves they are nothing. They have to abstain from unholiness and give themselves to the service of God (Rom. 6:13).

20 This verse elaborates the preceding. Christians are *bought with a price* (cf. 7:23; II Peter 2:1). The question as to the one from whom they have been bought is not answered here and need not be put. Not the transfer of ownership is the point of this figure but simply that they have no rights of their own. That is implied in *"with a price"*; a price is paid for them (Acts 20:28; I Pet. 1:19). It does not matter in this context whether the price was great or small nor even who paid it. Paul makes a general reference here, not to the fact of creation, but to the work of Christ. Gentiles who had come to Him should dedicate themselves to Him. By way of final conclusion we read: *glorify God*

152

with your body. No fornication, but submission to the law of God.

12-20 The main subject of this pericope is no doubt the matter of fornication. This sin is incompatible with the glory which the bodies of Christians possess in Christ. But with this subject Paul combines two more general points. For it first of all furnishes an occasion to condemn the Corinthians for making the rule *all things are lawful for me* a starting point for their general conduct. Secondly, the apostle ends with the summons to seek through the body the glory of God alone. Finally it should be noted that three points in this pericope are treated more circumstantially later on: the question of food (meat offered to idols), the relation of the sexes to one another and the resurrection. This is added proof of the importance of the concept of right or liberty (*exousia*) for the understanding of I Corinthians.

CHAPTER VII

CONCERNING WEDLOCK

7:1-7

1 Now concerning the things whereof ye wrote: it is good for man not to touch a woman.

2 But, because of fornications, let each man have his own wife, and let each woman have her own husband.

3 Let the husband render unto the wife her due: and likewise also the wife unto the husband.

4 The wife has not power over her own body, but the husband: and likewise also the husband hath not power over his own body, but the wife.

5 Defraud ye not one the other, except it be by consent for a season, that ye may give yourselves unto prayer, and may be together again, that Satan tempt you not because of your incontinency.

6 But this I say by way of concession, not of commandment.

7 Yet I would that all men were even as myself. Howbeit each man hath his own gift from God, one after this manner, and another after that.

1 In chapter 7 Paul begins to answer the questions the Corinthians had asked him. He does so only after having discussed problems about which the Corinthians had not asked questions but which, in Paul's opinion, were nevertheless more important than the difficulties that disturbed the Corinthian church. The emissaries mentioned in 16:17 probably conveyed the Corinthian letter to Paul.

Concerning the things whereof ye wrote: Paul is quite willing to answer the Corinthians but only after he had written about some weightier matters. *It is good*: the concept "good" plays a prominent part in this chapter (cf. vs. 8 and 26). The context determines its meaning. It does not mean: morally good, i. e., ordered by the law of God, as appears from vs. 28: *thou hast not sinned* and vs. 36: *He sinneth not*. It rather denotes an attitude which is commendable but not strictly commanded. Although

154

Paul wishes that all men might observe this attitude yet it may be forbidden under certain circumstances (cf. vs. 9). *Good* to Paul means being able not to use one's liberty. In starting out with the words: *It is good for a man not to touch a woman* the apostle makes clear that his aim is not to abolish the ordinance of marriage which God created (vs. 5, 9), since he does full justice to human nature, but, reckoning with sin, he points out that it may be useful not to possess or not to indulge in natural propensities. *To touch a woman*: a euphemism for sexual intercourse (Gen. 20:6; Prov. 8:29 LXX). The general nature of this expression shows that Paul does not speak about what should happen in marriage but about the question whether or not one should marry. Nor does he say: no woman, or: his wife, but: *a woman.*

2 *Because of fornications* i. e., to prevent fornication (I Thess. 4:3). The plural refers to various cases of fornication. *Each man . . . his own* implies a monogamous marriage. Chapters 5 and 6 discussed other illicit relations. *Let have* implies that monogamous marriage is a commandment. The same thing is then repeated with reference to *every woman.*[1] Vs. 2 states the reason why that which is commended in vs. 1 cannot be practiced under all circumstances. The question arises whether Paul's estimate of marriage is not rather low if he sees no other reason for marriage but to avoid fornication. Is it possible that this low estimate has caused Paul to prefer the unmarried state to the married state? We must realize that Paul does not speak about the purpose of matrimony. His statement in vs. 1 does not contain an absolute, universally valid rule. In vs. 2 Paul indicates why his rule cannot be an absolute one, why it is only "good." That is why he refers to fornications and limits his "good" by *because of fornications.* If there were no fornication the rule of vs. 1 could receive greater stress. But first of all it is necessary to prevent sin, especially in Corinth where Paul had issued so urgent a warning against unchastity. Vs. 2, therefore, has no other significance than that it elaborates upon vs. 1 and restricts its sense. Not until vss. 6 and

---

[1] The difference between τὴν ἑαυτοῦ γυναῖκα and τὸν ἴδιον ἄνδρα is worthy of note. Paul is consistent in this usage (cf. 7:37; Eph. 5:26, 28, 33; I Cor. 14:35; Eph. 5:22, 24; Col. 3:18; Titus 2:5). Perhaps ἑαυτοῦ implies subjection, ἴδιος only oneness.

7 do we read where the rule of vs. 1 can be applied. Moreover, according to vs. 15, there seem to have been Corinthians who were averse altogether to marriage or who abstained from sexual intercourse in marriage. Such people might appeal to Paul's statement in vs. 1 and so they must be made to see that not only their appeal was unwarranted but that there was also a great danger that they would lapse into fornication. If that should be the case there would be nothing "good" about it. The words: *because of fornication* are meant to be a warning at the very beginning of this passage.

3 In this verse the Greek offers a variant reading which is important for the interpretation. A. V. has: *due benevolence* which respects the obligation of husband and wife to each other. RSV has *her conjugal rights,* an expression clear in itself. The second reading is undoubtedly the right one. The implication is then that man and wife should not interrupt their sexual intercourse. The apostle aims at disclaiming the ascetic attitude as it was propagated and practiced by some of the Corinthians (cf. vs. 5). Paul reproves such an attitude. Married people are supposed to live as such and each of them has the same rights and the same obligations (cf. *likewise*). The use of the definite articles indicates that the reference is to the relation of one man to his own wife and vice versa. Moreover, our epistle does not seek to combat polygamy. Nor was that practice in vogue among the Greeks of this period, generally speaking. The question how Paul could write this to the Corinthians where there was so much unchastity must be seen in the light of vs. 9 where it becomes clear that at Corinth, as in sex relations generally, the extremes met. A wrong view of marital problems leads to fornication.

4 This becomes even clearer from vs. 4. *Has no power* touches upon the idea of right or authority again. The husband possesses right over the body of his wife and vice versa. The question whether they will use their rights is a different matter, not depending on that right itself but on the commandment of God. Paul teaches us here that a woman in conjugal matters has the same rights as a man so that she may do with her body according to her own will. But if she is married she has lost her right to the extent that her husband has the disposal of his wife's body.

Marriage, then, determines how the wife is to use her right which she does not lose in any absolute sense. Thus also the whole epistle assumes that every Christian keeps his rights but that he shall use them voluntarily according to God's commandments and according to the principle of love for his fellow-men. *The wife hath no power*: this is thus not a commandment but a statement of fact with reference to the existing situation in marriage. In matrimony a person does not have disposal of his own body. It should be borne in mind that Paul writes all these things to Christians. Our epistle inveighs against all manner of dissoluteness often enough (cf. vs. 5, 9). A married Christian has to live according to God's commandment. The main thing is here that husband and wife possess the same rights.

5 Vs. 5 shows that there was abstinence in marriage at Corinth. This happened perhaps out of reaction to pagan fornication. The words: *may be together again* implies that husband and wife were entirely separated for a while in order to refrain more easily from sexual intercourse. *Defraud ye not one the other,* a word directed by Paul to married people, refers to separation by mutual consent. Each party could take the initiative. The apostle approves of separation only if it complies with various conditions. It should be *by consent,* i. e., it should not be a separation in the proper sense of the word. It should also be *for a season,* not indefinitely but for a fixed time. Its goal should be definite, namely *to give themselves to prayer.* This last condition characterizes Paul's exposition. It is in this connection noteworthy that nowhere in the New Testament is any form of retreat demanded. Furthermore it should be noted that *prayer* has the definite article in the Greek, which implies that a certain prayer is meant. Vs. 33 teaches us that there is a certain solicitude in married life and a looking after worldly things which may hinder us from pleasing God. That is what Paul disapproves. So I Peter 3:7 demands of men that they dwell with their wives according to knowledge to the end that their prayers be not hindered. Married life may place such heavy demands on a person's life that he no longer has opportunity to pray. That should not be, and if a situation like that would exist, abstinence would be required, such, however, as answers the conditions of vs. 5. Thus Paul has nothing else in view than a brief interruption of the marriage relations if such a marriage would harm the relationship to God for lack of an opportunity for prayer. But that interruption should not be a long one under a mask of piety for that would lead a man to sin. Its goal from the beginning must be to come together again. Normal matrimonial relations must be continued.

The final purpose clause is of a different nature from the preceding clauses. It is more general and states the real reason for Paul's admonition, the thing which he seeks to prevent. Permanent separation would result in strong temptations on the part of Satan, who, during the absence of normal sex relations, would try to seduce to fornication. *Incontinency*: here with respect to sexual instincts. *Your*: not only of the Corinthians but of people in general since the apostle supposes that generally speaking a person does not possess the gift of continence. *Because of*: the incontinence exists always and everywhere and seeks expression. Satan uses it by urging people to give it an illicit expression. And then sin is near. It is therefore necessary to prevent temptation.

6 The demonstrative *this* cannot be taken of the immediately preceding words or even of the main clause of vs. 5 since the words *by way of concession* do not fit the peremptory words: *defraud ye not*. Since vs. 4 expresses a fact neither can "this" be taken of that verse. Coming thus to vs. 2-3, the words *by way of concession* of vs. 6 are certainly relevant to these verses. Moreover, they contain the principal rules on the matter which this chapter discusses; while the subsequent verses only contain further explanation. *Commandment* is the reverse of *concession* (II Cor. 8:9). Paul does not command every man and every woman to marry. His *concession* is not a reluctant admission but a full approbation. Here again it is a question of right. The Christian possesses the right to marry. Normal conditions dictate that he should use this right. Still it remains a right, i.e., there may be circumstances in which it is not necessary to use it. That is the case in vs. 7. There is here no question of a commandment without any exception.

7 In the new dispensation, however, a miracle may occur, and this is mentioned in vs. 7. This verse states Paul's real desire in this matter and explains why he could speak *by way of*

concession. By writing: *I would that all men were even as I myself* Paul implies that all Corinthians knew who and what he was. (cf. 9:5). They knew that Paul was unmarried but also that, through a special gift of the Lord, it was not necessary for him to marry and that he nevertheless did not need to fear he might fall a victim to fornication. *Even as I myself* receives much emphasis. It implies the possession of the same gift Paul had. Paul distinguishes himself from the Corinthians. He is able to do what they cannot do. This verse offers the key to the entire pericope. In the new dispensation God gives special gifts, charismata, gifts of the Holy Spirit (ch. 12-14), meant for the propagation of the kingdom of God (12:4-11). The apostle himself had several of these charismata, among other things the gift of continence. Paul wished that all men possessed this gift since then the kingdom of God would come with power but he respects the ordinance of God. He that has not received the gift of continence must marry, and must not try to remain unmarried. Just because continence is a gift of God there is no distinction implied here between Christians of a higher and a lower degree. But by granting the gift of continence God to a certain extent takes back what He commanded at the creation. That is why Paul wrote *by way of concession.*

Each man hath his own gift, i. e., his own charism (12:11; Rom. 12:6). Not every Christian receives such special gifts. But if anybody has a charism he has it from God. *One after this manner and another after that*: these words are further developed in 12:4f. There is a difference of gifts and everyone must be content with what God gave him. He that received the gift of continence should not boast as if he were more than somebody else. He that does not possess it should marry.

CONCERNING MARRIAGE

7:8-24

8   But I say to the unmarried and to the widows, It is good for them if they abide even as I.

9   But if they have not continency, let them marry; for it is better to marry than to burn.

10   But unto the married I give charge, *yea* not I, but the Lord, That the wife depart not from her husband

11   (but should she depart, let her remain unmarried, or else be reconciled to her husband); and that the husband leave not his wife.

12   But to the rest say I, not the Lord: If any brother hath an unbelieving wife, and she is content to dwell with him, let him not leave her.

13   And the woman that hath an unbelieving husband, and he is content to dwell with her, let her not leave her husband.

14   For the unbelieving husband is sanctified in the wife and the unbelieving wife is sanctified in the brother: else were your children unclean; but now are they holy.

15   Yet if the unbelieving departeth, let him depart: the brother or the sister is not under bondage in such *cases*: but God hath called us in peace.

16   For how knowest thou, O wife, whether thou shalt save thy husband? or how knowest thou, O husband, whether thou shalt save thy wife?

17   Only, as the Lord hath distributed to each man, as God hath called each, so let him walk. And so ordain I in all the churches.

18   Was any man called being circumcised? let him not become uncircumcised. Hath any been called in uncircumcision? let him not be circumcised.

19   Circumcision is nothing, and uncircumcision is nothing but the keeping of the commandments of God.

20   Let each man abide in that calling wherein he was called.

21   Wast thou called being a bondservant? care not for it: nay, even if thou canst become free, use it rather.

22 For he that was called in the Lord being a bondservant, is the Lord's freedman: likewise he that was called being free, is Christ's bondservant.
23 Ye were bought with a price; become not bondservants of men.
24 Brethren, let each man, wherein he was called, therein abide with God.

8 The words: *but I say* introduce a new subject. The apostle continues to give his own opinion. Vs. 1 stated a general rule which was limited in vs. 2. Vs. 3f. speaks further about this restriction and refers to married people. Our verse reverts back to verse 1 (*it is good*) leaving out of consideration for a moment the restriction just referred to. This is made possible by the fact that our verse refers to people who did not act according to the rule of vs. 2 and of whom it may therefore be supposed that they were able to abstain from marrying. This sort of continence is not the result of a charism for the apostle directs himself now to the unmarried and the widows. *Unmarried* may refer to both men and women. It refers here to men[2] who are not married and of women who lost their husbands. The latter are mentioned separately since they are in need of help and of remarriage. The fact that a widow did not remarry was indicative of a particular disposition (Lk. 2:36). For *"good"* compare vs. 1. *If they abide* expresses a general possibility: if it is possible for them to do so. *Even as I*, sc. remain. Paul is unmarried.

9 This verse offers a restriction of the same kind as the one in vs. 2. A difference must again be made between what is *good* and what is commanded. Under certain circumstances to pursue the "good" is even forbidden (note: *let them marry*). *If they have not continency* states a fact. Paul treats the case of persons who do not possess continence. It is not a sin to be such but rather the normal condition. Marriage is an institution of God, and is therefore permissible.[3] *For it is better*: a causal clause in the

---

[2] The Greek has τοῖς
[3] The Greek γαμέω can be used of both of men and of women. The aorist is ingressive: "let them seek marriage". The apostle does not state the precise way in which this can be done, least of all does he indicate how an unmarried woman would have to do this. That point is not at stake here.

161

form of a general statement, containing the ground for Paul's advice. The statement is of an ethical nature and names the evil that ought to be prevented. This is not given as a commandment of God but as a general appeal to common sense in the expectation that every one will agree with what is said (cf. 11:14). Since vs. 8 did not issue a command but only spoke of what was "good," this "good" may not be pursued at the expense of the claims of nature for that would be acting contrary to the very nature of the "good." *To burn*: to be consumed with passions which would hold the upperhand if there is no continence.

10 Paul turns now to the married. Comparison with vs. 12 makes clear that the reference is to the marriage between two Christians. The language is now very dogmatic: *I gave charge* and: *yea not I, but the Lord*. The antithesis expressed in the last words first of all has historical significance. More than once the apostle appeals to words of Christ (Acts 20:35; I Cor. 7:10; 9:14; I Thess. 4:15), words sometimes also appearing in our Gospels but at other times not found there. This is indicative of the fact that the apostles knew words of Jesus which have not found a place in the Gospels and that they delivered such words to the congregations. The word to which Paul appeals here is written in (Mt. 5:32; 19:3-9; Mk. 10:11, 12). But there must be still another reason for Paul to appeal to a word of the Lord, known to his readers. Upon other occasions the apostle does not fear to state his opinion and to demand obedience (cf. 9:1f.). This he can do because he receives revelations from the Lord which he can communicate to the churches (9:1, 2; II Cor. 13: 10). Paul's appeal to a word of Christ here is bound up with the special character of the argument. Twice Paul had spoken of what was "good," i. e., commendable, to be pursued under certain circumstances only. The statement of vs. 7 was again in the form of a recommendation since it presupposed the presence of a special charism given by God or of other special conditions (vs. 26). A commandment is necessary to prevent the Corinthians from thinking that for married people to remain together is only a "good." In order to emphasize this Paul reminds the Corinthians of a word of Jesus which he must have mentioned during his stay

162

at Corinth. The apostle may recommend, the Saviour commands. That this is Paul's meaning appears also from vs. 40.

As to the Lord's word, the subject is not the husband but the wife, i. e., Jesus assumed that according to Jewish custom the husband would dismiss his wife, which of course does not mean that the reverse is not equally implied in His words. The change of subject by Paul is in accord with the word of Jesus and is more readily understood when we remember that Paul has been speaking of unmarried women, especially widows. A more conclusive reason for the change is the fact that at Corinth a woman might leave her husband as well as a man might dismiss his wife. Other passages in this epistle bear out that the women at Corinth were very emancipated. The Corinthians may also have asked Paul whether a woman was allowed to leave her husband. In any case Paul must forbid the women in the name of the Lord to leave their husbands.

11 *But should she depart*: this cannot be an approval of the divorce. The meaning is rather: if, in spite of this, married people are divorced or seek a divorce. The Greek word indicates an act distinct from dismissing or leaving. It might be that at the moment the Corinthian church received Paul's epistle some were in the process of getting a divorce or had just got one. Such a divorce might be past being recalled so that it would be impossible for the wife to return to her husband. In that case Paul commands *to remain unmarried*, or, if possible, *to be reconciled to her husband*. After an illegitimate divorce the first marriage is not considered annulled. Reconciliation should be undertaken by the wife with whom the divorce started. Paul mentions two possibilities since it may be that the husband refuses to be reconciled. Since the husband's power over his wife is greater than that of the wife over her husband, Paul writes: *the husband shall not leave his wife.*

12 Since Paul has referred to the unmarried and the widows (vs. 8) and to the married (vs. 10), *the rest* must be a designation of the remaining cases, i. e., the mixed marriages. Marriages between two pagan spouses are not included in the scope of this epistle. The actual words of vs. 12 support this interpretation admirably. A mixed marriage in this context is not one

163

in which husband and wife belonged to two different religions at the time of their wedding but one in which one of the parties had become Christian during the time they were married.

I, not the Lord reminds us of vs. 10. Paul does not appeal here to a word of Jesus. He does not give any binding commandment, not having received a charge from the Lord concerning this matter during his apostleship.[4] A further explanation is given in vs. 15. If Christ had forbidden divorce in the case of which Paul speaks, then the unbelieving party would not be permitted to cooperate in a divorce either tacitly or by active approval simply because he or she would not be content with the existing situation. *If any brother,* i. e., at the time the epistle reaches Corinth. The first part of the conditional clause shows that there were Christians at Corinth who thought that they were permitted or even obligated to divorce their wives when the latter refused to abjure their paganism. But Paul points out the necessity for a distinction here. There is one condition, which if fulfilled renders divorce not only unnecessary but even forbidden. That condition is *to be content* with the present state of things, which implies not just an approbation for a time but constantly. The pagan wife resigns to the altered circumstances and she does so heartily. Then there will be peace in the home and the marriage will be good. The man must not dismiss his wife merely because she remains pagan, since the character of the marriage is not affected.

13 In this verse Paul says the same thing with respect to the wife. It is the wife who is now the subject of *"let not leave."* This may have something to do with the fact that Paul gives a place of honor to the woman who has become a Christian. The question as to what she can and shall do in civil affairs is not considered.

14 *Is sanctified* cannot mean: holy in Christ before God, because that kind of holiness cannot be predicated of an unbeliever. (cf. 1:2; 3:16, 17). Paul uses "sanctified" here as in I Tim. 4:5, i. e., more liturgically than ethically. In every marriage the two parties influence each other. If the unbelieving party dwells together in love with the believing party, the former shows that he

---

[4] The fact that Paul uses an imperative here does not alter the situation since these imperatives concern a special case.

is no longer at home in the circles of unbelievers. To a certain extent, externally, he belongs with believers. *Is sanctified* refers to a lasting condition. To become one flesh with a believer is for the unbeliever an important thing (6:16, 17).[5] That is why the marriage can be continued although this is not necessary under all circumstances. *In the wife*: through the close tie with her. It does not mean: *By* the wife, since the woman remains a creature. Due to the importance this matter has for Paul he repeats with respect to the wife what he had said of the husband. The believing husband is called a brother, namely of the other believers, the church. *Else,* an abbreviated form of a conditional clause which serves as the protasis of a coordinated causal apodosis (For if it were otherwise your children were unclean). *Your children*: all children, also the children born from mixed marriages in which husband and wife were content to live together. All those children belong to the congregation. Of course there were many mixed marriages in the beginning. *Unclean* reminds us of ceremonial impurity among the people of Israel. It is the opposite of "holy" and refers to people who are not connected with the church of God. *But now*: introduces the real state of things. *Holy* used of the children as a group has the same meaning as "sanctified" or as "holy" when used of the people of Israel. So Paul addressed the whole congregation as *sanctified in Christ Jesus* (1:2). This refers to the life within the covenant and to the right to baptism, but does not imply that each of those holy children will go to heaven (cf. Rom. 11:13f.).

Paul has now finished his discourse on mixed marriages. It is clear that he has turned in the first place against those Christians who thought that, when one of the parties in a marriage had come to the faith but the other one had not, the marriage was broken off. In our verse Paul takes his starting point in the holiness of the children, a fact which apparently was not contradicted by the Corinthians.

---

[5] Joh. Marckius, *Dissert. philol. exeg. ad sel. text. N.T.,* 1727, pp. 452-501, distinguishes between a *levissima,* a *media,* and a *plenissima sanctitas.* He assumes here a *media sanctitas* because every marriage is a sacred institution of God and because the *plenissima sanctitas* belongs to believers only.

15 Vs. 15 treats mixed marriages in which husband and wife do not agree. If in such a case the unbeliever would depart, *let him depart*. The Christian is under no obligation to prevent his departure. The fact that *the unbeliever* is the subject places the full burden on his action. To the unbeliever Paul cannot issue any commandment. The word "sanctified" cannot be applied to an unbeliever who departs. *Under bondage*: the brother or the sister, i. e., the members of the church of Christ are not subject to an unbeliever. *In such cases,* namely when the unbeliever departs. If the believing party were under obligation to prevent the departure he would be subject to the unbeliever and would virtually be forced to abandon his or her faith since only by dr ing that could a divorce be prevented. That price would be too high. If, therefore, circumstances are as Paul describes them, the Christian shall resign himself to the divorce. Note that Paul does not state that he should seek a divorce or even desire it. Possible economic and social objections which might keep a Christian from a divorce are not considered here, but solely objections which involve transgression of the law of God. *But God hath called us* introduces an idea of calling which is further developed at a later point. *Hath called* is used absolutely here and must consequently refer to the vocation to salvation. The perfect tense implies a lasting result. Paul addressed the Corinthians as: *Called to be saints* (1:2). *In peace* refers to the way in which this vocation took place and also describes the condition of those who are called, the members of the church (Eph. 4:4) since the result of the vocation is lasting. That is why the translation *to peace* has some merits here. Paul does not intend to set forth the chief characteristic of the divine vocation but only one which is important in this context. If, due to the conversion of one of the spouses to Christianity, peace has disappeared in a certain marriage, divorce is permissible according to the apostle. This element of a breach of peace is now related to the great change which comes into the life of one who has made the transition to Christianity. The result of such a transition is peace. Peace with God (Rom. 5:1) causes peace to prevail throughout the whole life (Rom. 12:18; Gal. 5:22). This peace is not the same as the absence of domestic quarrels, it is an internal peace granted by

166

God as a blessing upon a good marriage. If this peace would be disturbed by the continuation of a mixed marriage, then the yoke of bondage need not be shouldered but divorce is permissible.

16 Here we have a question, beginning with *for*. The verse must not be construed as stating the reason for the two latter parts of vs. 15. It is rather an additional reason for the statement in 15a: *let him depart,* on one line with 15b and c. The Christian party to the marriage might have conscientious objections. He might try to prevent divorce either by not insisting on separation or by trying to keep the unbeliever from divorce, since after the divorce the believer would no longer be able to preach the gospel to the unbelieving party. This consideration may very well have been used by others when speaking to people who had become resigned to the departure of the unbelieving spouse. Paul does not deem this a sufficient ground. Marriage is no missionary institution. Not as if this consideration would be without any significance but to be *"not under bondage"* and to be *"in peace"* is of greater import. This appears from the fact that the question introduced by *for how* follows after the legitimacy of divorce has been argued first. Husband and wife do not know beforehand whether they by their influence will save the unbelieving party i. e., win him or her for Christ. It is God Himself who determines such things without revealing them to us. Bondage and quarreling which are certain need not be accepted in order to achieve a highly uncertain goal.

17 *Only,* introduces a conditional clause which is not expressed here. We might paraphrase: if you do agree that you do not know whether you will save the unbelieving party, you should live according to your vocation, or, more briefly: if it is not so, i. e., the possibility implied in the preceding question. The apodosis is also somewhat obscure. Its meaning is: each man should walk in the way God has apportioned to him. Thus the words: *so let him walk* are properly the apodosis of the abridged conditional clause. Everybody individually must so walk as the Lord has distributed to him personally and as the Lord has called him. The glorified Christ governs the circumstances of man. The circumstances under which He calls differ. He distributes to the one this and to the other something else. The Christian should

167

acknowledge that it is God who rules the circumstances of his life and that he has to live accordingly. The repetition of *"each"* shows that Paul has the individual believers in mind. *Hath distributed* implies that it is God who determines everyone's life, spiritually and naturally. All things are from Him. In vs. 15 the words *"hath called"* were taken to refer to the vocation to salvation, and *"in peace"* to the circumstances of that vocation. In like manner must *"called"* in this verse be taken of the vocation to salvation and *"as - - so"* of the circumstances. *"In peace"* was very specific, but *"as"* refers to all the circumstances. Both clauses with *"as"* must be taken of all the circumstances after the vocation. Each person, according to the apostle, due to what God gave him and due to the vocation wherewith he was called is in special circumstances. Unlike vs. 18 this verse does not refer to the external circumstances since that would not agree with vss. 15 and 16 which permit a certain change to take place in the external circumstances after the acceptance of Christianity. They are rather internal circumstances, referring to the consequences of the vocation, and so *"as"* must refer to the Christian life. *So let him walk*: walk as a Christian because God has called him. You should walk according to your calling. The transition in the argument at this point should not go unnoticed. Previously Paul mentioned the circumstances of life in which a Christian may be; from now on he only deals with vocation, a subject which had only been mentioned in passing in vs. 15, but more intentionally in vs. 17, where it is connected with *"hath distributed."* Vs. 17 introduces a series of admonitions which end in another: *become not bondservants of men,* vs. 23 (cf. vs. 15). A Christian is unable to suffer slavery. He has to do every thing to avoid bondage. This verse, therefore, is of central significance. It does not treat a special case but deals in general terms, as in vs. 15 *"God hath called"* was also a general statement (cf. *hath distributed,* also general). This explains the words: *and so ordain I,* etc. Let not the Corinthians think that the apostle commanded them something special (cf. 4:17; 14:33). Paul does not insist on a special way of life which would be in accordance with a special vocation. There is one demand for all. *In all the churches* Paul ordains (note the present), now and always, that everyone must walk according to his vocation.

18 Vs. 18 enumerates various circumstances in which a person may find himself when his vocation comes to him. In each case enumerated, the external circumstances are said to be of no importance. Important only is the fact that a person is called and that he walks according to his vocation. The cases named by Paul actually occurred at Corinth. They are such as to deflect the attention easily to the change of a person's external condition rather than to his vocation. A person might be called in the condition of one circumcised, i. e., as a Jew. Such a one ought not to imitate the Hellenistic Jews who, by means of an operation, removed the effect of their circumcision so that in the gymnasium no one could see that they were Jews. Why should a Christian desire to do so? It is his honor to be *called*. If on the other hand a gentile is called, he must not be jealous of the Jews, the ancient covenant people. He must be content to be called by Jesus Christ.

19 Vs. 19 states the same thing in different words. *Circumcision,* i. e., to be circumcised or to be a Jew, and *uncircumcision,* i. e., to be a gentile, is for a Christian of no importance (cf. *nothing*). The important thing for him who is called is not to seek to be or to become what he is not, but to *keep the commandments of God.* The context indicates that with commandments here is meant the moral law, which is valid for everybody. The plural: *commandments,* not: law, implies that the Mosaic law is not meant.

20 After mentioning two cases Paul goes on to state what *each man* individually is supposed to do. He is *to abide in his calling,* i. e., he is to remain a Christian and emphasize his Christianity. However, more is involved than only to remain a Christian. To be a Christian is not something static, but something dynamic. It is to remain one who is called, to abide in that calling wherewith one is called not once, but always. It is always to hear the voice of God from heaven, which calls men to Christ and away from sin and ungodliness.

21 Now Paul deals with a special case which had special significance for the Corinthians because there were apparently many slaves among the members of the church. Those slaves naturally loved to be members of a church which preached the freedom of the Christian. Understandable is also their interpretation of the liberty propounded by the gospel as being in the first place a liberty from natural bondage. To the slave his vocation easily became a call to civil liberty. Paul, on the other hand, points out that a slave should not be concerned about his being called in that condition, since not slavery but vocation is the main thing. A slave may be a very good Christian. Just so he is called! Neither does slavery disappear when one is called as a slave, nay it need not disappear. Paul does not preach social revolution. The first thing is to be a Christian, and that is possible in all circumstances.

The next few words have been variously interpreted. The crux is in the phrase: *use it rather*. Those who supply the word "liberty" take the expression to mean that the slave, granted he becomes a free man, must use that liberty to its fullest advantage. Paul is then supposed to have said that the slave should be thankful for the freedom which he would be able to get, and that he, upon obtaining his freedom, should use his freedom better than his previous slavery. Those who, on the other hand, supply the word "slavery" favor the following interpretation: even if you can be free, use rather your slavery, i. e., remain a slave. Neither of the two opinions appears to us to be correct. The former view would demand at least the words: "better than your slavery." The second view is pressed by the objection that to say that a slave who could be free ought to remain a slave does not represent Paul's argument correctly. Moreover, what is meant by using one's slavery to advantage? We must keep in mind that in this verse the vocation stands in the center. This prompts us to supply the words "your vocation" after *use*. The phrase would thus mean: if you can be free, make a better use of your vocation.

22 Vs. 22 is added evidence of the central significance of vocation in this context. A Christian remains *called in the Lord*, i. e., called within the sphere of the Lord. It does not matter what he is besides, be he slave or free man. A slave, by virtue of his calling, is a freedman (of the Lord), and the free man is a slave of the Lord. This verse does not intend to imply that a slave in this world is really a freedman, while one who is a free citizen is not really free. It simply states that one's worldly position is not the important thing since one who is called is at the same time a freedman of the Lord and a servant of Christ, so that this fact should govern his attitude. This fact may appear to be paradoxical, it is nevertheless explicable.

This whole verse contains a reason for verse 21a in the first place, but, if our interpretation of vs. 21b was correct, also for 21b. A Christian must use his vocation to the best advantage for the first thing that matters is his relation to Christ. In the Greek text the words: *in the Lord* precede "called." This implies that all these things are only valid in the sphere in which the Lord rules and the people live in communion with Him. *The Lord's freedman*: a slave owner releases his slave but there remains some connection between him and his former slave. Christ redeemed us from sin and made us freedmen (vs. 23) and will still continue to claim us as his own. Those Christians who are free are the bondservants of Him who is the great Redeemer and who demands that all Christians shall follow Him and serve Him (Eph. 6:6). The words "slave" and "freedman" are used in the proper sense with reference to the subject, they are used in a spiritual sense with reference to the predicate. Spiritual liberty may be combined with earthly slavery, earthly liberty with spiritual slavery.

23 Vs. 23 repeats the words of 6:20 for the identical purpose of stating the ground which must prompt to obedience to Christ. This is followed by an admonition which is striking in this particular context. Its main thrust was that a Christian's condition is not determined by his social position of servitude. Hence the words: *become not bondservants of men*. This word constitutes a warning to those who, after having been called, are now slaves of Christ and are consequently obliged to live accordingly (Lev. 25:55), i. e., to keep the commandments of God (vs. 19). Slaves are apt to consider the wishes of men rather than their own vocation as Christians. Our epistle shows that this peril existed at Corinth. The Corinthians were slaves of men if they named themselves after Paul or Apollos, if they pursued worldly wisdom, if they thought it important to be either a Jew or a

171

gentile, if they supposed that liberty in the world was the highest good.

24 Vs. 24 contains a conclusion of this pericope. It repeats vs. 20 with just a slight change which does not alter the sense. He who is called of God can never become a servant of men. Paul knows this with respect to his own apostolic office. (Gal. 1:1) but it is also valid for Christians in general. *Abide with God* implies that to be called means to be in God's presence. *Wherein — therein* concern the circumstances that may exist before God, i. e., the spiritual circumstances which do not perish with the fashion of this world (vs. 31). It is clear that Paul considers vocation the determining factor in a Christian's life. He issues the warning to avoid circumstances which might endanger this vocation.

CONCERNING VIRGINS

25 Now concerning virgins have I no commandment of the Lord: but I give my judgment, as one that hath obtained mercy of the Lord to be trustworthy.

26 I think therefore that this is good by reason of the distress that is upon us, *namely*, that it is good for a man to be as he is.

27 Art thou bound unto a wife? seek not to be loosed: Art thou loosed from a wife? seek not a wife.

28 But shouldest thou marry, thou hast not sinned; and if a virgin marry, she hath not sinned. Yet such shall have tribulation in the flesh: and I would spare you.

29 But this I say, brethren, the time is shortened, that henceforth both those that have wives may be as though they had none;

30 and those that weep as though they wept not; and those that rejoice as though they rejoiced not; and those that buy as though they possessed not;

31 and those that use the world, as not using it to the full: for the fashion of this world passeth away.

32 But I would have you to be free from cares. He that is unmarried is careful for the things of the Lord, how he may please the Lord:

33 but he that is married is careful for the things of the world, how he may please his wife,

34 and is divided. *So* also the woman that is unmarried and the virgin is careful for the things of the Lord, that she may be holy both in body and in spirit: but she that is married is careful for the things of the world, how she may please her husband.

35 And this I say for your own profit; not that I may cast a snare upon you, but for that which is seemly, and that ye may attend upon the Lord without distraction.

36 But if any man thinketh that he behaveth himself unseemly toward his virgin *daughter*, if she be past the

173

flower of her age, and if need so requireth, let him do what he will; he sinneth not; let them marry.

37 But he that standeth stedfast in his heart, having no necessity, but hath power as touching his own will, and hath determined this in his own heart, to keep his own virgin *daughter*, shall do well.

38 So then he that giveth his own virgin *daughter* in marriage doeth well; and he that giveth her not in marriage shall do better.

39 A wife is bound for so long time as her husband liveth; but if the husband be dead, she is free to be married to whom she will; only in the Lord.

40 But she is happier if she abide as she is, after my judgment: and I think that I also have the Spirit of God.

25 *Concerning virgins*: the discussion of the main point of chapter 7 is here continued. The Corinthians may have asked Paul certain specific questions with regard to virgins. The apostle states that he has not received any special precept from the Lord concerning this matter. Not only had Jesus during His public ministry refrained from making any statement on the subject but likewise there had not been a special revelation concerning it. Paul, therefore, cannot speak with absolute authority but must give his *judgment* (II Cor. 8:10), i. e., his opinion or advice, at the same asking however that this advice be taken seriously since it comes from an apostle who has *obtained mercy of the Lord.* These words, while speaking of the significance of Paul as a person, nevertheless ascribe all glory to God (II Cor. 4:1; I Tim. 1:12). *As one*: Paul states his opinion but that does not mean that the case is uncertain or that the apostle is in doubt. The *Lord*: the risen Christ. *Trustworthy*: faithful to God (cf. 4:2). Paul always cleaves to his Saviour and walks in His ways. When giving advice the apostle does so in faithfulness to Christ. This advice must therefore be pleasing to the Lord (cf. vv. 32f.).

26 To *think* is here to be understood in the same sense as *judgment* in vs. 25. It implies a definite opinion, not just a supposition (cf. 7:36; I Tim. 6:5). *Therefore* indicates that

Paul is now stating his opinion.[6] Paul stresses two things. The first is that it is a good thing to be a virgin because of the present need, the second that it is a good thing in itself. *The distress that is upon us.* RSV has "the impending need." It is better to translate: the present need.[7] The reference is not to a need which was only present in Paul's own days nor to an imminent coming of the Lord whereby life on earth would lose its significance. Paul speaks in this chapter of the needs of all Christians in general (cf. v. 29 and 31). He has in view the distress which exists for every Christian at all times. That distress is described in several ways in this context: *tribulation in the flesh* (a consequence of sin; Gen. 3:16; Rom. 8:18f), vs. 28; a *shortened time,* vs. 29; *the fashion of the world passeth away,* v. 31. Due to sin there is need. The Christian lies bound in this need, it is a compulsion to him from which he cannot free himself. Although Christ has conquered sin, its consequences are still felt (cf. vs. 31). This makes the observance of a creation ordinance impossible without further qualification. As things are now people ought to marry *because of fornications* (vs. 2); special gifts of the Spirit are now needed in order to remain unmarried (vs. 7). *Continency* is possible in the present state but Paul also mentions *burning* (vs. 9). This points to a certain distress or compulsion. The Christian is caught in the midst of a struggle and his married life is not exempt. Certainly it is good for virgins to remain virgins. But only if they have received the gift of continency. Paul's mention of virgins only, and not of unmarried men, is not accidental. First, normally speaking, a young woman does not desire marriage as much as a young man, and second, the girl is passive inasmuch as she does not ask to marry someone but is

---

[6] The construction of this sentence is difficult. νομίζω is followed first of all by an accusative with infinitive. τοῦτο refers to the virgin state. The second clause, also dependent on νομίζω could not be expressed by means of an infinitive for that would require either the word ὑπάρχειν again or the word εἶναι which the apostle wants to use for a different purpose. Therefore he chooses an object clause with ὅτι and he writes ὅτι τὸ οὕτως εἶναι i.e. the virgin state καλόν sc. ἐστιν τῷ ἀνθρώπῳ.

[7] διὰ τὴν ἐνεστῶσαν ἀνάγκην, cf. Rom. 8:38; I Cor. 3:22; Gal. 1:4; Eph. 5:16.

asked by someone else. These words of Paul contain comfort for the unmarried woman. It is for her not disastrous not to marry. Paul stresses this point still further when he continues: *that it is good for a man*[8] *to be as he is,* i. e., even apart from the existing distress it is a good thing to be unmarried.

27 The general concept *man* forms the transition to vs. 27 which does not speak of virgins but of people in general. Here are some very clear precepts for every day life. The fact that our vocation is all important (vs. 24) does not in any way mean that the natural life must be condemned and that we should live a life of moral indifference as was the case at Corinth. Here again Paul, in close connection with the commandment of the Lord which he does not mention in so many words, issues very definite precepts. *Art thou bound* refers to a permanent state. When the husband is *bound unto a wife* he *must not seek to be loosed,* and vice versa. *Art thou loosed* need not refer to a marriage bond which had been previously dissolved by divorce or by the death of the spouse. It may not mean anything more than unmarried.

28 Vs. 28 shows that the second half of vs. 27 does not possess the same force as the first half. The second half moves in the sphere of that which is "good," the first contains a commandment. Vs. 28 speaks of men and women. The apostle states first in a general way that he who marries, in the first place the man, does not sin. Then he makes the same statement with reference to virgins since he is speaking of them in this pericope.[9] The statement which Paul makes here is remarkable and is intelligible only if there were some at Corinth who considered marriage sinful. Such an opinion might easily arise from a misunderstanding of Paul's own words. The Corinthians might think that Paul held that it was better not to marry because of the existing distress, and they would then construe these words as a prohibition of marriage. But actually Paul only states that continency is something good only if it is possible to have it without falling a victim to immorality. The last part of the verse makes this abundantly clear when Paul describes marriage as involving physical distress,

---

[8] Greek: ἀνθρώπῳ not ἀνδρί.

[9] Perhaps it is best to take these aorists as gnomic. The difference between γαμήσῃς and γήμῃ is too minute to be expressed.

not as a moral evil. *Tribulation in the flesh* we take of the bodily difficulties of married women (cf. Mt. 24:19). *I,* says the apostle, who myself have the gift of continency, *would spare you* the difficulties of marriage. He who marries does not sin but he will encounter difficulties. Especially virgins[10] will have that experience. Hence Paul's advice not to marry.

29, 30 Again Paul departs from his subject for a moment in order to return to it in vs. 36. He first makes a statement which is valid for everyone but in particular for married people. The latter have not received the gift of continency and are in close contact with life, and yet they should not consider that the main thing. *But this I say, brethren,* i. e., the following words, in any case, I say to everyone of you. *Brethren* indicates that Paul addresses the whole congregation with an important and tender message. There is no specific reference to marriage here but rather to general conduct. *The time is shortened,* i. e., compressed. That is a permanent quality of time: it is compressed and that means that it should be lived intensely (cf. Mt. 24:22). Time is compressed because we live in the period between the descent of the Holy Spirit and the return of Christ. This period demands the end of all things and also hastens towards that end. (Rev. 22: 20). Thereby time is characterized and our own life as well. For that reason our life should be free from the present time and direct itself toward life eternal (Heb. 11:13-15). *Henceforth* has the following import: because the time is shortened there remains only one thing we should be concerned about. That one thing necessary is to have the eye directed toward heaven. Marriage is a divine institution. He that lacks the gift of continency must marry. *That . . . may be* has the force of a commandment. *Those that have wives* should consider that in the resurrection they will neither marry nor be given in marriage but will be as the angels in heaven (Mt. 22:30).[11] The words: *though they had none* must not be taken as an exhortation to neglect marital duties, as the context clearly shows. They imply that it should be constantly kept in mind that marriage is something of this time, not of the proper abiding life of the Christian (II Cor. 6:10). That this is

---

[10] Not only the virgin, τοιοῦτοι.

[11] ὡς μὴ ἔχοντες ὦσιν, as being in the state of not having.

meant is borne out by the subsequent expressions. Even the Christian finds occasion to weep at one time and laugh at another. He may freely do so for he shares in the events of his own time (cf. 5:10). But the life of the world should not determine the character of the Christian life. In sadness as well as in joy the believer must direct his thoughts toward the heavenly fatherland (Heb. 11:16, 24f). For that reason it is quite proper for him to make purchases if he only remembers that he is not acquiring for himself a lasting possession. For that would make him like the ungodly (Ps. 49:7, 8).

31 *And* is summarizing. The world may be used[12] but it should be a *using to the full,* i. e., a using in such a manner that there is nothing more left. To him who uses the world to the full the world is his all and he has nothing beside it. We are bound to think here of worldly wisdom which Paul has rejected in chapters 1 and 2.[13] The Christian must not use the world as if he only had to live for this present era.

The causal clause which follows does not have in view the Christian vocation but rather the condition of that world with which he should not entangle himself. If he should do so, disappointment would be his share. *The fashion,* i. e., the form (RSV), the aspect. This refers not only to external character but also to attitude and conduct. This world is passing away (I Jn. 2:17). This does not refer to the constant change and motion to which this world is subject for this fact in itself would be no reason why we should not have a high regard for it. Passing away means that the world is under a judgment of transitoriness, it is under a curse. To pass away belongs to its character, more particularly to its attitude, its conduct. The world yearns for redemption (Rom. 8:18-25). To believers who partake of a new world the form of which will never pass away (Heb 12:27f), (II Pet. 3:7), the passing away of this present world must be a continuous warning not to set their heart upon this earth.

---

[12] χράομαι with an accusative, not uncommon in later Greek; in the N.T. only here.

[13] It should be remembered, however, that compounds with κατά sometimes differ but very little from the simple verb.

32-34 This passage presents Paul's thoughts as to the attitude all men should take toward the world which passes away. That attitude must be *to be free from cares.* In Matthew 6:25f. Jesus discussing the Christian's conduct says that it should include freedom from care and a confidence in our Father in heaven. By using *I would* Paul again moves in the sphere of that which is "good." The man who lacks the gift of continency should marry. In this respect there is a difference between our passage and Matthew 6. Jesus forbids all anxiety regarding a number of things which He specifies concerning human life. This prohibition is absolute. Paul infers that to be absolutely free from cares is possible only under certain circumstances. The apostle does not mean to imply that those who are married are bound to be wholly occupied with earthly things. He only states that a married man or woman is more likely to be bound to the things of the world than those who are unmarried. The words: *He that is unmarried is careful for the things of the Lord* following upon: *I would have you to be free from cares* cannot be taken to mean that the unmarried Christian would only care for the things of the Lord. This interpretation is also rendered impossible by the words: *and is divided,* vs. 34. The correct interpretation is that the unmarried Christian man or woman incurs less risk of becoming preoccupied with the things of the world, and so he or she will come more readily to a wholehearted service of God. The married person must reckon with the fact that he is married; he may not withdraw from the duties his family imposes on him. But it cannot be denied that those duties are somewhat distracting. The absolute statements in this context are not meant to be taken in an absolute sense. They only serve to emphasize the most important features of both the unmarried and the married state. Paul does not infer that a married man would have no other ideal than this world, for the obvious reason that worldliness simply cannot be identified with the married state, especially if the wife is a Christian. It is true, marriage is a thing of this world according to the apostle's exposition. So is a man's desire to please his wife (Lk. 14:20). But this desire only becomes a thing of this world and consequently a forbidden thing **if there** would be nothing else in the life of such a man. And Paul makes clear that that need not be so. This we conclude from the words *and is divided* which we connect with the preceding as is done by ASV and RSV.[14] The sense of "is divided" is the same as in 1:13. The married Christian wavers, wishing to please his wife and to serve the Lord. Now he will be engaged in a heavenly pursuit, then in an earthly. To say that this is sinful would be impossible following the teaching of vs. 28. The words do not imply that married people are too much attached to the earth, they simply state the fact that there is this division. Married people are necessarily and properly so much occupied with the affairs of this world that it becomes impossible for them to be absorbed with the things of the Lord. Thus we are back at vs. 7 where Paul spoke of the gift of remaining unmarried and of dedicating oneself to the things of the Lord. He that marries lacks that gift of the Spirit and consequently can do less for the kingdom of God, a fact which does not constitute sin.

The same thing applies to the unmarried woman, i. e., the widow or the divorced wife (vs. 15 and 16) and to virgins. The reason for this further elaboration on Paul's part may lie in the fact that properly speaking the subject of virgins is under discussion (vs. 25). It should be noted that in the passage concerning men there is nothing comparable to *that she may be holy both in body and in spirit*. This is partly due to the special subject of Paul's discourse, partly also to his desire to comfort the virgins. It should be to their comfort that they, who as young women cannot seek marriage as men do, need not think that they do not count quite as fully if they do not marry. They, after all, can dedicate themselves to a service of the Lord that is free from care. After a more detailed treatment of several points of importance we have now returned to vss. 25 and 26. The unmarried woman, the virgin, can give herself with all her gifts to the things of the Lord. In doing so she may have a very definite purpose in mind (*that* has a final sense). *Holy* need not be interpreted in the same way as *is sanctified* in vs. 14, i. e., of a relative holiness. Paul only states a fact and does not imply that those who are

---

[14] There are many difficulties here. First: the manuscripts differ. We follow Nestle's text: καὶ μεμέρισται καὶ ἡ γυνὴ ἡ ἄγαμος καὶ ἡ παρθένος. Second: μεμέρισται cannot be joined with the following words. γυνὴ and παρθένος are the subject of μεριμνᾷ.

unmarried are saints to the exclusion of others or are more saintly than others. Paul states that the purpose of the unmarried is to be holy. In this context that means that the latter actually perform more easily what every Christian should do. The holiness of which Paul is speaking is an obligation, it is not the holiness which Paul so often ascribes to the entire congregation. *Both*: the holiness concerns the *body* as well as the *spirit*. Paul does not plead for asceticism but he rather contends that the unmarried woman may have the ideal of serving the Lord with body and spirit. A married woman on the other hand tries to please her husband. This is a perfect parallel to what had been said with regard to the husband (vs. 33).

35 *This* refers to the immediately preceding words. *For your own profit* is a strong statement whereby Paul intimates that no ulterior motives, such as, e. g., the fact that he himself is unmarried, have prompted him to write as he did. His concern in writing is with the genuine interest of the Corinthian church. He does not want to *cast a snare upon them* (cf. vs. 5 and vs. 9). Paul has recommended the unmarried state in view of the service of the Lord, only then, however, when that state is possible, i. e., if there is a special gift, the gift of continence. The apostle does not recommend a continence which would lead to unchastity. This remark was made necessary because the Corinthians had already lapsed into immorality. It is safe to assume that a false asceticism had caused this to happen. An additional reason for this remark resides in the fact that Paul did not have a mandate of the Lord on this point but stated his own opinion, seeking in all things the *profit* of the congregation. This profit is more clearly defined by *which is seemly* (Rom. 13:13), *and that ye may attend upon the Lord without distraction.*[15] The peculiar mode of expression used by the apostle may be due to his desire to use the same words which the Corinthians used concerning conditions in society for his description of a proper relationship to God, thus stressing the purpose of his writing. That purpose was that the congregation might be true to the Lord without any hindrance. The

---

[15] Greek: εὐπάρεδρον τῷ κυρίῳ ἀπερισπάστως i.e. permanently remaining with the Lord without interruption or obstacle. εὐπάρεδρος only here, ἀπερισπάστως only here in the N.T.

181

apostle wants to attain that by his advice not to marry. It is his desire that all the members of the church should aim at the Lord's service and that they should be able to forego marriage to that end. But this should only be done where possible, lest one should receive a snare around his neck.

36 Vs. 36 introduces a new subject to the extent that the apostle begins to treat a special case relating to virgins. That which is called unseemly here is to restrain virgins from marriage. The pronoun *he* has been taken in two different ways, referring to either the father of the virgin or to her fiance. For the latter construction an appeal is made to the words *let them marry*. However, the idea of an engagement is absent here as much as in vs. 27. It would be strange to suppose that an engaged man would think of acting in an unseemly manner if he did not marry his fiancee, for the purpose of the betrothal is marriage. Besides, vs. 37 also excludes the thought of an engagement, since otherwise the words *to keep his own virgin* would have to indicate a permanent betrothal. This would be contrary to Paul's statements in vss. 7, 9 and 27. The expression *his virgin* would also be a peculiar designation of one's fiancee. On that basis we conclude that *he* must refer to the father. Thus also the ASV with its *virgin daughter*. RSV however has *betrothed*. The father receives the proposals for his daughter. He may have refused on religious grounds but later on he may have come to the opinion that it was better to accept because he would act unseemly if he kept refusing. *Past the flower of her age :*[16] this means that the time of marriage may not pass. The words *and if need so requireth*[17] which speak of a moral obligation also fit this particular thought. The father has a right with respect to his daughter but he is also responsible. Paul contends that nature itself as the years go by, shows that the father has a moral obligation not to hold up the marriage of his daughter. Thus he also combats the opinion that marrying would be sinful. The father *sinneth not* if he gives his daughter in marriage. The subject of *let them marry* is the virgin and the one who has betrothed her.

---

[16] Greek: ὑπέρακμος . For the Greeks the ἀκμὴ is the high point of life. The man is at his acme at the age of thirty, the woman at the age of twenty.

[17] Greek: οὕτως ὀφείλει γίνεσθαι.

37 In vs. 37 Paul indicates what he thinks is most commendable. Vs. 36 did not nullify what he had said in the preceding verses, but its advice was valid only under certain circumstances. In vs. 36 the apostle does not mention the desires of the girl in this matter but he places the whole affair in the hands of the father. Of every man Paul assumes that he will desire to marry and that this desire will be absent only when the Spirit has given continence (cf. vs. 7). The woman is much more passive, she cannot seek marriage herself and consequently the apostle assumes that she may remain unmarried even without such a special gift. That is why the circumstances under which it is permissible to remain unmarried are described in a slightly different way. Concerning fathers we read that there are some who are *determined in their hearts,* i. e., they will remain unchanged, since the heart is the center of life, ruling the whole life and all its expressions. *Having no necessity,* the father is under no compulsion to change his plan, as e. g., the financial situation which would make it impossible for him to support his daughter. Another possibility would be that his daughter's desires would become so strong that he would no longer dare to decline a proposal. In any case the reference is here to external circumstances and not to a fear on the part of the father that he might act unseemly if he would keep his daughter from being married. Nor is the father compelled by the *distress that is upon us* (vs. 26). When these conditions exist the man has the power to do as he desires. *Power (exousia)* may have a slightly different meaning here from what it has earlier in the epistle. Here it stands for the liberty or power to make decisions as one desires. The accumulation of expressions is due to the apostle's desire to indicate that he is thinking of actions taken in complete freedom. *This,* to wit: *to keep his own virgin daughter. Hath determined*: the father decides in full freedom and stands by it. This is no obstinacy but rather a decision resting on good arguments. *In his own heart* stresses again the complete freedom of the father. *Shall do well*: for *"well"* see vss. 1 and 26 (cf. Heb. 13:4). *Shall do*: the future indicates that what Paul writes here had not yet taken place. Apparently the Corinthians were in embarrassment. Some young women remained unmarried on ascetic grounds and this led to unchastity. Others simply refused to marry. When Paul is asked for advice (cf. vs. 25: concerning virgins) he states that he does not have any commandment of the Lord but he points to what he considers the best solution. And his advice is dominated by the idea that the Christian life ought to be directed not toward the earth but toward heaven. Marriage, however, is a creation ordinance and is also necessary to prevent sin in an ungodly world.

38 That this is the apostle's train of thought is shown by vs. 38. This verse contains two statements. The first one does not follow directly from the context, in fact it seems to exclude the second. Yet, Paul's conception of Christian life being what it is, the two do not exclude each other. The Christian has two fatherlands, one in heaven and one on the earth and with both he has to reckon. He should not live as if he were in heaven for then he might easily come to sin. More important still, he should not live as if the fashion of this world were not passing away (vs. 31). But since God distributes His gifts as it pleases Him, not all men are equal and so one may be able to do what the other is not. Hence it follows that the conclusion in this verse may state a double truth, one of which is described as "well" the other as "better" (cf. vs. 8 and 9). The two are not in the same realm. One person will have to reckon with the earth more seriously than another.

An additional argument for taking these verses of the father rather than of the betrothed is the fact that upon the second assumption the Greek verb translated with "to give in marriage"[18] must be translated by "to marry" which is at variance with its ordinary sense.

39 The point of vs. 39 has to do with marriage but is somewhat distinctive. It does not refer specifically to a Christian's conduct but touches upon the life of everyone, although immediately a clause is added implying that the ideal Christian life is in view here as well. We may suppose that the apostle is here discussing a difficulty often encountered by pagans who had become Christians (cf. Rom. 7:2). The marriage bond among

---

[18] γαμίζω.

pagans was not strong and divorce was a prevalent evil. The Christian had to learn that this was a sinful habit but it took some time before the Christians were convinced of this and so would observe the law of God in this regard. We have here before us the general commandment of God concerning the indissolubility of marriage. The woman is not free, there is a bond which she must not break. Remarkable it is that Paul first mentions the wife instead of beginning with the husband. This may be due to the fact that the Corinthian women were taking too many liberties and also that the wife is subject to the husband. Besides, the apostle reckons with death. *Only in the Lord* belongs to *to be married.* Paul does not say in so many words that a Christian woman may only marry a Christian but that is nevertheless implied in his words, since a marriage in the Lord is only possible if both partners are Christians (cf. vs. 12f. and II Cor. 6:14f).

40 In vs. 40 Paul takes up the main thought of the chapter. The wife who has lost her husband through death is, according to Paul's opinion, happier if she does not marry again, i. e., if she remains a widow. This "happier" is a corollary of "good" in vs. 1. This is not a question of a greater degree of bliss in heaven but simply of being happier on earth and of a better dedication to the service of God as the apostle had set forth in the preceding verses. This is not in the form of a commandment but only of advice (cf. vs. 25). The apostle does not appeal to his apostolic authority for then he speaks absolutely and issues commandments as is clear from many passages in I Corinthians. Paul is here taking a stand against others, perhaps those Corinthians who boasted that they possessed the Spirit of God (cf. chs. 12-14). If there were some among them who held a different opinion concerning widows, they did not sin although theirs was not the best opinion. Paul himself also received *the Spirit of God,* which is not here to be taken of complete inspiration but of the illumination which is given to all children of God (Eph. 1:17f.; I Jn. 1:27).

Paul points out in this chapter that the result of sin is an antinomy as far as marriage questions are concerned. Man has received

COMMENTARY ON FIRST CORINTHIANS

the mandate from God that he should marry. But God calls him to His service. The tension which arises from this can only be solved to a certain extent. Man must marry and he is only free from marrying if God gives him a special charism. The Christian is free to marry but he acts well if he, in special circumstances, does not marry.

CHAPTER VIII

THE EATING OF MEAT OFFERED TO IDOLS

8:1-13

1 Now concerning things sacrificed to idols: We know that we all have knowledge. Knowledge puffeth up, but love edifieth.

2 If any man thinketh that he knoweth anything, he knoweth not yet as he ought to know;

3 but if any man loveth God, the same is known by him.

4 Concerning therefore the eating of things sacrificed to idols, we know that no idol is anything in the world, and that there is no God but one.

5 For though there be that are called gods, whether in heaven or on earth; as there are gods many, and lords many;

6 yet to us there is one God, the Father, of whom are all things, and we unto him; and one Lord, Jesus Christ, through whom are all things, and we through him.

7 Howbeit there is not in all men that knowledge: but some, being used until now to the idol, eat as *of* a thing sacrificed to an idol; and their conscience being weak is defiled.

8 But food will not commend us to God: neither, if we eat not, are we the worse; nor, if we eat, are we the better.

9 But take heed lest by any means this liberty of yours become a stumbling-block to the weak.

10 For if a man see thee who hast knowledge sitting at meat in an idol's temple, will not his conscience, if he is weak, be emboldened to eat things sacrificed to idols?

11 For through thy knowledge he that is weak perisheth, the brother for whose sake Christ died.

12 And thus, sinning against the brethren, and wounding their conscience when it is weak, ye sin against Christ.

13 Wherefore, if meat causeth my brother to stumble, I will eat no flesh for evermore, that I cause not my brother to stumble.

187

1 The opening words of ch. 8 *now concerning things* recall 7:1, and it is safe to assume that Paul is treating here a second point concerning which the Corinthians had questioned him. Here again there were two opinions concerning the matter and both were wrong. Some thought that the Christian was allowed to do all things; others did not understand the doctrine of Christian liberty correctly. The church had consulted Paul concerning this matter in her letter to him and had apparently asked him for a precise statement as to how to act. But the apostle does not make such a statement. Starting from the right principle he turns against both opinions, condemning one as an undue inclusivism and the other as an undue narrowness.

The Corinthians, in speaking of *things sacrificed to idols* place themselves on a Christian standpoint.[1] At Corinth there was every opportunity to eat meat sacrificed to idols. This was so not only because there were banquets in the temples in honor of the idols, but also because sacrificial meat was consumed at home since the priests would sell their share of the sacrifice in the meat market. It was entirely impossible to determine whether or not a certain portion of meat had any connection with idols (10:25, 27). The question which arises is whether meat that has been sacrificed has become a special sort of meat since it was part of the sacrifice. A second question is whether everybody may eat all sorts of meat once it has been established that meat does not change when it is sacrificed to idols.

The words *we know that,* etc., have been explained in different ways. It appears best to assume that Paul is quoting a few statements from the letter which the church sent him, replying to them or perhaps refuting them. The objection that Paul does not indicate that he is quoting is removed by the consideration that everyone in Corinth would naturally know what they had written and thus would recognize their own words. Paul may have quoted here because there were a few things in the letter which needed correction, all the rest being true.

We know is an expression which fits the proud Corinthians (cf. 4:8). Just because they were of the opinion that everything was clear to them they had come to sin. And when writing to Paul about meat offered to idols they had indicated that they

---

[1] Pagans speak of ἱερόθυτα 10:28.

did not lack knowledge. Knowledge lacks the article, which implies that Paul does not mean knowledge concerning idols only but all knowledge. Knowledge was uppermost at Corinth. Why had the Corinthians sent a letter to Paul at all? Probably because they desired a solution of some practical difficulties, e. g., how to deal with people who refused to eat sacrificial meat. Paul's words *knowledge puffeth up, love only edifieth* are directed against this attitude.

Knowledge in Paul's vocabulary is not something purely intellectual, it is a knowledge which has results and leads to action, especially religious action. Knowledge and wisdom can be distinguished. The latter is practical insight, the former always has an intellectual starting point although it is not limited to intellectual action. Wisdom is a lasting quality, knowledge is an acquired good. The Corinthians had studied the question of the eating of sacrificial meat and they were convinced that they understood the problem except for a few minor details. Thus seen Paul's antithesis between knowledge and love is a real one. The starting point of the Corinthians was wrong. They began with the intellect and determined their conduct by means of their intellect. That sort of procedure leads to pride, a sin which was not rare at Corinth (4:6). Knowledge without love is sin (13:2, 8). The only right starting point is love. The question arises as to the kind of love Paul has in mind. Vs. 3 refers to the love to God: *if any man loveth God*, which justifies us in taking the love of vs. 1 as being closely akin to that love toward God, although it is at the same time, different as appears from the omission of *"of God."* The love of which vs. 1 speaks must refer to the love towards the brethren, which is rooted in the love towards God (cf. vs. 3 and 11). Of this love Paul can say that it *edifieth*, it accomplishes something. To be puffed up through knowledge is a vice. Love, on the contrary, has a good effect; it seeks the good of the community, it improves relationships and leads to good actions. Thus, before writing anything on the question under discussion, the apostle deals with its general background and analyzes the evil principle which has brought the Corinthians to their attitude. The verdict is that they have started with knowledge and have neglected love.

2 The word *thinketh* introduces a new element.[2] He who "thinketh" is of the opinion that others should hold the same views as his own, but that opinion is wrong. By using "thinketh" Paul renders faithfully the opinion of the Corinthians who had intimated to him in their letter that it was their opinion that they all possessed knowledge. After he has pointed out in vs. 1 the disadvantage of knowledge without love, he states in vs. 2 that the knowledge which the Corinthians thought they possessed is an imaginary knowledge. True knowledge is not pretentious and he who has it does not boast. He who thinks that he knows does not yet know as he ought to know (3:18; Gal. 6:3). *Anything* does not just refer to the question of eating sacrificial meat but to all kinds of knowledge. The absence of "anything" in the apodosis enhances the idea of the action of knowing.[3] He who falsely thinks he knows does not possess true knowledge for the latter implies that one continues to learn. *Ought* implies a moral duty. Paul does not infer that he who thinks he knows actually has no knowledge at all but only that the way he knows is not the right one. He does not know the way that God requires, for he does not have love.

3 This verse marks a surprising turn. What we would expect is an exposition of what true knowledge is. But since Paul has already intimated in vs. 1 that true knowledge goes hand in hand with love, he does not have to elaborate the point. He now goes on from here and teaches that love not only must be combined with knowledge but that a far greater benefit is implied in it. The love here referred to is no longer love toward the brethren but love toward God. Vs. 3 does not reveal something entirely new, for the point was implied in the preceding verses. The real difference is ultimately one of one's relationship to God. With him who loves the Lord according to His commandment all things are right. Such a one will have knowledge and much more

---

[2] Greek: δοκεῖ. We may translate: "thinks", if Paul writes *e mente Corinthiorum*. But the translation "appears to" is also possible, which would be *e mente Pauli*. The difference is insignificant but the translation "thinks" is nevertheless to be preferred since the second half of the verse shows that Paul in the first half introduces the man who thinks he knows.

[3] Notice ἐγνωκέναι, knowledge at rest, after ἔγνω, knowledge in action.

than that. Of the latter Paul gives an example by using the Greek verb "to know" in more than one sense. That verb also has the sense of "to recognize." Paul puts it this way: If any man loves the Lord he is known by God, i. e., recognized by Him. God accepts such a one so that he shares in God's grace. That is much more than an imaginary knowledge. He who loves the Lord will attain to that superior position, i. e., that of one who has the right starting point for his action.[4] *Is known* refers to a knowledge which has reached its acme and is not capable of augmentation. In God such knowledge may be assumed to exist even though in Him this knowledge will always be in action. It should also be clear that love is not the condition for being known by God. God's knowledge comes first (cf. Mt. 11:27; I Cor. 13:12). The two go together and it is Paul's purpose to inform the Corinthians of the great significance of God's love which surpasses all earthly knowledge. To know God as we should know Him is to love God and to love God is to know Him (cf. Rom. 8:28; I John 4:9).

4 Vs. 4 takes us back to vs. 1. After first speaking of the general principle the apostle now comes to the concrete subject of the *eating* of meat offered to idols. Again we read the words *we know,* followed by a sentence which is true in itself (cf. Rom. 3:30) but which nevertheless seems out of place in this context, for Paul has just stated that knowledge puffs up. Vs. 4 must therefore contain another quotation from the letter of the Corinthians to Paul. *No . . . anything* (RSV no real existence, i. e., nothing) may be used attributively or predicatively: there is not any idol in the world, or: an idol is nothing in the world. The first translation is preferred as being the most obvious. *Idol* was originally an image but it may also be the pagan god himself, and thus it is used here. To contend that there are no images of pagan gods in the world is contrary to fact. *World* must be taken in the sense of the ungodly world, as elsewhere in the Epistle. There must have been a definite reason why the Corinthians inserted the words: *in the world.* The question was: May a Christian eat sacrificial meat? Pagans commonly hold that their idols are present at the sacrifices and that they enjoy the vapors which arise from the burning fat so that those who participate

---

[4] We construe οὗτος with τίς and αὐτοῦ with God.

191

in the meal are actually communing with the idols (cf. 10:20f). The Corinthians contended that this idea was wrong since no idol existed in the world. There is no reason to abstain from sacrificial meat for there is but one God, our God whom we adore.

5, 6 Verses 5 and 6 also contain quotations from the letter sent by the Corinthians to Paul whereas in vs. 7 Paul gives his own opinion. *For though* introduces a clause which contains the ground for the preceding clause and counters at the same time an objection which could have been made against the preceding clause. The objection to the statement that there is but one God could be: there are many so-called gods. The reason why the Corinthians maintain their previous statement is that, since they only have one God, they have nothing to do with those idols. *There be that are called gods,[5] whether in heaven or on earth*: the Corinthians do not deny that there are beings in heaven and on earth which are called gods by their pagan countrymen, but those gods are no real gods and they certainly are not active in the world. By assigning to them either the heavens or the earth, the pagans themselves indicate that they rule over only part of the world. Even the pagans believe that there *are many gods and many lords*. The word "gods" refers to idols, "lords" refers to heroes and demi-gods as we know them from Hellenistic mythology. But not so the Christians, they have but one God, the *Father* of Christ and in Him our Father. He also is the origin of all things, for they are *of Him*. Everything that exists has its source in God. *We,* Christians, are *through* (better: to[6]) Him. *We* are a part of the things which are created by God. But as rational creatures and especially as Christians we have a task, namely a vocation to glorify God. Our life must be directed toward Him, we are *to* Him (cf. 15:28). We Christians, thus the Corinthians continue, have only *one Lord* and He is Jesus Christ, names which call to mind everything Christ has done and still does as the Saviour. But the Mediator also was active at

---

[5] εἰσὶν λεγόμενοι θεοί allows for the following two translations: 1) "for if there might be those, who (continually) are called gods"; 2) "for if there might be so-called gods." The meaning remains substantially the same.

[6] Greek: εἰς; RSV: "for whom we exist."

the creation. *Through* Him *are all things and we through*[7] *Him,*
i. e., by His mediation. The preposition *of* refers to the first
source (cf. 11:12), *through* has reference to giving something
its character (Jn. 1:3; Heb. 1:2). *We through Him*: This
second use of the preposition "through" cannot be for the purpose
of stating that we also, so far as our creation is concerned, are
through Christ. In the light of the context the "we" are always
the Christians. Added to this consideration is the fact that the
preceding words do not refer only to God's creative activity but
also have believers in view. In the light of these considerations
it seems best to hold that the Corinthians in their letter had first
written about their having been created through Christ, and afterwards about their salvation through Him. The use of the same
preposition in both cases is due to the character of these activities.
Like all men we are created by Christ but we are also redeemed
by Him (Rom. 11:36).

7 *Howbeit* indicates that Paul agrees with the Corinthians
only partially. Many things for which they contended for were
valid and the apostle does not deem it necessary to refute their
contention. But their starting point was not right. Vs. 1 already indicates that the Corinthians were of the opinion that
everything was all right provided one had a right view of things.
Paul contends, however, that to start with right knowledge is
insufficient for the very reason that *not in all men is that knowledge.* The Corinthians might think that knowledge alone could
determine their conduct. Paul makes clear that even upon that
assumption they were not yet ready. And in order to demonstrate
that, he points out that not everyone had the right knowledge
concerning idols and sacrificial meat. What he has in mind holds
true of *some,* i. e., not of the whole congregation. Yet there were
some and the Corinthians, when writing their letter, had not
thought of them, or if they had thought of these weak members of
the congregation, they had done so in the wrong spirit (Mt.
18:6). We receive the impression that the Corinthians in their
letter to Paul had evidenced the opinion that they, who were
strong, were naturally right and that the weak would have to

---

[7] Greek: διά, the usual preposition indicating the role Christ
played at the creation.

conform themselves to the strong. The apostle's standpoint is a different one. Although the weak only formed a minority the Corinthians had to reckon with that minority.

Being used until now to the idol, i. e., the service of those pagan gods. As a result of this these Christians were eating sacrificial meat as a sacrifice. Although no longer idolaters themselves, they were nevertheless Christians who at one time had been pagans and who had lived in a city full of idolatry. When they came in touch with idols again they were carried back to their former life. This is more than a weak person can endure. A former drunkard must stay away from strong drink altogether. Even so the ex-pagan cannot yet look upon meat offered to idols as ordinary meat. When he eats such meat it still is sacrificial meat to him and puts him in touch with the idols. This makes his way of eating sinful. *His conscience is defiled:* he pollutes himself. His conscience is weak, it falls into a trap. *Being* weak implies a permanent condition, which makes pollution possible. This is not a momentary lapse into sin but a living in it.

8 At vs. 8 the question again arises whether these words are Paul's own words or a quotation from the letter of the Corinthians. The words in question contain a positive statement which is not wrong in itself but which may easily lead to pride. Moreover, vs. 9 issues a warning, which, although it does not affect the contention of vs. 8, nevertheless mentions the abuse that could be made of it. This leads us to think that vs. 8 also is a quotation of a statement of the Corinthians. *Commend* etc.: what we eat does not bring us into contact with God (cf. II Cor. 4:14). It does not matter what we eat for by eating we do not come closer to God. And so we may eat what we like. This is a question of liberty which enables us to eat all meat including sacrificial meat. This statement is in line with the argument the Corinthians were using (6:12), an argument which is expressly applied to the eating of sacrificial meat in 10:23. If food does not bring us nearer to God, it is of no importance for our relation to God whether we eat or not.

9 One now finds Paul's answer to this contention of the Corinthians. Just as Paul had done previously, he begins by recognizing the liberty of the Christian and admits that it is true

that food does not change anyone's state before God. But here again this right cannot be the rule for a person's conduct. The Christian has to reckon with his brother. There is a development in Paul's argumentation here. First he indicated that knowledge should not be our starting point. Then he argued that knowledge as such cannot be the Christian principle because not all have that knowledge Now he writes that a Christian's liberty shall not govern his conduct. This is a point which the apostle has stressed throughout the epistle.

This liberty of yours: Paul recognizes that liberty but he points out that, although our eating may not affect our relation to God, it nevertheless may have certain results. It may be a *stumbling-block to the weak* brothers, i. e., it may lead them to sin. The apostle does not imply that the eating itself may be a stumbling block. On the contrary, back in vs. 7 we were informed that the eating of sacrificial meat in itself is no sin, but it may lead to sin if the weaker brethren eat it in a certain way. Here we have an identical situation. This stumbling block does not exist for everybody and in all circumstances. Only the wrong use of Christian liberty in eating sacrificial meat may become a stumbling block. And love for the brethren requires that we reckon with the difficulties of the weak (cf. vs. 11-13; Rom. 14:13; Gal. 5:13). That type of consideration the apostle may expect just because his opinion is that eating does not bring us nearer to God. It is not necessary to eat meat offered to idols. And if it might lead somebody else to sin one should refrain from it.

It should not escape us that both Paul and the Corinthians, instead of speaking of the eating of sacrificial meat, sometimes simply refer to eating without further addition. The reason is that Paul's arguments are valid for every kind of eating and the eating of sacrificial meat is only a specific case.

10 Vs. 10 explains how the weaker brother may come to sin when the strong would eat sacrificial meat. Paul takes one Corinthian as a representative of them all, one who *has knowledge*, i. e., a specimen of those who hold the opinion laid down in the letter of the church to Paul, namely that sacrificial meat is ordinary meat. The case which Paul describes might very well occur, and although Paul does not imply that this particular Corinthian actually existed, we must assume that the event here described did happen at Corinth. Otherwise Paul's words do not make sense. Today we may hardly be able to imagine that a Christian would go to a pagan temple to eat. Yet the occasion to do so may have been twofold. Paul may have had in view some official ceremony which in a pagan city could not happen apart from a meal in a temple. It is possible that a Christian could not withdraw himself from such a meal. Secondly, the situation here related agrees with the general conduct of the Corinthians. They held that since idols did not exist sacrificial meat was just like ordinary meat and hence a Christian could sit at meat in a pagan temple. Paul does not disapprove of that opinion in itself but he has objections because of attendant circumstances. Nor can we say that Paul approves of the standpoint of the Corinthians. Instead of rationalizing, as the Corinthians did, Paul uses love as his starting point. He poses the question what would happen if a weaker brother saw a stronger brother reclining comfortably at a meal in an *idol's temple* which might be the case whenever such a banquet was prepared in one of the open halls of the temple. The weaker brother will conclude that the eating of sacrificial meat is permitted to every Christian if it is proper for a Christian to take part in a temple banquet. Thus he will be brought to the eating of meat offered to idols. *He will be emboldened*[8] (RSV has "encouraged") : in the original Greek Paul uses a word which he always uses when speaking of the strengthening of one's faith. Here the apostle means that the weaker brother will be induced to the eating of sacrificial meat, not finding any valid reason why he should not, if his prominent brother even dines in the temple. The subject of *"be emboldened"* is not the weaker brother himself but his *conscience*, i. e., his weak conscience (cf. vs. 7). The voice of conscience will no longer have a restraining influence but there will be an inducement to eat. But that, according to vs. 7, is forbidden since the conscience of the weak is defiled by eating. The weaker brother must not follow him who is strong unless he is strong himself. Paul again does not imply that a case such as he mentions had actually happened but he warns that it should

---

[8] οἰκοδομηθήσεται.

not happen. The strong members of the church ought to consider what may be the consequences of their conduct.

11 In vs. 10 Paul asks the stronger brethren a question to which he expects an affirmative answer. This explains the rather strong words Paul uses in vs. 11 where he states what will happen if the stronger brethren do not consider the scruples of the weak. *For,* introducing a causal clause after an interrogative sentence, implies that it is self-evident that the answer to the question will be affirmative. *Perisheth through thy knowledge* implies that Paul calls those members of the congregation weak who lack the right insight into the nature of sacrificial meat and who consequently sin by eating it. But Paul does not endorse the opinions which the Corinthians had expressed in their letter to him. If he had he would have told the strong to go their own way and try to persuade the weak. Paul rather maintains as his opinion that knowledge is not the only thing at stake here. From the strong he asks love and sacrifice. He indicates what the consequence will be for the weak if the strong manifest a loveless conduct. *Perisheth,* i. e., comes to sin. It means: not to show oneself as a Christian. And he who perisheth by the loveless conduct of the strong is no one else than *a brother for whose sake Christ died!* If Christ gave Himself also for a weak brother, shall not the stronger brother have a proper regard for him?

12 *Thus,* i. e., by not regarding the weaker brother for whom Christ died, by *sinning against him, ye sin against Christ,* you regard the death of Christ upon the cross of little value. The strong do not commit anything sinful in itself but it becomes a sin in these particular circumstances. *The brethren:* the strong by their conduct sin against the church as a whole. It is the sin of *wounding the conscience* of believers, for this conscience is thus driven in a direction where the weak brother would not have gone of his own and where he is not permitted to go. The weaker brother sins if he eats meat against his conscience.

13 The last verse gives the conclusion. Paul uses the first person. For Paul himself there is no uncertainty and he hopes that the Corinthians will accept his opinion. He does not give a direct admonition, perhaps because he has done so already in vs. 7. If the Corinthians would heed that admonition they would come to Paul's standpoint. That standpoint is not just a preaching of abstinence in general but only under certain circumstances. *Meat*: here not only sacrificial meat but all food (cf. vs. 8). *To stumble*, i. e., to sin. He who stumbles falls; figuratively speaking, he falls into sin. Meat — Paul is still thinking of the eating of sacrificial meat — may lead a person to sin. A Christian in general may not lead astray his brother because of any food, and since that is so Paul makes a very definite statement concerning his own conduct. The apostle will not eat any *flesh for evermore* if he, by eating, would seduce his brother. The thing of which Paul disapproves especially is the ostentatious eating of sacrifices. Every Christian ought to omit that in order to help his brother. Thus Paul's pronouncement has the force of a strong admonition. Paul himself has shown his life long that he was willing to do and to leave undone all kinds of things in the interest of promoting the preaching of the gospel. That example the Corinthians had to follow.

1-13 Paul combats again the Corinthians' abuse of Christian liberty. There is such Christian liberty, the strong believers are right, but love has to rule our conduct.

CHAPTER IX

PAUL'S EXAMPLE IN SELF-SACRIFICE

9:1-27

1 Am I not free? am I not an apostle? have I not seen Jesus our Lord? are not ye my work in the Lord?

2 If to others I am not an apostle, yet at least I am to you; for the seal of mine apostleship are ye in the Lord.

3 My defence to them that examine me is this.

4 Have we no right to eat and to drink?

5 Have we no right to lead about a wife that is a believer, even as the rest of the apostles, and the brethren of the Lord, and Cephas?

6 Or I only and Barnabas, have we not a right to forbear working?

7 What soldier ever serveth at his own charges? who planteth a vineyard, and eateth not the fruit thereof? or who feedeth a flock, and eateth not of the milk of the flock?

8 Do I speak these things after the manner of men? or saith not the law also the same?

9 For it is written in the law of Moses, Thou shalt not muzzle the ox when he treadeth out the corn. Is it for the oxen that God careth,

10 or saith he it assuredly for our sake? Yea, for our sake it was written: because he that ploweth ought to plow in hope, and he that thresheth, *to thresh* in hope of partaking,

11 If we sowed unto you spiritual things, is it a great matter if we shall reap your carnal things?

12 If others partake of *this* right over you, do not we yet more? Nevertheless we did not use this right; but we bear all things, that we may cause no hindrance to the gospel of Christ.

13 Know ye not that they that minister about sacred things eat *of* the things of the temple, *and* they that wait upon the altar have their portion with the altar?

14 Even so did the Lord ordain that they that proclaim the gospel should live of the gospel

15 But I have used none of these things: and I write not these things that it may be so done in my case; for *it were good* for me rather to die, than that any man should make my glorying void.

16 For if I preach the gospel, I have nothing to glory of; for necessity is laid upon me; for woe is unto me, if I preach not the gospel.

17 For if I do this of mine own will, I have a reward: but if not of mine own will, I have a stewardship intrusted to me.

18 What then is my reward? That, when I preach the gospel, I may make the gospel without charge, so as not to use to the full my right in the gospel.

19 For though I was free from all *men*, I brought myself under bondage to all, that I might gain the more.

20 And to the Jews I became as a Jew, that I might gain the Jews; to them that are under the law, as under the law, not being myself under the law, that I might gain them that are under the law;

21 to them that are without law, as without law, not being without law to God, but under the law to Christ, that I might gain them that are without law.

22 To the weak I became weak, that I might gain the weak: I am become all things to all men, that I may by all means save some.

23 And I do all things for the gospel's sake, that I may be a joint partaker thereof.

24 Know ye not that they that run in a race run all, but one receiveth the price? Even so run; that ye may attain.

25 And every man that striveth in the games exerciseth self-control in all things. Now they *do it* to receive a corruptible crown; but we an incorruptible.

26 I therefore so run, as not uncertainly; so fight I, as not beating the air:

27 but I buffet my body, and bring it into bondage; lest by any means, after that I have preached to others, I myself should be rejected.

1 Paul does not begin a new subject, e. g., that of his apostleship, but he continues his argument, as chapter 10 also shows. He does not defend his apostleship but he explains what his rights are as an apostle and states that he does not use those rights. He does so to summon the Corinthians not to use their

Christian liberty if by using it they would cause their brothers in Christ to sin. *Am I not free?* is meant in a spiritual sense, it concerns Christian liberty, Paul is not bound to the ceremonial law but he is permitted to do all things. Being free in this sense means to be a Christian. *Am I not an apostle?* concerns his office. As an apostle Paul was free to ask many things from the Corinthians. But he did not ask for anything. *Have I not seen Jesus the Lord* is to be understood in the light of the context. It is not certain that Paul ever saw Jesus during his stay at Jerusalem (cf. II Cor. 5:16?). However this may be, Paul does not here refer to the time before his conversion but speaks of his apostolate. Therefore we must interpret this seeing of the Lord by what happened on the road to Damascus. There Paul saw the heavens opened and beheld a glorified Savior. There he was not only converted; he was also called to be an apostle. One of the marks of an apostle is that he must have seen the Lord so that he may be a witness in the full sense of that word (Acts 1:21, 22; Gal. 1:1) and that he may speak the things which Jesus Himself taught him. Paul does have that mark and that is very important to him (cf. 15:8). *Are not ye my work in the Lord?* An apostle must be able to show the fruits of his work, for Jesus gave the apostles a special task and promised His blessing (Acts 1:8). The Corinthian church is the fruit of the work of Paul. But only *in the Lord,* it is not Paul's own work for he worked in the sphere where the glorified Christ rules and dispenses His blessings. The work itself, however, makes Paul known to be an apostle.

2 To a certain extent Paul takes back what he just said. Paul knows that there are some who do not regard him as an apostle. This was not the case at Corinth for there everyone honored him as an apostle. But the Corinthians might have heard a different opinion. This is the reason why Paul could write as he did.

There also is an objective reason why the Corinthians could not deny Paul's apostleship. *They,* themselves, *are the seal of that apostleship.* A seal testifies to the truth of a deed. The Corinthians are the seal attached to the deed of Paul's apostolic office. The fact that there were those at Corinth who had turned away from paganism and had become Christians testifies that Paul is a true apostle. But again Paul adds *in the Lord* (cf. vs. 1). Paul himself shall not boast.

3 When speaking of a *defence* Paul cannot have the intention of defending his apostleship against those who denied it. For the word *this* refers to what follows, not to what precedes. There are those at Corinth who *examine* the apostle, i. e., they evaluate the merits and demerits of Paul's conduct and try him like judges (cf. 4:3). Paul inserts his personal defence into his treatment concerning Christian liberty, using his personal conduct as an example. Again he refers to the Christian's rights. In order to follow his argument we must first consider that at the end of ch. 8 the apostle stated that he would *eat no flesh for evermore* if that would lead his brother into sin. At the beginning of chapter 9 he indicated that such an abstinence would be a sacrifice to him inasmuch as he possessed the same rights every Christian possesses and besides those also the rights of an apostle. And now he is beginning to demonstrate that he has not been using many of his apostolic rights and that he was therefore justified in putting himself up as an example for the congregation. But Paul realizes that he cannot just proceed to demonstrate this. After first reminding the Corinthians that his apostolic power appeared especially at Corinth (vs. 2; cf. 2:4, 5), he must now pay attention to those who examine him, realizing that his conduct can only then be an example for the church as a whole if he defends himself against those who censure it. From this it also appears what those critics thought was wrong with Paul. Apparently it was thought that Paul did not give himself with all diligence to his work. These criticisms may have been of a twofold nature. Perhaps people said that Paul ought to marry just like all the other apostles and that he ought to accept a salary since that would be better for his work. They may also have desired that Paul should show more worldly wisdom. In a word, they may have wished that Paul would be a different man, one who would fit into this world a little more readily. But the opposite is also possible: they may have desired that Paul would be content with less than he asked for. This last assumption is, however, not very probable. In the first place, no one could demand more than Paul had already sacrificed. Secondly;

the apostle argues that, although he has the right to do all sorts of things, he has not used it for the sake of his work (II Cor. 12:16); the Corinthians should refrain likewise! This would also account for the reference to *Barnabas* at this point, who, according to the information available, had never been at Corinth. Barnabas could be used as an example because he also had not made use of his rights. Paul is thinking of the faithfulness which an apostle has to show according to 4:3f. It may very well be that the same persons who favored Apollos above Paul and who appealed to Peter, yea even to Christ Himself, were also censorious of Paul's conduct. But it is impossible to say exactly which one of the parties was guilty of this attitude. Not all Corinthians were guilty for Paul does not direct himself to all the members of the church but only to some. There were also Corinthians who defended Paul, though probably not always in a way agreeable to Paul; at least he makes his own defence. Our conclusion is that in the church of Corinth which was so proud of its liberty there were some who condemned the manner in which Paul used his Christian rights. The remarks which Paul is going to make may thus also serve as a defence against his censors.

4 Paul's question anticipates an affirmative answer:[1] "Have we no liberty?" The Corinthians were convinced that they had that liberty. *To eat and to drink,* without any object. Just like every Christian Paul has the right to eat and to drink everything he likes. That was the point of view Paul held when he treated the question of eating of sacrificial meat in ch. 8. That is what he repeats at the beginning of his defence. Apparently the Corinthians knew very well that the apostle did not eat every food under every circumstance. Therefore they could know also that what Paul wrote in 8:13 was true. In the present verse Paul speaks of his Christian liberty, in the following of his apostolate.

5 The question asked in vs. 5 concerns marriage, at least according to our opinion. The words: *a wife that is a believer* (literally: a sister, a wife[2]) have been interpreted differently. A possible translation would be: "'to take with me a sister that is a married woman," but this translation cannot be right. If Paul

---

[1] μή by itself implies a negative answer but οὐ an affirmative one.
[2] ἔχομεν ἐξουσίαν ἀδελφὴν γυναῖκα περιάγειν.

actually took a woman with him why would she have to be a married woman? She would at least have to be a widow since 7:5 forbids one to think that Paul took the wife of another man. However, the text says *wife* and not "widow." Furthermore, we read nowhere that the apostles were accompanied by married women. We know that Paul did not count on the help of others but that he made a living for himself. These difficulties are avoided if we translate: "*to lead about a sister* as our own wife," i. e., to be married while doing the work of an apostle. The first thing necessary is that this woman be a *sister*. Paul does not ask the right to lead about an unbelieving woman (7:39; II Cor. 6:14) but as Peter was married (Mt. 8:14) so Paul also may be married. *To lead about* refers to the many journeys which Paul had to make.

The apostle then mentions others who did what he has never done, namely taking their wives along to take care of them. Nobody objected to their doing so. *The apostles*: the men who were, like Paul himself, apostles in the technical sense of the word. *The brethren of the Lord*. exactly as in Acts 1:13, 14. We take this to refer to the sons of Joseph and Mary who at first did not believe in the Lord but afterwards were His faithful servants (Jn. 7:5; Acts 1:14; I Cor. 15:7). *Peter* is mentioned separately because there were some at Corinth who venerated him.

6 Vs. 6 shows that the ordinary way for the apostles to receive their subsistence was from the churches, a situation to which Paul had no objection (vs. 7f.; I Tim. 5:18). But he himself, and Barnabas who lived under the same conditions as Paul, did not ask for anything from the congregations. The apostle does not imply that he never received anything from a church but rather that he did not use his right, i.e., he did not ask for anything. Paul, the former Pharisee, worked as they all did to earn a living. To the Greeks, who detested all manual labor, this way of life was very strange.

7 Paul continues to give a series of examples. The normal way is that a preacher receives a salary from the churches in which he works. The first thing a general has to care for is that his soldiers have the food they need, otherwise his army will fall apart. The planting of a *vineyard* presupposes primitive conditions in which the countryman needs all the fruits himself (Deut. 20:6). No one, however, will drink all the *milk* of his *flock,* hence the preposition "of." The main point is that everybody lives off the proceeds of his business.

8 This verse states the grounds for the apostle's contention. The question: *Do I speak these things after the manner of men?* has in view a negative answer. *After the manner of men*: as men commonly take for granted. Divine revelation as it is embodied in the *law* may be of a different judgment. Here, however, human thought and divine revelation agree, which is not at all strange since it is one and the same God who created man and who also gave him His revelation (cf. also Is. 28:24f).[3]

9 *The law of Moses*: these words indicate that God's law and not some Greek law was meant. The quotation is from Deut. 25:4.[4] *Thou shalt not muzzle*: In oriental countries the way to thresh is to have oxen trample the grain with their feet or pull a threshing sledge over it. These oxen were not supposed to be muzzled so that they would have the opportunity to eat from the grain. The question Paul asks in this connection: *Is it for the oxen that God careth?* implies a negative answer. This is surprising in the light of Scripture passages teaching that God does care for the animals (cf. Ps. 104; 147:9, etc.). A commandment to take care of certain animals and to spare oxen while they are threshing is not strange. Yet tne question is legitimate whether the intention of Deut. 25:4 is to speak of oxen in the first place. The words quoted here are taken from a series of warnings concerning human relations. In view of this fact it is not impossible that Paul's application of these words to human relations is not at variance with their original meaning, which is the same as saying that Deut. 25:4 refers to human beings in a figurative sense.

10 This question implies an affirmative answer. *For our sake,* not only for the sake of the apostles and their helpers but for the sake of all men. *Assuredly*: RSV has a better rendering: "entirely," i. e., in every case. God's precept was given with a view

---

[3] Note that in the Greek the first interrogative is μή, the second οὐ. The second clause expects an affirmative answer.

[4] The Greek has here a variant reading. Some MSS have φιμώσεις following the LXX; the best witnesses have κιμώσεις. Either reading gives essentially the same sense.

to man. The clause introduced by *"yea"* states the reason why Paul expected an affirmative answer and the clause with *"because"* contains the ground. *Ought* does not refer to a natural necessity but rather to a duty which everyone has on the basis of the divine institution. God ordained that seed should bear fruit. Plowing must be a plowing *in hope*, i. e., he that plows must do his work in the hope that it will not be useless. Here again human practice agrees with the divine law. All plowing is done in hope. Yet this is an important link in Paul's argument for by using "ought" he implies that there is a duty to expect a reward upon one's labors. *Hope of partaking*: the threshing is a more advanced stage of the work than the plowing, hence this hope of partaking of the fruit. To *partake*: the word expresses the idea that the thresher expects to eat of the fruits himself together with others.

11 Vs. 10 concluded the argument that every laborer must earn his wages from his own labor. In vs. 11f., Paul defends his conduct, namely that he in distinction from others whose conduct he does not criticize, did not ask for any remuneration for his work. This is still a further elaboration of his statement made in 8:13. Paul grants that the Corinthians are right if they expect their teacher to do what their philosophers did, namely to receive an honorarium for their instruction. But he points out that for the sake of the gospel he did not make use of his right and refrained from asking any payment. Paul speaks here of his own work in figurative language in close connection with the figure of speech used in the preceding verses; only he uses two words not used before.[5] *Spiritual things*: the things of the Spirit of God, of which the Corinthians had not heard before. Those things Paul had brought as seeds rich in germinating power which bore fruit afterwards. Of those fruits he has a right to eat. There are two conditional clauses here: the first one expresses an established fact, the second contains a statement of what the apostle could have done but did not do.

What are the *carnal things* when compared with the *spiritual?* Paul says that after having given spiritual seed he certainly had

---

[5] *If*: the clause is a realis. Paul is firmly convinced that he and his helpers were the ones who sowed spiritual things. The second clause with εἰ comes close to an irrealis.

the right to receive carnal fruits. "Carnal" is not here identical with "sinful." The contrast is one between the heavenly and the earthly, or between the spiritual and the material. The Corinthians possessed those carnal things and they owed some part of them to Paul.

12 *Others* does not refer to Paul's opponents, for Paul seems to find no fault with what these "others" did. On the other hand, the sentence is not hypothetical either, for then it would not have any conclusive force. Apollos may very well have belonged to these "others" as also all other preachers who had preached or were still preaching at Corinth. The present tense and the plural person of *"partake"* point to a whole group. But all of them have come after Paul (4:15), which is the point of the argument. Paul views this right, which the teachers have of asking the Corinthians for an adequate remuneration, as one whole. in which each individual teacher has a share. Not as if each would only have a certain part of this right but rather that everyone has full right. Paul, who is the spiritual father of the church, has this right without any doubt but he did not use it. We may assume that others did use it by receiving living expenses. The clause with *but* indicates what the apostle did, and also, though indirectly, points out why Paul did not use his right. *We bear all things,*[6] i. e., Paul endures all things, and part of this attitude of endurance is to forego the right of using his right. The apostle refers to a conscious manner of acting: he could have acted otherwise but he chose to act this way. Paul's answer to the Corinthians who may have desired that Paul would act like the other teachers is that he did not want to do so because he wanted to avoid even the appearance of seeking to enrich himself through his preaching. The apostle does not want to *cause* any *hindrance to the Gospel of Christ* (II Cor. 6:3). He is fully aware that the gospel would be more easily accepted if he did not ask for payment but would rather suffer all things. This shows that Paul himself fulfilled the requirement of faithfulness posited in 4:2. *Of Christ*: Christ is the one who proclaims the gospel as well as being its contents.

13 Vs. 13 contains some further grounds for Paul's contention. The words *Know ye not?* imply that these grounds are solid. In

---

[6] Greek: στέγω, i.e. to cover by keeping silence.

the realm of temple-worship the rule that everyone shall live off his work is valid. *They that minister about sacred things*: not only the priests of Israel but all priests. These words are very general and it is not until vs. 14 that the commandments of the Lord are referred to. *The things of the temple,* namely: the *altar,* i. e., the sacrifice. Thus the last clause defines the first. To Paul it is entirely natural that the Christian ministers, like the priests in all religions, should receive their portion from the altar.

14 This universal practice is also according to Christ's own command. The apostle does not appeal here, as he does in I Tim. 5:18, to an explicit statement of the Lord, but he assumes that the Corinthians will have this in view. It is remarkable that Paul does not give this word of the Lord in the form of a commandment to the congregation but rather to the preachers of the gospel: they shall live of the gospel. Thus the point which is at stake here, namely the rights of the preachers, is enhanced. The fact that Paul is able to found this right on a well known commandment of Christ is important.

15 Vs. 15 Paul states what he himself did. He did not use his right. Thus he repeats vs. 12 and this repetition is necessary. For the contents of the preceding verses must serve to make the Corinthians understand the significance of what Paul has stated in vs. 12. Paul did not use[7] any of the prerogatives of gospel preachers.

Paul's first task is to prevent a misunderstanding at this point. Writing to the Corinthians required special care. Paul points out that he does not mean to speak of his rights in order that the Corinthians, seeing in how many things he had been wronged, would want to supply his shortage. If the Corinthians really thought that it would have been better if Paul had accepted support from the congregation, then it was doubly necessary for him to explain what he meant. That is why he states emphatically that his words must not be taken as a subtle attempt to secure financial support.[8]

---

[7] Greek: κέχρημαι in the perfect: the action is completed and its consequences retain their significance until the present.

[8] ἔγραψα: epistolary aorist. Paul is writing at this moment. ἐν ἐμοί: for me.

The following few words are difficult. The majority of modern interpreters assume here an anacaluthon. Then Paul, moved by the vivid impression of the manifold experiences he had while with the Corinthians, does not finish his sentence in a normal way. Instead he inserts an exclamation which interrupts the normal sequence of the words. The apostle says that it is *good*, i. e., ethically good, for him *rather to die than* to accept any remuneration for his work. Paul would prefer to die rather than to use his right. For by preaching without receiving an honorarium Paul guarded himself against suspicion and was able to accomplish much. There is an occasion for glorying here. Paul boasts of his conduct and he wishes to make sure that no one should *make void* that occasion, i. e., that he should modify it to such an extent that it would no longer exist. These words of the apostle point out again that the Corinthians were not unwilling to do something for Paul, but that he himself refused to ask or to accept anything. There might seem to be a contradiction between the way Paul speaks of his glorying and his words in Gal. 6:14. This is only so in appearance for it will soon appear that the occasion of Paul's glorying is not anything he himself performed but only the progress of the gospel.[9]

16 *For*: This clause contains the ground for the last words of the preceding verse, as is also clear from the repetition of the verb *to glory*. *For if I preach*: the context compels us to supplement: "like all the others," i. e. accepting living expenses. In that case Paul has no occasion to glory. For preaching is an obligation to him, there is a *necessity* from which he cannot withdraw himself. Paul does not speak of his duty, but of the necessity which is laid upon him. This may refer to the act whereby God called him to the apostleship (cf. Gal. 1:1f.; Phil. 1:16). The third clause with *"for"* states what will happen if Paul does not preach. That would mean a *woe unto* him. God has left man the liberty to resist a divine necessity. Paul could also have resisted if he had chosen not to preach. But that would have brought the judgment of God upon him.

---

⁹ We have followed the text of Nestle as does RSV. The Greek underlying the ASV reads: καλὸν γάρ μοι μᾶλλον ἀποθανεῖν, ἢ τὸ καύχημά μου οὐδεὶς κενώσει.

17 Verse 17 also begins with *for*. Paul approaches even closer to the ordinary realities of life. He now states his last ground which is the starting point of his argument. It is something of which he is completely convinced since it is a daily reality to him. *This*: the preaching of the gospel. The apostle must preach. If he does this preaching with all his heart, and so he does, then he has a *reward*. The question whether this is a reward of God's grace is not relevant to the subject treated (see vs. 18). Here it is Paul's purpose to intimate that he does not seek his reward in the receiving of financial compensation although he could do so, but in something quite different. *I have* implies that Paul has in mind a reward which he receives during his work. Parenthetically as it were Paul indicates under which circumstances he could not count on receiving a reward. That would be the case if he did not preach of his *own will*. *If not of mine own will*: supply "I do this." These words in vs. 17 refer to Paul's state of mind while he is engaged in preaching. *Stewardship* (cf. 4:1)[10] we take here of the task the Lord committed to Paul. That work continues regardless of the way in which Paul performs his task and it bears fruit. It does not matter in what frame of mind the apostle preaches, provided he preaches. However, the case is hypothetical since the apostle does his work with joy.

18 The following things have now been established: 1) that there is a reward for Paul in case of voluntary service, 2) that the apostle does not look for this reward by soliciting gifts of the congregation, and 3) that the apostle actually has a reward. namely in his occasion for boasting (vs. 15). The question quite naturally arises: *What then is my reward?* The answer is, that I in *preaching the gospel make the gospel without charge. So as not to use,*[11] i. e., so that, etc. The question of vs. 18 is answered, completely answered, by: *I may make the gospel without charge.* No other purpose needs to be stated. But since Paul is discussing his right he states one more fact which touches on it. Of Paul it can be said that he does not use his rights fully. And he summons

---

[10] οἰκονομίαν πεπίστευμαι, perfect. Paul refers to a completed action. Today he has his stewardship.

[11] Greek: εἰς τὸ μὴ καταχρήσασθαι. εἰς τό may have a final as well as a consecutive sense. We prefer the latter on the basis of the context.

the Corinthians to make his conduct their example. Paul's reward is not that he receives something. For that reason he could refer to his "glorying" in vs. 16; for that reason also he could omit an indication that his reward was one of grace (cf. vs. 17). The work itself is Paul's reward. And this is so because he only receives his reward if he is willing to do the work the Lord has committed to him. This willingness enables Paul to preach without remuneration. To be able to do just that is such a joy to him that he regards it as his reward. His reward consists in living in the consciousness that through his work the gospel can be heard everywhere freely. Of this reward, which must be distinguished from a future reward (3:12), the apostle states that he has it already (vs. 17).

The apostle has thus returned to his starting point. Paul does have a certain liberty but he does not use it to the full[12] for that would be abusing it and it would hurt the progress of the gospel (cf. vs. 4 and 5). These words of Paul are parenthetical in nature but they give us a deep insight not only into the soul of the apostle but also into his apostolic work.

19 After having thus returned to his self-sacrifice for the sake of the gospel the apostle continues to treat this point, giving new arguments of a more general nature. *For* has a summarizing force: all the preceding things could be said because the following facts are known to everybody. *Paul is free from all men,* that is his objective condition. He does not depend on anyone, not even for his sustenance. When he became a Christian he did not avoid the Jews and he overcame the initial distrust of the Christians. We must remember that Paul is still speaking of his liberty which is not unrestricted. He is not free from the law of God as he will soon affirm emphatically. The main point here is that he has maintained the liberty which he possesses generally speaking. There is a little shift of meaning between the word "free" in vs. 1 where it stands for complete Christian liberty, and the same word here, where it refers to an objective fact which Paul is able to assert because he has not used the liberty of vs. 1. *I brought myself under bondage* indicates what Paul did on his own, perhaps without being observed by others (II Cor. 4:5). That is his subjective condition, that is what he has done

---

[12] καταχρήσασθαι.

while being free. He became a bondslave to all in order to win them for Christ. *The more*:[13] probably Paul has in mind the many sorts of people with whom he came in contact through his missionary labors. Hence the enumeration of different kinds of people which follows. Thus *"the more"* may be the majority of the peoples which he reached by his preaching.

20 As everywhere else Paul begins this enumeration with the Jews. Although called to be an apostle to the Gentiles Paul never directs himself to the Gentiles before first fulfilling his obligation toward the Jews. The book of Acts shows us the meaning of *"a Jew to the Jews."* Paul is free from the ceremonial law through the work of Christ but he does not consider it a sin to observe the law, provided this was not done to acquire righteousness. To what extent Paul practiced this maxim may be known from passages like Acts 16:3, relating the circumcision of Timothy by Paul (cf. also 18:18, if that does not refer to Aquila) and 21:23f. Paul may also have observed the Jewish Passover (Acts 20:6). If Paul, who was the author of Gal. 5:2f and Col. 2:11 and 12, nevertheless performed the rite of circumcision, it is possible that he observed the Mosaic law also at other points. But we cannot determine precisely what Paul's conduct was. Certainly, this observance of the law cannot for Paul have been anything more than an accommodation to certain circumstances in order that he might win the Jews and avoid being a stumblingblock for his compatriots. The difference between *"the Jews,"* the whole nation, and "Jews," some of that nation, should be noted. *Not being myself under the law*: this implies that Paul remained inwardly free, accommodating himself only to special circumstances.

The question might arise why Paul, writing to the Corinthians who were Christians from among the Gentiles, speaks of the Jews instead of the Greeks as he does in Rom. 1:14. The answer is that to Gentile Christians no better proof could be given of Paul's accommodating spirit than by pointing out that he for the sake of his missionary work subjected himself to the difficult Jewish laws although he was free from them (Acts 15:10). *Law* in this context is the Mosaic law (cf. vs. 21). They *that are under the*

---

[13] Greek: τοὺς πλείονας, i.e. the majority.

law are those who are actually subject to the law of Moses and who observe it. That expression was readily understood by Gentile Christians since to them the Jews were a remarkable people with strange customs. The Jews are under obligation to observe the law because God commanded them to do so. With a view to such people Paul has imposed restrictions upon himself. Yet he was not bound to obey the law, he obeyed it voluntarily.

21 *They that are without the law* are the Gentiles. The latter had their own law to be true, but here the reference is to the law of Moses. Paul describes the condition of the pagans in relation to the Old Testament law. To the Gentiles Paul is *without law*,[14] not because he is actually without any law, but because he is accommodating himself to the conduct of those who are not bound to the Mosaic law. At this point a misunderstanding could arise, for the Gentiles not only refuse to be subject to the Mosaic law but also reject any commandment of the true God. With Paul this is different, therefore he adds: *not being without law to God but under law to Christ. Under law to Christ* is more important than *not being without law to God.* Paul is not only subject to God as God's creature, but, having been redeemed by the blood of Christ, he is also subject to his Saviour (7:22). As an apostle also he is a servant of Christ. This clause is of particular practical importance for the Corinthians who were seekers of freedom (II Thess. 2:8). *That I might gain*: this continues the main thought of the argument.

22 By referring to the *weak* Paul approaches the actual situation in Corinth. In that city there were some who could not eat sacrificial meat without burdening their consciences. Paul writes: *To the weak I became weak that I might gain the weak.* Paul did therefore what the stronger brethren at Corinth refused to do. Although agreeing that the strong are basically right he nevertheless refrains from using his right in order to win the weak. The difficulty which arises here lies in the fact that thus far the word "to gain" could be taken to mean: "to gain for Christ," whereas the weak cannot be gained for Christ since they

---

[14] Greek: ὡς ἄνομος (cf. vs. 20 ὡς Ἰουδαῖος, ὡς ὑπὸ νόμον ὡς). indicates the subjective condition: Paul is not actually without law but he is so in the opinion of the gentiles.

already are Christ's. This makes it necessary to give a different sense either to "to gain" or to "weak." In view of the fact that Paul for the sake of the weak respected their scruples and became weak with them, it is better to modify somewhat the meaning of "to gain." The same word "to gain," which the apostle uses throughout in this context, is here used in the sense of seeking the spiritual welfare of a person. But this is subordinate to the main thought, which is to gain for Christ. The following summary bears that out: *I am become all things for all men, that I may by all means save some.* Paul's conduct is clearly expressed by this thrice repeated "all." He was willing to help all men, with the obvious restriction only of the point made in vs. 21.[15] *Some,* not all, although Paul does all he can (cf. *the more* vs. 19, and Rom. 11:14). If the Corinthians will have to admit the truth of what Paul writes here, then the words of 8:13 will also appear to be anything but vain boasting.

23 Paul does *all things for the gospel's sake,* i. e., for the sake of the preaching of the gospel. The apostle's goal is to partake of the gospel, i. e., to partake of the effect of the gospel, of that which is propounded in the gospel, namely salvation (cf. Rom. 11:17; Phil. 1:7). Thus Paul returns to vs. 18. Paul's lot is not the worse for devoting himself to others. On the contrary, by his labor for others he makes spiritual progress (cf. vs. 16, also 3:15). Paul has his own salvation in view. The importance of this thought is emphasized in an elaborate figure of speech whereby the apostle not only exhorts the Corinthians by his example but also speaks of his reward so that he might show them that by following in the right way they will receive the grace of God. This accounts for the personal touch of the following words. It should be borne in mind that the apostles point the way not only by their preaching but no less by their walk. Their conduct, therefore, has normative force.

24 Paul begins his figure with a rhetorical question. It is a matter of course that the Corinthians agree with him. *They that run a race:* the well known Isthmian games, which were held in the neighborhood of Corinth may have induced Paul to the use

---

[15] οἱ πάντες, the whole; γέγονα, perfect, indicating the permanent result, the abiding attitude.

of this figure. The common thing is that all racers run but only one receives *the prize*. In Greece the prize awarded to the champions did not consist of money or objects of art but of a wreath. All the racers desired was to obtain the honor.

The following words seem to imply that there is a special running for the prize. This is remarkable in view of the fact that in a race all try to attain the prize. However, we may account for Paul's way of writing when we keep in mind that the Corinthians did not exert themselves; they were indolent. They might run in the arena but it was not a running for the prize (Gal. 5:7). Hence the necessity for Paul of pointing to his own example which was one of true Christian living (vs. 26). They all must run to get the prize.

25 *Striveth*, in the present tense, refers to the race as a whole: every one who is in the *race*. *Exerciseth self-control*, i. e., trains himself by doing or taking nothing that would harm. The first clause of vs. 25 must be taken both in a figurative and in a proper sense as is shown by the following words. Starting out figuratively the apostle makes a distinction later which enables him to set forth an additional thought. Earthly runners struggle for a wreath that withers after a short time.

26 Linking his remarks with what he wrote at the end of vs. 25 concerning Christians in general, Paul now sets forth what he does himself. He exerts himself as is his duty. The apostle is not driven by pride but by the realization that also by his example he has to edify the church. The figure he uses may be applied to him in the full sense of the word. The running of Paul himself will be recognized as a running for the prize, a running with full exertion. *Fighting* was one of the games of the Greeks. In that game *beating* must be striking; blows in the *air* are of no use. Thus Paul indicates that he labors with all his power.

27 After vs. 26 has dealt with Paul's action vs. 27 mentions his exercise of self-control. Paul *buffets*[16] his own body. The word "to buffet" is closely akin to "to fight, to beat" (vs. 26), but bears a different character. It does not mean that the apostle engages in a fight with himself but rather that he beats his body.

---

[16] Greek: ὑπωπιάζειν, to deliver a blow in that part of the face which is under the eyes; to beat black and blue.

I bring it into bondage: the apostle refers in strong language to his training. Just as an athlete keeps his body under control so does Paul in order that he may live as a true Christian. The word "body" is here used figuratively: Paul does not only aim at mastering his body but also his spirit. His great antagonist is sin, which always drives him in the wrong direction (cf. Rom. 7). Paul does not refer to fasting and bodily chastisement but to his struggle against sin. And the apostle summons the Corinthians to do the same.

In his final words Paul also refers to his apostleship. It is that apostleship which compels him to preach the gospel and to train himself as a Christian. Knowing the way of salvation so eminently himself, he makes a special effort to go that way that he *should not be rejected*, i. e., to be one of those who did not stand the test of God (3:13f.; 4:4f.). As previously (vs. 23) Paul brings in the matter of his own salvation. Paul's life is a unity: his apostolic work as well as his Christian life concern his whole personality.

1-27 This chapter bears out the great significance of the use of our Christian liberty. Chapter 9 bears a very personal character. Nevertheless it is of general interest. Paul could not have shown our vocation with respect to Christian liberty any better than by means of his own conduct (cf. 4:6).

CHAPTER X

THE EXAMPLE OF ISRAEL

10:1-13

1 For I would not, brethren, have you ignorant, that our fathers were all under the cloud, and all passed through the sea;

2 and were all baptized unto Moses in the cloud and in the sea;

3 and did all eat the same spiritual food;

4 and did all drink the same spirtual drink: for they drank of a spiritual rock that followed them: and the rock was Christ.

5 Howbeit with most of them God was not well pleased: for they were overthrown in the wilderness.

6 Now these things were our examples, to the intent we should not lust after evil things, as they also lusted.

7 Neither be ye idolaters, as were some of them; as it is written, The people sat down to eat and drink, and rose up to play.

8 Neither let us commit fornication, as some of them committed, and fell in one day three and twenty thousand.

9 Neither let us make trial of the Lord, as some of them made trial, and perished by the serpents.

10 Neither murmur ye, as some of them murmured, and perished by the destroyer.

11 Now these things happened unto them by way of example; and they were written for our admonition, upon whom the ends of the ages are come.

12 Wherefore let him who thinketh he standeth take heed lest he fall.

13 There hath no temptation taken you but such as man can bear: but God is faithful, who will not suffer you to be tempted above that ye are able; but will with the temptation make also the way of escape, that ye be able to endure it.

1 Seemingly the apostle in chapter 10 treats a different matter from that of the preceding section. Further on, however, it appears that he still deals with the eating of sacrificial meat (cf. vs. 25f).

Another difficulty is found in the fact that according to some expositors Paul seems to hold a much stricter view in I Cor. 10:1-22 than in I Cor. 8 and 10:23f. In I Cor. 10:1-22 Paul is said to forbid all eating of sacrificial meat as idolatrous; in the rest of his epistle he is supposed not absolutely to condemn such eating.

We suggest that the solution to this alleged difficulty be found in the following direction. So far the apostle had warned the strong Christians especially. Since Paul counted himself among the strong he could urge others to see in him their example. But in chapter 10 Paul turns to the weak believers. Those Christians, when eating sacrificial meat, actually ate it as meat offered to idols, and were therefore guilty of idolatry. Hence Paul's warning against idolatry. The church was a Christian church which had rejected idolatry. But in that church there were some, the weaker brethren, who by eating sacrificial meat reverted to idolatry. Eating sacrificial meat against the voice of one's conscience makes one an idolater.

This explains also Paul's reference to the ancient Israelites. Israel had been richly blessed by God but through its sins it merited the judgment of God. Paul mentions a case of idolatry, although it is not an example of pure idolatry, inasmuch as the worship of the golden calf was image worship, a sin against the second commandment. But with that image worship an idolatrous feast was connected (cf. vs. 7, also I Sam. 15:23). The worship of the golden calf may have been a return to the Egyptian type of idolatry (Lev. 17:7). Using the example of the golden calf as a parallel Paul is able to designate the eating of sacrificial meat on the part of those whose heart is still in the past as a case of idolatry, in the same way that calf worship by the Israelite people must be viewed as a case of rebellion and apostasy from the Lord.

If vs. 7 shows that Paul is here addressing the weak, his words nevertheless have meaning for others as well. *For* in 10:1 connects this chapter with the preceding pericope, the point of which was that an abuse of our Christian liberty may result in our rejection. 10:1 implies that that statement was not too strong inasmuch as the subsequent words point out that the Israelites also forfeited the grace of God. They did not do so, however, by abusing their Christian liberty. This proves again that Paul is addressing the weak in the first place, for the sin of the weak was not that they abused their liberty but that they ate against their own conscience. Thus vss. 1-12 form a transition, indicating the various grounds on which the preceding statements rest, but only in so far as they intimate that grace may be forfeited. At the same time these verses begin to warn the weak. Going on beyond that we may say that this warning against idolatry is a warning to the weak; the warning against fornication is connected with an abuse of liberty, not as concerns Israel but as concerns the Corinthians.

I would not have you ignorant, a litotes, which always introduces an important matter. The same is indicated by *"brethren."* A new subject is now introduced. Paul addresses himself to the weak. *Our fathers* cannot be meant of carnal descent, for Corinth was a Gentile Christian church as also appears from the antithesis which Paul draws between the ancient Israelites and the Corinthians. *Fathers* is to be taken in a spiritual sense therefore. The ancient Israelites were the fathers of the Corinthians because they were the people of God in the old dispensation. This unity is the reason why the apostle can admonish the Corinthians by reminding them of Israel's history. That is the general significance of this pericope: it shows how that which God did to Israel is of importance for the church of Christ in every age. Paul records some facts of the wilderness journey, particularly those facts which show the great mercy of the covenant God. And the way Paul writes emphasizes very clearly — witness the use of the word "all" which is repeated five times — that all the Israelites shared the same privileges but that they did not all enjoy the grace of God. (cf. vs. 5; also Mt. 3:9f). That this is also the case under the new dispensation a church like the one in Corinth, with its great pride, should know. That pride was evidenced not only by the strong but also by the weak. The latter would boast of

219

being the true people of God. They too should take care lest they sin; abstinence which is not justified may lead to godlessness, or — and that is what Paul seems to have in mind here — to boasting. That boasting of being the true people of God may bring them to actions that are sin *for them*, either by following in the footsteps of the strong or by doing things themselves which they condemn in others. Of that Rom. 2:17f gives an example. There Paul describes the Jews, who were weak in that they considered many things prohibited and yet did them themselves.

The first privilege Paul mentions is *that our fathers were all under the cloud*: the apostle has in view the pillar of cloud which led Israel on the way (Ex. 13:21). All Israelites enjoyed that favor of God. Even so when they passed through the Red Sea there was no distinction between believers and unbelievers: the entire nation safely reached the other shore.

2 Vs. 2 does not confine itself to purely historical facts but it interprets these facts by pointing out that the Israelites received something more than external things. *Were all baptized unto Moses*: the word "to baptize" in the N. T. may be used in the general, non-technical sense of "dipping." To baptize unto Moses means to immerse in Moses, i. e., to bring in close relationship with Moses. Paul uses this expression figuratively; the immediate occasion for this figure is the passing through the Red Sea. Moses is called by the Lord to lead Israel (Ex. 3:10). The Israelites, by following Moses' leadership and by passing behind Moses through the Sea which separates them forever from Egypt, have thus been joined to him forever and are compelled to follow him from henceforth. That is what Paul's words mean that they are immersed in Moses by[1] the cloud and by the sea. The whole nation shared in the gifts of God which He in Moses gave to His people.

3-4 Vss. 3 and 4 go still further. The apostle alludes to the eating of the manna and the drinking of the water from the rock. Those facts are not mentioned in so many words, Paul rather speaks of *spiritual food* and *drink*. For "spiritual" see 2:10f; 12:1 and 15:44. Here "spiritual" implies that the manna and the miraculous water were not of the natural order of things. In Paul's letters all manifestations of the grace of God in this

---

[1] Greek: ἐν with a local sense.

sinful world are spiritual (pneumatic) since they are manifestations of the Holy Spirit (cf. Gal. 4:29). At the creation the Spirit of God brought all things to their perfection. In the work of recreation it is again the spirit of God through whom things are perfected. Thus the miraculous bread and the miraculous water which were used to represent the salvation worked by Christ (Jn. 6:31) are pneumatic, spiritual. That made the enjoyment of them such a great privilege: God revealed Himself in them.

Paul states again that all Israelites in exactly the same way enjoyed the benefits of God (*all the same*). *Spiritual* is not used in this sense in the Old Testament. Seeking to clarify the use of the word here the apostle does not try to explain the reason why he uses the term nor what its contents are but he points to the spiritual background of this episode as a justification for his terminology. This interpretation rests upon the assumption that *the spiritual rock that followed them* is to be taken figuratively, i. e., the word "spiritual" in this clause does not apply to the rock from which Israel drank (Ex. 17). Arguments in favor of this position are: 1) The clause with *"for"* refers to the drinking only, not to the eating. If the rock had to be taken in the proper sense and the water in a spiritual sense since it flowed from a spiritual mountain, then Paul would have had to explain also why he called the food spiritual food. The fact that Paul does not do this shows that the reason why he calls the food and drink spiritual lies in the fact that wherever Israel went there was a spiritual background behind everything it received. This truth is described figuratively in terms of a drinking from a spiritual rock. 2) The second reason which prompts us to take this expression figuratively is found in the words: *the rock was Christ.*[2] Christ was the spiritual rock that followed and from which Israel drank. The benefits enjoyed by the people are spiritual because they came from Christ. Christ was the rock from which the people drank, not only at Meribah but everywhere, because that rock never forsook the people but followed on all its ways. Thus the apostle describes the significance of the work of Christ for Israel under the old dispensation in terms of water flowing from

---

[2] The Greek has two articles: ἡ πέτρα δὲ ἦν ὁ Χριστός, which serves to identify the rock with Christ.

the rock. Christ is the source of all blessings. He makes those blessings spiritual blessings.

Three things thus stand out: 1) the entire nation received the benefits of God; 2) those benefits had a spiritual character; 3) those benefits came from Christ. The apostle has now established two things: first, that we must distinguish between an enjoyment of the genuine benefits of God and a continuance in God's favor till the end (cf. vs. 5). Second, Paul has made it impossible for the Corinthians to say that all those things only applied to old Israel but that they no longer applied to them in the new dispensation. By recording past history the apostle is able to show that God punishes sinners more clearly than by direct admonition.

5 Vs. 5 presents the other side of the picture. Benefits, enjoyed by the people of Israel, do not mean that God's pleasure rests on all its members. God's gifts had for their purpose to lead Israel to Canaan but that goal was only reached by some. Paul writes this in order to warn the Corinthians so that they might take his admonition to heart. *Most of them,* the greater part. Those words do not refer to personal salvation; that point is not under discussion here. The subsequent words make clear that the expression: *God was not well pleased* refers to the fact that God, though granting His blessings to the entire nation at the beginning of the wilderness journey, in the end gave that kind of blessings to only a few. This makes the contrast the greater and the warning the more sincere. Nearly all of those who departed from Egypt died in the desert (Cf. Num. 14:16). This teaches us that it is possible, when God begins to grant His covenant blessings to a certain group of people, that some of that group do not share those blessings. God makes His covenant with a people but according to His inscrutable will not all those who belong to that people enjoy the blessings acquired by Christ. It should be noted that Paul does not speak of a loss of the gift of regeneration or salvation. That point is not in view here. Paul deals with the life in the congregation without speaking of the motive force behind that life. The main point of this pericope is the outward manifestation of that life. That is why Paul refers to the outward blessings Israel received.

6 *These things*: the facts mentioned in the preceding verses, and at the same time the entire history of Israel, especially the wilderness journey. *Example*: cf. our word "type" (Rom. 5:14). The Israelites actually existed and experienced the things Paul mentions. But the meaning of those things was that they should teach the people of all the ages. They contain a message for us (*cf. our example*).

Lust after evil things: a very general expression, covering all the sins forbidden by the tenth commandment. It includes the fully developed desire but also its first inception (cf. Jas. 1:15). *Evil* is used in an ethical sense. Paul had every reason to go right down to the root of all sinning in this letter to Corinthians who suffered from spiritual pride. *As they also lusted*: this points to the very core of Israel's sinful acts (Num. 11:4, 35). This same root sin is found at Corinth as it was formerly found in Israel.

7 This verse deals with certain concrete sins, especially those of which both the Corinthians and the ancient Israelites were guilty. In Israel's history the Corinthians could discern the coming of God's judgment. The first sin the Israelites and also the Corinthians committed was the sin of idolatry. The worship of the golden calf, which in itself was image worship, is treated here as a case of idolatry, since image worship is the first step to idolatry. The absence of any reference to the worship of Baal is remarkable. Paul may have preferred to choose his examples from the time shortly after Israel's exodus from Egypt in order to make a greater impression on the Corinthians who had recently become Christian. Besides, both in Corinth and at the time of worship of the golden calf, the idolatry was indirect. *Some of them*: not all the Israelites worshipped the golden calf nor did all the Corinthians eat sacrificial meat. The quotation from Ex. 32:6 again surprises us. Do those words actually prove Israel's idolatry? They do if we keep in mind that these words describe the high point of Israel's sin, namely the festivities after the offering. Apparently the people rejoiced in the celebration. Besides, the question at Corinth was also one of the meal after the offering. This made Israel's example so much more pertinent for the Corinthians.

8 Fornication was one of the special sins of the Corinthians Often fornication follows upon the debauchery of a sacrificial repast. It is no surprise that Paul uses the fornication of which some (Num. 25:5) of the Israelites were guilty as an additional ground for admonition. Apparently Paul has in mind the people's sin with Baal Peor, a case of idolatrous fornication (Num. 25). The tone of the warning is softened, as Paul does more often, by the use of the first person (*let us* etc.). The apostle records that there died on one day *three and twenty thousand*, but the O. T. lists four and twenty thousand as do Philo and Josephus. There are more of such small numerical differences, which we cannot always explain. Paul, the former Pharisee, knew the Scriptures. The main thing is that Paul describes a case of sin and consequent punishment which is applicable to the Corinthians.

9 This is also done in vs. 9. *Neither let us make trial of the Lord* to the end.[3] This sin consists of doing evil with the purpose of seeing what God's reaction will be. *To make trial* implies a formal evaluation of a particular sin. Even if there is no express intention of doing evil, still the character of a certain sin may be described as making trial. To a certain extent every sin is such a "making trial." Israel repeatedly made trial of the Lord (Num. 14:22; Ps. 95:9). In our verse, as the words themselves indicate, the reference is to Israel's murmuring described in Num. 21:5. It is true, the Old Testament does not call this a making trial but rather a speaking against God. Paul rightly qualifies this speaking against God as a making trial of Him. The Corinthians' pride, their abuse of Christian liberty, their glorying in their knowledge, all that is, well considered, a making trial of God.

10 Vs. 10 refers to Israel's repeated murmurings. There is an anti-climax in the enumeration: Paul mentions the most serious sin first. This verse may refer to the return of the spies (Num. 14), or, according to others, the rebellion of the company of Corah (Num. 16), cf. *some, destroyer*. The latter word occurs only here in the Greek[4] and refers to the destroying angel. If Paul has Num. 14 in mind the implication is that the plague

---

[3] Greek ἐκπειράξωμεν.

[4] ὀλοθρευτής. The Masoretic text of Num. 14:37 speaks of a plague, the LXX has πληγή, but in Exod. 12:23 the LXX reads ὁ ὀλεθρεύων (cf. Heb. 11:28). Paul must have followed Ex. 12:23.

recorded in Num. 14:37 was caused by an angel sent by God. The difference between Num. 14:2, which states that all the children of Israel murmured, and vs. 37 which records that the plague came upon the spies only, Joshua and Caleb excepted, must be explained by the abridged character of Paul's rendering of the familiar story. Paul does not refer exclusively to the murmuring of the spies. Thus the words *"some of them"* form the transition between the entire nation which wailed and lamented and the spies who died. Taking the murmuring of Corah's rebellion, the "destroyer" referred to may be found in Num. 16:30. It is difficult to determine which episode is meant, although there may be slight preference for the former of the two. The Corinthians, moreover, may have known very well what Paul had in mind which would be the case if "the destroyer" referred to a particular judgment. What is at stake is that the attitude of the Corinthians was like that of the murmuring Israelites.

11 Vs. 11 is very important for the understanding of the Old Testament. Not only does Paul refer back to vs. 6 (*by way of example*), but he also mentions the recording, the inscripturation of sacred history, i. e., he speaks about the Scriptures.[5] *These things*: the things mentioned; we are in the realm of history, cf. also: *happened*. Israel's history has a typical sense, i. e., there are real events, but those events also have a meaning for a later generation. This is seen more clearly at this point than in vs. 6 since Paul has pointed out by means of several examples how the facts of Israel's history had significance for the Corinthians. Those facts are important *for* the *admonition* of the believers of the new dispensation (cf. Rom. 4:23; 15:4).

Our admonition: to warn us, *upon whom the ends of the ages are come.* Paul indicates who the persons are whom he has in view. His words do not concern only the Corinthians but all those who live after Christ's incarnation. Hence our reference to the church of the new dispensation. The singular: *age* (aeon) means the world as it exists in time, the world in course of development, a period including the people who belong to that period. There may be more than one of such "ages," the one

---

[5] Note συνέβαινεν ἐκείνοις: the Israelites are related to the Corinthians and yet they are far off.

after the other or parallel with each other. Each one of these "ages" may reach its normal end. Paul is here writing to gentile Christians who according to vs. 1 call the ancient Israelites, to whom they are spiritually related, their fathers. There are therefore at least two ages for the Corinthians, two independent worlds of religion and culture, each of which have reached their proper conclusion. Israel came to its end and so did Greek paganism with its restless search. Paul does not limit himself to the Corinthians but speaks in general terms. That is exactly the reason why he can speak of *ages* (plural). As often as a nation comes in contact with the gospel, an age finds its end. Hence the plural: *the ends. Are come*: the ages hasten to their conclusion and that conclusion has reached us, i. e., it happens within our time. We find ourselves in a different age, on the borderline, so to say. Paul apparently agrees that the ends of the ages have come but he nevertheless maintains that the facts of Israel's history were types. The Corinthians cannot get away from the Old Testament (cf. 4:6).

12 *Wherefore,* i. e., since these things are so, and since the Corinthians have seen clearly how the ancient Israelites fared and have understood the warning which that contains for them, they should take care lest they meet with a similar judgment. *Him that thinketh*[6] *he standeth* correlates with *some* in vs. 7f. The people as a whole remain the people of God. But it is possible that a member of that people does not share the blessings which the people enjoy. At Corinth there were many who thought they stood and who determined their conduct starting with that assumption. They made bold to do all kinds of things since they were Christians and had Christian liberty (cf. 6:12f.) But they forgot not only that they had to reckon with their brethren but also that they themselves could not do many things without suffering harm. Israel's history bears this out. Since Paul uses this history typically in this chapter, the words "to stand" and "to fall" must be understood in a spiritual sense, i. e., of eternal salvation. The new dispensation does not know of merely external benefits of the church as the people of God. Paul warns the

---

[6] ὁ δοκῶν not "he who seems," but "he who thinks," because Paul refers to the opinion someone else has about him.

Corinthians and all who like them live in the new dispensation not to deceive themselves (cf. Rom. 11:20).

13 The preceding admonition is especially necessary when danger threatens. Such danger does exist, namely temptation. The Greek word[7] has a double meaning: trial and temptation. A trial comes from God who wants to purify His children, a temptation comes from the devil to seduce the people to sin. In our verse there is a twofold reference, both to trial and to temptation, as the context bears out. The words *hath taken you* imply that there was a certain temptation which had captured the Corinthians and which subdued them. *Such as man can bear*: Paul comforts the Corinthians by pointing to the nature of the divine temptations. In vs. 12 the apostle had spoken of things which were new to his readers and must have disturbed them, now he comforts them. The circumstances they meet with are temptations, such temptations, however, as befall all men, all Christians. Moreover, *God* is faithful, which is the third consolation.

Does Paul have any concrete facts in view in speaking of temptations? The only thing which might point in that direction is found in vss. 6-10. In those verses the apostle gives instructions regarding the sins into which the Corinthians could easily fall because of their surroundings. How easily could they entertain evil desires, eat sacrificial meat when their consciences forbade them, practice fornication or have a spirit of pride. These pagan surroundings offer a real temptation for the believers. For that reason Paul writes: *God is faithful*. He who called the Corinthians will also watch over them (cf. 1:8, 9).[8] The Corinthians will not succumb. The content of this verse does not militate against vs. 12. Scripture ever calls upon man to do those things for the performance of which God gives the strength. The Christian must lay hold on that for which he also was laid hold on by Christ Jesus (Phil. 3:12). God does not suffer the temptation to become too heavy, because He is our Father and also the Almighty One. He *will with the temptations also give the way of escape*. Here "temptation" means trial rather than temptation, in the full sense of the word. The future tense shows that the

---

[7] πειρασμός

[8] ἐάω not "to cause," but "to suffer." Paul does not make God the author of the temptation.

temptation is an active power which is continually working. But
every time it comes God gives the *escape*. The escape is that the
Christians *are able to endure* the temptations. That is why they
cannot fall. The temptation does not leave them but it is conquered.

1-13 The preceding pericope shows us the apostle's ability to
base a series of general remarks on a treatment of concrete difficulties. By drawing lines to the ancient Israelites he is able to
point out the unity of the people of God of all the ages. It is not
only the Corinthians that are thus admonished, we all see the
significance of ancient Israel for the church of Christ of all times,
in other words, we see the significance of the Old Testament for
the new dispensation.

ADMONITIONS AGAINST IDOLATRY

10:14-22

14 Wherefore, my beloved, flee from idolatry.
15 I speak as to wise men; judge ye what I say.
16 The cup of blessing which we bless, is it not a communion of the blood of Christ? The bread which we break, is it not a communion of the body of Christ?
17 seeing that we, who are many, are one bread, one body: for we all partake of the one bread.
18 Behold Israel after the flesh: Have not they that eat the sacrifices communion with the altar?
19 What say I then? that a thing sacrificed to idols is anything, or that an idol is anything?
20 But *I say*, that the things which the Gentiles sacrifice, they sacrifice to demons, and not to God: and I would not that ye should have communion with demons.
21 Ye cannot drink the cup of the Lord, and the cup of demons: ye cannot partake of the table of the Lord, and of the table of demons.
22 Or do we provoke the Lord to jealousy? are we stronger than he?

14 The apostle begins to admonish the weak. *Wherefore*: just because of this. The Corinthians could learn from ancient Israel that God does not leave sin unpunished and besides, vss. 12-13 imply that the exhortation, given in vs. 14, can be carried out through the faithfulness of God. *My beloved*: these words are used not only because something new is introduced at this point but especially because the congregation should know that even the preceding admonitions were inspired by love. Nobody should think it insulting when he, being a Christian, is warned against idolatry. Paul is obliged to write as he does. His warning is directed in the first place to the weak, who were guilty of idolatry whenever they acted against the voice of their conscience in eating sacrificial meat. Secondly, however, Paul also addresses the strong in so far as they, by compelling the weak to eat meat offered to idols, were also guilty. In view of this it is not strange

229

for Christians to be warned against idolatry; cf. I Jn. 5:21, where idolatry is related to not believing that Jesus is the Christ and to love for the world. *Flee from* implies a staying away from something as far as possible. One should not first introduce idolatry to condemn it afterwards, but rather avoid every connection with it. The present tense points to a continuation. The weak should not eat any sacrificial meat. The strong ought to abstain because of the weak and also in order to avoid becoming an idolater himself by causing others to sin (cf. II Cor. 6:14f; Jude 23b). When the Christian's attitude is as is here described, he will not fall into temptation.

15 In vs. 15 we have a different type of admonition. Paul submits the eating of sacrificial meat against one's conscience, as was done by the weak, to their intellectual judgment. They should decide for themselves whether it is possible for a Christian to eat sacrificial meat against his conscience and at the same time sit at the Lord's table. That this is the correct interpretation is shown on the one hand by the fact that Paul in this context speaks of a drinking of the cup of demons and on the other by the fact that the context make clear that eating sacrificial meat as a sacrifice is a case of conscience (8:7; 10:25, 28). *Wise,* here intelligent,[9] is the man who considers things in a calm manner. Paul's assumption is that the Corinthians are such people, as is indicated by the word *"as."* Whether the Corinthians are actually wise is not stated, Paul simply assumes that they are. The Corinthians must have agreed to Paul's words. According to their own opinion they were wise and therefore quite willing to listen to Paul and also to *judge* his words.

16 Vss. 16f. refer to the Lord's Supper, as a comparison with 11:23f. clearly teaches. The thing that should be kept in mind from the outset is that the apostle does not give an exposition of the meaning of Holy Communion. On the contrary, he starts with the fact that the congregation observes that ordinance, that it accepts its significance and that for that very reason the *wise* will *judge* that the eating of sacrificial meat is incompatible with the sitting at the Lord's table. Keeping that in mind we will not deduce from the fact that Paul mentions the cup first, that this must have been the precise way communion was celebrated so

---

[9] φρόνιμος

230

that the bread was given after the wine. The reason why Paul in this context mentions second the eating of the bread is that this enables him better to draw a comparison with the eating of meat offered to idols.

The cup of blessing: that particular cup, known everywhere, and set aside from other cups by the *blessing*. *Blessing*: the Greek word[10] denotes "eulogy," "benediction." The Jews used to pronounce a benediction when they drank from a goblet. So they did when eating the Passover. There are some difficulties at this point but in any case the cup of the Holy Communion received such a special benediction (cf. Mt. 26:26f; I Cor. 11:23f). This benediction contains a thanksgiving for the fact that God has given the cup. Just because this eulogy is a thanksgiving to God and does not say anything as such about the cup, Paul proceeds and writes: *which we bless*. Those words do not refer to something distinct from the benediction, they simply imply that every time, through our benediction of God as Christ has prescribed it, the cup becomes a special cup. It is also possible to take *"blessing"* of the eulogy to God and *"we bless"* of a special word, connected with that eulogy and constituting the cup as the cup of Holy Communion. Perhaps this last interpretation is the best because of what we read in 11:24f. The apostle points expressly to the sacred act which is done by and in the midst of the congregation. That act in itself is inconsistent with the eating of meat offered to idols. The rhetorical question: *is it not,* etc., expects an affirmative answer from those who are *wise*. *Communion* is to be explained in the light of the context. Paul, in connecting a cup with the blood of Christ, wishes that to be understood spiritually: the apostle speaks of a cup rather than of the drink in that cup: more important is the character of the cup and of the blood. The nature of the connection cannot be deduced from the word *communion*, neither are we here primarily concerned with that question. The only purpose of the apostle is to deduce from the connection between the cup and the blood of Christ the incompatibility of sitting at the Lord's table and eating sacrificial meat as meat offered to idols. It should be borne in mind that the shed blood and the broken body of Christ do not exist anymore. *Communion*, therefore, cannot refer to a mystical connection

---

[10] εὐλογία

with an existing thing or an existing person, e. g., the risen Lord. Bread and wine speak of Christ's sacrifice. The connection between the cup and Christ's blood is in that respect indissoluble. Holy Communion does not bring the congregation in contact with Christ, for the church is Christ's body, but Holy Communion signifies the connection with Christ's suffering and death. Paul implies that the Christian, because he partakes of the Lord's Supper, is in connection with the death of Christ. The apostle apparently presupposes a certain act on the part of the believer. Only if the cup is drunk in faith is there communion with Christ.

No mention is made of the bread being blessed. This is probably omitted not so much because the bread was not actually blessed but because Paul wanted to write something else about that holy bread, namely that it is *broken*. If the bread was not broken it could not be distributed as this should be done with communion bread. The connection between wine and blood is much more apparent than between bread and a body. Hence the breaking of the bread. Christ did not use meat but bread. It should also be noted that both here and in other places wine and bread are not mentioned side by side, neither are the dish and the cup, but rather the cup and the bread. This requires a different treatment of each. The description of the sacrament is not abstract but graphic. The minister holds in his hands the bread and the cup, not the dish or the wine. The word *body*, in distinction from "flesh," contains the thought of unity; it refers to an organism. The breaking of the bread is a sign of Christ's suffering upon the cross. If the word "flesh" had been used here it would have been less appropriate to mention the blood, since the flesh contains the blood. As things are, there is on the one hand a reference to the shedding of the blood, signifying a violent death and on the other to the destruction of the body.

Our Lord is called *Christ* because His suffering is viewed as His official work, as an act of propitiation, which again implies that His people are called upon not to have communion with anything that is foreign to Him. The person who drinks from the cup and eats the bread has a spiritual communion with the fruits of the work of the risen Lord. For that reason it is im-

232

possible to sit at the Lord's table and at the same time to eat sacrificial meat with a burdened conscience.

17 The combination of the various parts of vs. 17 presents some difficulties. One possible translation is: For one is the loaf (bread), we, who are many, are one body. Another translation is: Because the loaf (bread) is one (or: because there is one loaf (bread), we, who are many, are one body.[11] The latter translation is the best in view of the fact that the former translation leaves open the question as to the causal connection between this verse and the preceding. It is, on the other hand, quite natural to assume that Paul after mentioning the breaking of the bread also refers to its unity. That this bread is the bread of Holy Communion does not have to be indicated here. Just as the loaf, before it is broken, is a unity and remains a unity even after it is eaten since all pieces have the same quality and the same origin, so also is the congregation one, because it is one body although consisting of many members. *One body;* here not the body of Christ, for the apostle does not speak about that point, but rather of the organic unity of the congregation. The ground of that unity is not that all are members of Christ, but that all *partake* of the same bread. The two causal clauses,[12] one before and one after the words: "we who are many are one body," are practically parallel with each other. The former refers to the unity of the loaf, i. e., it demonstrates that unity, the latter mentions the partaking of the loaf, in close conjunction with the words: *we; who are many.* The latter clause gives special emphasis to *"all"*: Although there may be many, they all partake of the same bread.[13] Each member eats a piece of the loaf and in that way partakes of the loaf in its entirety. The rendering: to partake of the one body on account of the one loaf, must be rejected for what Paul

---

[11] ASV: seeing that we, who are many, are one bread, one body. This is very unclear, neither is it correct. Better with RSV: "because there is one loaf, we who are many are one body."

[12] Greek: ὅτι εἷς ἄρτος...οἱ γὰρ πάντες; RSV: because there is one loaf . . . for we all.

[13] οἱ πάντες and οἱ πολλοί because the words are in apposition with a personal pronoun implied in the verb. Certain expositors prefer to distinguish between μετέχειν: "to possess a part of the whole" and κοινωνεῖν: "to have a connection with the whole." The words are however used interchangeably.

233

wishes to do is to prove the unity of the body by means of the unity of the loaf.

The question why Paul brings up this point of the unity of the congregation somewhat parenthetically must still be answered. Perhaps in vs. 17 Paul wants to point out, in spite of the fact that he is directing himself mostly to the weak, that the church is a unity after all, as is clearly demonstrated at the Lord's table and that for that reason his words are important for the stronger brethren as well. The latter may not eat sacrificial meat against their conscience; their eating of it may not be incompatible with the sitting at the Lord's table. Yet it is better if they, for the sake of the weak, and, in some respects, also for their own sake, refrain from eating such meat.

18 Vs. 18 takes up the main point of the argument, which is the admonition of the weak. By calling their attention once again to ancient Israel the apostle points out not so much the judgments of God as the connection between the sacrifice and him who eats of it. *After the flesh*, i. e., the apostle does not refer to that Israel which is an example for the church of God at all times (cf. Gal. 6:16), but he rather mentions certain facts which follow from Israel's ceremonial laws which are now abolished. The rhetorical question here used anticipates an affirmative answer (cf. vs. 16). *They that eat the sacrifices*: not only the priests are meant, for there were sacrifices from which the offerer also ate (cf. Lev. 7:15, 16). The animal becomes a sacrifice when it is put on the altar (Mt. 23:19). This accounts for Paul's words: that there is *communion with the altar* through the eating of sacrificial meat.

19 This reference to the communion of the ancient Israelites with their sacrifices had to serve to point out the communion with idols which is obtained through the eating of sacrificial meat. This element, the second part of this argument, was introduced by vs. 18. In vs. 21 the two parts meet and the conclusion is drawn. In vs. 19, before drawing a parallel between the sacrifices of Israel and pagan sacrifices, Paul seeks to prevent a misunderstanding. Vs. 18 had spoken of a real communion, based on God's own ordinance, the communion with the holy altar which God had commanded Israel to build. The Corinthians might think that Paul considered the communion between a pagan offerer and his idol to be of the same nature as that in Israel, thus attributing a real existence to the demon. The fact that he wishes to prevent this accounts for his strong terminology. It should be remembered that there was no clearcut demarcation between the theogony and the cosmogony of the Greeks. The myths of gods and heroes had their place in national history. The Greeks, upon becoming Christian, found it hard to abandon all those stories and they continued to maintain the existence of those gods and heroes. Paul has no zeal to strengthen them in that error. Everyone will know that he himself does not believe in the existence of idols. *What say I then?* Although Paul had not actually made any statement concerning idols everybody could understand what was implied in vs. 18. Paul states in so many words that an idol is nothing, i. e., it does not exist. The Corinthians argued the same way (cf. 8:4f.). However, those were words of the stronger brethren and Paul had deemed it necessary to point out that the weak did not yet see those things clearly. The weak basically believed that idols did exist so that sacrificial meat to them was a special kind of meat. This part of the letter being addressed more particularly to the weak, a clear statement on the part of Paul is necessary: there are no idols. The solution which Paul is going to offer will not take the standpoint of the weak for its starting point.

20 *But* is short for "I do not contend that idols exist, but I do contend etc." The verb *sacrifice* does not have a subject. The Corinthians knew that Paul had none other in mind than the surrounding Gentiles. *To demons,* the absence of the article makes the expression more abstract.[14] The fact that the Gentiles did not bring their sacrifices to the one true God was clear in itself. Therefore we must translate: *to a god,* and not: *to God.* The absence of the article before *god* is conclusive proof of the correctness of this translation. The implication of all this is that we must not think of these *demons* as actually existing evil spirits but as the powers of darkness in general. Another argument in favor of this interpretation is the fact that Paul clearly refers to Lev. 17:7 in the Septuagint; a passage which mentions the things

---

[14] The Greek not only lacks the articles with δαιμονίοις and Θεῷ, but it also uses the word δαιμόνιον instead of δαίμων, the former being more abstract.

235

that are vain and nonexisting. Dt. 32:17 is quoted literally (cf. also Ps. 106:37). The apostle apparently has in mind the situation as it prevailed in Israel. The people deviated from the law of God and sacrified to demons, who are "nothings" according to Ps. 96:5 (ASV: idols). So do the Gentiles at Corinth; worse yet, they sacrificed to evil powers. Paul does not want the Corinthians to become partners with idols. By this he means the evil spirits about which he wrote, as the use of the article bears out. There is not the slightest intimation at this point that sacrifices would ever be brought to particular and actually existing idols, much less that such pagan idols would really be demons as the church fathers read this passage. True, mention is made of evil powers to whom the pagan sacrifices were directed, but no personality is attributed to them. *To have communion with demons* does not mean to be companions of the idols but rather to be partners of, to belong to, the world of the evil spirits, to be connected with the powers of darkness. That is the horrible character of idolatry and that is the reason why we should flee from it (vs. 14).

21 The last words of vs. 20 virtually contain already an application of Paul's discourse on sacrifices to idols. But the full application is given in vs. 21. Here the two parts of his argument are joined together. After the general exhortation: *Flee from idolatry*, v. 14, Paul had begun to discuss the communion established in the Lord's Supper and after that the communion established through the sacrifice to idols. In vs. 21 he asserts emphatically that those two are wholly incompatible and he may assume that now everyone agrees with that assertion. It is Paul's purpose to keep the weak from committing idolatry, i. e., from the eating of sacrificial meat, and to exhort the strong to be prudent. Paul proceeds upon the assumption that after everything he has written the congregation will recognize the absurdity of desiring to have communion with Christ through the Lord's Supper and to have communion with the evil spirits through pagan sacrifices. There is no communion between Christ and the idols; those two exclude one another. Greek literature uses the word *"table"* also of pagan altars. The thought behind that was that the offerer pictured himself as sitting at a table with the idols during the sacrificial meal. A view different from

236

this is one which conceived of the idols partaking of the flesh which was offered. The Corinthians were familiar with such views, which makes Paul's argument a very strong one.[15] Not as if there would not be any difference between *the table of the Lord* and *the table of demons*. The latter is a sacrificial meal, the former is a meal to which the glorified Lord invites His people to remember His death (11:25). But that does not affect the matter of communion and of partaking as such. One table symbolizes communion. There is a kind of parallelism in this verse. First the *cup* is mentioned as part of the meal, then the whole *table* on which the whole meal rests. This repetition strengthens the argument.

22 One other possibility is that one would silence his conscience and so eat of the sacrificial meat. This may have occurred out of a misplaced feeling of shame, for Paul calls it a *provoking of the Lord,* i. e., an arousing of His jealousy. (cf. *let us make trial* vs. 9). The person who would eat sacrificial meat without having renounced idols completely would be an idolater and arouse God's wrath (Is. 42:8). The positive thought contained in Paul's question is that the Corinthians will not have such a desire, simply because Christians in general do not desire such a thing. Here is another quotation from Dt. 32, this time vs. 21 (LXX with some changes as the context demanded). Because this is a quotation the word *"Lord"* is to be taken of God, not of Christ. The quotation serves to point out which sin the weaker brethren commit when they eat sacrificial meat.

Then follows the question: *Are we stronger than He,* namely God? If it is impossible to serve God and the idols at the same time we should not think that we can conquer Him. This is not an invitation to make a choice; the apostle assumes that the Corinthians have chosen already. His purpose with these questions is that they should do nothing against their choice which they made previously. Thus they will recognize the gravity of their sin.

14-22 By calling the eating of sacrificial meat against one's conscience idolatry and by pointing out the incompatibility of sitting at the Lord's table with the eating of a sacrificial meal,

---

[15] Cf. my *De Eerste Brief van den Apostel Paulus aan de Kerk te Korinthe* (KNT, Amsterdam, 1932).

this section points out the seriousness of the sin of the weaker brethren when the latter eat sacrificial meat. This eating is a religious question. This is not a question of causing a brother to sin, but of committing sin personally. Along with chapter 8, ch. 10:1-22 presents a new treatment of the point under discussion, this time for the benefit of the weak. This was necessary, for besides the ones who gave offense there were also those who took offense. If all the believers at Corinth had been strong the whole argument of ch. 8 would have been superfluous; the presence of the weaker brethren was its only reason. But if that is so one could a priori expect Paul to treat the question for the benefit of the weak as well. Paul points out that in these questions of Christian liberty there are also weaker brethren and that the latter sin grievously if they allow themselves to be seduced by the strong. The strong sin likewise, when they do not consider the possibility of abusing their liberty due to a lack of love.

PRACTICAL RULES ABOUT IDOL-MEATS

10:23-11:1

23 All things are lawful; but not all things are expedient. All things are lawful; but not all things edify.

24 Let no man seek his own, but *each* his neighbor's *good*.

25 Whatever is sold in the shambles, eat, asking no question for conscience' sake;

26 for the earth is the Lord's, and the fulness thereof.

27 If one of them that believe not biddeth you *to a feast*, and ye are disposed to go; whatsoever is set before you, eat, asking no question for conscience' sake.

28 But if any man say unto you, This hath been offered in sacrifice, eat not, for his sake that showed it, and for conscience' sake:

29 conscience, I say, not thine own, but the other's; for why is my liberty judged by another conscience?

30 If I partake with thankfulness, why am I evil spoken of for that for which I give thanks?

31 Whether therefore ye eat, or drink, or whatsoever ye do, do all to the glory of God.

32 Give no occasion of stumbling, either to Jews, or to Greeks, or to the church of God:

33 even as I also please all men in all things, not seeking mine own profit, but the *profit* of the many, that they may be saved.

11:1 Be ye imitators of me, even as I also am of Christ.

23 In the preceding verses Paul addressed himself primarily to the weak. But that was not the main thrust of his argument. That is why he once again takes up the point, treated in ch. 8, thus concluding this section dealing with the eating of sacrificial meat with a concrete precept for daily use and with an exposition of the general principles which should rule a Christian's life. The main point was that there were some at Corinth who abused their Christian liberty by regarding it as a general principle for their actions and who did so also in the matter of eating sacrificial meat. To this point Paul now reverts by quoting once again the slogan which the Corinthians used (cf. 6:12). Again Paul admits that that slogan is right, but again he also offers two restrictions which serve to demonstrate that no one can permit his life to be ruled by the slogan *all things are lawful*. The first limitation is the same as that of 6:12: not all things are useful. The only distinction is that in 6:12 the apostle had in view the profit of the possessor of Christian liberty, here the profit of the brother (cf. vs. 23).

Not all things edify adds something new, although 8:1, 10 also mentioned the point of edification. *To edify* is to cause to advance spiritually. Paul uses the word always of causing some one else to advance. The meaning of the word is similar to "to be expedient." Both verbs imply that it is not only necessary to ask what one may do, but also to consider the effect of such an action upon some one else. Every Christian has to consider his brother (cf. Rom. 14:19; 15:2).

24 Vs. 24 sets forth this same demand as a general principle. *No man*: no member of the congregation. *The neighbor*: everybody God puts at my side, another member of the church. *Seek*: here used of an intensive seeking. Thus Paul makes love the principle of man's every action. This is a general principle according to which the Christian has to use his liberty.

25 Speaking more concretely the apostle now indicates how the Corinthians had to act. This he can do after he first has pointed out what the implications of this great principle are for the strong (ch. 8) and for the weak (ch. 10). Both know what they have to do. That is why Paul can now link up the statement of the general principle with some practical admonitions. The first one of these is: *whatsoever is sold in the shambles eat, asking no question for conscience' sake.* In order to understand these words we must keep in mind the conditions at Corinth. Every animal that was killed was a sacrifice inasmuch as the butchers burnt at least a few hairs of every animal they slaughtered by way of a sacrifice to the gods. Furthermore, the priests, who received their portion of the sacrifices, often had more than they could use and so they sold a part of their portion in the meat market. It could therefore happen quite easily that a Christian, who went to the market to buy meat, received sacrificial meat. If that meat was really

different from any other meat, or if there were no Christian
liberty (as the Jews asserted, Acts 10:14), then the Christian
would have to abstain religiously from any such meat, yea it would
be better for him if he did not buy any meat. But such an attitude
need not to be taken, as Paul already pointed out.

The words: *asking no questions* may be taken in two ways.
They may be connected with "for conscience' sake" and then the
implication would be that a scrupulous investigation would not be
necessary. To examine something on account of the conscience
means to inquire in order that the conscience will not be violated,
to prevent one from acting against the voice of his conscience. But
if the words: *asking no questions* are combined with *eat* then Paul
meant to say that one should eat without further examination. The
words: *for conscience' sake* would then come at the end of the
clause and their meaning would be that if a person would inquire
he might find out that his conscience was violated and that experience Paul wants to spare his readers. The difference is not great
but the latter interpretation best fits the context. What Paul is
saying is that they must go their own way for the Christian is free.
And should it appear later that they had eaten sacrificial meat, they
still would not have committed any sin.

26 In order to demonstrate that, Paul quotes Ps. 24:1 in the
Septuagint. *For*: the chief purpose of the verse is to indicate that
no examination is necessary. The whole earth and everything that
fills it is of the Lord, i. e., everything the earth produces stands in
exactly the same relationship to God: it is His (I Tim. 4:4). At
the creation already God gave the whole world to man (Gen.
21:28). Through sin it became necessary that Israel, as a separate
people, should abstain from many things. But Christ set aside
those commandments, the whole world is Christ's (Mt. 28:18).
This means that the Christians, who rule with Christ over all
things (3:23), may freely use them (Rom. 14:14, 20). But they
must use them according to the law of God.

27 However, it may also occur that not only he who buys or
uses sacrificial meat comes in touch with it, but also someone else.
This brings up not only a metaphysical question concerning what
sacrificial meat actually is, but also the ethical question concerning
my behavior with regard to that other person. In such a case the
rule of vs. 23 must be applied: not all things are expedient, not all

241

things edify. Vs. 27 mentions one case of this kind. A Christian may be invited by an unbeliever, i. e., by a pagan. Of course, every Christian has pagan relatives and friends. He is under no obligation to break off his relations with them (5:9f). Now, if such an invitation is made, the Christian may accept, if he cares to go,[16] and he may apply the rule: eat, without asking questions.

28 Vs. 28 mentions a case that may arise when the conditions of vs. 27 are fulfilled. It might happen at such a dinner in the house of a pagan that somebody would say to the Christian: *This hath been offered in sacrifice.* Paul has in mind a pagan or a weak brother saying this.[17] What should the guest do? A pagan might say this to a Christian to warn him, knowing that idols are an abomination to him. He might also do it to embarrass the Christian and to see what he would do. In such a case the Christian ought to confess his faith and abstain from such sacrificial meat. An other possibility is that a weak Christian, wanting to keep his brother from sin, warns him that that is sacred meat. In that case the Christian should also abstain from eating, this time in order not to violate the conscience of the weak brother. In any case: *eat not, for his sake that showed it,* i. e., on account of the other. The principle of vs. 23 and 24 must now be applied, and the Christian liberty may not be exercised. The whole thrust of Paul's argument throughout is that the other person, especially the brother, shall not suffer any harm. In the light of this the man who says: *this has been offered,* is most probably a weak Christian, not a pagan. But the other possibility must not be excluded altogether. For would a weak brother be found in the house of a pagan? Or could he know that some meat was sacrificial meat?

At the end of the verse we read: *and for conscience' sake.* This *conscience* cannot be the conscience of him who eats, for in the preceding verses the ground for not eating was sought not in the person himself but in others. It must therefore be the conscience of "him that showed it" or of someone else. This separate mention of the conscience by Paul is remarkable. He had already mentioned the other person, now he mentions his conscience.

---

[16] "And ye are disposed to go": perhaps Paul means: you are considering the advisability of going, with a view to possible difficulties.

[17] It is noteworthy that Paul speaks of εἰδωλόθυτον whereas the pagan calls it ἱερόθυτον.

This he does with the purpose of placing this matter on a higher plane. A Christian need not allow his liberty to be curtailed by somebody else. But he is obliged to take care that that other person does not fall into sin and if he would hurt that other person's conscience he has not fulfilled that obligation. By adding: *for conscience' sake* the words: *for his sake that showed it* are interpreted. Just because "he that showed it" has a conscience, must he be respected.

Indirectly this also bears upon what we wrote earlier concerning the identity of the man who says: this hath been offered. The addition of the words: for conscience' sake, substantiate the view that this man was a weak Christian and not a pagan. This also prepares the way for vs. 29 and 30 where the weak are in view.

29 Vs. 29 makes clear that the *conscience* which was meant in the preceding verse was that of him who spoke to the guest, at least it was the conscience of *another*.[18] This also does full justice to the contrast: *not thine own — the other's.*

The rhetorical question of the second half of vs. 29 must serve to prove that Paul gave his precept for the sake of another. Now the apostle uses the first person. *My liberty* (cf. 9:1), i. e., the right which I as a Christian have to use all of God's gifts. (vs. 26). The conscience of another should not judge that liberty. The fact that the one may have objection to the eating of sacrificial meat has no significance for another who is strong. The conscience of the strong need not feel burdened just because the conscience of the weak is burdened. On the contrary such a conscience remains free, whether the person eats or does not eat. This means therefore that the strong is not obliged to abstain

---

[18] ἑαυτοῦ presents some difficulty. It is not necessary to take it in the sense of the classical σεαυτοῦ for although the use of the plural ἑαυτῶν for the first, the second and the third person has been established, this is not the case with the singular ἑαυτοῦ. We should keep in mind that in vs. 28 Paul speaks in the plural but that in vs. 29 he no longer directs himself *to* the Corinthians but speaks in the singular *concerning* them. ἑαυτοῦ may very well have the meaning: someone himself. The apostle would then mean: I do not have in mind the conscience of the person himself, i.e. of him who eats, but rather of the other, namely of him who warns not to eat sacrificial meat, or of him who cannot attend the meal.

from sacrificial meat for his own sake, although he may be obliged to do so for the sake of the brother.

30 *Thankfulness,* cf. *thanks* at the end of the verse,[19] is not grace but gratitude. Paul speaks of a *partaking* of something, i. e., of food, with gratitude to God. Although a Christian be in the house of a pagan and eat meat offered to idols, yet he thanks God by whose grace he has received that gift. And if Paul eats with thanksgiving to God, if he eats with a prayer in his heart, he need not be concerned about the calumny of others who reproach him for eating without having a right to it. Paul, like every other Christian, may do what he likes to do, he is free in his conscience and he does not need to abstain from any food. That is the Christian liberty in theory, which must be distinguished from its practice. In the words: *why am I evil spoken of,* which must refer to what the weak did, we hear an indirect warning to the weak to recognize this Christian liberty in principle and not to offend the strong in the latter's relation to God.

31 Thus the apostle, in a very practical manner, has expounded how a Christian has to act in the matter of meat offered to idols. From 8:1 it appears that the Corinthians had asked Paul to write to them what their attitude should be concerning this point and that question has now been answered. But going on from that point Paul issues a general admonition by way of conclusion, thus linking his words to the immediately preceding which also spoke of a general maxim. Entering into the realm of principles Paul recognizes two: the glory of God and the well-being of one's fellow man. Whatever man may do let him seek the glory of God. Since the context mentioned the matter of eating it is also mentioned first in our verse, before the drinking. *Do all:* this is the general conclusion and at the same time the basic principle that must rule the whole life of God's children (Col. 3:17). It should be noted that Paul seeks to promote the glory of God in the ordinary things of life. It is precisely in that realm that the law of God must govern our entire life.

32 The consequence of this love toward God is and must be love to the neighbor. That love will not in the last place manifest itself herein that one should not cause his neighbor to sin. This makes it necessary to impose upon oneself a voluntary limitation

---

[19] Χάριτι...εὐχαριστῶ.

244

of the exercise of Christian liberty for the sake of the brother. This is the second admonition, the one which Paul really intended to give, and which can be viewed in its right light only after we are first admonished to seek the glory of God. *Give no occasion of stumbling.* RSV has: give no offence,[20] i. e., do not place a stumbling block in anybody's way over which he might trip. Not only in the matter of food, which after all is only one of many cases. Paul now utters a general principle, using his treatment of the question of sacrificial meat as a basis. The reference to *Jews, Greeks* also points to the general character of this remark. Instead of limiting himself to the brethren as he had done hitherto, with the exception of vs. 28 where a pagan may have been meant, Paul now takes account of the total environment of the Corinthian believers. They have to reckon not only with the members of the *church,* the church in general, but also with *Jews* and *Greeks.* They are obliged to try to convince everybody (cf. vs. 23: expedient, edify).

33 Again Paul speaks of his own conduct (cf. the exposition of ch. 9). We repeat that this is not Pharisaism, but that the apostles know that they have to do their missionary work not only through their preaching but also through their example. *Even as I also please all men in all things:* this is as comprehensive as is possible. As far as Paul is concerned, he tries to please everybody in every respect. Paul need not make it clear that he does not mean the pleasing of men. For in the first place his conduct is also governed by the rule of vs. 31. The context shows that Paul does not have his own profit in view, as that is the case with those who are man pleasers in the bad sense of the word. Paul, on the contrary, is thinking of *the many,* i. e., the majority. That which Paul seeks to obtain for the majority is *that they may be saved.* That is clear enough. In passing it should be noted that Paul does not imply that this majority comes to salvation.

11:1 The Corinthians should act as Paul himself does. Not that the apostle points to his own example as such, but he asks the Corinthians to be his *imitators* because he himself is an imitator of Christ. In his own life he shows what Christ requires of His servants. That is very important for the subject at stake here. The

---

[20] ἀπρόσκοποι...γίνεσθε is in the present tense, and so applies always.

Scriptures never ask to imitate Christ without adding some qualification. They ask us to follow Christ in His bearing of the cross, in His gentleness, in His offering Himself for the brethren (Mt. 10:38; Jn. 13:15; Phil. 2:5; I Pet. 2:2f). Christ gave His life for His people (8:11). Then we must be quite ready to seek the well-being of our brother, even if that implies not using a part of our Christian liberty.

10:23-11:1 This section is important not only because Paul teaches very concretely how we must act, but especially because he mentions the two great principles which ought to rule the Christian life as a whole and therefore also the use of Christian liberty. Other parts of the Scriptures (e. g., Gal. 5:1, 13; cf. I Pet. 1:16) warn against the abuse a Christian might himself make of his liberty. All things shall promote the glory of God. In our context the restrictions concern the welfare of the neighbor and are consequently much farther reaching, which made it necessary for Paul to recommend a very particular line of conduct.

CHAPTER XI

THE VEILING OF WOMEN

11:2-16

2 Now I praise you that ye remember me in all things, and hold fast the traditions, even as I delivered them unto you.

3 But I would have you know that the head of every man is Christ; and the head of the woman is the man; and the head of Christ is God.

4 Every man praying or prophesying, having his head covered, dishonoreth his head.

5 But every woman praying or prophesying with her head unveiled dishonoreth her head; for it is one and the same thing as if she were shaven.

6 For if a woman is not veiled, let her also be shorn; but if it is a shame for a woman to be shorn or shaven, let her be veiled.

7 For a man indeed ought not to have his head veiled, forasmuch as he is the image and glory of God; but the woman is the glory of the man.

8 For the man is not of the woman; but the woman of the man:

9 for neither was the man created for the woman; but the woman for the man:

10 for this cause ought the woman to have *a sign of* authority on her head, because of the angels.

11 Nevertheless, neither is the woman without the man, nor the man without the woman, in the Lord.

12 For as the woman is of the man, so is the man also by the woman; but all things are of God.

13 Judge ye in yourselves: is it seemly that a woman pray unto God unveiled?

14 Doth not even nature itself teach you, that, if a man have long hair it is a dishonor to him?

15 But if a woman have long hair, it is a glory to her: for her hair is given her for a covering.

16 But if any man seemeth to be contentious, we have no such custom neither the churches of God.

2 This is the beginning of a new section. And not only that, it is introduced in a special manner. The familiar phrase: *concerning the things*, which might make us think that Paul was again treating certain questions which the Corinthians had asked him, is not used here, a fact which is the more remarkable because chapter 12 deals again with difficulties which the Corinthians had subjected to the apostle's judgment. Nor does Paul rebuke the Corinthians as at other points, e. g., at the beginning of his letter, for asking him questions concerning unimportant matters but ignoring the fact that they were living in great sin. On the contrary, Paul begins to praise the Corinthians (cf. 1: 4-9). This lends to this section a special character. Probably Paul treated this point simply because he was writing about other things, although he himself did not consider it a point of great importance. The reason why this question is treated at this point in the epistle becomes clear upon comparison of vs. 2 with vs. 17. Vs. 2: *I praise you*, vs. 17: *I praise you not*. In vs. 17 Paul deals with the evils in connection with the Lord's Supper, a subject which quite naturally follows after the section about the eating of meat offered to idols. Paul had already mentioned the Lord's Supper in that section (10:14f). It is not improbable that Paul, before beginning to expose another evil, namely that concerning the Lord's Supper, first wishes to deal with a subject which can be introduced to his readers with a word of praise.

I praise you: the apostle does not omit to praise where that is possible. *In all things*, i. e., with respect to all things.[1] The Corinthians remembered Paul; there is no disloyalty in the congregation, on the contrary, Paul's praise is all-inclusive. Generally speaking, the apostle in this letter does not complain of lack of appreciation. Nor was a defense of the apostolate against those who did not accept it found in ch. 9.

To remember the apostle is to keep and to observe his doctrine and moral commandments. This encomium is not in conflict with the admonitions given by Paul so liberally in I Corinthians. Those admonitions regard, for the greater part, new areas of conduct. The congregation had grown much, it was called upon

---

[1] πάντα, accusative of limitation. The Greek has a perfect, μέμνησθε, which indicates that the Corinthians remember continually.

to define more precisely its line of conduct and it had not succeeded in keeping its balance. By abusing its Christian liberty it had made its life easier, simpler. There were no heresies at Corinth; the only thing of the kind is mentioned in 15:12. Thus Paul's eulogy is understandable. In the second part of the verse the apostle writes that the Corinthians *hold fast the traditions* (RSV: "maintained"), *even as Paul delivered them.* These words contain a clear reference to Paul's missionary work. The new churches possessed only the Old Testament. The Gospels did not yet exist. That made it necessary to keep most minutely the preaching, the traditions of the apostles. Those traditions constituted the Word of God. By using the word *tradition* the apostles indicate that they do not come in their own name but that they hand down what Christ commanded them to preach. That is why Paul may demand that the traditions be obeyed. As concerns the contents, the traditions do not differ from "the gospel" or "the preaching"; the word views the same thing from a different angle.

3   This and the following verses show that Paul has especially in view the Christian relation between husband and wife, a point concerning which the pagan Corinthians needed instruction badly. *I would have you know,* a solemn expression which becomes understandable if we assume that what Paul wished to say at this point did not yet belong to the tradition since it had arisen in connection with what had happened at Corinth. The words might be paraphrased: I will that you also know. The new thing is not that the husband is the head of the wife; that is taught already in the Old Testament. The new point is that there is a certain gradation of which the marriage relationship is a part. That offers the key to the subsequent words. *Of every man*: no matter who. Paul does not refer to Christians only but to all men. The fact that non-Christians do not know these things and do not even want to know them does not do away with the truth of this statement (compare I Cor. 2:14 with 15:25; Phil. 2:10, 11). *The head is (the) Christ,* note the article: head and Christ are identical. Every man has one head and that one head is only and always Christ. *Head* is used figuratively: it means a governing, ruling organ. Paul does not use the figure of the head and the members, but distinguishes the head, from everything

249

that is not the head. *Christ*: designating Him in His office. We take these words of Christ's mediatorial work, the wonderful consequence of which is that the Mediator is the head over all things, not only over the church but over everything (Mt. 28:18; Eph. 1:22; Heb. 2:8f.) and therefore also over every man. Paul's words: *and the head of the woman is the man* cannot refer to the relation between man and woman as God created it. That point is treated in vs. 8, at least to a certain extent; from the use of *"for"* in vs. 8 it is clear that the apostle uses that created relationship as the ground of something. This makes it impossible to find that relationship in vs. 3 already. In the second place, the words which precede and which follow this phrase refer to the work of recreation. Finally, if at all possible we will have to give the word *head* the same meaning in all these parts of the text. This prompts us to take the words *the head of the woman is the man* as implying that in the realm of recreation the man rules the woman. This does not particularly regard marital relations, but the relation between man and woman everywhere especially where Christ is worshipped as Head, i. e., in the church. *Head* lacks the article, nor does *woman* have the indefinite pronoun *every*. That means that man's headship over the woman is not as absolute as Christ's headship over all things. *The man*, not the husband of a woman, but every man, man as man. Of every man it can be said that he is above the woman. Also in the realm of sacred things the authority of the man is not abolished. Paul had a special reason to add these things to the tradition. True, in Gal. 3:28 we do not read: male *or* female, but: male *and* female, but this does not alter the fact that Paul must have preached to the Corinthians also that in Christ Jesus the woman is made free. Unlike the Roman woman the Greek woman lived in the background. This resulted in wide spread prostitution. The preaching of the gospel restored to woman her place of honor. But now it appears that the Christian women at Corinth abused their liberty; there was a desire to put man and woman on the same level. (cf. 7:3, 11, 39). This makes it necessary for the apostle to write: *the head of the woman is the man*, i. e., Paul places the man above the woman, also in the church. The difference which God has created continues to be valid in the church.

Then follows: *and the head of Christ is God.* God sent Christ into the world as a Mediator and as such Christ is subordinated to the Father (Jn. 14:28; I Cor. 3:23; 15:24f.). This is the order God has instituted. The Saviour, who acquired for Himself the whole creation, is its Head under God. And according to God's ordinance the woman shall be under the man also in the world which is recreated. The recognition of the fact that God is the Head of Christ should make it easier for the women to recognize the superiority of the man, also in the church.

4 Vs. 4 speaks of *praying* and *prophesying.* The question whether this refers to the meetings of public worship or to the worship in the homes must not be put in exactly that fashion. In 14:34 Paul expressly writes: *in the churches.* But in our context there is not the slightest indication that the church is meant. It is true, in vs. 16 we read: *neither the churches,* but the point there is not one of praying or prophesying, but of not being contentious. Our starting point must be another one. The praying of which the apostle speaks, be it a form of supplication or of praise, is clearly a praying with and for other people. And the nature of New Testament prophesying, especially as it is described in I Corinthians, is clearly that of intercession for others in public. This gift of prophecy is one of the charismatic activities, which was given not for the good of the individual but for the benefit of the whole church (12:10f., 28: "in the church"). A prophet does not speak to himself but to other people (14:3), he edifies the congregation (14:4, 22f.).

Chapter 14 in its entirety shows that both glossolalia and prophecy took place in the meetings of the congregation. That agrees with what we read elsewhere concerning the prophets, e. g., in Acts 11:27f.; 13:1; 15:32; 21:10f. The impression one gains from all these passages is that prophets are those men who, during the time the New Testament was not yet in existence, were called and prepared by God to preach to the churches what should be done or believed at that particular moment. The fact that the work of the prophets was for the benefit of the churches does not imply that their prophetic utterances were made or should be made only in the churches. On the contrary, the Scripture teaches us that there are other possibilities. An appeal to Mt. 26:6 is not relevant, because that is a case of mockery which is based upon that which the people knew concerning the prophets of the old dispensation. Of special importance is Acts 21:11f., where the activities of Agabus are not pictured as taking place in a meeting of the congregation. This leads us to the conclusion that Paul in ch. 11 speaks of a praying and a prophesying (of women) in public rather than in the meetings of the congregation. This interpretation has in its favor that it avoids a conflict with the absolute language of 14:34; it makes clear why Paul in this chapter argues from the divine ordinance of creation, as he points out that a Christian woman shares in the blessings of Christ (vs. 11), but does not touch upon the conditions in the congregation.

Praying refers to an ordinary action, *prophesying* to a charismatic action in public life. The point of the apostle is that a woman must so conduct herself in praying and prophesying as she always would when appearing in public.

Some scholars, e. g., Bachmann, have argued that Paul is giving rules for domestic worship at this point. Bachmann's principal grounds are: 1) 8:1-11:1 discusses domestic problems and our pericope follows upon that, without any indication of a change of subject. However, 10:31-11:1 forms the conclusion of the preceding section and in 11:2 Paul begins to speak of an observing of his ordinances in *every* realm. Moreover, this new section will have to show for itself whether or not it has the same character as the preceding. 2) Bachmann appeals to the nature of prophecy as it manifested itself not only at Corinth, but also at Thessalonica (I Thess. 5:20) and most probably in many other cities (cf. Rom. 12:6). The character of prophecy is said not to forbid one to assume that it was practiced in smaller meetings, i. e., in domestic worship. Earlier we noticed that the nature of prophecy demands a public exercise of it. Since there is no scriptural evidence of a private use of the prophetic gift such use is not very probable. 3) Bachmann argues that vs. 17 begins to refer to the meetings of the congregation more particularly. Indeed it does, but that does not prevent us from taking the preceding verses of such meetings as well. 4) Bachmann also points out that girls are not mentioned in this context, only women, and he points to the emphasis which is placed upon the relation between the married man and the married woman. The first contention is correct, the second one not quite (cf. v. 3), but we fail to see the relevance of this consideration to the point under discussion. The most it could prove would be that actually only married women prophesied. We feel justified in maintaining that Paul refers to a public action and fail to understand what objection Paul could have against a married woman performing certain functions in her own house, i. e., in the presence of her husband and children, *with her head unvailed*, i. e., without having her head covered or with loose hair. That that should be a dishonor, nature certainly does not teach (vs. 14). But everybody will understand that it must have been very objectionable for a woman to speak in public with her head unveiled in a country where custom dictated that honorable women wore a veil or a fillet in public. See also vs. 5.

The man who *hath his head covered,*[2] *dishonoreth his head.* Many ancient pictures show that men walked in public with uncovered head, women on the contrary were veiled in public. A man going with his head covered acts like a woman and dishonors his head. This refers only to something that may have happened.

5 Vs. 5 deals with an actual occurrence, as appears from the extensive treatment and from Paul's clear disapproval. It also shows that Paul is not formulating a rule that a woman, when praying or prophesying, must cover her head. His point is that a woman, who ordinarily has her head covered when appearing in public, must also have it covered when she prays or prophesies, i. e., when she is in ecstasy. It is possible and necessary to regulate the expressions of ecstasy (14:26f.) for it seems that the Corinthian women had laid aside their veils during their prayer. The reasoning behind such action was that if a woman like a man engages in praying and prophesying she also may wish to be like a man in the manner in which she prays or prophesies. But in doing so a woman degrades herself. If a woman

---

[2] Greek: κατὰ κεφαλῆς ἔχων, most probably a standing expression. ἔχων, sc. τι ἔχων κατά, refers to the hair or the veil of the women hanging down from the head. The verb is not mentioned in so many words in this context, but a veil or a ribbon for the hair belonged to the ordinary headgear of women.

dresses like a man, she has to shave herself like a man.[3] Probably prostitutes used to or were compelled to cut their hair and to keep it very short.[4] The causal clause implies that the fact that such prostitutes wore their hair short shows that a woman who prays or prophesies with uncovered head dishonors her head.[5] Paul's argument may be summed up as follows: If immoral women were shaven and if they behaved like men, then honorable women should cover their heads and distinguish themselves in all things from men or else they place themselves on a level with immoral women.

6 That type of argument appears too strong and so vs. 6 adduces further proof. The causal clause with *for* is subordinate to the one in the preceding verse. If *a woman is not veiled* she acts so unwomanly that she should cut her hair as well. Everyone agrees that it is shameful for a woman to have her hair cut short or to be shaven. If that is so, a Christian woman should cover her head. This reasoning is not strictly logical, it is based on analogy: A woman who once begins to act like a man (by having her head uncovered in public), should be consistent (by letting her hair be cut short). She will then see that the end of her behavior is a *shame*. Paul does not refer particularly to praying or prophesying here, he speaks in general. This shows even more clearly than vs. 5 did, that Paul does not have public worship in mind (cf. 14:33f). Paul's argument is: that which a woman is obliged to do under different circumstances, she must do also when she worships, when she prays or prophecies. The apostle appeals to common sense. It is shameful for a woman to have her head uncovered in public.

7 Vs. 7 points in the same direction when it argues that, by virtue of creation, there is a difference which puts the man above the woman, a difference we should never forget. Obviously this is a stronger reason than that based on common sense, which was used in vs. 6. Paul's argument increases in depth when in

---

[3] Paul writes: she is one and the same as the shaven one, i.e. she may as well be shaven.

[4] Paul uses two different words, vs. 5: ξυρᾶν (ASV: to shave), vs. 6: κείρειν, (ASV: to shear, i.e. to cut short).

[5] Joh. Weiss states that women who were guilty of unnatural prostitution wore their hair short in any case. If that is true Paul's argument is even stronger than it seems at first sight.

our verse he comes to his last and most potent reason: the creation of God. The man has the duty, prescribed by God Himself ("ought"), to have *his head uncovered*. This does not imply that the wearing of a hat is forbidden for a man for the word *"ought"* does not imply a duty which must be performed always and everywhere, but something which is becoming, decent[6]. A duty before God in this case is also a duty before men. The man is not obliged to cover his head. Paul regards this covering of the head as a token of subjection, not so much because every subordinate would always have his head covered (e. g., slaves) but because Paul is considering the woman first, for whom the wearing of a veil signifies subjection. A man degrades himself by wearing such a token of subjection which the woman is supposed to wear. In the preceding verse Paul declared that a woman should not act like a man; here he states: a man shall not act like a woman. *Forasmuch as he is the image and glory of God*: God does not require the man to wear a token of subjection. The man is subject to God who has distinguished him from the woman who is equally subject to God.

Vs. 7b contains the ground for the first part of the verse: the man reveals continuously[7] that he is *the image and glory of God*. Those words remind us of Gen. 1:27. But there we read: God created man in (after) His own image, in the image of God created He him, whereas Paul writes: the man *is* the image of God.[8] The apostle implies that a man, by virtue of the manner of his creation can be called the image of God; he has received some features of God only in a secondary sense. If Paul had used the word "image" only, the woman might point to Gen. 1:27 and say that she too was the image of God. But Paul writes: *image and glory of God* and he adds in vs. 7c of the woman that she is *the glory of the man*. That means that according to Paul a man is not only the image but also the glory of God, a woman is the glory, not the image of a man. *Glory* does not here have the meaning of the full divine majesty. The word used alongside the

---

[6] ὀφείλει denotes more an obligation (*obligatio*) than a duty (*officium*) in this context. It implies that a man shall behave like a man.

[7] ὑπάρχων, present participle.

[8] Gen. 1:27 (LXX): κατ' εἰκόνα Θεοῦ.

word "image" points to that which is not only God's image but also honors and magnifies Him. Man, created last, is the crown of creation (Ps. 8). But this regards the man only, for the woman was created in a way which was different from everything else: she was formed by God from the man. That is why Paul can write that a man, who is the image of God, reveals how beautiful a being God could create, which makes him the crown of creation, the glory of God. A woman, on the other hand, reveals how beautiful a being God could create from a man. Thus Paul makes everything a question of creation. Besides, we notice that although actually the first woman was the wife of the first man, Paul does not base his argument on the marriage relationship but rather on the created relationship between man and woman.

8, 9 Vs. 8 teaches us why a man is the glory of God and why a woman is the glory of the man. It all follows from the way in which God created woman. Vs. 9 offers a second ground for the thesis of vs. 7. This second ground is found in the purpose for which Eve was created. She was created *for the man,* to help him. The man alone cannot replenish the earth (Gen. 1:28). Both times Paul states the matter negatively and thereby emphasizes the actually existing situation. To state that the first created man was not created for the woman was in itself not necessary.

10 *For this cause* i. e., because the woman is created from and for the man. Here we have a case in which that which follows from a causal clause (vs. 9) is stated as a ground after that causal clause. Materially this conclusion is the same as that for which the causal clause gave the ground. In our case this means that the words *"the woman is the glory of the man"* coincide with *"the woman ought to have a sign of authority on her head."* A new element is expressed by the words: *because of the angels,* which is of the same order as *for this cause.* The woman has an obligation with respect to the angels, namely that she should wear something on her head. The apostle does not refer to the matter of praying or prophesying but he says what a woman should do in all circumstances by virtue of the ordinances of God given at the creation. That which she ought to do by virtue of this ordinance she is to do always and everywhere, also when she prays or prophesies.

A woman's head cover in this verse is called *exousia,*[9] authority. As we met this word earlier in I Corinthians we noticed that Paul used it to designate Christian liberty. In more than one passage the question arose as to the rule according to which the Christian is to use this liberty and the answer was: according to the law of love. By writing that a woman's head cover is to be viewed as an authority, Paul indicates that she is entitled to approach unto God with a covered head. That head cover is an *exousia,* because it is an ornament for the woman (cf. vs. 15). God permits the woman to approach Him with her glory or to prophesy in His service. But because this glory, this ornament of the woman, is the sign of her subjection to the man at the same time (and it is God's grace that this is so), and because it is necessary that this subjection to the man appear at every moment, also during worship, the woman is *obliged* to exercise her Christian liberty by appearing in public with her head covered, i. e., also by praying and prophesying in that way. Thus the word *exousia* in this context implies three things: a) the relation to God, b) the relation to the man, c) the demands of nature. But Paul's choice of the word *exousia* shows that he has especially in view the relation to God. The matter is thus lifted out of the earthly sphere and the woman may view this question in the light which is from above, knowing that she, in the ultimate analysis, is accountable to God and not to her husband. It is God who has given a certain liberty to her, as He also allowed her to worship Him and to prophesy in His name. Her relation to the husband only implies that she is obliged to use her liberty. Chapters 8-10 taught us that the Christian may have the duty not to use his liberty because of his brother; the woman likewise is obliged to use it under certain conditions. If this interpretation is correct the words *because of the angels* do not surprise us, for they contain an additional reason why the woman must use her *exousia.* Scripture often mentions the service which angels render. The law was ordained through angels by the hand of a mediator (Gal. 3:19). The angels are ministering spirits, sent forth to do service

---

[9] Greek: ἐξουσία, ASV: a sign of authority; RSV: a veil (Mg.: Greek: authority, the veil being a symbol of this).

for the sake of them that shall inherit salvation (Heb. 1:14). The angels of the little ones always behold in heaven the face of the father who is in heaven (Mt. 18:10). Angels also had a task at the creation, especially in the further preparation of the created things (Job 38:7). The angels, therefore, were witnesses of the creation of the woman from the man and thus it was ncessary for the woman to cover her head on account of the angels when she approached the Lord, thus to make use of her *exousia* (cf. 4:9; Eph. 3:10; I Tim. 5:21). And in so doing she recognizes before the angels the right of God. This reference to the angels must serve to make things easier for the woman. Not just for the sake of the man does a woman have to cover her head, but the Corinthian woman, who desired to be like a man, has to cover her head also because of the angels.

11 Although the woman is given a place below the man, vs. 10 makes abundantly clear that she is not the slave of the man. Her inferior position is not because the man has a greater degree of dignity than she. On the contrary, the apostle fights on two fronts. On the one side it was necessary to put the emancipated Corinthian ladies in their places, but on the other Paul seeks to prevent the woman from being considered inferior. There is a creation ordinance which must be maintained and if that is done the woman who is a creature of God, will have a position of honor, a position far better than that which Greek paganism was able to offer.

The woman is *in the Lord,* just as much as the man. *Nevertheless,* i. e., in spite of what was said in the preceding verse.[10] *In the Lord* is stressed, as its place at the end of the clause indicates. To be in the Lord is to live in the sphere of the glorified Christ, i. e., to be subject to Him and to enjoy the benefits He acquired. To be in Christ is to live in the sphere of faith (Gal. 5:6; Eph. 1:7). In that sphere *the woman is not without the man nor the man without the woman.* The absence of the articles in the Greek shows that these words do not refer to a man and his wife but to men and women in general. Both are in the sphere of Christ. The question arises whether the difference between

---

[10] Greek: πλήν, i.e. the apostle writes something new and is anxious that we should keep that in mind in order that wrong conclusions from the foregoing may be prevented.

man and woman existing since the creation disappears in the
Lord. Another question is why, if both are in Christ, the woman
is to be distinguished from the man when she prays or prophesies.
The answer is that the apostle does not imply that in the Lord
every difference disappears. The only thing Paul implies is that
both are in the Lord and that both for that reason share the
benefits of salvation. Christ gave Himself unto death not only
for men but also for women, and so in the higher things man
and woman are equal.

12 Vs. 12 states the reason for vs. 11. Why are man and
woman both in the Lord? Because both are created by God and
thus are related to one another. Certainly, *the woman is of the
man,* according to God's disposal. But no man was ever born
without a woman. Every man has a mother, he is *by the woman.*
That Adam is an exception does not matter. Paul speaks of the
ordinary conditions. The main point is, that *all things,* Adam
included, *are of God.* Adam too is a son *of God,* therefore man
and woman can be and should be in the Lord.

13 In vs. 3 Paul began with a general maxim from which he
deduced the thesis that a woman is obliged to have something
on her head when praying or prophesying. In vs. 7 the question
was viewed more generally in the light of what God did at creation. In our verse the apostle appeals to the common sense of
the Corinthians. This threefold treatment of the question on the
part of the apostle points to the importance which he attributed
to it: God's ordinances, given at the creation, must not be
transgressed. Secondly, Paul apparently expected contradiction.
The pride of the Corinthians may very well have led to an obstinate attitude on their part. The Corinthian women were not
prepared to let go of their presumed liberties. In view of this
fact the apostle writes: *Judge ye in yourselves* (cf. 10:15). The
Corinthians were wise in their own eyes and so Paul invites
them to consult their own wisdom. *In yourselves* may be in your
own circle as well as in your own heart. *Seemly:* there are things
a Christian does and others he does not do. Not because they are
forbidden but because everybody feels they should not be done.
It is not seemly if *a woman prays to God unveiled,* as everybody
agrees. We remember that Paul considers the long hair of a

259

woman as it was bound together with a string or a net in those days to be a *veil*.

14-15 *Nature* stands for the general notion all people have by virtue of their being human beings. Vs. 13 appeals more to the intellect, vs. 14 to the general consciousness. Paul does not mention prayer here for "nature" does not give any decisive answer about that. Nature does teach that the wearing of long hair dishonors a man, but that it is an ornament for a woman. That holds true of every nation. It is true that there are deviations at certain periods, and it is not that nature would prescribe the precise length of a woman's hair. But it is true that, generally speaking, as is clear from pictures and reports, women all over the world wore their hair much longer than men. The long hair is a *glory* of the woman, i. e., the thing that distinguishes her as a woman from the man. The reason (*for*) is that *the long hair is given her for a covering*. The meaning of the words *"is given"* cannot be that God gave to the woman and not to the man the possibility of having long hair. A man's hair *may* grow long. We understand *is given* of the *exousia* or right (vs. 10). The woman has received the liberty to wear long hair and that is at the same time her glory and that which distinguishes her from the man. When the words: *the hair is given for a covering to the woman* are compared with some of the preceding verses it will be clear that in the earlier verses it was impossible to take "covering" of the hair only. Vs. 4 reads: having his head covered, lit. from the head; vs. 6 distinguishes between a not covering of the head and a cutting short of the hair, apparently assuming that even if the head is not covered the hair may still be long. The solution of this question must be sought in the two different words for hair which the Greek uses.[11] The first one means hair as such; the second, which is used here, means the hairdo, hair that is neatly held by means of ribbon or lace. That also fits the context which shows that the Corinthian women did not cut their hair short (vs. 6), but that they took it down in ecstasy. In the foregoing verses, therefore, Paul has in view what necessarily must be added to a woman's hair to make it look neat, whereas in our text he refers to the hair as it requires such an addition because of its condition. That means that the apostle does not

---

[11] τρίχες and κόμη.

imply that a ribbon or a veil is required; what is required is an orderly hairdress which distinguishes a woman from a man. All women should have that sort of a dress always, also when they pray or prophesy.

16 Vs. 16 concludes this section with a general remark. *Seemeth*: it may be that someone through his conduct appears to be contentious, without being it. In the Corinthian scene, where customs existed which were defended by the one and disapproved by another, this might easily happen. In his defense of an existing custom a person may easily go too far, though he does not mean to do so. But, after all, only that which appears to the eye can be taken into account.

It may be that Paul writes these things to warn the Corinthians and that he does so because he fears opposition. The apostle did not approve of what happened when women prayed or prophesied. Assuming, or knowing, that the conduct of these women is ardently defended the apostle states that he does not agree and that it is not his (*we*) custom nor that of the churches of God *to be contentious*.

Another interpretation is that, although there be many in the world who are *contentious,* he and his helpers are not thus characterized. Thus viewed the words of the apostle do not imply any uncertainty on his part, they show no sign of willingness to give in to others, for the argument is too positive for that. It is only a question of behavior. Paul does not act contentiously; the point at issue is the only thing that matters. And because that point is so important the apostle may not give in, even though he may thus appear to be contentious.

This interpretation is the better of the two for it does not assume the existence of opposition against the apostle of which the text has nothing to say. There may also be a transition to the following section in the word *"contentious."* The naming of *the churches of God* implies that the apostle does not ask anything special of the Corinthians; what he asks of them he asks everywhere (7:17; 14:33). These passages concern the position of the woman. The Corinthian women should not think that Paul demands of them what he does not demand of others.

2-16 A case which does not appear very important in itself is treated very seriously by Paul, not because the conduct of the

Corinthian women raised unrest in the church, but because they violated the ordinance of God's creation. That is also the lasting significance of this section. An injunction concerning what the hairdress of women should be is not given, but Paul teaches that women are wrong if they in any respect neglect their difference from the men, a difference which remains also in the church. This admonition is true in all circumstances, even if one might judge that Paul does not refer to public conduct but rather to services at home.

ABUSES AT THE LORD'S TABLE

11:17-34

17 But in giving you this charge, I praise you not, that ye come together not for the better but for the worse.

18 For first of all, when ye come together in the church, I hear that divisions exist among you; and I partly believe it.

19 For there must be also factions among you, that they that are approved may be manifest among you.

20 When therefore ye assemble yourselves together, it is not possible to eat the Lord's supper:

21 for in your eating each one taketh before *other* his own supper; and one is hungry, and another is drunken.

22 What, have ye not houses to eat and to drink in? or despise ye the church of God, and put them to shame that have not? What shall I say to you? shall I praise you? In this I praise you not.

23 For I received of the Lord that which also I delivered unto you, that the Lord Jesus in the night in which he was betrayed took bread;

24 and when he had given thanks, he brake it and said, This is my body, which is for you: this do in remembrance of me.

25 In like manner also the cup, after the supper, saying, This cup is the new covenant in my blood: this do, as often as ye drink *it*, in remembrance of me.

26 For as often as ye eat this bread, and drink the cup, ye proclaim the Lord's death till he come.

27 Wherefore whosoever shall eat the bread or drink the cup in an unworthy manner, shall be guilty of the body and the blood of the Lord.

28 But let a man prove himself, and so let him eat of the bread, and drink of the cup.

29 For he that eateth and drinketh, eateth and drinketh judgment unto himself, if he discern not the body.

30 For this cause many among you are weak and sickly, and not a few sleep.

31 But if we discern ourselves, we should not be judged.

32 But when we are judged we are chastened of the Lord, that we may not be condemned with the world.

33 Wherefore, my brethren, when ye come together to eat, wait one for another.

34 If any man is hungry let him eat at home; that your coming together be not unto judgment. And the rest will I set in order whensoever I come.

17 As we look for the connection with the preceding we notice as a point of agreement that Paul here as well as in the previous section omits any reference to the source of his information. Not until 12:1 is there any reference to questions which the Corinthians asked of Paul in their letter to him (*now concerning*). Our present pericope, therefore, constitutes another interruption of Paul's reply to the Corinthians. By writing: *in giving you this charge,* Paul connects this verse with the preceding verses. *This* (charge) cannot refer to vs. 16, because that verse did not mention any special case. Therefore it is better to take *"this"* of the whole preceding pericope, vss. 2-16, but to note particularly the connection between vs. 17: *I praise you not,* and vs. 2: *I praise you.* We may paraphrase: Now that I am commanding you these things, I first have occasion to praise you, but I also must mention something that is not worthy of praise, because you do not observe in all things the tradition I gave you. The trend of Paul's thought is the following: the long series of admonitions, including the answer to the questions of the Corinthians which also had the character of an admonition, is interrupted for a moment by the treatment of a case which gave occasion for praise. But Paul cannot continue in this vein for he knows that not everything the church does is worthy of praise (cf. vs. 23). Treating that point in the same breath, the apostle will resume the reply to the letter in 12:1.

The *coming together* about which Paul writes must be understood of the meetings of the congregation as such (cf. vs. 18). Whether these were ordinary services or congregational meetings is less important. It is not known whether the two were distinguished at that time. The sequel teaches us that discussions were held in those meetings but that also the Lord's supper was administered. These meetings of the church were *not for the better but for the worse,* i. e., instead of being beneficial for the members, as they should be, they were harmful.

18 Vs. 18 explains the reason why Paul could say this. There are two reasons given, first, of the fact that Paul wrote the way he did, second, of the fact that these meetings had evil results. The words: *for first of all,* introduce the first reason. The second is not mentioned in so many words. It is not to be found in vs. 20 for that verse, as appears from the word *"therefore,"* speaks about the same point as the preceding verses. Vs. 34b points to a better solution. There Paul states that there were yet many more things which he could mention, but they are either not very important, or they cannot be treated in an epistle. *First of all* must mean therefore: this is the main thing and that I must discuss with you. *Church*: here the organized congregation, meeting in that capacity. The wrong which has resulted in much evil for the church is found in the abuses which have caused the decline of the church. The evil is that there are *divisions.*[12] The latter need not have a sinful reason, neither does Paul mention any reason for them as yet, nor does he connect them with the divisions referred to in 1:12. If such a connection existed Paul would have mentioned it. To think of these divisions as being the same as those of 1:12 is out of the question. The fact, also that Paul in 1:10f. characterizes the divisions as quarrels but in our text says that *"there must be factions"* forbids us to identify the one with the other. Besides, while in ch. 1 the apostle mentions the source of his information, he does not do anything of the kind in our pericope, again an important consideration against identifying the two. The situation in ch. 1 was apparently one of quarrels concerning certain points, quarrels which tore up the church, whereas the question which is at stake here is the fact that the official meetings of the church did not form a unit. The Corinthians formed separate groups which, although they did not engage in fighting each other, still lived in comparative isolation from each other. Vs. 21 seems to warrant the assumption that there were social contrasts at Corinth which led to divisions. It seems that the few who were rich refused to sit beside the poor who may have been slaves of the well-to-do. The sin here signalized had nothing to do with material difference as in ch. 1,

---

[12] The Greek word οχίσματα is rather neutral (cf. 1:10). Yet it appears at once that the apostle does not approve of the existing divisions.

but consisted in a refusal to sit together at the same table. The only connection between our chapter and ch. 1 is that both point to the divisive character of the Corinthian church.

I hear that divisions exist among you: it is hard to tell why Paul expresses himself in such a cautious manner. Perhaps his source of information was less reliable than usual, or he may have distrusted the message because of the form in which it came to him. Paul adds: *I partly believe it.*

19 *Must* implies a moral obligation. What Paul writes here is a duty of the church. *There must be factions,* but they do not exist; there are divisions, but they should not exist.[13] "Factions" does not refer to different groups as in Acts 5:17, etc. The meaning of the word is choice, selection, distinction.[14] Paul is opposed to divisions as well as to uniformity. There must be action in the church, expressing itself in discussions but not in separation. Discussions will not break up the church's unity, their consequence will be quite different from that, namely that *they that are approved,* the believers who have proved to be reliable, *may be made manifest* (confer Dt. 13:3). A good discussion will show which Christians are the best founded in their faith, but it does not create divisions. This is the reason why Paul inserts vs. 19. It is to prevent the Corinthians from saying: there must be factions. Indeed, factions must be, but not those which end in divisions.

20 *When therefore ye assemble*: this is not a new point but a further explanation of the nature of these evil divisions. The latter did not appear so much during the preaching as during the love-feasts, where the whole church used to meet (*assemble together*). The way in which the congregation met was not the right way *to eat the Lord's supper.*[15] The divisions among the Corinthians made this impossible.

---

[13] The Greek has σχίσματα (vs. 18), αἱρέσεις (vs. 19). αἵρεσις does not yet have the sense of heresy as in I Pet. 2:1, but it is used in a good sense.

[14] See: Moulton & Milligan, Lexicon, s.v.

[15] The construction is remarkable, for the genitive absolute is the subject of the clause. We translate: your meeting is not the eating of the Lord's Supper, or: when you meet there is not an eating of the Lord's Supper. The sense is: when you meet, it is not possible, etc.

The expression: *the Lord's supper* is not immediately to be understood as a technical term designating a sacrament. Since Paul is introducing the expression here we shall have to take it first in its literal sense. The supper is the main meal, the dinner of the Greeks, served in the evening. The addition *Lord's* supper implies that the meal is not an ordinary meal but that it received its character from the Lord. The context elucidates this further: the church ate its meal in an official meeting. The Lord's supper, as Paul uses the word here, is not to be restricted to what we call Holy Communion, for the following words do not fit the description of a sacrament. Vs. 21 teaches us that the meal, meant by Paul, is in the first place a love feast, i. e., a special kind of poor relief. The members of the congregation brought the food they otherwise ate at home to the meeting of the church and then they dined together in the name of the Lord. Rich people brought many items, poor people only a few, and there resulted a kind of equality, since all those who were present divided the available food (cf. II Cor. 8:14). This is about the same kind of relief as that mentioned in Acts 2:44 f., where we read that as often as a poor person was in need a brother was prepared to sell his real estate to help the poor. Whether such a love feast was held every day, or only now and then, e. g., on the first day of the week, is not known (cf. 16:1). Only the Lord's supper was more than a love feast. Jesus instituted Holy Communion at a meal. And at Corinth Holy Communion was served at a love feast. It is the Holy Communion which made the meal a supper of the Lord.

21 Vs. 21 describes the evil: everybody brought something, but when the assembled multitude began to eat then *each one taketh before his own supper*, i. e., they took what they had brought along and did not permit others, the poor, to eat from their portion. That was a violation of the character of a love feast. The spirit of holiness was absent and the result was that the poor, who had counted on receiving a meal, were still *hungry* after the meal was over. Another one, on the contrary, ate too much and so he *is* (present tense) *drunken*. Drunken, not only inebriated but implying that he took too much so that the other had nothing. It should be kept in mind that wine was the most common beverage among the Greeks. What happened was that the rich were averse to the food brought by the poor, nor did they think it necessary that the poor should receive such excellent food.

22 If the Corinthians were not able to observe the character of a love feast, why did they serve them at all? If their only purpose was to eat and to drink, they could do that at their homes. Vs. 22a is directed to the well-to-do, who had something to eat and to drink and who spoiled the love feasts through their misdemeanor. By their "taking before" they showed disrespect for the church, which is the *church of God*. They violated the unity of the church, they thought only of themselves, forgot brotherly love and gave rise to divisions. They disappointed the poor, who came in the firm expectation of receiving food, but obtained nothing. With caution the apostle writes: *What shall I say to you?* He does not begin with an austere punishment. Presently, when discussing the Lord's Supper in the proper sense of the word, he will speak more strongly. This lack of severity is due to the fact that love feasts did not belong to the church's prescribed duties, since other ways and means could be found to relieve the poor. But if love feasts are organized they should be held in the right way. Besides, it may be that Paul is not sure whether he is rightly informed. Hence the calm question: *shall I praise you?* The answer can only be: *In this I praise you not* (cf. vs. 2 and vs. 17). Note that Paul does not just rebuke the rich but the entire congregation. The poor were also guilty, perhaps because they also had a part in the divisions.

23 Vs. 23 sets forth the reason why Paul does not praise the Corinthians. In this verse the apostle no longer writes about the love feasts but begins to mention more explicitly Holy Communion, showing the very close connection between the two, inasmuch as Paul speaks of a keeping of the Lord's Supper in a wrong spirit (vs. 27). Paul need not mention this point specifically for every Corinthian is informed concerning this matter. The sin which Paul rebukes is that the Corinthians celebrated Communion after their love feast had been spoiled, and thus desecrated the Lord's Supper. When speaking of those love feasts the apostle did not say that they were instituted by Christ. With Holy Communion, however, institution by Christ is the main point.

I received and I preached to you, i. e., I know that the Corinthians are well informed, for I myself *delivered unto you,* what I received from the Lord. There is an unbroken chain of tradition.[16] It is not impossible that the apostle knew already something about the Lord's Supper before his conversion. In a later time pagan writers show some acquaintance with the Christian ceremonies. In any case, as soon as Paul moved in the circles of the church, he has heard about communion and he has served it himself (Acts 20:7). *In the night in which he was betrayed*: Paul refers to his preaching and affirms anew that the Holy Supper is not an institution of men but of Christ Himself, who gave this sacrament at a very important moment, while he was at death's door.[17] All these considerations show how important a thing Holy Communion is and how great is the sin of the Corinthians if they make a wrong use of it. *The Lord Jesus,* who is now in glory, but then in the days of his humiliation *took bread.* Subsequently Paul does not stress the manner of the institution as much as the significance of the sacrament. Paul cannot praise the Corinthians *for* they desecrated Holy Communion. Jesus took a piece of ordinary bread, the Corinthians did likewise when they held their love feast which also was a supper of the Lord. This explains why Paul needs no further transition when coming to the subject of the Lord's Supper. A love feast ill-observed is a Lord's Supper ill-observed.

24 *When He had given thanks,* (see 10:16), refers to the prayer of Jesus, spoken before the breaking of the bread (Jn. 6: 11) by which He made ordinary bread communion bread. Jesus did so by giving thanks to God, who gave this bread and who consented to use it for the Communion. This thanksgiving did not change the bread for of the bread it is said: *this is my body for you,* but of the cup: *this cup is the new covenant in my blood.* If a change had taken place the reference to such a change should

---

[16] The Greek words παραλαμβάνειν and παραδιδόναι imply that the apostles actually preached to the churches what they received from the Lord (cf. 15:15f). ἀπὸ τοῦ Κυρίου, not παρά. Paul does not imply that he had a direct revelation of the Lord concerning Holy Communion, but that what he preached had its origin with the Lord, and so he can state that he received it from the Lord.

[17] The imperfect παρεδίδοτο implies that this betrayal was still going on. Note παρέδωκα in contrast.

have been made in a similar way. Besides, Jesus was present in body at the table. He held the bread in His hand, and thus we are prevented from understanding *this is my body* in a literal sense. The words of the thanksgiving are not recorded, which would have been an unpardonable omission if they were words of consecration. Since this thanksgiving precedes the breaking of the bread, it must therefore certainly precede the words which were pronounced upon that occasion. So it is impossible to identify the thanksgiving with the breaking of the bread or with the words which were spoken. The breaking is mentioned separately. It is an important action, because it speaks of the breaking of Christ's body. *This*: the bread Jesus holds in His hands. *For you*:[18] the body of Christ is for others, for the disciples. Since *this* refers to the bread and *for you* is joined to "body," the word *is* cannot imply complete identity, but must refer to a very close connection, between the bread and Christ's body.[19] The nature of this connection is not expressed by Paul. *This do*: the Holy Communion is a perpetual institution. *In remembrance of Me*: to remember Me, and this in such a way that the communicants have before their eyes a vivid picture of Christ and His work. The Communion leads to Christ, especially to His death as follows from the manner in which it is celebrated. Holy Communion is not just a meal of remembrance (see vs. 26); it is also a confession. Besides, we must not forget that Paul does not present here a theory of the Lord's Supper. Rather he records the words of Christ in order to teach the Corinthians the greatness of their sin. Only a few remarks are linked with his admonition to set forth the value of Holy Communion.

25 *In like manner* as happened with the bread. There is no verb in this clause and so we must supply the verb of vs. 23: *took,* and: (omitting the less appropriate "brake") *had given thanks* (cf. 10:16). *After supper,* not after the whole supper was over, for that does not suit the context, but after the eating of the bread.

---

[18] In the Greek μου precedes ἐστιν τὸ σῶμα; ὑπέρ ὑμῶν are the last words of the clause.

[19] The presence of the article before σῶμα does not justify the conclusion that the head is identified with the body. The article is necessary because 1) a certain body is meant, 2) ὑπὲρ ὑμῶν can be joined to σῶμα only by means of an article.

The words must mean that Jesus, as they were eating, took bread and distributed it and after that, i. e., after the eating of the bread and the giving of the bread of Holy Communion, He delivered the cup and made that cup the cup of the Lord's Supper. This interpretation agrees with the customs of the Jewish Passover where food and drink were used alternately.[20] The Lord spoke of a cup and not of wine because it was impossible to distribute wine without a cup, whereas bread could be held with the hands. Upon distributing the cup Jesus also spoke the same words, indicating that this cup was a special cup. For *is* cf. vs. 24. This time Jesus did not say: the cup, or, the wine is my blood, but: *the new covenant in my blood*. That proves that there is no change of quality, a cup can never become a covenant. The nature of the connection is not explained. But in order to understand it, it is important to note that our Saviour speaks of a *new* covenant. The new covenant is not a covenant of grace over against an old covenant of works; it is the new manifestation of the covenant of grace in the work of Jesus Christ, who died for the sins of His people. In the old dispensation there was a revelation of the covenant in the desert (Ex. 24. cf. Heb. 8:6f). That was an incomplete revelation in so far as it demanded a fulfilment in a Messiah. It was not the covenant itself, but a shadow of things to come. For the law was given through Moses; grace and truth came through Jesus Christ (Jn. 1:17). Christ initiated the new, the final dispensation and He revealed that in a special way by instituting the Holy Communion and connecting that with His blood. *The new covenant in My blood*: It was necessary for Him to give His blood as the firm foundation of the covenant. It was necessary that He should die, yea, die a violent death so that His blood

---

[20] See e.g. Strack-Billerbeck, IV, pp. 56 f.

[21] In the LXX διαθήκη is the translation of ברית. διαθήκη comes closer to "will" or a one-sided agreement; ברית on the contrary is more an agreement between two persons. The use of these two different words helps to determine the meaning. The covenant has one side inasmuch as all things come from God, it has two sides insofar as the believer in the covenant is called to do God's will.

See e.g. TWNT on the word; F. W. Grosheide, *De Brief aan de Hebreen en De Brief aan Jakobus* in KNT (Amsterdam, 1927), pp. 209f.

flowed. Paul does not quote any word of Christ which might indicate that there was no other way to reconcile our sins but the flowing of Christ's blood, but the simple: *in my blood* quoted by the apostle is clear enough. *In my blood* is on the same level with *He brake it,* vs. 24. *In my blood*: because I die I give my blood.[22] By saying that the cup is the covenant Jesus indicates that this covenant is the guarantee of the fact that He is willing to shed His blood in order that this covenant may be executed. The cup is the sign of the covenant.

Jesus also declared that Holy Communion must become a permanent institution; *for as often as ye eat this bread* (vs. 26); *this do*[23] *as often as,* etc. *This*: not the cup, but the act of drinking it, an expression which is clear in spite of its brevity (cf. vs. 24). There is not a complete parallel with vs. 24, but a material analogy. That which is new in vs. 25 is developed at length, whereas elements mentioned in the preceding verses are passed over briefly. In its complete form the clause would read: Drink frequently the cup of the Lord and do so always in remembrance of Me.

26 The question in this verse is whether Paul is using his own words or quoting the words of the Lord. A simple comparison with the words of the evangelists will not suffice. We have before us the oldest account of the institution of the Lord's Supper. It is conceivable that Paul would mention certain words of Jesus not found in the synoptic gospels. But it is also possible that Paul, continuing in the second person plural, added some words to those of Jesus in order to explain certain things more clearly. The words here are almost literally the same as those given by Luke (22:19, 20, ordinary text[24]); the differences with Matthew and Mark are much greater. Further comparison shows that in none of the gospels is there anything corresponding to I Cor. 11:26. It is probable, therefore, that at least the words at the beginning of vs. 26 are words of Paul, the more so because those words seem to be an elaboration of the preceding thoughts. *The Lord's death till He comes*: these words fit better in Paul's mouth

---

[22] ἐν τῷ αἵματι belongs to the predicate, because there is no article.
[23] ποιεῖτε imperative, not indicative.
[24] Certain witnesses of Luke 22: 17-20 place the verses 17 and 18 after vs. 19. There are some other smaller variants.

than in that of Jesus. The whole phrase, indeed, points to a time after Jesus' death rather than before. On the other hand, one could hold very well that the idea expressed in "till He comes" was that of Jesus Himself. The question cannot be solved with absolute certainty.[25]

Ye proclaim refers to the same thing as *in remembrance of Me*. Holy Communion shall be served in remembrance of Him, according to His own commandment. This can be done because every Communion proclaims His death. By speaking of proclaiming Jesus' death Paul implies that the Lord's Supper is not just a meal in commemoration of the Lord but also a meal of confession. He that comes to the Lord's table declares that he not only believes that Christ died to pay for the sins of His people, but that he also believes that Christ lives and that His death has significance for all times. This is implied in the use of the word *"Lord"* in *the Lord's death*, for it points to the glorified Lord in heaven. Likewise: *till He come* is not merely a chronological indication as to the time during which the Lord's Supper must be served, it also points to the Lord's return. He who comes to the Lord's table confesses that he believes that the glorified Lord will come from heaven. How great is the sin of the Corinthians who desecrate this Holy Communion!

27 Earlier we contended that Paul does not in this section offer an exposition of the institution and the significance of the Lord's Supper, but that he is concerned merely to set forth the value of the Communion that the Corinthians may rightly see their sin. That this is the apostle's purpose becomes especially clear from vs. 27, in which a conclusion is drawn (*wherefore*).

The bread, i. e., the bread of the Lord's Supper and also the cup, as appears from *of the Lord* which must be connected with "bread" as well as with "cup." *Unworthy*: this implies that a certain worth, or value, is connected with the bread and the cup. He who uses them without counting their value uses them *in an unworthy manner*, i. e., not in accordance with their value. Such an unworthy use the Corinthians made of the Communion when

---

[25] A second question regards καταγγέλλετε. If vs. 26 contains words of the Lord, it may be an imperative, as well as an indicative, but if they are the words of Paul then an indicative is the more probable. γάρ also points to an indicative. We translate therefore: "for as often as you eat ... you proclaim" (as ASV and RSV have it).

they served it after a love feast marred by quarrels. There is no indication in the text that this profanation was intentional. The apostle simply states that it actually occurred. That this is so follows from *shall be guilty*. To a certain extent these words take back what was said in the preceding clause: It will happen, it has not yet happened. Paul's only reason for expressing himself in this particular way must be his purpose of showing the Corinthians in the first clause what they actually did, and in the second what would happen if they did not obey his admonition. This does not conflict with vs. 30. That verse, to be sure, does speak of a judgment which is already present. But that is not the kind of judgment which will descend upon those who are *guilty of the body and the blood of the Lord*. It serves to arouse the people and is of the same nature as Paul's admonition. *Guilty of* has as its object that against which the offense was directed and, consequently, that which renders the offender liable to punishment. To be *guilty of the body and the blood of the Lord* means to break the body of Christ and to shed His blood. This guilt arises from a wrong use of the Lord's Supper, which is not strange in view of the close connection between the Supper and the death of the Lord. On the other hand, elsewhere the Scriptures also teach that, by scorning the sacrifice of Christ, we assume responsibility for the death of Christ on the cross. Stephen calls those who oppose Jesus to the end "betrayers and murderers" of the Lord (Acts 7:52; cf. Heb. 6:6; 10:29; Mt. 27:25). This involves a declared antagonism against the blood of Christ. He who thus despises it intentionally will be terribly punished by God.

28 Paul sets forth here the right use of Holy Communion. The shortcomings of the Corinthians are indicated and the way to improvement is pointed out. *To prove*: the Greek word[28] implies a special kind of proving, namely such as implies the conviction on the part of him who proves that the result of his proving will be good. It implies the purpose of detecting the good and consequently of recognizing it as reliable. Paul demands that every member of the church (*a man*) shall so prove himself that he will sift out the evil and will arrive at the condition of one who is "proved." To prove is not in the first place to search oneself whether he is worthy to sit at the holy table, although in

---

[28] δοκιμάζειν.

practice this is what it amounts to. Paul calls this act in vs. 31 : *to discern oneself.* This act of "proving" cannot have as its result staying away from the Lord's table, for its result is always good. *And so* : in that state of one who is "proved." *To eat of the bread and drink of the cup* implies the use of both elements at the Supper. Each of the communicants is to do this in the right manner.

29 The word *unworthy* (so AV, not in ERV, ASV, RSV) does not appear in the better manuscripts and had better be omitted. This verse, consequently, says nothing about those who do not use Holy Communion in the right manner. *Judgment* is the object not of the former pair of verbs but of the latter.[29] If it were the object of the former Paul should have mentioned this point previously, which is not the case. The protasis reads : *for he that eateth and drinketh.* The context indicates that the meaning is : he who eats without proving himself, he who eats as if he sat at an ordinary table. *Such a one eats judgment unto himself* : a figurative expression in which "judgment" is treated as if it were food. The reference is to such eating as causes a judgment for the eater. *Judgment* is a judgment of God. They who abuse the Holy Supper cause the judgment of God to come upon them (cf. vs. 27). *To discern* : here to determine the value of the Communion by regarding it as something different. By not coming to the table in the right manner one does not regard the body (i. e., the body and the blood) as it should be regarded.

30 *For this cause,* i. e., because he who eats, without discerning the body, lies under the judgment of God, there are *many weak and sickly among* the Corinthians. The fact that many are ill among them is a judgment of God because of their abuse of the Holy Supper. In vs. 21 Paul had stated his objections against the conduct of the Corinthian Christians directly. Now he argues from what God had brought upon them in order to show that his remarks were well founded. *Weak and sickly* :[30] the two words do not differ much in meaning. It is not certain whether they denote two kinds of persons. *Sleep,* also in 15 :18 euphemistically for "die." The present tense implies that there are constantly

---

[29] According to the Greek text both are possible grammatically.
[30] ἀσθενής, ἄρρωστος.

some that die. *Not a few*[31] a sufficient number, more than normally could be expected. The Lord caused His judgment to come upon the Corinthians in many diseases and deaths. The church should see that as a judgment of the Lord in order that they might come to conversion.

31 Vs. 31 has the form of a *modus irrealis*: if it were not so, we should not pass through this judgment. The use of the first person is evidence of the apostle's carefulness. It is used here because this statement is general and is valid for many other cases as well. *If we discerned ourselves,*[32] *we should not be judged* by God and punished by Him, when He would find sin in us. The verbs: to discern and to judge are used in a pregnant sense.

32 *But when we are judged* and eventually punished, as is the case with you Corinthians at this moment. The One judging is *the Lord,* hère referring not to Christ but to God. *Chastened* implies that the Lord has a purpose in judging His people. They lack something, they are not where they ought to be. That is why God educates them by means of a judgment. That judgment, therefore, is not a punishment, but a chastisement, a token of God's grace (3:11; Heb. 12:5f.; Rev. 3:11). If God did not chasten we would be *condemned with* the unbelieving, sinful world. God did not yet deliver us up to judgment (Rom. 1:24, 28), but He leads us so that we may come to conversion.

33 This verse and the following contain Paul's final admonitions. The Corinthians are told what they ought to do, i. e., how it will be possible to abolish the existing evil. *Wherefore* introduces a conclusion. *When ye come together to eat*: not only for Holy Communion but for every meeting of the congregation where all eat together. *Wait one for another*: no one must hastily take the food he himself had brought to the meeting, all shall begin their meal at the same time. If that rule is observed the spirit for the observance of the Lord's Supper will be right. Then the judgment of which vs. 27 spoke will not come. Paul recommends them to *wait,* not because he wishes to spare the brother, but in order to keep Holy Communion from being desecrated.

---

[31] ἱκανοί.

[32] Greek: ἑαυτούς. It is used in the koine for the three persons in the plural. ἑαυτοὺς διεκρίνομεν is stronger than a middle.

34 *If any man is hungry*: one would feel inclined to take these words of those who were poor but this is ruled out by the fact that it would presume that the poor did not receive at those love feasts what they needed, and that they had to go home where they had sufficient food. To take the words of the rich is equally difficult, for to the rich Paul would then have said that it would be better for them to remain at home. In either case a love feast would be impossible. Nor is it possible to render: if any man is still hungry, i. e., after the love feast. For it would still be true that the poor did not have anything to eat at home. We prefer the following paraphrase: If anybody is only hungry, i. e., if he attends the meetings of the congregation only to eat and to drink and not to enjoy the communion of the saints, let him eat at home. For it is that very attitude that spoils the love feasts. This regards the poor as well as the rich; no one shall try to get more than is seemly in the meetings of the church. For then the church would bring upon itself the judgment of the Lord, vs. 29. *And the rest I will set in order*: If Paul had written these words at the end of his letter they might be taken as referring to a number of questions he could not treat in his epistle. But at this place they can only refer to a further treatment of these church suppers. Paul went into the matter only so far as was absolutely necessary, writing about the worst abuses alone. Later on he will have more to say. *Whensoever I come*: a vague statement; the apostle does not indicate when and under what conditions he will come to Corinth (cf. 4:21; 16:5).

17-34 This section concerning the Lord's Supper has become very important in later times. Although it may be true that Paul does not offer an exposition concerning the significance and the right use of Holy Communion, yet it is no less true that many lessons regarding these points can be deduced from this treatise. Concerning the necessity of proving oneself in particular, no place contains as much information as this. The sin which is rebuked, moreover, also throws light on the character of the Holy Supper. It should finally be noted that, though the words "right" or "to be puffed up" do not occur in this section, nevertheless the abuse of the Lord's Supper is a consequence of the chief sin of the Corinthians, who thought that they were entitled to do all they liked.

CHAPTER XII

CONCERNING SPIRITUAL GIFTS IN GENERAL

12:1-3

1 Now concerning spiritual *gifts*, brethren, I would not have you ignorant.

2 Ye know that when ye were Gentiles *ye were* led away unto those dumb idols, howsoever ye might be led.

3 Wherefore I make known unto you, that no man speaking in the Spirit of God saith, Jesus is anathema; and no man can say, Jesus is Lord, but in the Holy Spirit.

1 *Concerning spiritual gifts*: the Greek text allows for the translation: concerning spiritual men. The context, however, bears out that the apostle has a neuter in view: spiritual things, i. e., spiritual gifts. These words form the heading for the chapters 12-14, a heading which resembles those of 7:1 and 8:1. Paul must be coming to a new subject. Chapter 13 fits into this context very well for in it the apostle sings of love as it is compared with other spiritual gifts. *Brethren* also indicates a new beginning. There is no connection between this section and the preceding. Paul here answers a question of the Corinthians.

Spiritual is in the New Testament always used of what regards the person and the work of the Holy Spirit, also the work of the Spirit in the believers (cf. 2:13). The one exception is Eph. 6:12. The word may be used of all believers (2:15; 3:2; Gal. 6:1). But there are also passages where it is used of a group of Christians, e. g., 14:37: *prophet or spiritual*. Generally speaking, chapters 12-14 do not refer to what all Christians have in common but to the spiritual gifts which are given to some, the so-called charismata. Some expositors hold that all Christians had received such spiritual gifts of the Spirit and they appeal for their view to vs. 7: *each one* (cf. 7:7). But that view is clearly refuted by 12:28f. where we read that those who had received the charismata were *in the church*. In other words, not all received such gifts,

278

only some. Comparing 12:31a with 12:31b leads to the same conclusion: Paul points to a way which is better than the longing for charismata. This implies that if the special gifts are lacking, love must not be lacking.

This whole difficulty can be removed only if we assume that "spiritual" does not have only the ordinary sense applicable to the state of all Christians as they receive the Holy Spirit, but also a special sense, implying the possession of special gifts of the Spirit, namely the charismata. Passages like Mt. 22:43 and II Peter 1:21, dealing with the Old Testament prophecy, also use the word "Spirit" of extraordinary activities of the Spirit. The context must decide every time which meaning must be adopted and this decision is nowhere difficult. In chapters 12-14 Paul has in view the special gifts of the Spirit. Finally it should be borne in mind that basically there is no difference between the two kinds of spiritual gifts. It is one and the same Holy Spirit who gives His grace to every Christian and His special gifts to some (cf. vs. 11). *The spiritual gifts of* 12:1, therefore, are the charismata, the extraordinary gifts.

I would not have you ignorant: a litotes, often used by Paul (Rom. 1:13; I Cor. 10:1; II Cor. 1:8; I Thess. 4:13) for the strengthening of his argument. Paul wishes very definitely that the congregation shall know. Perhaps the Corinthians had asked Paul's opinion about these charismata, in any case the apostle gives them a clear answer.

2   The structure of the verse is difficult and has inspired many variant readings,[1] but the meaning of the sentence is not uncertain. *Ye know*: Paul appeals to the Corinthians themselves (10:15; 11:13). They knew very well the situation they were in when they were still pagans. Continually they were *led away* from the right way *to the idols* which are *dumb*, i. e., they cannot *speak* and thereby demonstrate that they are dead (Ps. 115:4f; 135:15). *Idols*: to the heathen the image often is the god himself. *Howsoever ye might be led*: the Corinthians followed every teacher but

---

[1] We follow the text ὅτι ὅτε with Aleph B C D g etc. (other readings are ὅτε, ὅτι) and we assume that ἦτε is to be joined to ὅτε ἔθνη (ἦτε) as well as to ὅτι ἀπαγόμενοι (ἦτε). Then ὅτι... ἀπαγόμενοι becomes a clause dependent on οἴδατε and the two clauses ὅτε ἔθνη ἦτε and ὡς ἂν ἤγεσθε are dependent on ὅτι ἀπαγόμενοι ἦτε.

279

the end was always idolworship. That is the sad condition of paganism.

3 *Wherefore*: introduces a conclusion. Paul notices the contrast between the uncertain state of the Corinthians during their pagan period (howsoever ye might be led) and the firm principle of their Christianity. In former times nobody could say which way they would take. The Christian, on the contrary, has one certain way, he confesses that *Jesus is Lord. I make known*: a somewhat solemn expression.[2] Paul mentions what is important above all else. This leads us to the assumption that here we have the point about which the Corinthians had asked a question. Further support for this opinion may be found in the fact that the apostle, though writing about spiritual things in the subsequent verses, does not answer any further questions but warns against an overestimation of glossolalia. The question of the Corinthians must, upon this assumption, have concerned speaking in the Spirit. This *speaking in the Spirit,* as follows from our interpretation of vs. 1, must be taken as a speaking under an extraordinary impulse, a special guidance of the Holy Spirit. In any case, Paul does not mean a speaking in the Spirit such as is given to all believers (cf. 2:12f), for the context speaks of things only given to some. *In the Spirit* (cf. Mt. 22:43). For the Corinthians this was the difficult question. Speaking in the Spirit can be checked only to a certain extent. He who uses the gift of glossolalia is not always able to interpret what he is saying, since he does not know it himself. This gave rise to the question whether everything spoken in the Spirit was good and to God's glory. This question was justified for Greece knew of the wild ecstasies of the cult of Dionysius, and in II Thess. 2:2; I Jn. 4:1 mention is made of false spirits in the church. This enables us to understand the question whether all things spoken in ecstasy were good and whether they all came from the Spirit of God. Paul's answer is definite: it is impossible that one who speaks in the Spirit of God would say *Jesus is anathema,* for there is in the Christian faith one firm principle, one work of the Spirit which remains always the same (cf. vs. 4) and never turns away from Jesus Christ. Paul writes: *Spirit of God,* i. e., indirectly he acknowledges that there are other spirits as well, but at the same time he indicates where the Christian can find

---

[2] γνωρίζω.

the certainty that he is on the right path. The real point is that we have the Spirit of God.

Anathema:[3] strictly speaking, that which is set apart for the deity, the present which is consecrated or devoted to a god. In the second place: that which is given up to a god may have in view a curse. That which is cursed is abandoned to the gods. Thus "anathema" can be used of curses. Paul could hardly mean that a Corinthian had actually said: Jesus be cursed! In the first place, the words of the text do not support this view. Secondly, the point of Paul's argument is such that the only thing we can assume is that the Corinthians who did not understand glossolalia feared that something might be said that was wrong or irreverent. The correct interpretation is that Paul, without referring to an acual statement, assures his readers that no one who speaks in the Spirit of God will say: Cursed be Jesus. *Jesus is anathema* is simply a brief statement, summarizing everything that could be said against Jesus. *Jesus is Lord* on the contrary, is a real confession, through which the Christian church distinguishes itself from Jews and pagans; we find this confession often in the New Testament (Rom. 10:9; II Cor. 4:5; Phil. 2:11). That confession nobody can make except he be in the Spirit of God. In this context these words are not to be taken of the ordinary confession of the believer, but of the confession in glossolalia. This is not strange, for the speaking in tongues is a speaking to God's honor (14:2). The question whether it is not possible to confess Jesus as Lord with the lips only (cf. Rom. 10:9) is not under discussion here and is therefore irrelevant. The apostle speaks of the extraordinary gifts of the Spirit and he does this upon the presupposition that there are real gifts of the Spirit. Paul states that if anybody has these gifts he can in no wise blaspheme and that, if anybody confesses Jesus as Lord, that must be in any case the work of the Holy Spirit. This is then a means whereby to discern the spirits (vs. 10), a means such as the Corinthians had been anxious to have.

---

[3] ἀνάθεμα: the Hellenistic form of the classical ἀνάθημα.

THE DIVERSITY OF GIFTS

12:4-11

4 Now there are diversities of gifts, but the same Spirit.

5 And there diversities of ministrations, and the same Lord.

6 And there are diversities of workings, but the same God, who worketh all things in all.

7 But to each one is given the manifestation of the Spirit to profit withal.

8 For to one is given through the Spirit the word of wisdom; and to another the word of knowledge, according to the same Spirit:

9 to another faith in the same Spirit; and to another gifts of healings, in the one Spirit;

10 and to another workings of miracles; and to another prophecy; and to another discernings of spirits; to another *divers* kinds of tongues; and to another the interpretation of tongues:

11 but all these worketh the one and same Spirit, dividing to each one severally even as he will.

4 After having offered a solution of the Corinthian difficulties Paul begins to speak positively about the spiritual gifts. The first thing is that the Corinthians overestimated the speaking in tongues. Certainly, Paul himself also honors this gift as a precious gift of the Spirit but it is wrong to place it above all other spiritual gifts. There are many gifts, but they are all given by one and the same Spirit. This agrees with the last words of vs. 3.

Diversities: The Greek word[4] has the sense of distributing. This accounts for the plural here, for Paul does not refer to the one work of the Spirit as He is distributing His gifts but rather to the various distributions of these gifts. Whether this refers to the fact that the Holy Spirit, every time a charism is given is dispensing that gift at that very moment, or to the different gifts that are given to different persons is irrelevant here. The thought conveyed is that there are various charismata and that all those

---

[4] διαίρεσις

charismata are given by one Spirit. The idea is one of distribution and this implies that no one gets everything.

In which sense are we to understand charismata here: in a general sense, of all the gifts of the Spirit, or in a special sense, of the extraordinary gifts which God gave to the early church? It should be noted that in 12:9, 28, 30 the word *gifts* is qualified by *healings*. This implies that the word gift, charisma, is used generally, whereas the qualification points to a special use of the word. In 7:7; 12:31 on the contrary, the word is used in a special sense. For these reasons the word had best be taken in a general sense as in 1:7, of all the gifts of the Spirit, but with the understanding that Paul had particularly in view the special gifts such as prophecy, glossolalia, etc. This interpretation also shows the propriety of the use of this word at the head of an enumeration such as is given in the following verses.

There is no clear statement here that it is the Spirit who gives all those charismata, since the context calls for a contrast between the oneness of the Spirit and the diversity of His gifts. Nevertheless the fact that they are gifts, charismata, which we receive from the Spirit, is stressed. And in view of vs. 8 we may say that it is one and the same Spirit who distributes all the charismata. The apostle's standpoint, therefore, appears to be that there are many gifts of the Spirit and that it is wrong to esteem any one of them more highly than the rest.

5 There is also a distribution of *ministrations,* services. This point is stated only briefly, for the sake of comparison. Paul knew that the Corinthians were convinced that it was one and the same glorified Lord who called to various services.[5] Thus it is also with the charismata.

6 Vs. 6 makes a similar reference to the *workings,* which are the various kind of forces working in the church. The reference may even be in general to all the forces which God has given, not only those that work in His kingdom (cf. *all things in all*). Paul's argument gains strength through this remark. In order to

---

[5] The Greek text has διακονίαι. The word διακονία does not exclusively denote the work of the church-officers, it may denote every service to the good of the church. Be this as it may, it is very important that "Spirit" and "ministration" are mentioned in the same context. It is not so that the church in the first period was governed by the Spirit apart from church-officers.

set forth the diversity and the unity of the gifts of the Spirit the apostle mentions first the work of Christ in His church and afterwards the work of God in creation. Everywhere there is difference and yet it is God who *works all things in all.*[6] The church sees and knows this; let her see it also in regard to the gifts of the Spirit.[7]

7 In vs. 7 we have the second link of the argument. After first calling attention to the unity of the work of the Spirit the apostle now speaks of its diversity. Hence: *to each one is given.* That which is given is first called in general: *the manifestation of the Spirit.* These words may refer to the Spirit's manifesting *Himself* (subjective genitive) or to the revealing of the works of the Spirit (objective genitive). The difference is not important in this context: in either case *"manifestation"* is the subject of *"is given"* so that the action of the Holy Spirit is in view. The apostle may very well have both the subjective and the objective sense in mind. The verse implies that there is a special manifestation of the Holy Spirit in the life of every Christian. The works of the Spirit that appear outwardly are different, be it that every Christian may have more than one charisma, just as Paul himself did (7:7; 14:18). Since vs. 8 is to enumerate the various workings of the Spirit, Paul's words *"to each one is given"* must mean: to everyone who has special gifts of the Spirit is given. This will appear less strange if it is kept in mind that certain words, such as the word spirit (*pneuma,* cf. 14:4) are often used in the chapters 12-14 in a special sense, namely in connection with the charismata.

Vs. 7 mentions the purpose of the gift of the working of the Holy Spirit: *to profit withal.* That reminds us of what was written in 10:23 and parallel texts. With his treatment of the charismata Paul thus comes back to the leading principle of our letter. That principle is throughout that everything one possesses or is allowed to use must be used in such a manner that it is to the glory of God and the well-being of one's fellow-creatures. That principle is put here very generally, in accord with the

---

[6] ἐν πᾶσιν: the context shows that Paul has in view persons, not things.

[7] Vs. 4: τὸ πνεῦμα: vs. 5: ὁ κύριος; vs. 6: ὁ Θεός; perhaps an allusion to the Holy Trinity (cf. II Cor. 13:13; Eph. 4:4-6).

general tone of these verses. The brethren or the church are not mentioned specifically, just well-being in general. It is important that we should encounter this principle here too. It is the third thing Paul mentions as he prepares to admonish the Corinthians because of their undue esteem of glossolalia. These three things we now know: all charismata descend from one and the same Spirit; there is a diversity of gifts; they are given "to profit withal," i. e., for the common good (RSV), not to the end that one should boast of them.

8 The apostle begins to enumerate different manifestations of the Spirit as consequences of the gifts of the Spirit. Paul does not enumerate such manifestations only as were present in the first period of the church. There is one Spirit from whom descend all spiritual gifts (cf. vs. 11). *For* is used because the diversities referred to, and perhaps also the fact that they were given "to each one" is now proved from generally known facts. *Through*[8] *the Spirit*: God is the One who gives but He does so especially through the Spirit, who dwells in the church since the day of Pentecost and who determines the character of the gifts (cf. Rom. 5:5; then Rom. 8:12; Eph. 4:4 f.; I Thess. 4:8). *Through the Spirit*: I Cor. 2:10; II Tim. 1:14. *The word of wisdom* as in ch. 1 and 2. Only in this verse the expression is used in a favorable sense by means of a change of the governing word and the word governed (cf. 1:17). *The word of wisdom* is the word or speech which has wisdom as its contents. It appears that in this context wisdom is not just the virtue of the right intuition, the right insight, but also the result which is acquired through practicing this virtue. The reference is not to a word spoken with wisdom as is clear from a comparison with *word of knowledge* which cannot indicate the word spoken with knowledge, but rather the word which has knowledge as its contents. Not only the words but also their contents are gifts of the Spirit (cf. 2:13). Knowledge implies, more than wisdom does, research and investigation, although knowledge too should not be taken in a purely intellectual sense; it has an existential character. And it is more suitable than "wisdom" to indicate the result. However, the context compels one to give to both words similar meanings (cf. with 1:5). It is noteworthy that Paul

---

[8] διά, not ὑπό, presently κατά and ἐν

285

does not use the words *through the Spirit* here, but: *according to the same Spirit,* i. e., the Spirit who works also in wisdom. For *"according to"* see Rom. 1:4; 8:4, etc.; it carries with it the idea of an agreeing with the Spirit who works in the church. The Spirit of God is the standard which determines whether a thing is good or valid. The wisdom and the knowledge with which the word is filled both descend from God. Since wisdom is primarily a virtue the emphasis is on how it is effected (*through*), whereas knowledge, being the result of inquiry in the first place, is characterized by *"according to* the Spirit."

9 There is a difference between the pronouns at the beginning of vss. 8, 9 and 10. Vs. 8: for to one — and to another; vs. 9: to another — and to another; vs. 10: to another (four times). The only reason for this difference, in our opinion, is the desire for variation.[9]

It strikes us that in vs. 9 *faith* is named among the charismata. According to Rom. 1:17; 3:22 et al., faith is given to all believers. How then is it possible that Paul writes: *to another faith?* The use of the word in this context proves that it, just like the word "spiritual," has a special meaning. It must mean a faith that has special, visible results, a faith that enables one to do miracles (cf. Mt. 17:20 et al. I Cor. 13:2). Of such a faith the expression *in the same Spirit* is understandable: the preposition *in* has an instrumental sense as well as designating the sphere in which the Spirit works. *In* expresses action more than "through" and "according to" (cf. Rom. 9:1f.). *Gifts of healings*: the charismata given by God to the primitive church to perform miracles of restoration to health. The plural "gifts" may indicate healings of various illnesses. Each illness requires a special charisma.

10 *Workings of miracles* (better, with the marginal note: *of powers*). There are certain powers which are not merely bestowed but which also work. In the believers who received charismata there appeared certain workings that must be attributed to special powers, given by God. The expression may also refer to

---

[9] In the Greek the differences are much greater: vs 7: ἑκάστῳ; vs. 8: ᾧ μὲν...ἄλλῳ δέ; vs. 9: ἑτέρῳ...ἄλλῳ δέ; vs. 10: ἄλλῳ...ἄλλῳ [δέ]...ἄλλῳ δέ...ἑτέρῳ ..ἄλλῳ. The difference between ἄλλος and ἕτερος has disappeared in the koine.

the enduring of extraordinary exertion, as we witness in the life of Paul and in that of his companions (e. g., II Cor. 11 :23f.).

Prophecy in the New Testament is of a somewhat different nature from that under the old dispensation. It is that special gift that calls and enables certain persons to convey revelations of God to His church. Only a few prophetic utterances are recorded in the New Testament (Acts 11 :28; 21 :11) but those few show us that the prophets did not receive the same kind of revelations as the apostles received, i. e., revelations of fundamental importance for the whole church, but rather such as proclaimed to the primitive church what it had to do and to know under special circumstances. Those revelations did not have a permanent significance and that may be the reason why so few prophecies are mentioned in the New Testament. The primitive church did not yet have a New Testament; hence her need of prophecies. After the New Testament canon was closed, about 200 A. D., the Montanists tried to revive prophecy artificially, but then the phenomenon disappeared. At that time the church knew what the standard was for her action and confession, because she found it in the New Testament. *Prophecy,* as Paul describes it, was of a permanent nature; there were prophets at Corinth. This may justify the conclusion that the other charismata also had a permanent character.

Another gift of the Spirit was the *discerning of spirits.* I Jn. 4:1 gives an explanation. There were also evil spirits at work as, e. g., in those who were demon-possessed. But there were also evil spirits working in the churches of gentile Christians (I Thess. 2:2; I Jn. 4:1). Such evil spirits may have manifested themselves in false prophecies but also in the performing of miracles (Acts 19: 13 f.). In general there was a devilish imitation of the charismata and of the work of Christ. From 14:29 we learn that a prophet had the gift of discerning the spirits (cf. 14:37). It is not always easy to discern the evil spirits from the good ones. This is implied by the admonitions of Acts 20:29; I Jn. 4:1, but also statements such as II Cor. 11 :14 f. where we read that the devil and his servants often disguise themselves in a comely appearance. Jesus Himself already warned His apostles to be on

287

their guard (Mt. 24:33). He who received the gift of discerning the spirits received a special insight, a special ability to distinguish between good and evil spirits. Both kind of spirits operate in and through human beings.

The last members of this enumeration are *kinds of tongues* and *interpretation of tongues*. The word "tongue" does not do full justice to the Greek original.[10] The Greek word indicates the speaking tongue, the tongue in action. From the preceding we know that to the charismata of which Paul speaks belongs the gift of a tongue that is moved by the Holy Spirit and is thus enabled to proclaim unusual things. This gift we call after the Greek word "glossolalia." It is that point that Paul wants to treat in the first place. Glossolalia is, as the preceding verses bear out, a gift of the same Spirit who also gives the other charismata. While honoring glossolalia, this fact implies at the same time that there are other gifts of the Spirit besides glossolalia. It is not feasible to treat the phenomenon of glossolalia fully here, since this cannot be done without treating all the relevant passages. Thus limiting ourselves to the exposition of I Corinthians we are unable to compare with it the data found, e. g., in the book of Acts. I Cor. 12-14 mentions glossolalia among the extraordinary gifts of the Spirit. It cannot refer to what we now call inspiration. For in the first place, prophecy precedes glossolalia and prophecy is used of the speaking by inspiration of the Spirit. Secondly, Paul mentions the interpretation of tongues as a gift of the Spirit, i. e., not every one could understand those speaking tongues. The reason for this cannot have been that, e. g., a Greek speaking person could not understand an Aramaic speaking person or the reverse, for if one did not know Greek or Aramaic one could learn that language as every language can be learned without a special gift of the Spirit. Paul speaks of Christians who received an extraordinary gift of the Holy Spirit, a charisma, to speak or to understand a language which did not have the ordinary human characteristics, a special language formed by the Spirit, unintelligible for ordinary people. The speaking in tongues, therefore, is the speaking of a miraculous spiritual lan-

---

[10] γλῶσσα.

guage that had its own sounds.[11] The plural *tongues* may imply
that this miraculous language of the Spirit was spoken at inter-
vals, the word *kinds* implies the existence of various sorts of
tongues, i. e., with one and the same person the tongue did not
always have the same character. It cannot be determined whether
kind refers to the contents or to the sounds. Two things are
clear: Paul has in view a "tongue" which under the influence of
the Spirit speaks in a way different from a normal tongue. And
it is possible that he who received the gift of tongues did not
possess the gift of interpretation, although both charismata could
be given to the same person (14:5, 13).

11 Vs. 11 sums up and states the main point again. That
point was that all the charismata are gifts of one Spirit. That is
implied in *"all these"* on the one side and in *"the one and the
same"* on the other. *All these* is to be taken of the gifts enumerated in vss. 7-10, which are all attributed to one and the same
Spirit. That this is so is clear from the fact that vs. 7 begins a
section which enlarges upon the first part of vss. 4-6. *Ministrations* are not mentioned any more. The one reference to "workings" in vs. 6 stands alone and is a formal word which has no
connection with the ones listed in vs. 10. *Worketh*, in the present
tense, implies that the Spirit gives these gifts continually. They
remain where they are given but only because the Spirit keeps
them in existence. There is a difference, to be sure, as Paul also
mentioned earlier. The one person has this, the other another
charisma. But that diversity is also from the Spirit. He and only
He distributes the gifts according to His will (7:7, cf. Mt. 25:15;
Rom. 12:3-6).

No one, therefore, should be dissatisfied or put the one charisma above the other. That would be a finding fault with the work
of the Spirit. This is Paul's foundation on which he rests the
right evaluation of glossolalia.

---

[11] More than once expositors have contended that this miraculous
language was the language spoken in Paradise. We do not deny
the plausibility of such a view but maintain that it cannot be proved
from the words of Paul but goes beyond them. Paul does not speak
about the nature of the sounds.

ILLUSTRATION OF CHRISTIAN UNITY

12:12-31a

12 For as the body is one, and hath many members, and all the members of the body, being many, are one body; so also is Christ.

13 For in one Spirit were we all baptized into one body, whether Jews or Greeks, whether bond or free; and were all made to drink of one Spirit.

14 For the body is not one member, but many.

15 If the foot shall say, because I am not the hand, I am not of the body; it is not therefore not of the body.

16 And if the ear shall say, Because I am not the eye, I am not of the body; it is not therefore not of the body.

17 If the whole body were the eye, where were the hearing? If the whole were hearing, where were the smelling?

18 But now hath God set the members each one of them in the body, even as it pleased him.

19 And if they were all one member, where were the body?

20 But now they are many members, but one body.

21 And the eye cannot say to the hand, I have no need of thee: or again the head to the feet, I have no need of you.

22 Nay, much rather, those members of the body which seem to be more feeble are necessary:

23 and those *parts* of the body, which we think to be less honorable, upon these we bestow more abundant honor; and our uncomely *parts* have more abundant comeliness;

24 whereas our comely *parts* have no need: but God tempered the body together, giving more abundant honor to that *part* which lacked;

25 that there should be no schism in the body; but *that* the members should have the same care one for another.

26 And whether one member suffereth, all the members suffer with it; or *one* member is honored all the members rejoice with it.

27 Now ye are the body of Christ, and severally members thereof.

28 And God hath set some in the church, first apostles, secondly prophets, thirdly teachers, then miracles, then gifts of healings, helps, governments, *divers* kinds of tongues.

29 Are all apostles? are all prophets? are all teachers? are all *workers* of miracles?

30 have all gifts of healings? do all speak with tongues? do all interpret?

31 But desire earnestly the greater gifts.

12 In vs. 12 we have the beginning of an elaborate figure of speech. It is true, Paul makes his application immediately but in vs. 14 he returns to the figurative way of speaking. The point which this figure is supposed to illustrate cannot be the work of the Spirit but rather the truth that unity and diversity quite naturally go together. It is clear that this constitutes a leap in the argument. Until now Paul spoke of the one Spirit who gave different charismata. The recipients of those gifts were only mentioned in clauses such as "to one," "to another." Here the apostle assumes that the church as a whole is the recipient of those gifts. The Spirit dwells in the church and works His gifts; the church is thereby constituted a unity but manifests also a great diversity. That thought Paul had not yet brought out. One might contend that only the apodosis *so also is Christ* contains that thought, since *"so"* corresponds with "as" of the protasis. Although this is a correct observation yet vs. 12 is only understandable if Paul had this thought in view from the very beginning, otherwise *"for"* is out of place. The argument is that the truth of the one Spirit and the many charismata appears in the congregation which is the recipient of the gifts. For that congregation is one and yet manifests a rich diversity which in turn presupposes the work of the Spirit as it was described.

It is generally known that *the body is one,* that the one body has *many members* and that all those *members, being many,* form *the one body.* In modern language that would be: the body is an organism, it has many members but it can only be what it is if it possesses all those members and if all those members are governed from one center; there is one life in all of them.

So also is Christ: Christ is also one body that has many members. This cannot be applied merely to the person of our Savior.

Paul does not make mention of Him either in this verse or in the following. This statement concerning Christ does not fit in with what is revealed to us in the Scriptures. For that reason we understand "Christ" as having reference to the body of Christ, in accordance with vs. 27 (cf. Eph. 1:22, 23), it is Christ *with His church* (cf. 6:15). The apparent reason why Paul does not write "the body of Christ" is that then the figure of speech would no longer be a figure, since the word "body" would then occur in both the figure and in the reality portrayed by the figure. For that which holds true of the one body also holds true of the other. Paul would then have to write: the church can be called the body of Christ because it possesses the nature of a body. But that is not the point Paul wishes to make; he is anxious to demonstrate the presence of unity and diversity among those who have received the gifts of the Spirit. Nor could the word "church" be used very well, for the organization of the church is not the point in question, and it would be impossible for the apostle thus to refer to the unity of the one King, Christ, and His many officers. For those reasons Paul, taking account of the close union between Christ and the believers, writes: so also is *Christ.* This interpretation does not exclude Christ but it thinks of the church and of its Head, namely Christ.

13 *For* adds a new reason to the preceding one, stating why Paul could write: *so also is Christ,* i. e., why the church manifests both unity and diversity, which makes the figure of a body appropriate. That is the consequence of the way in which the church manifests itself. In reality the subject *we* implies a great diversity. *We all* who today form the one congregation, in former times were quite diverse; we were Jews or Gentiles, according to our religion or nationality, slaves or free men, according to our social position. The analogy between the first two groups and the last two consists in the fact that the position of both the *bond* and the *free* does not alter after the Corinthians have become Christians. This prompts us to take *Jews or Greeks* not so much of their respective religions as of their nationality which is also something permanent. All those different people become one body by baptism, they form the body of the church and that is accomplished by[12] the one Spirit. Baptism receives significance only if there is an activity of the Spirit, hence the addition: *in one Spirit.* Paul does not imply that baptism incorporates into the body of Christ, but he writes that all are baptized by one Spirit (cf. Mt. 3:11), unto one body, i. e., that incorporation does not depend on the administration of baptism but on the work of the Spirit. Where that work of the Spirit is wrought, people entirely different from one another form one body, a body which according to vs. 12 may be called "Christ." In the first century A. D. the unification of so varied a multitude was very remarkable; such a thing only took place in the Christian church. No wonder therefore that that church also manifests that other unity combined with multiplicity, which exists in the realm of the spiritual gifts. What Paul does is to borrow his argument from the well known fact of the unity of a congregation which is of such a composite nature. After this has been done the apostle can go on and draw a conclusion with regard to the charismata of the Spirit and that the more easily since the unity wrought by baptism is also a work of the Spirit.

We were all made to drink:[13] these words do not refer to any particular action in the Christian church, and so we assume that this is figurative language. For *"to drink"* cf. Jn. 6:53; it implies a very close communion. Subject of that communion are *we;* of all the members of the congregation it can be said that they are made to drink of the same Spirit. The closest union is this that we all are united as closely as possible with one and the same Spirit of God, who dwells in us all (3:16)[14]

---

[12] Greek: not ὑπό but ἐν, because baptism as such is not performed by the Spirit. But baptism is only valid if there is a working of the Spirit. Therefore ἐν ἑνὶ πνεύματι is employed.

[13] The Greek verb ποτίζω governs a double accusative, "to cause somebody to drink something." Literally: one made us all drink one Spirit.

[14] The aorist ἐποτίσθημεν is not to be taken of baptism but of the receiving of the Spirit at baptism (Acts 10:44f.; 19:5f.). That is the historical fact which Paul has in view.

14ff Vs. 14 carries us back to the figure of vs. 12.[15] This figure can be used again both because of its many implications and also because the church itself is the body of Christ so that what applies to a body also applies to the church. The truth that *the body is not one member* is universally accepted. Paul then puts into the mouth of the various members of the body statements which are absurd because they failed to appreciate the unity of the body, a unity which cannot be abolished. The *foot* is right when it says that it is not a hand, for there is a difference between the members, but it is wrong if it does not like to belong to the body simply because it is not a hand. Underlying the argument is the assumption that the hand does belong to the body. *Of the body*: a part of the body.[16] The ear might speak in a similar way to the eye. In both cases the inferior member seems to suppose that the superior member certainly must belong to the body. This indicates diversity.

17 Vs. 14-16 was based on the existence of a difference between the members. Vs. 17 on the other hand supposes that this difference does not exist. *If the whole body* were only one member the condition would be sad. Then certain functions could not be performed.

18 Vs. 18 is similar to vs. 11 and, in figurative language, it interprets vs. 11, by pointing out that the truth stated in vs. 11 is not exceptional since there is a corresponding phenomenon in the body. *God hath set the members,* i. e., God created the body in such a way that it has members and more particularly these members. God gave to each of the members its special place in the body, making them a part of the body. And He did so according to His own good pleasure. Paul adds those last words in order to emphasize that we cannot explain why all things are the way they are.

19 The figure is still continued, this time in close connection with vs. 17. Hypothetically the apostle had placed on a par the

---

[15] καὶ γάρ is difficult. Vs. 14 is neither a reason for vs. 13, nor is it like vs. 13 a reason for vs. 12. But vs. 14 has a similar content to vs. 12. This prompts us to take καὶ γάρ as a γάρ following upon and coordinated with vs. 12.

[16] *Therefore* is in the Greek παρὰ τοῦτο: against that, i.e. contrary to what it says (cf. also παρὰ τοῦτο in vs. 16).

whole body and one of its members. Now he calls attention to the distinct nature of a member and of a body. Suppose there were unity of all the members but that unity were "one member"— then the whole could not be distinguished from its parts, but all the members would be one homogeneous mass. That would mean that the unity, the organism of the body, would not exist. The body is not just the total of the members, it is something different from the members.

20 Vs. 20 describes the actual situation: one body, many members. In other words, the generally accepted truth stated in vs. 12 is repeated again, this time with more certainty after what has been said. The order is different from what it was earlier. In vs. 12 Paul started with the unity, here with the diversity.

21 Vs. 21 draws a conclusion from the fact that the body is one. If the body is a unity then the members are related just because they are the members of one organism. Here again Paul mentions those members which are visible, external and most frequently functioning. If the head does not lead the feet cannot walk.

22 *Nay, much rather* (RSV, less literal: on the contrary), introduces an antithesis which is not fully expressed. Besides, although still using figurative language, Paul no longer personifies the members, but makes a general statement. We paraphrase: the members cannot say that they do not need one another for they all have to perform their own task in the organism of the body. No member is superfluous, yea, all *those members* that *seem to be*[17] *feeble are necessary. Seem:* appearances are deceptive; human opinion deems certain members of the body more important than others. But that opinion is not always right, a fact which is often recognized upon further reflection. *More feeble*, to wit: than other members. It is difficult to say which members Paul has in view in this verse, perhaps the arms and legs which enable the hands and the feet to do their work, but seem to have no independent function outside of that. One might also think of the intestines, without which no man can live.

---

[17] Greek: ὑπάρχειν, indicating a continual condition.

23 In vs. 22 Paul mentioned a widely held incorrect opinion, here he mentions the right opinion also held by Paul himself.[18] That right opinion leads to a *"bestowing of honor." Less honorable* is not the same as *more feeble*. With *honor* is meant the value we attribute to certain organs of the body and in consequence of that the respect with which we treat them. We value one member higher than another, be it that the opinions may differ. In the second part of the verse Paul clearly refers to the consequences sin has had for the evaluation of our members. Assuming that this also applies to the first half then the words *upon these we bestow more abundant honor* become more intelligible, for their implication is then that we cover with a special care some of our members, e. g., the sex organs and the organs of secretion, and in so doing we bestow more honor on them than on other members which we do not cover. That, in any case, is the meaning of the second part of the verse, for that part characterizes certain members as *uncomely*. The function of those members is not indicated by Paul, but rather in what position they are. Their uncomeliness shall not be revealed.

24-25 The text-division is not right at this point, for the first part of vs. 24, asserting that our comely members, e. g., our face, do not need any special care or cover, belongs to the thought content of vs. 23. A new thought follows in which the actual situation is attributed to the good pleasure of God. This thought is another important link in Paul's argument. After pointing out in an elaborate figure of speech that unity and diversity can go together, yea that such is in the nature of things, the apostle makes clear that God has ordered it thus (cf. vs. 11, 18). The repetition of this thought indicates its importance.

God, says Paul, *tempered the body together*: God mixed the members of the body.[19] The fact that the body is what it is, is due to God's disposal, and we human beings ought not to find fault with it. God has constituted the body a unity by giving each member a special privilege. There is an equilibrium; some mem-

---

[18] ASV has "seem" in vs. 22, "think" in vs. 23 whereas the Greek has δοκεῖν in both verses. This makes for a greater degree of parallelism than we have in English; the two words "to seem" and "to think" must both be taken in the same sense.

[19] Greek: συνεκέρασεν τὸ σῶμα.

bers come behind, e. g., because they are not to be seen. But even to those God gives a special privilege because they are indispensable for the working of the body. And the result of it is that there is no division in the body (there were divisions in the Corinthian church); all the members of the body take care of one another. It is impossible for them to perform their task if any member is lacking. The verb: *to have care for,* is used by way of analogy, in connection with the personification of the members (vs. 15f.). All the members *have the same care one for another.*

26 Vs. 26 mentions some consequences which result from the fact that God thus shaped the body. That consequence is self-evident: a close connection means to suffer and to enjoy honor together. That this consequence is chosen with a special application for the situation at Corinth which was far from healthy is apparent.

27 After drawing the conclusion Paul makes an application. *Ye* Corinthians are not the body of Christ but a *body of Christ.*[20] Paul does not have the universal church in view but the local congregation at Corinth, in which the universal church manifests itself. The Corinthian church as such is a *corpus Christi,* an organism made by Christ and maintained by Him, having the complete character of a body as that was described. If the church does not want to be guilty before Christ it will have to show its character. It must be what it is. The individual Corinthians are *severally,* each for his part, members of the body. The apostle does not here use the well known figure of Christ as the Head of His body the church, but he speaks of the fact that the Corinthian church is an organism instituted by Christ. The word "body" is not used in quite the same way as in vs. 13: there it is used of the universal church, at least in its primary reference, here more of the local church. But the distinction between the two should not be made absolute, they are two sides of the same thing. The Corinthians are also members of the universal church.

28 In vs. 28 there is a change in the argument: the apostle abandons figurative language and its application. *And* indicates a change of subject. However, Paul does not change the subject

---

[20] Greek: σῶμα, not τὸ σῶμα. It is true that σῶμα is part of the predicate. But if Paul had in view Christ's body he would have written the article.

too radically for he continues to lay the foundation on which afterwards he can build his conclusions concerning the glossolalia question. The elements in that foundation were: first, there is one Spirit, who gives different charismata. Expanding that thought a bit the apostle pointed out that there is one church which, besides having these different gifts of the Spirit, also has different members. In vs. 28 the apostle begins to speak about the diversity of offices and gifts which God had given to that one church that it might be governed by them.

Some:[21] God is the One who distinguishes. In vs. 27 we were compelled to take "body" of the local church, but we cannot do the same with "church" in vs. 28, for Paul's enumeration far exceeds the limits found in any local church. *Church* in vs. 28 is the world-church as is also indicated by the use of the article. The objection based on the fact that the local congregation at Corinth is also called the body of Christ (vs. 27), is not valid, for by putting the universal church first and by speaking about the diversity found in it, the apostle also speaks concerning the church at Corinth by implication. This is therefore a new picture of the church which must serve to teach the Corinthians that glossolalia is not the only gift of God. God desires diversity as appears from His own institution.

He set, first of all, *apostles,* men directly called by Christ to be His witnesses. The *prophets,* who follow next, have in common with the apostles that they only have a task to perform in the first period of the New Testament church. Their office is not as important and not as universal as that of the apostles, but, like that of the apostles, it is not restricted to one locality. The *teachers* are among the ordinary officers in the church, they are the men who teach and preach the revelation which was once received. This teaching may have been based on a special *charisma* (cf. vs. 8), but it must have been done without such a special gift of the Spirit as well. The information concerning the teachers which the rest of the New Testament furnishes indicates that their office may have been merely local, as could be deduced from Acts

---

[21] Greek: οὓς μέν. It is impossible to understand this as introducing a relative clause which would form the protasis of the apodosis which begins with πάντες in vs. 29. It is better to translate the expression by "some" (cf. vs. 28)

13:1 and from the close connection of the teachers with the *pastors* (Eph. 4:11). In Jas. 3:1, we read that the office of a teacher was open to everyone's ambition, and the requirement of a special charisma is not mentioned. The office of a teacher is based on a vocation rather than on a *charisma*. It is one of the most common among the ordinary offices in the church.

Then indicates that a different class follows next. There is no further mention of the names of offices but rather of gifts. This is partly due to the fact that Paul no longer refers exclusively to office bearers, and also to the fact that Paul does not use any special names designating the bearers of the gifts which he is now to enumerate. The list includes services performed for the good of the church, some of them ordinary, others extraordinary in nature. All those services may be performed by means of a special charisma but that is not at all necessary, although the ability to fulfill the several tasks comes from the Spirit. The point which Paul stresses is not that all those services require a special charisma, but that there is a great diversity among them in the one church.

Miracles, miraculous powers (cf. vs. 10), *gifts of healings* (see vs. 9). *Helps*:[22] referring to continual aid rendered by special persons. The context requires us to think of help which was rendered to the church. There were apparently people, who, without holding a particular office, rendered many services to the church enabled by the special gifts of the Spirit which they had received. Those services may have included the care for the church's finances and the arranging of the divine services. Then follow *governments*: comparison with I Tim. 5:17 indicates that there were elders who ruled without laboring in the word and in doctrine. Those men were charged not so much with the administration of the external things as perhaps the "helps" were, but rather with the spiritual leadership. *Kinds of tongues*: see vs. 10. It is worthy of note that Paul is now back at the first part of his argument, dealing with the spiritual gifts and emphasizing especially the fact of the one Spirit giving a diversity of gifts. At first this was done in a rather direct discourse, now the attention is drawn to the actual situation in the church. Yet progress has been made, for the various *charismata* are now considered in their relationship to the offices which, as everybody

---

[22] Greek: ἀντιλήμψεις.

agrees, have been given to the church. Thus the true nature of the diversity is more clearly set forth. It indicates that the difference in the distribution of the gifts of the Spirit is not an unrelated phenomenon; on the contrary, it is analogous to the diversity of the offices. Apostles, prophets have received charismata but the main point is not that they have those special gifts but rather that they are the officers of the church. This enables the Corinthians to see the diversity of the charismata so that they will understand that the gift of glossolalia, so highly esteemed by them but mentioned last by Paul, is but one of the charismata given by God to the church.

29, 30 The questions in vss. 29 and 30 clarify the contention made in vs. 28. Not everybody, only some received charismata. With respect to the apostolate the Corinthians would immediately agree. But once that point is granted, then it has been established that God Himself makes the distinction and that the one *charisma* should not be extolled at the cost of the other.

The meaning of the questions is clear from the preceding verses, but the main question : *do all speak with tongues?* requires some elucidation. This is the first time Paul uses the expression : *to speak with tongues,* from which the phenomenon of glossolalia derives its name. The phrase is remarkable since everybody uses his tongue while speaking. This proves that "tongue" must be taken in a special sense, as also was shown by the words "spiritual," "Spirit," "faith." He who has received the *charisma* of glossolalia speaks with a special tongue, moved by the Spirit. This calls a language into existence which is different from ordinary languages, a language which needs interpretation. Glossolalia is not the speaking of a foreign language, for nobody needs a charisma to understand that sort of language. Foreign languages are spoken with an ordinary human tongue. Thus Paul returns to the point of speaking in tongues (see vss. 4-11), and its interpretation, which is the main point in this context.

31 Vs. 31 lists two distinctive marks of the charismata. Paul refers to *the greater gift,* or, as another and better translation reads: *the greatest gift* (RSV: highest gift[23]), cf. 14:1. This points to a difference between the gifts of the Spirit. The fact

---

[23] The comparative μείζων has the significance of a superlative.

300

that the Corinthians also made a difference is consequently not in itself worthy of rebuke. But this distinction must be made in accordance with God's standard and not man's own. The fact that the apostle in his enumeration of the gifts of the Spirit twice gave the lowest place to the gift of glossolalia is important. Apostles and prophets rank higher than those Christians who speak in tongues. But what is the meaning of *desire*? Was it possible to strive for those charismata, yea to give preference to some while striving for them? The context points out that the church at Corinth valued the gift of glossolalia very highly, i. e., the church hoped that that gift might be given to it abundantly. That desire would have to be changed, for it was wrong to put the speaking in tongues above all the other gifts. That is why Paul now summons the Corinthians to realize which gifts were the most important and to pray the Lord that they might receive them. The church must leave it to God (cf. vs. 11) to determine which gifts were most necessary at Corinth. The context forbids one to take vs. 31 as an admonition aimed at stimulating the individual Corinthians to strive for special charismata.

1-31 Paul propounds one thesis in this chapter. He combats the abuse of the gift of glossolalia, only first in a preparatory way. Three times the apostle points out that there is unity but also diversity in the work of the Holy Spirit and therefore also in the church. By means of that thought the apostle challenges the Corinthians' wrong estimation of glossolalia but maintains at the same time that the speaking in tongues is one of the gifts of the Spirit. Against that background the aforementioned gift appears as only one among the precious gifts of God.

Special attention should be given to the fact that words such as "charisma," "spiritual," "faith" have a special sense in this section. The great significance of this is that it prevents us from separating the giving of the charismata from the work of the Spirit in general. There is one great work of the Spirit and the church and the charismata are the exponents of it. That is precisely the reason why love can be called the highest of all the charismata (cf. Gal. 5:22). Love is also a gift of the Spirit, a gift given to all Christians.

CHAPTER XIII

THE SIGNIFICANCE OF LOVE

12:31b-13:13

12:31b And moreover a most excellent way show I unto you.

1 If I speak with the tongues of men and of angels, but have not love, I am become sounding brass, or a clanging cymbal.

2 And if I have *the gift of* prophecy, and know all the mysteries and all knowledge; and if I have all faith, so as to remove mountains, but have not love, I am nothing.

3 And if I bestow all my goods to feed *the poor,* and if I give my body to be burned, but have not love, it profiteth me nothing.

4 Love suffereth long, *and* is kind; love envieth not, love vaunteth not itself, is not puffed up,

5 doth not behave itself unseemly, seeketh not its own, is not provoked, taketh not account of evil;

6 rejoiceth not in unrighteousness, but rejoiceth with the truth;

7 beareth all things, believeth all things, hopeth all things, endureth all things.

8 Love never faileth: but whether *there be* prophecies, they shall be done away; whether *there be* tongues, they shall cease; whether *there be* knowledge, it shall be done away.

9 For we know in part, and we prophesy in part;

10 but when that which is perfect is come, that which is in part shall be done away.

11 When I was a child I spake as a child, I felt as a child, I thought as a child: now that I am become a man, I have put away childish things.

12 For now we see in a mirror, darkly; but then face to face: now I know in part; but then shall I know fully even as also I was fully known.

13 But now abideth faith, hope, love, these three; and the greatest of these is love.

302

Chapter 13 is not to be regarded as interrupting the discourse concerning the charismata. On the contrary, it is a necessary link in the argument which has as its purpose to assign to the glossolalia its rightful place. Chapter 12 laid the general foundation. Glossolalia was thus listed as one of a series of spiritual gifts and given its proper place. This brought out the truth that glossolalia is not the principal gift of the Spirit, a truth which is further enhanced when in our chapter love is put above all charismata, i. e., also above glossolalia.

The last words of chapter 12 are often taken with chapter 13. In any case they constitute the transition between the two chapters. When Paul writes : and moreover a most excellent way show I unto you, the words "moreover" and "most" (RSV: a still more) clearly refer to the earnest desire to which the apostle had incited his readers. The way which Paul now points out surpasses all other ways, i. e., all kinds of action and of conduct, by its excellence. The greater eminence of that way is not that it would be a better means of achieving the charismata than the way of earnest desire, for that is not the point at issue here. No, this way is even better than the desire for charismata itself. Paul does not command here, but by extolling love he shows its excellence. His purpose is to incite the Corinthians to seek love in the first place. The apostle is so overpowered by the greatness of love that he gives to his thoughts a most wonderful form.

1 Vs. 1 does not concern itself primarily with the reality of things. It merely states that if such and such were the case then something would follow. As to the tongues of men, Paul actually possesses the gift of glossolalia as is stated in 14:18; moreover in 12:10 Paul declares that one person may have several gifts of the Spirit. It is different with the reference to the tongues of angels. The apostle does not contend that the angels actually received the gift of glossolalia. He only implies that if he had at his disposal not only a type of glossolalia as it is found among men, but also one which might be found among angels and yet, despite all this, would lack love, that then all those benefits would be of no avail to him. Moreover, Paul uses the first person singular here not to designate himself in the first place but rather with a more general reference of what is true of others or of everybody

303

(cf. 4:6). It is especially appropriate for Paul to do this because he is going to say certain less agreeable things.

I am become: I have come to that point and remain there; I am ultimately no more than sounding brass. *Sounding brass* (RSV noisy gong): a sounding brass instrument. *Clanging cymbal*: an onomatopoetic word designating a loudly rattling cymbal. The figure implies that a man gifted with glossolalia, who has no love, is no more than an inanimate, impersonal instrument, which makes noise or may give certain signals (cf. 14:8), but has no heart.

The purpose of this verse is not to place glossolalia without love over against glossolalia with love but rather to compare glossolalia as such with love. About the same thing can be said of the subsequent verses. A person may have received many gifts from God, he may use them to advantage, but if he has no love all those gifts cannot prevent that ultimately he is nothing but a dead instrument.

2 In 12:10 and 30 Paul assigned the last place to glossolalia and in so doing he put it below other gifts of the Spirit. In chapter 13 the apostle mentions glossolalia first and ascends from there to the gifts which involve a greater degree of consciousness. The first one is prophecy, frequently referred to in chapter 12. The phrase: *to know all mysteries,* did not occur previously. It is followed by *"knowledge"* which points to 12:8 where Paul speaks of *the word of wisdom.* A mystery in the New Testament is generally speaking something that was hidden before but revealed afterwards. The knowledge of those mysteries rests upon revelation (Mt. 13:11 cf. 16:17; Eph. 3:3f.). For that reason it may be given a place among the charismata. The "mysteries" refer especially to the work of Christ which appeared to be not only for Israel but for the world (Jn. 3:16). *Knowledge* in this context is also to be regarded as a *charisma.* This word, after the preceding, refers less to the character of the revelation than to the active use of what was revealed. "Knowledge" in the New Testament must not be taken in a purely intellectual sense, it contains a mystical element (see e. g., Jn. 17:3; also I Cor. 2:12). *Faith* (cf. 12:9): here faith to perform miracles. This word reminds us of Mt. 17:20; Lk. 17:6. It should be remembered that an absolute distinction between the extraordinary gifts (the charismata) and the permanent gifts of the Spirit cannot be made. They all descend from one Spirit and the borderline between them is not clearly marked. Paul does not imply that he received all those gifts himself but he simply states that if he should have them all but should not have love he would be *nothing*, i. e., without any value. The contrast is stronger than in vs. 1. In vs. 1 Paul asserted that he would at least be something even though he lacked love, but after he has enumerated the gifts which surpass glossolalia, he states that he would be nothing if he would be without love. The highest charismata do not in themselves lend any dignity to a person.

3   With a slight change of subject Paul omits any reference to the charismata in the protasis, but speaks of an extraordinary evidence of love for the brethren and for the Lord's work. The climax of the previous verse is thus interrupted but it is maintained in another respect. First, because it is more difficult to do the things mentioned here than those mentioned in vs. 2. Second, because this protasis forms a transition to what follows and teaches us provisionally that the love of which Paul speaks is love to the neighbor as well as love to God, it is love as a principle. The apostle has thus made a transition from the realm of the intellect to that of the will. *I bestow all my goods to feed the poor*: The Greek word[1] means either: "to spend everything on food." or "to break into crumbs." A choice between the two is not necessary for in any case Paul uses the word of a giving to others one's entire property. *I give my body to be burned*: history does not record any major persecution which would have taken place at the time Paul wrote these words. We only know of the martyrdom of Stephen and of the stoning of Paul at Lystra (Acts 14:19), but there is no record of anyone being burned at the stake at this early time. Paul uses the words hypothetically: To him they stand for the acme of self-sacrifice, an interpretation which agrees with vs. 1. It also applies to the distribution of goods to the poor, likewise a hypothetical case for Paul who was a poor man himself. On the other hand, we should not forget that though this may be hypothetical it is not by that same token unreal or incapable of fulfilment. Paul could have distributed the few things he possessed. And of the possibility of true lovers of

---

[1] ψωμίζω.

God giving their bodies to the fire we know from the story of the three men in the fiery furnace (Dan. 3). Apparently Paul is thinking of the worst that could happen, both with regard to his possessions and with regard to his body. But all those sufferings do not *profit*[2] without love. Everybody who gives himself to the work of the Lord will receive his reward, but only if he has love. That is the reverse of 3:15.

4 Paul now no longer uses the first person singular but enumerates the works love performs. *Love suffereth long and is kind*:[3] opinions differ on the question whether the second "love" should be taken with *is kind* or with *envieth not*. This question does not affect the meaning of the words in either direction, although the rhythm of the clause pleads for a combination with *is kind*. A similar alternative presents itself with the third reference to love. Here considerations of rhythm plead for taking it with *envieth not* instead of joining it to *vaunteth not*. Apparently Paul continues to put the subject after the verb and avoids the repetition of the subject in the negative clauses. The Greek word for *"to envy"*[4] may be used of a virtue, namely of an assiduous striving for the good (12:31). Here it implies an envious striving which is incompatible with love, for envy and love are mutually exclusive. Since love implies contentment it causes one to esteem someone else better than himself (Phil. 2:3). *To vaunt* and *to be puffed up* remind us of the sin of the Corinthians who boasted in their pride (ch. 4). Love cannot do such a thing and consequently the Corinthians' boasting is not in harmony with love.

It is also worthy of note that Paul, instead of speaking of human beings and of their love, rather speaks of love itself. Perfect love is his subject and its qualities he depicts. This is love personified, for after all it is love which manifests itself in human conduct even though it is never perfect in human life. Christian love is witnessed in the Christian's life. The Corinthians should

---

[2] οὐδὲν ὠφελοῦμαι is middle: I am not profited by it.

[3] μακροθυμεῖν is passive suffering, it is waiting for what comes, as against ὑπομένειν, which is the active persevering. χρηστεύεσθαι to show kindness. μακροθυμία and χρηστότης: II Cor. 6:6; Gal. 5:22 (cf. Rom. 2:4). Paul joins related ideas together.

[4] ζηλοῦν.

search themselves to see if they are ruled by that Christian love. In this part of the chapter love is especially love to one's fellow men.

5 In vs. 5f. we find the same words as in the earlier part of the epistle. Those words must have had a particular appeal to the Corinthians. *To behave unseemly* (cf. 7:36), to treat somebody in a wrong way. Perhaps the reference is to the many irregularities at Corinth. *To seek one's own* is a genuinely human sin which love alone can conquer. *To provoke* (RSV: to be irritable) is the consequence of the real or the imaginary suffering of injustice. *Taketh not account of evil*: to ponder the ways and means of doing somebody harm. Love has nothing to do with all those evils. Love also keeps away from the powerful influence of injustice and sides with the truth (cf. vs. 6). The situation in the world is different (I Jn. 3:4f.).

6 Vs. 6 speaks of the joy of love. Love does not rejoice in *unrighteousness* but rather *with the truth*. Those two words are not to be taken in an abstract sense, for love simply cannot rejoice in abstract virtues. Both words must be understood concretely of the doing of injustice, or of the whole complex of unrighteous acts, and, in clear contrast with that, of the speaking of the truth. Injustice is falsehood for it denies rightful claims. Love and truth belong together, the one is the ethical, the other the intellectual good. Christ, the loving Savior, is a witness of truth (Jn. 8:40f; 18:37. cf. also II Thess. 2:12). *To rejoice with* (not "in") implies a personification of truth. Love cannot be neutral, it takes sides.

7 *Love beareth all things* (or: covereth, cf. I Pet. 4:8). The Greek word means: "To bear," or "to cover with silence," "to suppress." Both meanings fit the context. *To believe all things*: to trust, taken in a general sense. It certainly is remarkable that both faith and hope are here predicated of love (see vs. 13). This implies that in him who hopes and trusts hope and faith arise from love. When we love somebody we trust him fully, we expect nothing but good things from him even though appearances be against him. Vs. 13 also gives rise to the question whether Paul has not in view love in the fullest sense of the word. love toward God and toward our fellow man.

The passive notion of "suffering" (vs. 4) is supplemented by "enduring," which has an active sense: the overcoming of all difficulties. Love is inventive. The scope of *"all things"* is naturally limited to that which love can and may suffer, as is clear from vs. 6. The oft repeated *all* expresses the absoluteness of the thought.

8   In vss. 4-7 the connection between the subject and the charismata was tenuous, but it was not entirely lost out of sight as appears from vs. 8, which carries us back to the subject of the gifts of the Spirit. Vss. 4-7, therefore, are not so much a digression as an enlargement of the thought aimed at showing more clearly how love surpasses all charismata. Love makes man a man of God, it teaches him to live to the glory of God and the well-being of his brother. Everything that was said about love bears that out. The significance of this is that Paul, with respect to glossolalia, has defended the position that there should only be glossolalia if the church is edified by it (14:15).

In vs. 8, therefore, a new strophe begins, this time the last one, which leads us to the top and reveals to us all of love's glory. This appears from the words: *love never faileth* (never falls; RSV: never ends), i. e., it never disappears. Love is always present and where it is present it works. The context supports this interpretation of Paul's words: three charismata are mentioned; they are among the most highly reputed; of each of them the temporal character is indicated. *Prophecies*: not the single utterances of the prophets, but the cases of prophecy, prophesying as such. *Be done away*: the Greek word[6] means: to render inactive, inoperative. There will no longer be any prophecies for there will be no need for them. The time that this shall occur is indicated in vs. 10. Of the tongues Paul states more simply that *they shall cease. Knowledge* too will not any longer perform its task.

All these words, as we will understand, refer to the charismata, as everywhere else in this context. However, this should not prompt us to separate the ordinary work of the Spirit from His extraordinary work. Especially with respect to knowledge the difference between the ordinary and the extraordinary gift of the Spirit is rather slim. There is therefore no objection to

---

[6] καταϱγεῖν.

taking "knowledge" in this and the following verses as referring to knowledge in general, although concretely the Christian's knowledge is always in view.

9 Vs. 9 states the reason for what vs. 8 contended (*for*). That reason is that all our knowledge and all our prophesying (including the glossolalia, but about that Paul speaks in ch. 14) are *in part*, i. e., they do not reach their highest attainment; they do not become what they could be. In what respect these gifts are only in part is not indicated. The gifts themselves are perfect since they are given by the Spirit. The context forbids to think of the imperfection of sin. Vs. 12 speaks of the development of a child to manhood, vs. 13 of a seeing of an imperfect image. In view of this it appears best to take the phrase *in part* as having reference to the nature of this dispensation. And since this section deals with the affairs of the kingdom of God and with the church of Christ, we may go one step beyond this as we assume that Paul has in view the fact that the kingdom and the church have not yet come to the acme of their development. The question is not whether this is caused by the sin of man; Paul only states what has been revealed to him. This interpretation is supported by 15:24f. *We know in part* means that all human knowledge, even if it be given by way of charisma, is incomplete, unfinished. The words do not imply that we only know a part of that which is to be known, but rather that the knowing itself is imperfect (cf. we prophesy in part). Implied in this is (*for* we know, etc.) that when the zenith is reached those gifts will no longer operate. Note, however, that Paul does not imply that we need the charisma of prophecy only in this dispensation, a thing which could hardly be said of knowledge, but that both prophecy and knowledge, as they actually exist, bear the mark of this imperfect dispensation.

10 *When that which is perfect is come,* i. e., when the zenith has been reached, then by that very fact *all which is in part shall be done away.* The protasis and the apodosis refer to the same thing, the positive side explaining the negative. The world does not stand still nor does time, all things hasten toward the end as Paul has declared more than once. In 1:7 Paul gloried in the subjective expectation of the Corinthians; in 7:31b and in 15:24f. he stated the same truth objectively (cf. also Eph. 1:9f.). All things hasten to the end, to the culmination point; the Christian must reckon with that fact. Once the acme has been reached and this dispensation come to an end, then all that belonged to this dispensation, including the charismata, will terminate.

11 A figure of speech serves to illustrate that truth. A child becomes a man, but that child also has the desire to become a man whereas the man does not wish to be a child again. Using the first person singular again the apostle states that *when he was a child* he acted as a child.[7] Both his speaking and his disposition were that of a child. Youth marks the beginning in every respect. But as Paul's life developed, as he became a man and remained one,[8] he wiped out everything childish, he canceled it because it was powerless. The illustration is not applied; this was not necessary for it was used primarily to illustrate the preceding verses and only in the second place the following, and such only in part.

12 *For*: this verse can hardly contain a reason for the image of vs. 11, but it may very well furnish the ground for what was said in vss. 8-10. The many astounding things stated in those verses could well be in need of a special clarification. The causal clause contains another figure of speech. In vs. 11 the figure was used by way of comparison, but in vs. 12 the truth itself is expressed in figurative language, of which we have to avail ourselves whenever we treat subjects which are beyond this present dispensation. *To see* refers to Christian life in general, to thinking and speaking as well; the intellectual side is emphasized (cf. *I know*, in the second part of the verse). The contrast is one between *"now"* and *"then,"* this dispensation and the future, the latter being the period of perfection (vs. 10). It is true, the seeing of God is in the Scriptures identified with the highest of bliss (I Jn. 3:2) but it should not be forgotten that Paul does not speak of the seeing of God in the narrow sense of the word ("see" is without an object). Moreover Paul's use of this particular language (mirror, etc.) may have elicited the word "to see." The word stands for the Christian life as a whole, the charismata not excluded: prophecy, glossolalia, knowledge.

---

[7] Greek: νήπιος, little child.
[8] Greek: γέγονα (cf. vs. 1): to become something and to remain in that condition.

Our seeing in this dispensation is *in a mirror darkly.*[9] The mirror in antiquity gave a very poor image. Seeing something through a mirror only was not seeing the reality (II Cor. 3:18). It was like considering a riddle, which makes one wonder what one really sees. Our vision is hampered by a twofold darkness and hence it is *in part.* We are unable to determine what in our vision is precisely lacking, for if we could we would have freed ourselves of the imperfection of the mirror. The only thing that can be said is that our Lord reveals in a figure which is formally perspicuous that we, when we see, have not reached perfection. Our vision is not untrue, but it is imperfect as to its degree. When perfection has been reached *then* we shall see *face to face,* i. e., we shall with our eyes look straight into the face of things; there will be nothing between us and the things. Here again we are reminded of I Jn. 3:2. Passages like Ex. 33:11; Dt. 34:10 (confer also Gen. 32:30; Is. 52:8)[10] point in the same direction. The subsequent words also support this interpretation. Nevertheless we maintain that the vision of God, the knowledge of Him, although not entirely excluded, still is not the only thing Paul has in view. The reference is broader, Paul refers to a seeing in which our face is in immediate opposition with the face of things. "To see," as appears anew, implies a Christian's entire intellectual life, as is also clear from the word "to know" in this context. Paul quite naturally speaks of knowing here instead of prophecy or glossolalia. In the first place, knowledge does not bear a charismatic character quite as clearly as prophecy or glossolalia. It is hard to separate the charismata nature of knowledge from its ordinary side as it is the possession of every Christian. In other words, every Christian "knows" in a sense. Secondly, knowing implies the activity of the subject more than prophecy or glossolalia. And thirdly, knowledge implies both the action and its result. In vs. 9 Paul wrote that the reason why knowledge must be done away is the fact that it is in part. In our verse the thought is rather that knowledge may be used to characterize the new dispensation. During the latter there will not just be knowing, but knowing *fully,* intensely. This knowing

---

[9] ἐν αἰνίγματι, in a riddle.
[10] The LXX in Ex. 33:11 has ἐνώπιος ἐνωπίῳ; in Dt. 34:10 πρόσωπον κατὰ πρόσωπον.

will be superior also because it will no longer be in part. Knowledge in the present dispensation (perhaps even when it is charismatic in nature) is acquired with difficulty, but "knowing fully" is of a more immediate nature.

How that will be is demonstrated by Paul as he points to the manner in which we are known in an absolute sense, i. e., by God. *Even as also*[11] does not imply a full equality. Again Paul has in view the knowledge of God and yet it must be repeated that we should not think of such knowledge exclusively or it would have to be the knowledge of God and of His works. God knows everything that is in man; we shall know likewise (cf. 8:3). The purpose of omitting the words "by God" here may have been to cut off every thought that our knowing would be divine. Even in the realm of glory, as vs. 13 points out, man remains distinct from God. Our knowledge is determined by God's knowledge, which is of the first order. But this much is sure, we shall see things as they are.

13 Vs. 13 contains the conclusion, the final statement concerning love, which, in connection with the preceding verses, shows that love far surpasses the charismata. *Now*, not to be taken temporally in this context, but as introducing a conclusion. Paul does not mean to say that *faith, hope and love*, which abide at this moment, will later on be succeeded by something else, but rather, on the basis of the preceding verses, that they remain for evermore, i. e., not just to our death, or to the end of this earthly dispensation when they will be present at the last judgment, but even to all eternity. As far as love is concerned that conclusion can be made from vs. 8: *love never faileth*. As to faith and hope the conclusion is indirect inasmuch as vs. 7 predicated faith and hope to that love which never fails.

The question arises how it can be that faith and hope will remain if they really belong to the dispensation in which all things are in part. In order to answer this question we must bear in mind that "faith" in our epistle is used in a very broad sense. In 1:21 "to believe" is to be understood of saving faith; so also in 2:5. But in 12:9 faith is the charisma to perform miracles, so also 13:2. And in 13:7 it has a very general meaning. We should not be surprised at this diversity of meanings. Faith is not yet a

---

[11] καθὼς καί.

technical term in the New Testament, used exclusively of saving faith, it is used in a variety of connotations, such as "trust" and "confidence." Similarly in vs. 13 "faith" does not have the sense of saving faith, nor that of faith to work miracles, but must be interpreted in the light of the context especially vs. 7. That faith, as the apostle indicates, will remain with us. It is a human characteristic not to lose faith; Adam in paradise had faith; Christ is the author and finisher of our faith (Heb. 12:2). Faith in the general sense of the word refers to the relation between man and God, man and nature. We believe that God is as He reveals Himself. We believe that creatures are as they appear to be. And although in this dispensation faith is spoiled by sin so that the natural relation between man and his environment is violated, Paul knows of an antithesis between *now* and *then*. Living in the new dispensation we shall experience that we know fully, i. e., that relationship will then be freed from all that is in part. But it remains faith, for even then we shall not know the deep things of God (2:10).

The same thing holds true of *hope.* Our hoping is attended by uncertainty, our expectations are accompanied by the knowledge or the apprehension that the result may be quite different from what we expect it to be. But that uncertainty does not belong to the nature of hope (cf. vs. 7; Heb. 6:19; I Pet. 1:13). Hope's real character is drawn up by Paul in Rom. 8:24: hope that is seen is not hope. Just as faith indicates the relation between God and the Christian at any given moment, so hope implies that this relation will remain what it is. We hope that all will remain as it is not because we doubt but because we are certain. The fear inspired by thought of the future is definitely removed by Christian hope. This hoping is more than knowing, for it involves the whole person and is akin to faith. This hope remains together with faith.

Love has a somewhat different nature from faith and hope. Love is basic for it does not just refer to a certain relation, but it governs and sustains all relations, because it indicates a direction of life. Love will enable a person to do many things, such as to believe and to hope (vs. 7) but it will make it impossible for him to hate anything else except sin. Love is the root of all good actions. Where it manifests itself, and it must needs be

313

manifest, it displays a certain quality, i. e., it operates in a certain area. There it adds color to things, it determines the nature and the direction of every action. Love does not seek its own but is directed toward somebody else. For that reason it is superior to faith and hope. This sheds light on the climax of this chapter: *the greatest of these is love. These three* (cf. I Thess. 1:3; 5:8; Col. 1:4, 5) is the subject of *abideth*: only those three remain. This is part of the apostle's conclusion since he had written before that even the most excellent charismata will *then* no longer operate.[12]

12:31b-13:13 I Cor. 13 occupies a most important place in the discourse on the charismata. It furnishes the foundation both for a warning against overestimating glossolalia and for a summons to use that gift rightly. Love to God and to the neighbor is to govern this use. In the second place this chapter has its own significance due to its excellent description of the nature, the strength and the working of love. Because the apostle writes to sinful men his treatment is for the greater part negative. Furthermore, we are informed that the charismata belong to this dispensation, love to the future one. The church possesses love (Rom. 5:5), it must therefore strive for its highest attainment.

---

[12] μείζων τούτων may be translated "the most of these" (three) or "greater than these" (three). We prefer the first translation because love is described in the context.

CHAPTER XIV

LOVE AND SPIRITUAL GIFTS

14:1-19

1 Follow after love; yet desire earnestly spiritual *gifts*, but rather that ye may prophesy.

2 For he that speaketh in a tongue speaketh not unto men, but unto God; for no man understandeth; but in the spirit he speaketh mysteries.

3 But he that prophesieth speaketh unto men edification, and exhortation, and consolation.

4 He that speaketh in a tongue edifieth himself; but he that prophesieth edifieth the church.

5 Now I would have you all speak with tongues, but rather that ye should prophesy: and greater is he that prophesieth than he that speaketh with tongues, except he interpret, that the church may receive edifying.

6 But now, brethren, if I come unto you speaking with tongues, what shall I profit you, unless I speak to you either by way of revelation, or of knowledge, or of prophesying, or of teaching?

7 Even things without life, giving a voice, whether pipe or harp, if they give not a distinction in the sounds, how shall it be known what is piped or harped?

8 For if the trumpet give an uncertain voice, who shall prepare himself for war?

9 So also ye, unless ye utter by the tongue speech easy to be understood, how shall it be known what is spoken? for ye will be speaking into the air.

10 There are, it may be, so many kinds of voices in the world, and no kind is without signification.

11 If then I know not the meaning of the voice, I shall be to him that speaketh a barbarian, and he that speaketh will be a barbarian unto me.

12 So also ye, since ye are zealous of spiritual *gifts*, seek that ye may abound unto the edifying of the church.

13 Wherefore let him that speaketh in a tongue pray that he may interpret.

315

14   For if I pray in a tongue, my spirit prayeth, but my understanding is unfruitful.
15   What is it then? I will pray with the spirit, and I will pray with the understanding also: I will sing with the spirit, and I will sing with the understanding also.
16   Else if thou bless with the spirit, how shall he that filleth the place of the unlearned say the Amen at thy giving of thanks, seeing he knoweth not what thou sayest?
17   For thou verily givest thanks well, but the other is not edified.
18   I thank God, I speak with tongues more than you all:
19   howbeit in the church I had rather speak five words with my understanding, that I might instruct others also, than ten thousand words in a tongue.

1   Already in chapter 12 it became apparent that because of a misunderstanding of glossolalia at Corinth, Paul deemed it necessary to write about the charismata. After treating this subject in chapter 12 in general, and after pointing to the "most excellent way" in chapter 13, thereby assigning to the charismata their proper place and indicating the principle according to which they must be used, the apostle bases his further treatment on this general foundation: he first speaks about glossolalia and, in connection with that, about prophecy and about the task of women in the church. The advantage of this method is that Paul, without treating glossolalia in the special sense of the word, has assigned it to its proper place in relation to other spiritual gifts. The Corinthians know already that they shall not give glossolalia the first place for love deserves a higher one. Using this as his starting point the apostle writes: *Follow after love.* "To follow after" is much stronger than to *desire earnestly spiritual* gifts. "To follow after" indicates a never terminating action, while "to desire earnestly" stresses the intensity rather than the continuity of the action. *Spiritual* gifts: see at 12:1. Since chapter 13 spoke of the universality of love, while in 14:2, 3 Paul refers to some special persons possessing the gifts of glossolalia or prophecy, the conclusion may be warranted that "to follow after" is a commandment to the entire congregation, whereas "to desire earnestly" is enjoined upon him who has spiritual gifts. This earnest desire may then have special reference to the use of the charismata. the

316

more so because Paul teaches us afterwards that we must distinguish between the possession of spiritual gifts, between receiving a prophecy or some other working of the Spirit at any given moment, and giving utterance to them (cf. vs. 26f.).

Rather conveys a thought related to 12:31 (*greater gifts*). There is apparently a difference of degree between the charismata and now Paul assigns the highest place to *prophecy,* another indication that the Corinthians were wrong in giving that place to glossolalia.[1]

2 Vs. 2 bears this out more clearly for the apostle states the reason for his assertion of vs. 1. *To speak in a tongue*: see 12:30. The plural *tongues* which was used there was in harmony with the subject (all) and served to designate all possible cases of glossolalia. Here the apostle has a single case in mind, as may be found with one person. That teaches us at the same time something of the nature of glossolalia. In order to speak we must use our tongue and express ourselves in a particular language. The word *tongue* must therefore be used in a special sense, namely of a tongue which is moved by the Spirit. The expression does not indicate a foreign language but it points to a language given by the Holy Spirit, whatever its sounds may have been. *Speaketh* implies that in this context the sounds are more important than the contents. *He that speaketh in a tongue,* i. e., he that is accustomed to do so, not, he that speaks in a tongue occasionally. Not that which takes place the moment a person speaks in a tongue is the important point in this and the following verses, but rather the quality of such a person. That is why we do not read with the ASV: *unto men,* but: *for men*[2] and also: for God, i. e., to His honor (cf. vs. 28). That glossolalia does not direct itself to men is evident from its very nature. Neither does "unto men" go well with "he that speaketh in a tongue." *For men,* on the contrary, renders a good sense, after love has been placed above all charismata. He that speaks in a tongue with no one else to interpret his words is not driven by love to his fellow men. Though he may honor God his magnifying of God is of no use to men and there-

---

[1] ἵνα depends on ζηλοῦτε: prophecy is one of the charismata. The word does not have a final significance in the strictest sense of the word.

[2] Greek: ἀνθρώποις, Θεῷ.

fore he that speaks in a tongue has to avoid such speaking in the presence of others if there is no interpreter (cf. vs. 28). This touches again upon Christian liberty. The one endowed with the gift of glossolalia undoubtedly has the liberty to use his charisma. But he must be guided by love, i. e., in certain circumstances he must refrain from using his gift.

The second clause with *for* has a particular reference to the words *not unto (for) men. In the Spirit*: in vs. 14 Paul writes: *my spirit,* (cf. vs. 15) ; the reference must be to the spirit of the believer which is sanctified and driven by the Holy Spirit. There is a possibility to speak *in the spirit,* i. **e.**, without the cooperation of the mind (understanding) (cf. vs. 15). Words that are uttered *in the spirit* only do not touch others. That is why it can be called a speaking of *mysteries.* Paul uses the latter word of those things which were hidden first but revealed later. In our context, however, the reference is not so much to the great mysteries of salvation but rather to those things which, though they have been expressed, are not clear to everybody. This explains the fact that the words spoken in glossolalia, although they were audible and had a spiritual content, yet were not understood by everybody. At the same time we notice that glossolalia was not a speaking of an existing foreign language, for then someone might be found to translate that language.

3 Quite different is the prophet who speaks for the benefit of his fellow men, i. e., in such a way that others may understand and use his 'message to their profit. A series of abstract nouns with a concrete significance is used to point out which profits are meant. *Edification* is the promotion of the spiritual life. *Exhortation* and *consolation* are the translation of Greek words which have approximately identical meanings.[3] All three are definitely of spiritual use. Earlier we noticed that prophecy is that gift of the Spirit whereby that which believers need to know at a certain moment is revealed to them. Our verse is another argument in support of that interpretation.

4 Vs. 4 points to a second contrast. Glossolalia also has this use that it edifies the one who speaks in a tongue himself. The

---

[3] παράκλησις καὶ παραθυμία. Since the latter of these nouns has the special sense of "consolation," it is better to translate the first with "exhortation" (cf. I Thess. 2:12).

manner of this edifying is not disclosed. Paul only warns not to
speak in tongues if there is no interpreter. This implies that the
person speaking in tongues was not able to understand and to
interpret what he was saying, except when he had received the
charisma of interpretation. "Edification" apparently is not to be
understood as if the contents of what such a person said was to
his own profit, but rather that the fact of speaking in tongues is
edifying in itself. We may assume that the reason for this lies in
the fact that the person who speaks in tongues may be assured
that he possesses the Spirit who enables him to do so. This view
is given added support by the consideration that, according to the
Acts of the Apostles, as often as the gospel of Christ came to a
new circle the Spirit revealed His presence by giving charismata
(Acts 10:46; 19:6). So far as is known glossolalia was always
among those charismata. In view of this fact we interpret *edifieth
himself* in the sense that glossolalia assures the person who speaks
in tongues of the possession of the Holy Spirit (cf. vs. 22). On
the other hand, when speaking of "him that prophesieth," Paul
repeats about the same thought as he expressed in vs. 2, with this
difference only that here an explicit reference is made to the
church. If a prophet speaks in a congregation the church, the
ecclesia, i. e., the organized church, is edified. It is in agreement
with this that in 12:28 the prophets are classified among the
officials of the church, while speaking in tongues is mentioned
afterwards as one of the charismata given by God.

5 Vs. 5 continues to develop the same theme, but it constitutes
an indispensable link in the argument. Paul's battle is on two
fronts: on the one hand he must warn against an overestimation
of glossolalia but on the other he must assign to it the place which
it deserves as a charisma of the Spirit. This explains why he
praises glossolalia and immediately thereafter places prophecy
above it (*rather,* cf. vs. 1).

I would have: this implies that, though there were many at
Corinth who spoke in tongues, not all had received that gift. It
would be a good thing if all had that charisma, but prophecy is
more valuable. For prophecy is not only to him who possesses it
proof of the presence of the Holy Spirit, but it is also profitable

for the congregation.[4] *Rather*: because Paul mentions something that cannot be accomplished (cf. I should like; RSV: I want) It appears that there were not too many at Corinth who had the charisma of prophecy. *Except he interpret*: does not refer to a particular interpretation of a message spoken in tongues, but to a permanent gift of interpretation, just as *he that speaketh with tongues* possesses the permanent gift of glossolalia. Paul has in view a person who has received two gifts, that of speaking in tongues and that of interpretation. Apparently not every possessor of the gift of glossolalia was able to interpret his words. Interpreted glossolalia has the same value as prophecy. Glossolalia is apparently not just words without any sense, its meaning is such that it may edify the congregation. No wonder, for it is a charisma of the Spirit.

6 *But now* introduces a conclusion. Paul wishes to sum up the state of affairs. Let the Corinthians, who had such a high esteem for glossolalia judge themselves! What would have been their profit if Paul had spoken to them only in tongues or if he would do so when he came to them the next time? The apostle does not imply that he never spoke in tongues. Paul may have done so at Corinth, see on vs. 18. Paul is only speaking of a possibility. *Speaking with tongues*, i. e., speaking with tongues exclusively. If that which is expressed in the protasis really happened, Paul would not be of any profit to the Corinthians. The clause beginning with *unless I speak* contains those things which were the most important for Paul's missionary work. The enumeration is not exhaustive, only the principal gifts which the apostle received for the benefit of the church are named. The four things mentioned are not all of the same nature. It depends whether the apostle has in view the origin or the manner of his preaching. But all four are distinct from glossolalia because they are addressed to the conscious life. *Revelation*: the new revelations which were given to Paul during his preaching. On the opposite side stands *knowledge*, which may be of a charismatic nature but remains a lasting possession. It is difficult to distinguish *prophesying* from *revelation*. The former had best be taken

---

[4] θέλω: I should like. Θέλω is first followed by an infinitive (λαλεῖν γλώσσαις) and afterwards by a clause with ἵνα (with a weakened final sense)

of a giving utterance to the things which were revealed. The word is thus somewhat restricted in meaning as is understandable because revelation is also mentioned. *Teaching,* i. e., the teaching of the knowledge which is at hand.[5]

7 Using a simile Paul shows that nobody benefits from indistinct sounds.[6] There are *things without life* which *give a voice,* e. g., musical instruments, a *pipe,* or a *harp.* But if there is not a difference in pitch (lit., if they do not give any difference through the voices) it is impossible to distinguish them and nobody knows what is played on the flute or on the harp. The application is: a sound alone is not sufficient, that sound should communicate something.

8 Vs. 8 continues the figure. *For*: an additional reason, after vs. 7 had already adduced a reason for not speaking in tongues if there is no interpretation. The *trumpet* in antiquity called the people to arms. But the people were only willing to fight if they were convinced that they heard the war cry.[7]

9 An application with respect to glossolalia is not yet given in vs. 9. The verse does not mention that point; the real application is given in vss. 13f., or perhaps beginning with vs. 12. Vs. 9 simply continues the figure of speech; perhaps we might say that Paul furnishes us with yet another example or simile. In any case, he derives his words this time from human speech. But that speech itself is compared with the sound given by inanimate things The first clause is more directly related to vs. 7, the second to vs. 8.

So also ye is to a certain extent an independent clause, with the meaning: so things are with you (cf. 12:12), namely, just as

---

[5] διδαχῇ is without ἐν, probably because the word is the most formal of the four. The teaching does not add any new content to the apostle's knowledge, it is only a means to communicate what is present with him.

[6] The translation of ὅμως gives difficulty. In the koine the meaning is: nevertheless, but that does not suit the context. This has made some think that Paul uses the word in an archaic sense: "in the same way." Others (Lietzmann, Heinrici) circumscribe τὰ ἄψυχα, καίπερ φωνὴν διδόντα, ὅμως οὐ γνωσθήσεται ἐὰν διαστολὴν μὴ δῷ. The sense of the clause as well as the intent of the simile are clear. "Even" in the ASV and the RSV is not correct.

[7] πόλεμος in this context the word should perhaps be taken in the sense of battle rather than war.

with sound-producing instruments. Wherein this equality exists is then pointed out by Paul. The apostle does not imply that the Corinthians do speak unintelligible words, he only says that it may be that they do so.[8] Instead of using the expression "to speak in a tongue" or a similar one, the apostle writes more indefinitely: *unless ye utter by the tongue speech easy to be understood*. The Corinthians are to make the application to glossolalia themselves. It is true, *by the tongue* has some similarity with "speaking in tongues," but "tongue" must here be understood of the organ of speech as such. If that tongue does not give a clear sound, then it is impossible to distinguish what was spoken. The subsequent clause indicates a reason (*for*), in so far as the preceding clause implies the answer: no, it cannot be known because etc. *Speaking into the air*, cf. 9:26: *beating the air*. All speaking is a speaking into the air, but the clear sense of the words is: "entirely in vain."[9]

10-11   The verses 10-11 do not yet give the application. In a sense they are still figurative in nature. Only Paul moves closer to his subject: glossolalia, vs. 11 containing at least a direct reference to glossolalia. The apostle makes use of the fact that "voice" may be taken of the human voice but also of the sound uttered by non-humans or instruments. *It may be* (RSV: doubtless): the omission of these words would make the sentence too strong. *There are many kinds of voices*, (or sounds, distinct from each other), in the well-ordered world (kosmos) and properly speaking, no thing is without sound.[10] *So many kinds of voices*, nobody knows how many. *The meaning of the voice*: the contents of the spoken word (cf. the effect of a command).

The second part of the sentence proceeds on the correct assumption that in ordinary conversation there must be one who speaks

---

[8] The conditional clause expresses eventuality.

[9] Ye will be speaking (ἔσεσθε λαλοῦντες) implies continuation.

[10] Many expositors take οὐδὲν of γένος, but that does not give a good sense. It is better to keep in mind that Paul was speaking of the voice of instruments and so Paul returns to that subject after mentioning the human voice. Thus it becomes clear that the voice is always a means to distinguish. οὐδὲν ἄφωνον does not refer to the human voice, οὐδέν has a general sense: no thing. ἄφωνον: every object makes a sound, which is distinct from other sounds, when someone strikes it.

and one who understands; both must comprehend the signification of what is said. If such comprehension is lacking with either of the two no conversation is possible. We should expect that Paul would say: then the speaker is a stranger to me. But since in Greek the first person preceded the second and since Paul always takes the blame upon himself he continues: if I do not understand the signification of my own words, i. e., if I do not know the sense of the language I speak. If the man who speaks in a tongue lacks the gift of interpretation he cannot explain his own words. The main point which Paul wishes to make is that the speech will not be clear not only if a sound itself is unintelligible but also if both speaker and hearer are strangers with respect to the sounds that are made. *Barbarian*: the original sense of the Greek word is: one who does not speak Greek, then more general: strange, ununderstandable.

12 *So also ye,* is first to be taken as an independent clause: your condition is as was described. If there is no connection between the hearer and the speaker the speaking is of no use. The form of this verse, which is one of exhortation, shows that here the application is made.[11] Nevertheless, this application is only provisional. It is couched in general terms and does not yet mention glossolalia, the main point of the discussion. The verse is a kind of introduction to vss. 13f. which name the things that really matter.

Since ye are: that assumption is the startingpoint. *Spiritual gifts*: the Greek has "spirits," referring to the individual spirits, of which each Corinthian endowed with special gifts of the Spirit, possessed one or more. Paul assumes that the Corinthians are eager to receive such a spirit. This does not run counter to passages like 12:31 and 14:1, for the exhortations which are found there acquire a special sense from their context, somewhat like this: do what you may have been doing thus far, only now with special earnestness. This explains why Paul may presuppose here a zeal for spiritual gifts. Significant is the fact that Paul speaks of the striving after spiritual gifts, the Corinthians of striving after spirits. It is Paul's assumption that they have received the Holy Spirit (cf. Rom. 8:15; I Cor. 2:12), and that that Spirit

---

11 ζητεῖτε cannot be taken as indicative, for it mentions something that the Corinthians did not do.

323

can give special gifts, charismata, to their spirits; the Corinthians strive after spirits which possess or procure special gifts. It is not impossible that the Corinthians attributed each charisma to a special spirit. That may be deduced from 12:4f., where the apostle maintains that all the charismata descend from one and the same Spirit. The difference is not very significant as appears from the fact that Paul does not correct a presumably incorrect terminology but only urges them to do increasingly what they were doing already. The apostle is anxious that the Corinthians should apply what he has written to the spiritual gifts. He has a higher regard for that which proceeds with regularity than for the sudden outbursts which could occur with glossolalia. What you do, do it in a good and regular fashion, that is an oft repeated adage in Paul's epistles (cf. Rom. 15:13; I Cor. 15:38, etc.). The goal is always *the edifying of the church*. The context points out that the sense here is that the church must understand what is spoken in tongues, otherwise there is no edification. *Church*: Paul has in view what is to happen in the official meetings of the congregation, a case different from 11:3f.

13 In vs. 13 we have the real application: what is the duty of him *that speaketh in tongue? Wherefore* introduces this admonition as a conclusion, i. e., this specific exhortation which Paul has in mind is deduced from and proposed as a part of a general admonition. This admonition results logically from what Paul wrote about speaking in an understandable language. *He that speaketh in a tongue* (cf. vs. 4), not: whenever one speaks in a tongue, but rather: he that is able to speak in tongue (cf. vs. 26). The singular "tongue" implies that this person speaks in one of the tongues that occur. He who possesses the gift of glossolalia shall *pray that he may interpret*. This is not the same as praying for the charisma of interpretation, for then the Corinthians might think that it would be proper to pray for a charisma (cf. 12:31b; 14:1). But it is perfectly proper to start from the gift of glossolalia and then to pray for the ability to interpret what was spoken in a tongue. God is free to answer such a prayer either by giving the required charisma or without it. We should pray only that God may perfect His own work. It appears evident that usually he who spoke in tongues did not possess the gift of interpretation.

14 Paul sets forth the abuses which arise when one speaks in a tongue without being able to interpret what he has said. That was the evil which actually prevailed at Corinth, as appears from the admonition of vs. 13. Since the thing Paul is going to say is not agreeable to the Corinthians, Paul uses the first person singular. Vs. 19 bears out that the apostle himself is not in the habit of doing that which he says about himself in this verse. He only speaks in terms of general possibility.

He who speaks in a tongue shall pray that he may interpret what he is saying, *for* if Paul *prays in a tongue,* his *spirit prays but his understanding is unfruitful.* This is carrying the argument one step further for while vs. 13 has *speaketh* vs. 14 has *I pray.* But there is no difference in meaning because vs. 2 implies that glossolalia is adoration, a speaking to God. The subject of this adoration is the spirit that dwells in the Christian, as it not only is sanctified but also endowed and moved by God's Spirit. The fact that Paul speaks of his understanding as opposed to his spirit forbids us to think here of the person of the Holy Spirit. But it is that person of the Holy Spirit who endows the spirit living in the Christian. When a Christian spirit speaks in a tongue the understanding is not left out. We cannot comprehend that, and no wonder for glossolalia is a miracle. It should be kept in mind, however, that the apostle does not present a psychological system in which spirit and understanding each would have their own well-defined place. *Spirit* and *understanding* look at man from two different angles. "Spirit" denotes the acting subject in the center of his life. It is the spirit which makes man man and makes the person person. That appears in glossolalia: the one "understanding" has contact with the other, but the one "spirit" may not touch the other "spirit" at all, if the "understanding" does not cooperate. In regeneration the spirit of man is touched by the Holy Spirit and made a new spirit. This results in the renewal of the whole man (7:6; Eph. 4:23, 24). That renewed spirit is the organ of the charismata. It is exactly that point which Paul has in view here, as appears from the contrast between understanding and spirit. "Spirit" views man as a personality, "understanding" as a knowing and thinking being. The understanding is discriminating, sifting. When the spirit is renewed the understanding is also renewed, without however changing its operation.

The renewed spirit may use the understanding, but it is not compelled to do so. Normally man, apart from the special gifts of the Holy Spirit, works through his understanding. But in glossolalia the understanding is inactive. This leads to the following conclusion: if a person prays in a tongue, worships in it, he does well, but because such a prayer does not use the understanding it is incomprehensible to another.

15 *What is it then?* In the answer to this question Paul states what he himself will do. Paul is accustomed to honor glossolalia as a gift of the Spirit, but at the same time he has in view the well-being of the church. He accomplishes this by praying *with the spirit* but also *with the understanding.* The latter he does in the meetings of the church. Paul does not imply that he prays with the spirit only when he is alone, for he not only possessed the gift of glossolalia but also that of interpretation. That is the reason why Paul can cite himself as an example without causing confusion. The preceding verses make abundantly clear that Paul wishes to indicate that where there is no interpretation, glossolalia should not be used in the congregation. The main point is that both are good, the speaking in a tongue, i. e., with the spirit, and the speaking with the understanding. For a Christian both are sanctified by the Holy Spirit. Circumstances will dictate which particular course of action must be followed.

16 Vs. 16 changes to the second person, making a clearer reference to what happened at Corinth possible. *To bless* and *to give thanks* are related in thought to *to pray* and *to sing* (vs. 15); the former also refer to the adoration and the thanksgiving which are implied in the speaking in tongues. The words *"to bless"* and *"to thank"*[12] are not used in the same sense as in 10:15. Paul does not speak about Holy Communion in our verse; moreover, the words of 10:14f.; 11:24f. are derived from Jewish customs which do not enter in at this particular point. Paul assumes that a Corinthian *blesses with the spirit* in a meeting of the church and he pictures the ensuing scene. An *unlearned* man, i. e., the man who has no knowledge of a certain thing or question. Which question that is the context points out; it is glossolalia. *To fill the place of* is a difficult expression. We take the words not of a special place in the meeting but figuratively in the sense of holding

[12] εὐλογεῖν, εὐχαριστεῖν.

a position. Instead of simply using the words "an unlearned man," as in vs. 23, the apostle uses the circumlocutory phrase *he that filleth the place of the unlearned.* The Corinthians overestimated glossolalia and considered those who lacked that gift to be incomplete Christians. Paul, on the other hand, gives to the unlearned their rightful position. They too are fully members of the church. The context bears out that the unlearned man was the one who did not have the gift of speaking in tongues or the gift of interpretation.

In I Chron. 16:36 and Neh. 5:13; 8:6 we find an early record of the congregation responding to a prayer by saying "Amen." The same custom prevailed in later times in the synagogue and from the synagogue it came into the Christian church.[18] To say "Amen" only makes good sense if the hearer understands what is preached or prayed. Paul's assumption is that someone in the congregation would offer a prayer and the whole congregation would express its agreement by saying "Amen." But this cannot be done if the one who offers prayer uses an unintelligible tongue. This leads to the conclusion: there shall be no glossolalia in the meetings of the church.

17 Paul again honors glossolalia for its worth but also assigns it its proper place. This verse contains the reason (*for*) for the maxim implied in vs. 16: no glossolalia without interpretation in the meetings of the church. *Thou . . . the other*: with thee everything is all right but others, i. e., all who lack the gift of glossolalia and of interpretation, are not *edified in the faith.*

18-19 These verses point out the solution which Paul has found for himself and which he also recommends to the Corinthians. Paul *thanks God that he speaks with tongues more than all the Corinthians.*[14] As also in many other places, Paul uses his own example as an object lesson, and he does so with great prudence. In the matter of glossolalia he certainly surpasses the Corinthians but every gift is one of grace so that boasting is ruled out. *Tongues*: the diverse kinds of tongues (cf. 12:10); Paul

---

[13] Justin, *Apol.,* I, 65, 3; Terullian, *De Spect.,* 25.
[14] Here again it appears that glossolalia is not a speaking in foreign languages. Paul could speak Greek at Corinth and then everybody would understand him. If it were a matter of speaking in foreign languages Paul would not have written: I speak **more** (adv., more often), but: I speak with **more tongues.**

had received the charisma of glossolalia in a special measure. *More than you all*: this means not merely "more than one of you," but rather "more than occurs among you."

Paul, however, does not make a wrong use of this privilege. He uses his gift only for the good of the church. Here we notice that the one who received the gift of glossolalia had to a certain extent power over his charisma. He could delay giving utterance to it until he was at home or until there was an interpreter. Vs. 19 furnishes no conclusive ground for assuming that Paul did not have the gift of interpretation. The verse only implies that Paul preferred to utter five words with his understanding than to speak in uninterpreted glossolalia (cf. vs. 5). Other considerations make us think that Paul did have the gift of interpretation, otherwise he could not have written about glossolalia as he does. *In the church*, i. e., in an official meeting of the church, where the goal is edification and instruction. *With my understanding* includes prophecy but also teaching, in fact every speaking a person does with his understanding. Such speaking is understood by the hearers. *Others also*: the word "also" implies that the glossolalia had a primary significance for him who spoke in a tongue (vs. 4). *A tongue*: particular type of tongue, used at that particular occasion.

DECORUM IN THE EXERCISE OF GIFTS

14:20-25

20 Brethren, be not children in mind: yet in malice be ye babes, but in mind be men.

21 In the law it is written, By men of strange tongues and by the lips of strangers will I speak unto this people; and not even thus will they hear me, saith the Lord.

22 Wherefore tongues are for a sign, not to them that believe, but to the unbelieving: but prophesying *is for a sign*, not to the unbelieving, but to them that believe.

23 If therefore the whole church be assembled together and all speak with tongues, and there come in men unlearned or unbelieving, will they not say that ye are mad?

24 But if all prophesy, and there come in one unbelieving or unlearned, he is reproved by all, he is judged by all;

25 the secrets of his heart are made manifest; and so he will fall down on his face and worship God, declaring that God is among you indeed.

20-21 The new pericope, introduced with *brethren* is indicative of a change of subject. Paul no longer speaks about the uselessness of speaking in tongues in church meetings. He first issues a general admonition concerning the motives that should lead the Corinthians to speak in tongues or to refrain from doing so. Then he sets forth in the light of the Old Testament the meaning of glossolalia in church gatherings and thus he points out the distinction between glossolalia and prophecy.

Be not any longer *children in mind*: the Corinthians behaved like children by placing a one-sided emphasis on glossolalia and by speaking in tongues when there was no interpreter. Children usually look at the outside and boast to each other of things external. An adult Christian must not do so (cf. Jer. 4:22). He must not live in a childish naivete, certainly not if that would mislead or harm others. If he wants to be childishly naive, let him be a *babe in malice* (Rom. 16:19; Eph. 4:14). Improvement in that respect was both necessary and desirable at Corinth as we

329

learn from Paul's rebuke of several sins in this epistle. Note that Paul uses a stronger word the second time: *children* first, *babes* later. *Mind*: the Greek word translated thus occurs only here in the N. T. It means properly: midriff or diaphragm, a concrete term, much more concrete than the word translated by "understanding." It designates not only the thinking mind but also the heart as the seat of the emotions, the complete man, who is filled, heart and soul, with something. The apostle is thinking of the direction of a person's life.[15] In the background of *"mind"* is "love" (13:5), which takes no account of evil. Paul's writing here is not that of the discursive Greek, his summons has the concreteness of the Semite (cf. Phil. 2:5) and thus they prepare the way for the quotation from Is. 28:11, 12.[16] *Law*: here the Old Testament (cf. Jn. 10:34; 12:34; 15:25). This Jewish designation confirms our opinion concerning the nature of this section. God *will speak by men of strange tongues and by the lips of strangers, i. e.,* by non-Israelites, in this case the Assyrians. The quotation does not speak of glossolalia but of foreign languages which are indicated in a twofold way. The question arises whether this quotation does not imply that glossolalia was the speaking of an existing foreign language rather than a language of miraculous sounds, taught by the Holy Spirit and spoken to the glory of God. Along with the many objections we encounter with respect to the former view, vs. 18 definitely pleads in favor of the latter. The reason for the use of this quotation, we assume, must lie in the twice repeated *other*.[17] Isaiah is referring to other sounds, i. e., sounds distinct from ordinary sounds. Such sounds are also heard in glossolalia. Although Isaiah refers to foreign languages and glossolalia is of quite a different nature, the middle term of the comparison is that in both "other" sounds are uttered. The judgment upon Israel was that it, after it had heard the voice of the Lord, delivered by the prophets, would not listen even if the Lord spoke through foreign nations. This speaking of God was intended as a new token of His grace thereby to arouse the

---

[15] This may be a quotation. But the words the apostle uses we may at any rate interpret.

[16] The quotation does not agree with the Massoretic text nor with the LXX.

[17] ἑτερογλώσσοις καὶ ἐν χείλεσιν ἑτέρων.

attention of the people. But Israel disregarded this grace of God (*even thus*).

22 *Wherefore* introduces a conclusion from the quotation. From this word of Isaiah Paul deduces that glossolalia has still another meaning from the one mentioned in vs. 2f. *The tongues are for a sign*, i. e., they are a sign to the believers of today in the same way as the strange tongues were a sign to Israel. Those foreign sounds were a token of the grace of God to stir up the people of Israel to fear the Lord. Thus the speaking in tongues is a *sign* not to the congregation itself but to the *unbelieving*. Not as if glossolalia were intended to show to the unbelievers how much grace the church possesses in Christ, for Paul then would have insisted that, as soon as an unbeliever would enter a meeting of the church, believers ought to speak in tongues. Verses 22, 23 imply just the opposite. We should keep in mind that glossolalia, according to Acts 10:46; 19:6 is one of the signs of the presence of the Holy Spirit in persons who may be compared with unbelieving Israelites. This kind of speaking in tongues was not necessarily limited to the meetings of the church. On the contrary, it might occur at home and still observe the rules laid down by Paul for its use. Believers do not need such a sign. The objection that in the quotation others, non-Israelites, speak in strange tongues is not in its place for the "sign"-character of both types of speaking lies in the fact that the speaking is different. A further consideration is the difference between the two dispensations. In the old dispensation God uses more than once foreign nations to chastise His people.

For the believers, who are assured of the indwelling of the Spirit (2:12), there is another sign, namely prophecy. That prophecy convinces them that they, after having once received the Spirit, still enjoy the grace of God. God speaks to them through His prophecy (whether they receive the gift of prophecy themselves or hear the prophecy from others) and He tells them what to do. The conclusion is (cf. vs. 20) that glossolalia has its value, they are not to seek it but rather to desire prophecy.

23 With *if therefore* Paul returns to his subject, which concerns the use of glossolalia in the meetings of the church. But he utilizes the thoughts he just expressed, as it were parenthetically. Suppose the whole congregation is gathered in an official meet-

331

ing[18] and all speak in tongues. Such a case, although it actually does not happen, yet is not among the impossibilities. If the speaking in tongues were as desirable as the Corinthians thought, they should desire that the whole church would speak in tongues. If at such an occasion *men unlearned*[19] or *unbelieving* would come in, they would come to only one conclusion: those assembled *are mad*. And there would be every reason to speak thus, else Paul would not have made these words his own. It would not be a guilty utterance of an evil heart as in Acts 2:12f.; if the Corinthians would speak in tongues only, they would be the guilty ones. For God wishes that one of the purposes the meetings of the church must serve is to attract unbelievers. Here we see anew that glossolalia cannot have been a speaking in a foreign language but that it consists of uttering strange sounds which repel strangers.

24-25 Paul argues that also in view of strangers, prophecy is to be preferred to glossolalia. Suppose that all prophesied — another of these things which might happen although it does not actually happen — how good a thing that would be. That demonstrates how great a good prophecy is. The unlearned or the unbelieving person would be instructed, for he would be *reproved* or *judged* by all. The word of the prophet, spoken by the Holy Spirit, would reveal the unbeliever and would rebuke him and admonish him to be converted. *The secrets of his heart*: what is hidden in his heart. Paul apparently wishes to enumerate the successive effects of the words of the prophets. After the initial rebuke an account is drawn up by means of which the evil which lies hidden in the heart is made manifest. This is another disclosure of the effects of prophecy. It discloses to a person his sins infallibly, as he is inspired by the Spirit of God. These may be the particular sins of that particular person (cf. Acts 5:3f.; 8:20f.). But it is also possible that the unbeliever recognizes his own image in the general picture of the sinner and thus is con-

---

[18] *Together,* ἐπὶ τὸ αὐτό: they are not to speak in tongues except in the meeting.

[19] Greek: ἰδιῶται. The word cannot have the same meaning here as in vs. 16. There it refers to people who did not receive the gift of glossolalia, here to people who do not know what is going on in the church.

verted (converts himself to God), which would mean that the things hidden in his soul were only revealed to himself and not to the whole church. *And so*: in that condition, after experiencing these overwhelming and convicting effects. Then the unbeliever will humble himself, he deserts his idols (or his Jewish religion) and he glorifies the only true God. This may happen at once in the meeting of the church, but also later on. He will cry out that God dwells in the midst of the congregation. *Indeed*, i. e., different from a meeting of pagans, where God is sought but is not found (Acts 17:27). Paul makes an allusion here to Is. 45:14 (cf. also Dan. 2:47; Zech. 8:23; Jn. 4:19).

Note that Paul does not mean to say that all these effects are wrought every time an unbeliever casually strays into a meeting where someone is prophesying. The whole congregation must be prophesying and thus they must turn toward the unbeliever. That is why Paul's words will serve the purpose of providing a better evaluation of prophecy. The latter is truly for the edification of the church and for the help of unbelievers. It is also worthy of note that Paul, when speaking about glossolalia, was very positive in his tone (vs. 22), whereas in his comparison of glossolalia and prophecy in our section he deals with hypothetical cases in his concern to show the greater worth of prophecy.

ORDER IN THE ASSEMBLY

14:26-33a

26 What is it then, brethren? When ye come together, each one hath a psalm, hath a teaching, hath a revelation, hath a tongue, hath an interpretation. Let all things be done unto edifying.

27 If any man speaketh in a tongue, *let it be* by two, or at the most three, and *that* in turn; and let one interpret:

28 but if there be no interpreter, let him keep silence in the church; and let him speak to himself, and to God.

29 And let the prophets speak *by* two or three, and let the others discern.

30 But if a revelation be made to another sitting by, let the first keep silence.

31 For ye all can prophesy one by one, that all may learn, and all may be exhorted;

32 and the spirits of the prophets are subject to the prophets;

33a for God is not *a God* of confusion, but of peace.

26 The new section which begins in vs. 26 is introduced in the same way as vs. 15. The verse contains a conclusion. The change of subject is also indicated by *brethren* (cf. vs. 20). In a comprehensive admonition Paul tells the believers how their conduct must be in the meetings of the church, a conduct which takes account of circumstances and of Paul's directives. It deserves our attention that Paul again expressly writes that he is dealing with the meetings of the church (*when ye come together*). This does not mean that from 11:17 to 14:40 Paul has in view the divine services rather than Holy Communion and the charismata. But this much is true, the apostle lays down a definite rule for those services, namely that all shall be done to the edification of the church. The Corinthians have the liberty to use the charismata, including glossolalia, according to their own insight. But that liberty is not unrestricted, it is circumscribed by what is for the benefit of the church. Here also liberty shall be ruled by love.

334

One is not allowed to act in those services as he would like, but everybody will have to take into account the purpose of the meetings (*together — each one*).

The form of the apodosis is unexpected. We would have expected the following construction: when you come together and some one has a psalm, then, etc. Instead we read: when you come together, each one has a psalm. This is a statement of fact which may mean that every Corinthian, though he may not have had a special charisma, had at least his own personal gift of the Spirit. Or, if the element of diversity is more in the foreground the sense would be that everybody has his own gift peculiar to himself. We prefer the latter interpretation (cf. 12:4f.).

Then follows an enumeration of what each member of. the church may have. *To have* is used here in a special sense; its direct object is an activity which is at least partly charismatic. This applies to all the activities listed. *To have*, therefore, is to have on the basis of a special working of the Holy Spirit. Yet it is not so much its suddenness of origin as its continuity of possession which is expressed in the words: to have a psalm, etc. This clarifies our understanding of the nature of the charismata.[20] They were not just a sudden impartation of certain words or proverbs, but also a permanent ability to do a certain thing. This also explains how Paul can prescribe certain limitations in the use of charismata, which would be impossible if the charismatic person were suddenly overpowered by the Spirit. The condition is as follows: a service is held which is attended by people with special gifts. One possesses the charisma of uttering a psalm in special manner (he may even have composed a psalm or have sung a Christian hymn). Such a gift should not be despised: Corinth was a church of gentile Christians, which had been in contact with the Old Testament for only a short time. Hymn books did not exist, they were in any case very rare.

[20] The question might be asked if the gift of singing a psalm can be called a special charisma. This also applies to the teaching. That question cannot be answered with full certainty. Earlier we noticed that there is not a hard and fast distinction between the ordinary and the extraordinary gifts of the Spirit (cf. 12:31). Prophecy is not named here, it probably is subsumed under revelation (cf. 14:6, 30). This verse does not contain the various elements of a service of worship (cf. e.g. Acts 13, Col. 4:16; I Thess. 5:27).

Perhaps there was only one copy in the whole church. In such a time the appropriate singing of a psalm is a gift. *Teaching*: instruction in what had been preached earlier. *Revelation*: the setting forth of a new truth (cf. vs. 6). We may suppose that the members of the church who possessed special gifts abused the divine services to make themselves heard. Although Paul values the charismata, he forbids such practices. In the service all things shall tend to edification, as has been Paul's sustained emphasis from vs. 3 on. The verse, therefore, contains a foundation, a standard of which the subsequent verses give the application. Liberty shall be governed by love.

27 The first words of vs. 27: *if any man speaketh,* do not mean: if a person in one of the services suddenly begins to speak in tongues, but rather, as the context bears out (cf. vs. 13: him that speaketh): if a person is able to speak in tongues.[21] Following strict logic the apodosis does not fit the protasis, but the sense is not obscured. The protasis refers in general to a case that may occur in a meeting of the church, hence it uses the singular. The apodosis issues a concrete injunction as to what ought to happen. In every service no more than two or three shall speak in tongues, and this should not be done at the same time but alternately,[22] so that there will be no disturbance (cf. vs. 40). There shall be one interpreter. No further mention is made of this interpreter; it may have been one who also spoke in tongues, but he may have been another. Here also there ought not to be any jealousy or confusion. Again we see that glossolalia is not a blind power but a gift of God which can be controlled by him who receives it.

28 *If there is no interpreter* nobody shall speak in tongues in a service (cf. 5:13). Not as if the person who speaks in tongues may then not use his charisma at all. He may only use it for his own profit. *To himself* does not mean that he must address his words to himself, but that he speaks for his own benefit (cf. vss. 14, 22). Glossolalia is a sign of the presence of the Holy Spirit. Since speaking in tongues gives a blessing to him who received that charisma, let him therefore use his glos-

---

[21] The first εἴτε is not followed by a second, but it is clear that Paul as previously puts prophecy next to glossolalia. Vs. 29 really contains the remarks that could have been made after a second εἴτε.

[22] κατὰ δύο distributively; ἀνὰ μέρος every one at his turn.

solalia at home; it will then be to the glory of God (cf. vs. 4). Apart from the conclusion, vs. 39, this is the last time Paul mentions glossolalia.

29 In vs. 26 Paul wrote that all things must serve the edification of the church. That this is to be taken seriously appears in vs. 29, where the apostle, who repeatedly had placed prophecy above glossolalia, now subjects prophecy to that same rule. The context bears out that that is implied in Paul's words here. The Greek text begins with the word *prophets,* i. e., concerning the prophets, etc. Just as with speaking in tongues, only two or three shall prophesy in one service. This rule appears strange after all the good things Paul said about prophecy. Apparently the apostle does not wish to single out any charisma, neither does he desire a congregation governed by charismatic functions. That which the prophets speak, according to Paul, is not absolutely necessary for the government of the church; a service shall not be completely taken up with prophecy. The latter may offer divine instruction which is helpful *hic et nunc,* but it is put beneath the apostolic preaching, beneath the gospel, which must occupy the place of honor (cf. 12:28). All other words have to make way for the gospel and the prophets have to wait, though their word may edify the congregation (vs. 4). These statements are clear when considered in the light of vs. 3: prophecy means edification, exhortation, consolation but not always, perhaps not primarily, new revelations (cf. however Acts 13:2). If prophecy is meant to give words of consolation (Acts 15:31), it is understandable that it could be deferred or even repeated (cf. vs. 31: may), in spite of its great importance. Does not the preaching of the Word also afford consolation and edification, though in a different way? It is the Lord Himself, who gives the prophecy and who restricts its use.

Let the others discern: reminds of 12:10, where the apostle speaks of the discerning of the spirits, and of I Jn. 4:1: "prove the spirits whether they are of God." The latter passage implies that there were evil spirits at work in the congregations, not indeed in the true members of the church, as is excluded by 12:3, but in them that joined the church without really belonging to it. It was possible that such an evil spirit said or cried something during a service. This made proving of the spirits necessary (see on 12:10). But this does not exhaust its meaning here, for Paul does not speak here of discerning the spirits, but of discerning the words of the prophets. Even if a prophetic utterance is correct, inspired by the Spirit of God, the congregation has the duty to "discern" what must be done with such an utterance, namely whether it is of value for the church. In Acts 21:10f. we read that Paul hears the word of the Spirit, uttered by the mouth of Agabus, and that he does not obey it but travels to Jerusalem. Nowhere in I Cor. 12-14 is there a warning against false glossolalia or false prophecy; "prophets" are *true* prophets. Nevertheless it may be necessary not to follow up the utterance of true prophets.

Since 12:10 counts the discerning of the spirits among the charismata of the Holy Spirit, *the others* must refer not to the members of the congregation but to the other prophets, as far as they had received that second gift. This charisma, just like that of interpretation, will have manifested itself of its own accord; misunderstanding was excluded. Generally speaking we may say that prophecy, just like glossolalia, needed a complementary charisma, although it was understandable in itself.

30 Vs. 30 contains a limitation of a different nature. It may be that something is revealed to one of the listeners (*another sitting by*). Prophecy and revelation are closely connected (vs. 6). Our verse implies that the revelation precedes and is thereupon given utterance in prophecy.[23] The Greek has no subject, the meaning is: if another receives a revelation. Here we have another case of a sudden revelation which expresses itself in prophecy. In such a case the first prophet must keep silence, obviously because God Himself gives a new revelation at the very moment the other prophet is speaking. This also rules out the possibility of a prophet receiving a revelation while the third prophet is already speaking (vs. 29). God Himself has commanded that no more than three prophets shall speak. God, who gives prophecy, also controls it.

31 This verse states the reason why *keeping silence* is sometimes demanded (vs. 28). *Ye all can prophesy one by one*: this is

[23] ἀποκαλύφθη may be translated with *was revealed* or with *is revealed*. Because of καθημένῳ the latter translation is the most probable one.

338

looking at it from the human standpoint. In the preceding verse the interruption of a prophecy was approached from God's side, in the form of a command. Vs. 31 tells us that such an interruption is very reasonable, since prophets can speak one after the other. The apostle apparently militates against the evil of two prophets speaking simultaneously, in case one of them received a revelation when the other was speaking. Such a thing is prohibited, nor is it necessary, for it is possible for the one to follow the other. The only thing Paul has in mind is the possibility of stopping prophesying and of waiting until some one else, who has observed that a second person also received a revelation, keeps silence. There is no further information as to what the first speaker is to do with his interrupted prophecy; the fact that God Himself interrupted it is enough.

God has made it so that prophecies can be uttered seriatim, in order that thus prophecy might fulfill its purpose. For in this way *all may learn* (more intellectually) and all are *exhorted* or consoled (more mystically). The use of *all* implies that the revelation the second prophet received was destined and suitable for a different category from that which the utterance of the first prophet had in view. That is the way God controls prophecy, and the prophets are to observe the divine injunction when they speak.

32 Vs. 32 implies that God ordained that *the spirits of the prophets are subject to the prophets*. The Greek text lacks articles. indicating that Paul speaks about the genus prophet rather than about the species. *Spirits of prophets* are the spirits which received a prophetical charisma. God subjects those spirits to the prophets. Is this a subjection to other prophets or to the prophet who possesses that charisma himself? The former view finds support in 12:10, dealing with the discerning of spirits. But the second view is more strongly supported by the consideration that. while in vs. 29 and 30 the element of subjection of the one prophet to the other was expressed, vs. 31 emphasizes the prophet's relative independence. We conclude that God subjects the spirits. endowed by Him with prophetic charismata, to the prophets themselves. Thus there is a complete parallel between the prophets and those endowed with glossolalia.

The difference in expression between vs. 26 and vs. 32 should not escape us. In vs. 26 the present tense indicates something durative, here it refers to what is for a moment only. The apostle has in view an act of God. The very moment that the prophetic spirits are working God subjects them to the prophets.

Vs. 32, together with vs. 31, contains the reason for vs. 30. In vs. 33 we read why God effects this kind of subjection. Paul's words are very general and objective here: *God is a God not of confusion but of peace*. This points us to two of God's virtues. Because God desires peace He himself subjects the prophetic spirits, lest the one work the destruction of the other. Confusion in the services will thus be prevented.

WOMEN TO KEEP SILENT

14:33b-36

33b As in all the churches of the saints,

34 let the women keep silence in the churches: for it is not permitted unto them to speak; but let them be in subjection, as also saith the law.

35 And if they would learn anything, let them ask their own husbands at home: for it is shameful for a woman to speak in the church.

36 What? was it from you that the word of God went forth? or came it unto you alone?

33b A new sentence begins in vs. 33. Since the words of vs. 33a refuse to take any further qualification, the clause: *as in all the churches* cannot be taken with the preceding, as some have tried to do. Taken with what follows the words are an appropriate reminder that this commandment is not given to the Corinthians alone but to all the churches (cf. 7:17). The sense is then: let that which happens everywhere, also happen with you. This also accounts for Paul's sudden transition from the subject of prophecy to that of the women. Already in 11:5 we learned that some Corinthian women had the gift of prophecy. Our pericope implies that some of them desired to prophesy in the services. Paul's aim has been to restrict prophecy in its use and in accordance with that the women should not prophesy at all in the services. Women are allowed to prophesy but not when the congregation officially meets (cf. chapter 11). This prohibition shows some analogy with Paul's statement concerning glossolalia, namely that it should not be used in the services except under very special conditions. This time the prohibition is absolute which is due to the fact that it is given not because of anything inherent in prophecy itself but simply because women ought not to speak in the services. Women who have received the gift of prophecy, are not to use their *exousia* in the meetings of the church.

341

The view has been expressed that Paul does not issue an absolute prohibition of women's speaking in the church for 1) the verb the apostle uses connotes speaking[24] rather than the giving of an address, and 2) it should be remembered that the special circumstances at Corinth may have demanded special measures. It should be granted that Paul writes of speech not of prophecy. But it is inconceivable in this context that Paul's words should imply no more than that women may not speak during the services. Such an admonition would ill accord with *subjection as also saith the law*. Does not the context speak of using the gift which God has given to the church's profit? Secondly, the expression "speaking in tongues" implies that "to speak" is more than simply expressing oneself. Much more plausible is therefore the view that Paul uses the general word "to speak" because he is of the opinion that any kind of speaking in the services is forbidden to women. Vs. 35 even forbids asking questions in the meeting. And as to the second argument, conditions were indeed unusual at Corinth, but at the beginning Paul stated that the rule which applies at Corinth applies everywhere. Our verse, it should now be clear, contains an absolute prohibition against women's speaking in the services.

The question as to the agreement between this apostolic injunction and the words of 11:5f., where the apostle seems to assume that women pray or prophesy, must be answered with the consideration that chapter 11, although undoubtedly referring to public activities of prayer and prophecy, does not mention them as taking place in the official services of the church. Those services are not mentioned there, whereas in 14:34 they are explicitly referred to.

Another objection has been that 14:34 should not be detached from its context and that this context discusses glossolalia and prophecy and how to use those charismata. Women, it is then alleged, are forbidden to enter into such discussions during the services. But this interpretation is too far-fetched, for Paul speaks in very general terms and does not think of the Corinthian conditions alone (*as in all the churches, for it is shameful,* etc.). And furthermore; here as well as in chapter 11, Paul has in view married women in the first place.

---

[24] λαλεῖν.

342

To be in subjection: the present tense implies a lasting condition. To whom the woman's obedience is due, is not stated here but from 11:3-15 we already know that it is to her husband. On the other hand, Paul's omission of the words "to their husbands" is significant since it serves to emphasize the dependent position of women in general. A command of this nature is found in the law (Gen. 3:16). *As also*: the Old Tesatment, already teaches something which is now in use in all the churches (vs. 33). That adds to the force of the commandment and relates it to a divine institution, given after the fall for all times (cf. 11:18f.).

35 It might be that women did not desire to express themselves but merely to be better informed. Is it forbidden for a women even to ask a question? Paul answers yes, if they wish to *learn* something they are to *ask their own husbands at home*. The apostle assumes that the husband will be able and willing to answer those questions. The implications of this word of Paul are thus equally far reaching for the men as for the women. Again Paul adduces a reason: he appeals to the *shamefulness* of the Corinthian practices (cf. 11:5, 6), i. e., Paul appeals to the ordinary course of nature. Everybody will agree that it is unbecoming for a woman to speak in a public meeting of the church.

36 From vs. 36 it appears that the abuse, which the apostle rebukes, did exist at Corinth. The thought of vs. 36 is related to that of vs. 33b. The Corinthians had their own customs. Why? Did the Corinthian church have a different character from other churches? Did it occupy a leading position? That would be so if the word of God *went forth* from Corinth. Everybody knows that the word of God came from Jerusalem. Neither has the word of God come to Corinth alone. Therefore the Corinthian church has to take into account the other churches.

CONCLUSION AND EXHORTATION

14:37-40

37 If any man thinketh himself to be a prophet, or spiritual, let him take knowledge of the things which I write unto you that they are the commandment of the Lord.

38 But if any man is ignorant, let him be ignorant.

39 Wherefore, desire earnestly to prophesy, and forbid not to speak with tongues.

40 But let all things be done decently and in order.

37, 38 After having treated all questions connected with the charismata, especially those regarding glossolalia and prophecy, the apostle now comes to his conclusion which is also an exhortation. Paul faces all those who have received charismata with responsibility to submit to his words. He himself does not determine whether a certain person has a particular charisma. That is left for every person to decide: *If any man thinketh himself to be a prophet,* etc., i. e., whether this be true or false, he is to observe the things Paul wrote in his letter. *Spiritual* here has reference to one who speaks in tongues, as appears from the context. The Corinthians' esteem for glossolalia may have been so great that they considered him who spoke in tongues as spiritual par excellence (cf. *thinketh,* and also 2:13). He who thinks he is spiritual has to observe Paul's remarks about the charismata for they are *commandments of the Lord.* Thus the apostle first of all assigns to the spiritual person his proper task and duty according to his charisma (cf. I Jn. 4:6). But he also implies that what he writes is destined for the whole congregation to whom Paul, to a certain extent, gives a kind of supervision. The main point is that those gifted with charismata are to adhere to the ordinances of the Lord.

If anybody does not observe those ordinances then he will not be recognized,[25] he belongs to the perishing (1:18). Not to be

---

[25] The words of ASV: If any man is ignorant, let him be ignorant, do not render the original εἰ δέ τις ἀγνοεῖ ἀγνοεῖται correctly. The RSV is better: "if any one does not recognize this, he is not recognized."

344

recognized is the opposite of "to be known by Him" (8:3; cf. 13:12).

39 This verse contains an admonition for the whole church. *Desire earnestly to prophesy* is almost a repetition of vs. 1 but this exhortation which in vs. 1 applies to prophecy in a general sense, carries more weight after Paul's exposition on prophecy. The words do not mean that the congregation, which is potentially able to prophesy, must desire that it may actually prophesy. Vs. 37 indicates that not the whole congregation, but only certain of its members were prophets. On the other hand, it is significant that Paul does not speak about being a prophet but about *prophesying*, i. e., the point in question is not to be considered a prophet, but rather to speak as a prophet to the congregation.

After the positive commandment with respect to prophecy there follows a negative one concerning glossolalia. Glossolalia, indeed, is also a charisma of the Spirit and has its place as such, but because glossolalia is either wanting in fruits for the church, or remains behind prophecy in that respect, due to the abuses which have arisen around it, Paul does not encourage them *to speak with tongues*.

40 Vs. 40 contains a general exhortation by way of conclusion (cf. vs. 33). *Decently and in order* reminds us of 7:6, 17, 25, 35, 36, where the general background is formed by the charisma of remaining unmarried. Charismatic activities shall not disturb good order in the services. The meetings of the congregation are to serve the edification of the church. Everything which conflicts with that principle shall be excluded.

The lasting importance of this chapter lies in the fact that Paul sets forth what the character of the divine services must be. That which he writes about that subject is still valid. Furthermore we learn that God the Holy Spirit had endowed the early Christians with special gifts, charismata, and that He guided the ancient church by means of them. We also notice how great the dangers connected with those gifts. That should make us grateful that in the Holy Scriptures of the Old and New Testaments we have all that we need.

CHAPTER XV

DECLARATION OF THE GOSPEL

15:1-11

1 Now I make known unto you, brethren, the gospel which I have preached unto you, which also ye received, wherein also ye stand,

2 by which also ye are saved, if ye hold fast the word which I preached unto you, except ye believed in vain.

3 For I delivered unto you first of all that which also I received: that Christ died for our sins according to the Scriptures;

4 and that he was buried; and that he hath been raised on the third day according to the Scriptures;

5 and that he appeared to Cephas; then to the twelve;

6 then he appeared to above five hundred brethren at once, of whom the greater part remain until now, but some are fallen asleep;

7 then he appeared to James; then to all the apostles;

8 and last of all, as to the child untimely born, he appeared to me also.

9 For I am the least of the apostles, that am not meet to be called an apostle, because I persecuted the church of God.

10 But by the grace of God I am what I am: and his grace which was bestowed upon me was not found vain; but I labored more abundantly than they all: yet not I, but the grace of God which was with me.

11 Whether then *it be* I or they, so we preach, and so ye believe.

1 Thus far Paul has treated only those abuses which prevailed in the whole Corinthian church, either because he had heard of them himself or because the Corinthians had asked for information. In chapter 15, however, Paul treats the resurrection of the body, of which he expressly states (vs. 12) that the latter is denied only by some among the Corinthians. Besides, we have here the first error of a doctrinal nature. According to vs. 12 this was not

346

a system of error but rather a single contention, on one point only. But nevertheless we are here in the realm of doctrine.

The solemn beginning of this chapter must be understood against this background. *I make known* is not "I remind you." but "I make known emphatically" (cf. Gal. 1:11). Paul speaks here expressly about facts already proclaimed to the Corinthians. The import of the introductory words is: I bring to you the old gospel, the one and only true gospel, whatever may be adduced against it or whatever preaching may seem to conflict with it. It is the gospel which I must preach to you also now, in relation to the error which has arisen in your midst. In other words: I preach to you now what I must preach to you at all times.

The word "gospel" is qualified by various clauses, which do not touch upon the content of the gospel, as is done in vs. 3, but which predicate something of the gospel and thus point out its value. Paul preached that gospel to the Corinthians "as glad tidings." The Corinthians experienced the gospel as such and they accepted those tidings, and thereby became true Christians. They also *stand* in that gospel, i. e., they took a stand on that gospel (cf. Rom. 5:2) so that it became their foundation, which determines both their spiritual position and their conduct. Paul's words imply the high esteem he has for the gospel which he preached and the Corinthians accepted.[1] The resurrection of Christ is an essential part of this gospel.

2 *By which* refers to the working of the gospel. The Corinthians *are saved* by the gospel, i. e., saved from sin and endowed with eternal life. In 1:18 we read that the word of the cross, i. e., the gospel, is the power of God (cf. Rom. 1:16, power of God unto salvation). *By* does not indicate here the ultimate efficient cause, but the means through which something is brought about. The gospel itself does not save, but God saves by the gospel. He begins His work with man by calling him through the gospel (Rom. 10:14, 15). Paul's use of the present tense *"are saved"* as in 1:18 is noteworthy. It implies that the Corinthians are at this moment on the way to salvation. But the gospel does not save all

---

[1] παραλαμβάνω is the special word for the acceptance of the gospel; παραδίδωμι, to deliver, the word for the preaching of the apostles who received the gospel and handed it down to the churches.

men, only those that *hold fast the word* preached by the apostle.[2] *To hold fast,* (cf. 11:2), corresponds with "to be saved." But if the latter is conditioned upon the former the question arises how such a thought agrees with the sentiment expressed in the words: *wherein ye stand.* This apparent contradiction seems to disappear if we consider that Paul begins by speaking of the church as a whole and of its actions, after that, as elsewhere (cf. 3:2f in the commentary), he sets forth that everybody personally has to render account of his own conduct, asking himself whether that which is true of the church also is true of him (cf. Phil. 3:11, 12). If Paul had meant *wherein ye stand* absolutely of all the members of the congregation the addition *by which also ye are saved* would have been superfluous. In connection with the doctrinal deviations this basic truth needs renewed emphasis.

The following words: *except ye believed* continue in the same admonishing tone. These words introduce a new element in that Paul states now that to accept the gospel means to come to faith. That faith is not defined but it is certain that in this context we are to think of it not as faith in the gospel but rather as faith in Jesus Christ. Thus the matter is carried to the realm of the subjective faith of the church. Secondly, Paul appeals to the church, as he is going to many more times (cf. especially vs. 12f.). Paul knows so certainly that the Corinthians are convinced not to have believed *in vain,* that he makes it his startingpoint for the following argument (cf. Gal. 3:2f.). Thus the apostle has gradually shifted from the objective to the subjective, from the gospel to faith. The Corinthians experienced subjectively the objective value of the gospel; as the beginning of vs. 2 was meant to elicit a positive answer on their part, so the conclusion a negative one. From the very outset they are to realize, on the basis of Paul's words, the objective value of the gospel. It should be noted that Paul does not lean upon a subjective experience. Vs. 12 teaches us that he wishes to start his argument against that wrong asser-

---

[2] τινι λόγῳ εὐηγγελισάμην ὑμῖν, i.e. τούτῳ λόγῳ ᾧ. εἰς has the meaning of ὅστις. The sentence could have read: εἰ κατέχετε τούτῳ τῷ λόγῳ ᾧ εὐηγγελισάμην ὑμῖν; cf. οἶδά σε τίς εἶ in Lk. 4:34. Λόγος, manner, way. The Corinthians are saved by the gospel if they hold it fast in the way, i.e. with the same contents as Paul had delivered to them.

tion with an appeal to a most objective truth. But that argument is so strong because that objective truth is of the greatest interest to the church.

3 *To deliver* and its correlate "to receive" (vs. 1) refer to the way in which in ancient times the gospel was preached. In a period in which there existed few, if any, scriptures, this mode of transmission was a matter of importance. The apostle received the gospel from Jesus Himself (Gal. 1:12) and delivered it to the congregations (cf. also 11:23), who in turn delivered it to others. There is a constant handing down of the gospel. Thus by writing "I delivered that which I received" Paul reminds us of the divine origin and of the truthfulness of the gospel.

It is not feasible to consider the words that follow as a summary of what Paul preached. The apostle only records that which is required by the context. It is significant that the apostle does not formulate a doctrine but records facts: death, burial and resurrection, facts which will serve to combat the error regarding the resurrection of the body. *First*:[3] not because Paul was the first one to preach at Corinth, but because the things he mentioned were the "first" i. e., the most important things he preached. Implied in this is that the error of the Corinthians did not agree with Paul's preaching.

The four clauses which follow tell us what the apostle preached at Corinth. In vs. 6 the construction of the sentence changes although it is clear that the thought is continued even there, for we can be sure that Paul preached about Christ's appearance to him near Damascus (vs. 8). The reason why Paul uses the name Christ in this context, when referring to the Saviour, is that he wishes to designate His work as to its official quality and its consequences for those who believe in Him (cf. Rom. 5:8; 8:32; 14:15; II Cor. 5:14; Gal. 1:4: Eph. 5:2, 25; Tit. 2:14). It is striking that Paul, although writing to a gentile Christian church, says: *according to the Scriptures* (cf. Is. 53; Mt. 26:24: Jn. 20:9). Paul attaches much value to this phrase as appears from its repetition (vs. 4; cf. also Rom. 1:2). Even to gentile Christians Paul is anxious to demonstrate that God performs His atoning work in Christ as the prophets had announced. There is unity and for that reason also strength in the work of God (II Pet.

---

[3] πρώτοις may be masc. or neuter.

349

1:19). The apostle does not quote a particular text, but refers to the analogy of all the Scriptures. Nothing in this area is accidental, everything is contained in God's decree. If the death of Christ is what the apostle says it is, it is a foregone conclusion that His resurrection also has great significance.

4 The burial is also mentioned in order to demonstrate the genuineness of both death and resurrection. The phrase "according to the Scriptures" is here omitted because Christ's burial is only an interlude between His death and His resurrection. *He hath been raised*: God was the author of it. The perfect tense implies that Jesus lives at this moment, thus pointing to the special significance of the resurrection. The words *according to the scriptures* also go with *on the third day*. Even the day agrees with the prophecy. Most probably Paul has in view Jonah 1:17 (Hebr. and LXX 2:1) (cf. Mt. 12:40). There are no further references to the three day period in the Old Testament. Hos. 6:2 cannot be understood of Christ's resurrection; moreover the New Testament does not quote it.[4]

5 Coming now to the appearances of our Lord the apostle discusses them at great length because they guarantee the truth of the resurrection. On the other hand, this lengthy reference is somewhat striking in view of the fact that the truthfulness of Christ's resurrection was not doubted at Corinth. Paul probably did not intend to argue the truthfulness of the resurrection by means of these appearances but only wished to place the resurrection of Christ in the fullest light since it was the starting point for his argument. Besides, we ought not forget that these appearances are expressly mentioned as part of the preaching. If Christ's resurrection had not been of far-reaching significance Paul would not have preached about these appearances. That accounts for the reference to them here; all of them bear an official character and are designed to make the preaching of the resurrection to the churches possible. Christ Himself took care that His resurrection should be proclaimed. *He appeared*: he could be seen by human eyes, the appearances were not just visions.[5] *Cephas*: cf. 1:12. Paul does not relate the appearance to the

---

[4] On the three days, see further Grosheide, *Mattheus* in KNT, p. 157 and *1 Korinth.* in KNT, p. 494.
[5] ὤφθη

350

women, not because he did not know of it but because he is only selecting (cf. *first*, vs. 3). The appearance to Peter was here more important because Peter was the first apostolic witness to the resurrection (Lk. 24:34), and it prepared for the appearance to the twelve.

The clause of the direct object ends here, marking a separation between the preceeding and the following appearances, which are of a different nature. The appearance to the apostles authorizes and charges the apostles to preach the resurrection (cf. Mt. 28:16; Jn. 24:19). We cannot say with precision which appearance is meant, perhaps Paul takes all of them together. *The twelve*: these words designate the body of the apostles even though there were only eleven present.

6 After relating the appearances which made the apostles witnesses of the resurrection (Acts. 1:8, 22), the apostle mentions one to a great number not holding a special office but representing the church. The greatness of the number is stressed there can be no mistake. The Corinthians may check this story because the majority of the *five hundred brethren* is still alive. Paul cannot have meant that the Corinthians should go to Palestine to meet those brethren. This was not feasible, nor was it necessary because the Corinthians did not doubt Christ's resurrection. And even if they had, Paul would have been more interested in a faithful acceptance of the preaching of the apostles than in an on the spot interrogation of the five hundred. The resurrection can only be accepted by faith, not by simple reliance upon man's authority (cf. vss. 2 and 11). Besides, we must not forget that of the apostles who saw Jesus after the resurrection some were still alive, and yet Paul does not speak of them. Paul's reference to the five hundred is for the purpose of pointing out that there were many others besides the apostles who were deigned worthy of seeing Jesus and of being with the apostles as witnesses and preachers of His resurrection (cf. vs. 11). Perhaps some of the five hundred were known at Corinth. This appearance is not recorded in the gospels.

7 Of still another character is the appearance to James. In view of the words that follow (*then to all the apostles*) we are compelled to think of the apostle James. However, it is highly improbable that one of the twelve should be meant, namely James the son of Zebedee, or James the son of Alpheus. Much more obvious is the view that this is James, the brother of our Lord, who was the leader of the church at Jerusalem. In the beginning the brothers of the Lord did not believe in Him (Jn. 7:5) but after the resurrection they are found with the apostles (Acts 1:14). From this we conclude that Paul has in view an appearance of the Lord to His brother, who, just like Paul near Damascus, was converted by this means. The unbelieving James saw his Brother, just like Peter who saw the Lord whom he had denied.

The next appearance is one *to all the apostles.* Since vs. 5 mentioned the twelve we prefer to think here of a larger circle. Paul's use of the word apostle is not restricted to the twelve only. This interpretation also fits our view concerning James, for the latter also belonged to this larger circle. There is thus an analogy with vs. 5: there it was Peter first and then the twelve; here James first and then a greater circle of apostles.

8 Paul directly joins the appearance of Christ to himself to the one to all the apostles: *and last of all —* He *appeared unto me. Last of all:* the last one in this series. Paul was the last one to see the glorified Lord with his own eyes, in order that he might be a true apostle. Hence the words: *the child untimely born.* The article before *child* shows us how Paul designates himself in relation to the other apostles. The expression may also imply that there were no more of such children afterwards. In any case, Paul pictures himself as the unworthy one (cf. vs. 9 also Job 3:16; Ps. 58 (LXX 57):9; Eccl. 6:3[6]). Others have taken the expression to refer to Paul's sudden conversion which resembled the untimely birth of a child; still others of a birth from a mother which was already dead, namely, Israel. But those views fail to do justice to the context: the purpose of *"as to"* can only be to describe the relation of Paul himself to the others who also received an appearance of the Lord. Just as a miscarriage cannot be called a child so Paul could not be called an apostle at the time (cf. vs. 9). The other apostles were converted when they were called. They never opposed Jesus as did Paul, their birth as apostles was normal. With Paul this was otherwise. Paul's words do not intend to prove the truth of his apos-

---

[6] In the first and last of these texts the LXX also has ἔκτρωμα

tolic office but he is simply overwhelmed as he comes to speak of the appearances of the Lord and as he is obliged, to the glory of God's grace, to speak of the appearance which he himself received and of all God had given him. Ultimately these things are also witnesses of the truth and the significance of the resurrection. Even to Paul Christ deigned to reveal Himself.

9 Paul's statement about himself was very strong and was consequently in need of some additional proof. Further clarification was also desirable because the expression *child untimely born* should not be used to diminish the grace of God. *For I am the least of the apostles* (cf. Eph. 3:8; I Tim. 1:15), implies that Paul, and Paul alone, was the least[7] of the apostles. This "least" is based on his conduct. But still, he was an apostle even though he had *persecuted the church of God*, a terrible thing because it was *God's* church. But Paul knows that he is converted, that his guilt is expiated (cf. Rom. 7:24, 25). He knows he is a true apostle, and yet, not only the fact that he once was a persecutor, but also the consequences of it for today depress him. He remains the least of the apostles, though God has glorified Himself in Paul.

10 Everything Paul is, he is *by the grace of God* (II Cor. 3:5). That does not refer to his conversion alone, not even to his vocation to be an apostle; but God's grace appears especially in the work he has been allowed to do. Paul's sin serves the glory of God, who forgave him his transgressions and made him an outstanding apostle (cf. Rom. 9:17). God's grace toward Paul was *not found vain*, without contents (II Cor. 6:1); on the contrary, Paul *labored*, i. e., toiled[8] *more abundantly than they all.*[9] Two thoughts stand side by side: a) God's grace is extolled in Paul's life in a special way; all glory is due to God so that Paul can boast in spite of his sins. b) But in *"more than they all,"* which refers to the other apostles, Paul places himself on the same level with the other apostles. Summarizing we may say: it is to the glory of the grace of God that the least of the apostles could do so much.

---

[7] ἐλάχιστος not the last called, for the word is not the same as ἔσχατον in vs. 8.

[8] κοπιᾶν.

[9] αὐτῶν may be "more than one of them" as well as "more than they all." The context pleads for the second.

More abundantly does not refer to a greater measure of fruit, or to the performance of more important or heavier work. These words are consequently no evidence that Paul is conceited. He states the fact because he knows that he has toiled more than the other apostles. To such a work God called him and the *grace of God was with* him on all his journeys and with all his labor.

11 Paul had digressed for a brief moment that he might glorify God in the things he wrote about himself. But in vs. 11 Paul returns to his subject: the resurrection of Christ. *Whether — or*: however these things with Paul and the other apostles may be, the main point is that they all unanimously *so preach* the gospel, i. e., they preach it (present tense) in the way that Paul has just defined it in vs. 1f. It is in that way also that the Corinthian church believed it. *So ye believed*, because the resurrection of Christ was the contents of the preaching and at the same time the contents of their faith (cf. vs. 12). There is unanimity and absence of doubt.

Thus the apostle has laid the foundation for his subsequent argument directed against false doctrine: the resurrection of Christ is true, it has been preached, it has been believed.

THE PLEDGE OF OUR RESURRECTION

15:12-19

12 Now if Christ is preached that he hath been raised from the dead, how say some among you that there is no resurrection of the dead?

13 But if there is no resurrection of the dead, neither hath Christ been raised:

14 and if Christ hath not been raised, then is our preaching vain, your faith also is vain.

15 Yea, and we are found false witnesses of God; because we witnessed of God that he raised up Christ: whom he raised not up, if so be that the dead are not raised.

16 For if the dead are not raised neither hath Christ been raised:

17 and if Christ hath not been raised, your faith is vain; you are yet in your sins.

18 Then they also that are fallen asleep in Christ have perished.

19 If we have only hoped in Christ in this life, we are of all men most pitiable.

12 *If Christ is preached,* i. e., if it is true, as the facts which Paul has just called back to mind clearly demonstrate, that the resurrection of Christ[10] is preached. *Hath been raised:* (perfect tense) He lives at the present as the risen Saviour.

Say: there is no reference to the preaching of a false doctrine but only to "saying" something erroneous. This is the first and the only time that Paul writes about a doctrinally unsound assertion in I Corinthians. So far only aberrations in the moral sphere had been treated. Moreover, the false contention is found only with *some,* which points to an exception (cf. 4:18; 8:17; 15:34). There was at Corinth a group, either small or somewhat larger, but probably not very large (*some!*), which denied the resurrection of the body. That is all the information which is available. How

---

[10] Paul writes *Christ,* as in vs. 3, and thus brings the office of Christ to the foreground.

Paul received this information is not known. We assume that the false doctrine had not yet spread very far in view of the fact that Paul waited until now to mention it. The error, moreover, cannot have been a very serious one for Paul remains composed. The fact of Christ's resurrection was not denied, only that of the resurrection of others (cf. *resurrection of the dead*, i. e., literally: of corpses). It was assumed that death was the last thing that happened to the body, the soul (pneuma) was thought of as living on. Death meant death, for believers as well as unbelievers. This must be a remnant of a pagan belief. Some Greek philosophers believed that the souls would continue to exist, others that the soul perished with the body. As the body was publicly burnt on a pile the conclusion could soon be drawn that that was the end. Again another school held that the soul must be liberated from the body, then the body was allowed to perish. Besides, the assumption is justified that the question of *exousia* or "rights" also played a part here. As we noticed earlier, the Corinthians thought that they were entitled to all things. And perhaps, rationalists as they were, they may have reasoned that a resurrection of the dead was impossible. Though it is not stated in so many words, we must conclude from the context that there were some at Corinth who denied the resurrection of the *body* without denying that the souls continued to exist. Paul's argument as a whole is guided by the thought that such a separation between spirit and body is not permissible. *We*, the Christians, are the subjects of the resurrection (vss. 22, 51), as much as the "corpses" that are raised. That becomes even clearer when Paul mentions in one breath that Christ was raised, and that the dead are raised, and when he draws a parallel between the two.

It is not known whether the apostles often preached about the resurrection of the dead. In their letters they do not often touch on this point. The remarkable feature of Paul's argument here is that he formulates the main point of his refutation of this error at the very beginning. That error is impossible (*how say some*). But in spite of that he demonstrates at grea: length that faith in the resurrection of Christ actually includes .aith in the resurrection of the body. It is that absurd situation, of an acceptance of the one and a rejection of the other, which exists at Corinth. Paul assumes that the erring members of the church will come to the insight that they accept an impossible viewpoint. At the same time, however, by drawing up such a sharp contrast (Christ raised, the dead not raised) he implies that the erring Christians are doing violence to the Christian faith.

13 The conditional clauses which follow in this and subsequent verses do not, as in vs. 12, end in a question, but in a conclusion which follows clearly from what is posited in them. *If there is* really *no resurrection of the dead* (lit.: "corpses," Paul speaks of dead bodies) *neither has Christ been raised*, because His body also was dead and returned to life only because God raised it. Now the Corinthians are convinced that Christ rose from the dead, and so their assertion must be false; there *is* a resurrection of the dead.

14 Vs. 13 might have this wrong consequence that the Corinthians might still hold to their error and conclude from that that Christ was not raised. In order to prevent this Paul takes over the contemplated conclusion and uses it as a premise for his own argument. Suppose Christ is not raised, he argues, as would follow from the wrong premise, then a whole series of other facts would follow of which the Corinthians immediately would cry out: they are not true! And that again must lead them to the conclusion that the premise of vs. 14 and consequently also of vs. 13 is not true. *If Christ hath not been raised our* apostolic *preaching is vain*[11] and also the *faith* of the Corinthians. *Then* implies the inevitable nature of the conclusion. The Corinthians will disagree with this last conclusion, they know for themselves that they believe and are convinced that that preaching is true (cf. vs. 11). Not as if the truth of Christ's resurrection would here be made to rest on the apostolic preaching or on the faith of the Corinthians. Paul does not discuss the question as to the grounds on which the resurrection is based; he does not prove that Christ is raised. But in his argument Paul carries that which he has just posited *ad absurdum.*

15 Vs. 15 enumerates still other consequences of the assumption that Christ was never raised from the dead, consequences of which the Corinthians again will say that they are not true. *We are found,* i. e., we appear. *Witnesses,* when used of the apostles, invariably means that the apostles have seen certain

---

[11] κενός, without contents; vs. 17 has μάταιος, without effect.

357

things and that they speak of what they saw (Acts 1:22). *False witnesses* are those who contend they have seen or heard what they actually neither saw nor heard, since what they mention never happened, or because they falsify the actual facts (Mt. 26:59f.; I Jn. 5:10). *False witnesses of God*: people who give their false witness in God's name not only speak an untruth but they hold God in derision by covering their false witness with His name. Thus the apostles would then appear to have presented themselves as witnesses of God, while God actually did not send them. The object of the testimony is the resurrection of Christ. That was the message Paul and his co-laborers brought.[12] The fact that the apostles preached the resurrection of Christ is taken for granted both by the apostles and by the Corinthians. If that testimony is not true then they would be false witnesses, who abused God's name. But the Corinthians would never accept that, though they have not always given Paul his proper place. If the apostles are true witnesses the Corinthians are to accept their preaching that Christ was raised up. *We witnessed of God* (lit.: we witnessed against God[13]) is a further clarification of the words: false witnesses of God. If Christ was not raised (a), and if the apostles preached that he was raised up (b), then the apostles are false witnesses (c).[14] In order to emphasize that his assertion is the conclusion of two mutually dependent clauses the apostle repeats them at the end: *If so be that,* i. e., if that wrong assumption would really be true.

16 In view of the importance of this point Paul repeats what he wrote in vs. 13, which was also given by way of appendix at the end of the preceding verse. Thus vs. 16 serves to stress the fact that what holds true of all the rest of the dead must hold true of Christ also. *Whom he raised not up* (vs. 15) was with all its terrible implications also against the truth. But if the assertions of some of the Corinthians were true, namely that there is no resurrection of the dead, then this other thing would be

---

[12] In this context Paul always uses the verb ἐγείρω rather than ἀνίστημι, evidently because he is concerned to argue that God also will raise up men.

[13] ἐμαρτυρήσαμεν κατὰ τοῦ Θεοῦ, i.e., against what God did.

[14] The first ὅτι introduces a causal clause, the second an object clause.

358

true too. *For*: by means of this concise repetition Paul offers a reason for his previous statement.

17   Vs. 17 begins with a new series of conclusions drawn from the proposition, Christ is not raised, as they followed from the opinion of certain Corinthians. This new series is of a more subjective nature, i. e., it sets forth the condition in which the Corinthians would find themselves if the assertion of "some" were true. *Your faith is vain* (cf. vs. 14) : if the Corinthians' faith, here taken of the act of faith, is without result, then they are *yet in their sins* (Jn. 8:12; Eph. 2:1). For faith alone makes one enter into communion with Christ, the only One who delivers from sin (Acts 4:12). Yet Christ can only deliver from sin if, after He died, He also rose from the dead (Rom. 4:24; 5:1f.; 8:11, etc., cf. also I Cor. 15:3, 4). All those passages imply that Christ's death is only of value if He also conquered death and as the Living One applies the benefits of His death to sinners. If Christ died only, but did not rise from the dead, then sinners are no better off than the men of Emmaus (Lk. 24:21). The Corinthians are apparently convinced that they would be *yet in their sins* without the resurrection of Christ. And to be in sin means to be under the power of death. Again the Corinthians know that this cannot be said of them, they had the assurance of faith.

18   Vs. 18 mentions another result of the tenet that Christ did not rise from the dead, a result of which the Corinthians are likewise convinced that it is not true. *Then*, namely if the Corinthians are yet in their sins because their faith was vain. *They that are fallen asleep in Christ*: the deceased Christians who died hoping in Christ, those who were in Christ at the moment of their death. *Have perished*: see 1:18, cf. II Cor. 2:15; 4:3. The Corinthians are convinced that they who died in Christ are saved. Paul does not speak here of the resurrection of the body of them who died in Christ, but rather of their being doomed, because if Christ had not been raised, they had died in their sins (Rom. 4:25). We might ask whether the Corinthians did not realize that Christ's resurrection, which they did not deny, was necessary to salvation. But Paul does not imply that they denied even such necessity. He only shows the consequences to which they would be led if they denied the resurrection of the dead.

359

19 Vs. 19 still is related, though indirectly, to the erroneous supposition of vss. 16 and 17. It is most intimately connected with vs. 18. If they who died in Christ have perished, it follows that Christ's work is only of importance for our life on earth. That is the presupposition underlying vs. 19. *If we have only hoped*: the Greek[15] implies: if we must conclude from our argument that at this moment we are such as have until now hoped in Christ in this life only, and if there is no reason to expect anything after this life — and that is the case if Christ did not rise from the dead — then there is no real hope left. Again every Corinthian will deny such a possibility emphatically. This also renders it unnecessary to inquire concerning the sense of the words: *to hope in Christ only in this life*, for such a thing does not even exist. If hoping in Christ does not guarantee the resurrection, it is better to remain Jew or gentile and to enjoy this present life.[16] Then there will be no disappointment at the moment of our death. If that which Paul writes here were true, the Christian would be put to shame when he dies. It would be of no use to forsake the world and to deny many things that are agreeable to the flesh and make life comfortable. *To hope,* cf. 13:13. Hope is one of the essentials of Christian living.[17]

We notice that Paul in his entire argument assumes that the main points of the Christian doctrine were accepted at Corinth; the error had not assumed serious proportions. Not only had the consequences not yet been drawn, but those consequences had been realized so little that Paul, by pointing them out, is able to combat the error itself.

---

[15] ἠλπικότες ἐσμέν.

[16] ἐλεεινότεροι πάντων ἀνθρώπων. We can translate, "more pitiable than all men," or "the most pitiable of all men."

[17] μόνον must not be joined with ἠλπικότες. It is to be construed with ἐσμέν: "we are only," and thus it is virtually linked with ἐν τῇ ζωῇ. Because of its position μόνον is stressed and underscores the contrast between this life and the future one.

FUTURE PROSPECTS

15:20-28

20 But now hath Christ been raised from the dead, the firstfruits of them that are asleep.

21 For since by man *came* death, by man *came* also the resurrection of the dead.

22 For as in Adam all die, so also in Christ shall all be made alive.

23 But each in his own order: Christ the firstfruits; then they that are Christ's, at his coming.

24 Then cometh the end, when he shall deliver up the kingdom to God, even the Father; when he shall have abolished all rule and all authority and power.

25 For he must reign, till he hath put all his enemies under his feet.

26 The last enemy that shall be abolished is death.

27 For, He put all things in subjection under his feet. But when he saith, All things are put in subjection, it is evident that he is excepted who did subject all things unto him.

28 And when all things have been subjected unto him, then shall the Son also himself be subjected to him that did subject all things unto him, that God may be all in all.

20 Paul now comes to the end of his lengthy argument. It cannot be continued any further for no Corinthian denied the resurrection of Christ, and an argument presupposing such a denial might prove to be unbearable in the end. The Corinthians had to admit that the "some" of vs. 12 erred.

Coming now to the positive side of his treatment Paul not only discusses the resurrection of Christ, or the resurrection of the body, but the end of all things in general. The latter, as Paul will demonstrate, also bears upon the resurrection of the body. There is a shout of rejoicing: *but now hath Christ been raised from the dead!* That is the glorious reality which is generally accepted; Paul has taught us its precise import. Not until now

361

is Paul able to deduce the resurrection of the body from the resurrection of Christ. *But now*, followed not by an assumption but by a reality. The premise of vss. 13, 14 is false. Now Paul draws a conclusion from a true premise. The name *Christ* refers to the quality of Him who rose from the dead. Because *Christ* is raised He is raised as the *firstfruits* of them who died as He did. and who have the same nature as He (Heb. 2:14). Paul uses the figure of the *firstfruits*, derived from the Mosaic law, elsewhere, (cf. Rom. 11:16 and Ex. 23:19; 34:26; Lev. 2:12; 23:10, 17, 20; Num. 15:20, 21). Christ is the first One to rise from the dead but Christ is never without His people (Rom. 6:5). The offering of the firstfruits symbolized the offering of the entire harvest. In the old dispensation, however, the greater part of the harvest was not sacrificed. But in the work of Christ all symbolism is abolished. If He is the firstfruits His people must follow Him (Col. 1:18). The resurrection of Christ, which was accepted by the Corinthians, means the resurrection of *them that are asleep*. That this applies to the believing dead needed not to be said, because Christ is not the firstfruits of the others. Besides, in Paul's epistles "they that are asleep"[18] always refers to believers; the fate of the unbelievers is not discussed in this chapter. And finally our verse, as it is contrasted with vs. 18, leaves no doubt on this point. Note that Paul in this whole context speaks of the divine action (*hath been raised*, not: arose).

21 *For since*[19] introduces a causal clause which, strictly speaking, does not contain the reason for vs. 20 where it was stated that Christ is the firstfruits of them that died. Vs. 21 presupposes the following thought: and for them who are asleep there can only be a resurrection if Christ is raised as the firstfruits. Thus Paul deduces a necessary condition from the fact stated in vs. 20. And the reason for that condition in vs. 21 is also formulated as an existing fact (cf. vs. 22). So instead of writing: because death is by a man, the resurrection *must* also be by a man, Paul writes: the resurrection *is* by a man. Paul does not argue that such and such must be so, but he places the existing facts in causal connection. The twice repeated *man* without the article

---

[18] κεκοιμημένοι.

[19] ἐπειδὴ γάρ: γάρ belongs to the apodosis; ἐπειδή introduces the protasis.

receives much stress. The absence of the article before *death* and *resurrection* implies that Paul is speaking about qualities: something like death came into the world by one who belonged to the genus man. Likewise the resurrection. Dying and rising from the dead are not essential to nature. Not that which nature does with a corpse should have the attention of the Corinthians, for it is a man who is the agent here. Thus we see that it is God who raises from the dead as it was He who sent death.

22 After mentioning death and resurrection in their basic quality Paul mentions them as facts. *For*: the facts bear out that vs. 21 was true. As vs. 21 furnished the reason for vs. 20, so does vs. 22 for vs. 21. It appears that the one "man" is Adam, the other Christ. The Corinthians knew those names; they serve to point out that two real men are meant. Furthermore special emphasis rests on the twice repeated *all* and on the contrast *death* — *life*. There is a similarity of result in the actions of the man Adam and of the Man Christ. *All*: not all without any qualification, but all those who are connected with either Adam or Christ; the latter appears from vs. 18: *In Christ;* vss. 20, 21: *firstfruits;* vs. 23: *that are Christ's.* Paul speaks here, as already was mentioned, only of the resurrection of those who are connected with Christ.

In view of the fact that Paul earlier referred to them that are asleep we are inclined to take *die* of the natural death. *Made alive* would then refer to the resurrection of the body. As to the latter element of this interpretation it is supported by vs. 23: *then they that are Christ's at his coming.* To die must therefore also refer to the end of our earthly existence. Implied in this interpretation is that *in Adam* — *in Christ* does not mean: at the moment Adam dies, or: at the moment Christ rises; the preposition *in* refers to the efficient cause, not in the sense that Adam is conceived of as causing to die, or as being the means whereby men die, but in the sense that through Adam's death all those who are connected with him also die. The present tense *die* implies that the dying is going on at the moment Paul is writing and that it keeps going on. The future: *shall be made alive* refers to the future resurrection on the last day. Christ's work has its analogies in earthly life. But with Christ there is perfection and glory, not death but resurrection.

363

23 Paul does not again refer to Adam; the subject of death had only been introduced for the sake of comparison. The apostle develops the thought that in Christ all will be raised. That will be the result of the communion between Christ and His people. The whole resurrection is a unity. Paul apparently takes for granted that the error of the "some" of vs. 12 has been refuted. That refutation is a good occasion for some further remarks about the resurrection of the body.

A distinction must be made : *each* is not used in a strictly logical sense, for it does not refer to either Christ or Adam, or to both of them. The context points out that it refers to Christ and all who are in Him. The meaning is that each is raised. *Order*: group, class, implies that there are two groups, two resurrections. It is difficult to determine whether Paul has in view an order of time or an order of degree. Perhaps both : the word *firstfruits* would point in that direction and also the use of a simple *then*. In any case, Paul speaks about two orders, to the first order Christ belongs, to the second His people. For *firstfruits* see vs. 20. *They that are Christ's* : the nature of the communion with Christ is no more specified than was the nature of the firstfruits. The apostle assumes that all these things are well known to the Corinthians (6:11). The Corinthian Christians knew that they were Christ's own as is proved by 12:3 (cf. 1:30; 7:23). The earlier parts of the epistle are here presupposed. *At his coming* : lit. at this presence[20] (II Cor. 7:6, 7; 10:10). Christ is at this moment in heaven, but He will return. He will be present again on earth (cf. Col. 3:1-4). In connection with our interpretation of the firstfruits (vs. 20) we paraphrase : Christ is already raised, He as the firstfruits, i. e., through Him all will be raised and that will happen at His return. Paul does not imply that the resurrection coincides with Christ's return but that it happens at His return.

24 Joh. Weiss takes *the end* as the third link of the series of which *Christ* and His people form the first two links. Paul is thus supposed to have referred with these words to the remnant, the third group, i. e., those who did not believe in Christ. The advantage of this view is that it enables us to take *all* in vs. 22 absolutely, instead of restricting it to the believers only. The rea-

---
[20] παρουσία

364

sons why we nevertheless reject this view are, first, that Paul has not made any previous reference to the unbelievers, he has not disclosed the moment they will rise, yea he has not intimated whether they will rise at all, as is done in Jn. 5:29. Not until the second part is there any reference to the powers inimical to God but even there the ungodly are not mentioned. Furthermore: *order* cannot refer to a rest, a remnant. The commonly accepted view that *the end* refers to the absolute end is much better; thus the word "cometh" needs to be inserted. Christ is risen from the dead. After that, at His return, the believers will rise. Then comes the end of this world order. Denial of the resurrection implies a denial of the normal end of history. Added support for this interpretation comes from the clause introduced by *when,* which qualifies *the end* and refers to something that is expected in the future, at an unknown moment. It is true, if this interpretation is followed, the nature of that which follows after *then* is different from what follows upon the identical word in vs. 23. There it was the resurrection, but after "the end" there is no resurrection. Moreover, "the end" itself is an important element in the argument since it includes the annihilation of death. Not as if this annihilation would take place after the resurrection, on the contrary, the end, the delivering of the kingdom, occurs when the enemies are destroyed. It is well for us to remember, however, that great caution should be exercised in applying the same chronological order as that in which we live up to the events of the final judgment. The main point is that *the end,* the normal end of history, is only present when death is abolished and the pious are raised. The present tense: *delivers*[21] implies that the end will be there when the kingdom is being delivered.

The reference to the kingdom is worthy of note. It calls to mind the beginning of the preaching of John the Baptist and Jesus. Jesus' work is to destroy the work of the devil (1 Jn. 3:8) and to found the kingdom of God. Christ effects the general recognition of the kingdom of God, by believers and ungodly alike (Phil. 2:11, "every tongue"). When that has been accomplished the work of Christ with regard to the kingdom will be finished and He will offer His kingdom to the Father (cf. vs. 28). That is the end of

---

[21] ASV has "shall deliver up," according to the T. R. παραδῷ. RSV, "delivers," according to the better reading παραδιδοῖ.

the development of the world, for that is its natural end. Quite normally, therefore, the words: when he delivers, circumscribe "the end."

God, even the Father: the Greek text has only one article, God, who is also Father (Eph. 5:20; Js. 1:27). Father may refer to the Father of Christ, or to God as the Father of His people. The two cannot be separated, although the former is most prominent. Do not the Scriptures teach that Christ does His work as He is sent by the Father (Jn. 5:23)? And secondly, there was every reason for referring to Christ's special relation to God in this section dealing with the delivering up of the Kingdom (cf. Rom. 15:6, also II Cor. 1:3; 11:31; Eph. 1:3; Col. 1:3 (var.).

A second clause with when[22] follows. Paul has first indicated when the end will be reached, then he described its accompaniments, and finally he intimates what must precede the end. The abolishing of all rule and authority is already going on (cf. are coming to nought, 2:6, in the present tense). The words rule, authority and power need not be taken of different powers (cf. Eph. 1:21). But it should be noted that rule and authority are closely connected, since both are preceded by all. "Power" may refer to the existing government, while "rule" and "authority" have reference to the abstract notion of authority. Christ delivers His kingdom to the Father, when He shall have abolished all rule etc., i. e., deprived them of their power (not: finished their existence). Although the God-opposing character of these powers is not expressly stated, vs. 25 points out that Paul has that in mind. Christ delivers His kingdom when He has conquered all sinful powers (cf. I Chron. 29:11; Ps. 22:29; 145:13; Ob. 21; I Jn. 3:8; Rev. 11:15; 12:10). This victory Christ will gain at His return but He has gained in principle through His resurrection as appears from the fact that the reference to the end (then — then) is preceded by mention of the firstfruits. The work of the glorified Saviour during the period between His resurrection and His return consists of applying the fruits of His glory (see the following verses).

25 Vs. 25 contains the reason (for) why Christ surrenders the kingdom to the Father. He is to be king until He has sub-

---

[22] καταργήσῃ in the aorist indicates that the abolishing precedes the deliverance expressed in the present form παραδιδοῖ.

366

jected all enemies. That is a part of His work as the Saviour, it is His obligation. This means that in this and the following verses His task, His duty as the Saviour is set forth. Paul does not imply that Christ will lose or abandon His kingship, but that He will possess it until the kingdom is consummated (cf. vs. 24). That point should not go unnoticed because it explains why Paul inserts this section on general eschatology into his argument. Christ's kingship points to the task which He fulfills today. The fact that Christ rose as the firstfruits signifies that there is more to follow. That which Christ is doing right now is but the prelude of the absolute end. Christ's life and work is real and it is by that same token a warrant that He is the firstfruits and that they who are Christ's will be raised.

Till: the word does not in itself refer to the end of a certain period (cf. I Tim. 4:13). The following quotation from Ps. 110[23] deserves attention for the reason that it is used to describe the fulness of Christ's work in an epistle which otherwise does not abound in Old Testament quotations. Christ is under a moral obligation because Ps. 110 (a psalm quoted by Jesus Himself (Mt. 22:44) for the purpose of instructing the Jews in the nature of His ministry) had written what the Saviour was to do (cf. Lk. 22:37; Jn. 13:1f.). And precisely because that was written of Him the Messiah is both able and obliged to abolish the hostile powers. God Himself, as appears from the prophecy, determined that He would put all enemies under the feet of the Messiah, an oriental way of indicating complete subjection. This act of subjection to the Messiah is not the victory itself but the public indication of the victory. God proclaims that the Messiah has gained the victory. The time of that event is also fixed by God. The Messiah will return at a certain hour. Just as the apostle stressed the activity of God in the matter of the resurrection by using the verb to raise instead of to rise, so he quotes here a psalm which again refers to an action of God rather than that of the Saviour. Christ as Mediator is subordinate to the Father (Jn. 14:28). This also serves to make the Corinthians understand that the resurrection of the body is a part of the great work of God. When

---

[23] The quotation is not wholly according to the LXX. The first person is altered into the third in view of the context. The LXX has ὑποπόδιον τῶν ποδῶν.

the Mediator, as was prophesied of old, will have exercised His dominion to the end because He has conquered His enemies, the resurrection will come.

26 Vs. 26 defines the time element expressed in *till* still more precisely. Of the various enemies that are to be conquered by Christ death will be the last one. *Death* is here used in the full sense of the word: spiritual, temporal and eternal death, as it came into the world by sin (cf. vss. 21, 22, 56). That death, in which we see concretely the power of sin, must be abolished (II Tim. 1:10; Rev. 20:14; 21:4) and then there can be a resurrection of the dead, for in it the victory over death becomes apparent. The words: *the last enemy*, imply that death is our special enemy.[24] Death is in this respect the last enemy in that temporal death, in spite of the resurrection of Christ, continues in power over the children of God (Rom. 5:14). That will end when Christ comes on the heavenly clouds. This brings us back to vs. 23. The coming of Christ is the complete victory over death because then He reveals Himself as the living Messiah to the whole world. After His resurrection only His disciples saw Him, at His return it will be otherwise (Zech. 12:10; Jn. 19:37; Rev. 1:7; 20:1f.). Then Christ's victory over all powers hostile to God and over all that has come into the world through sin will be manifest, and that will mean the full liberation of the people of God from all consequences of sin, also from temporal death, which means that the resurrection of the body will then take place.

27 The present tense in vs. 26 implies that death *is being abolished*.[25] The action has begun already because Christ has been raised up as the firstfruits. But by way of an additional argument (*for*) Paul offers another quotation, this time of Ps. 8:7 in the LXX version, with alterations of a nature similar to those in vs. 25. Hebrews 2 points out that the primary reference of Ps. 8 is to Christ. That is also the way Paul uses it. The subjection mentioned in Ps. 8 is first of all a subjection to Christ, who is the last Adam. Because all things are subjected to Christ, death is also subjected. Thus vs. 27 proves from the Scriptures the truth of vs. 26. It should be borne in mind that a subjection wrought by

---

[24] G. Heine, *Synonymik d. neutestl. Griechisch*, 1898, p. 154.

[25] Greek: καταργεῖται; ASV, "shall be abolished," RSV, "to be destroyed."

God does not exclude the activity of Christ, as appears from the context. God ordains it thus.

The second part of vs. 27 contains a self-evident truth (*it is evident*). *When he saith*: the "when" does not refer to the moment God speaks to Christ, but to God's speaking in the Psalm. Otherwise the temporal order would be disrupted, for then the event mentioned in the protasis of vs. 28 would precede in time the event of the protasis of vs. 27. All that vs. 27b does is to give a further interpretation of the quotation with a view to what follows later. When God subjects all things, then all things *are put in subjection*. Earlier in the verse *all* was taken absolutely. This might create the impression that God Himself was also included in "all things" and the rejection of such a possibility might detract from the validity of Paul's argument concerning the resurrection of the body. This causes Paul to make his remark that God Himself is exempt from this subjection.

28 But *when all things* that exist *have been subjected to Christ, then the Son shall be subjected* to God. To subject has an eschatological connotation in this verse, for Paul writes about that time when the work that God is doing now, the application of the resurrection of Christ (cf. vss. 25 and 26), will be finished. There is a certain tension between *put in subjection* (vs. 27), *are put in subjection* (vs. 27), and *"when . . . have been subjected"* (vs. 28),[26] but it is the same tension we meet elsewhere in the work of Christ. His resurrection is a complete victory, nevertheless the evil still has power to work; not until the end will Jesus' victory appear.

It strikes us strangely that Paul designates the Saviour as *the Son* while hitherto he referred to Him as "Christ." This is done that we might realize that Paul actually has in view that Christ who is the Son of God. The apostle does not imply that the Son will be subjected to the Father. He keeps referring to Christ's work as Mediator (*subjected to him that did subject*) but he designates the Mediator by His highest name. The Bible contains little about the subjection of the Mediator to the Father after the former's work is done. We might put it this way, that the Mediator will lay down His office at the feet of the Father, when He has finished His work as such. This interpretation does not

---

[26] ὑπέταξεν aor.; ὑποτέτακται, perf.; ὑποταγῇ, aor.

conflict with the teaching concerning Christ's eternal kingship (II Pet. 1:11). In our context Paul writes about that particular dominion of Christ that will terminate, since it serves to protect His people on earth and to conquer the ungodly. This dominion will end at the absolute end of history.

The goal of Christ's subjection is *that God may be all in all.* There will be no opposition any more. God's glory will then only be fully accomplished when all resistance has been frustrated by the mediatorship of Christ. Then God will be the One before whom *all* will kneel. God will be *in all*, i. e., with all, in the sense that He will rule them and possess them. There will be no room for anyone except God. *All in all* is to be taken absolutely (Col. 3:11). All people, both the ungodly and the pious, all devils will be compelled by the work of Christ to recognize God as the One and Only. Paul does not speak of God's blessed nearness but rather, as appears from the repeated "to subject," of God's dominion. The latter will be universal and universally accepted. This end manifests God's absoluteness; higher than this Paul cannot go. But then it must also be considered as proof for the certainty of the subjection of death and of the resurrection of the body. Indirectly Paul also warns the Corinthians that they should not think it strange if they do not now witness any resurrections of the dead. That will have to wait, for not all Christ's enemies are yet subjected to Him.

BAPTISMS FOR THE DEAD

15:29-34

29 Else what shall they do that are baptized for the dead? If the dead are not raised at all, why then are they baptized for them?

30 Why do we also stand in jeopardy every hour?

31 I protest by that glorying in you, brethren, which I have in Christ Jesus our Lord, I die daily.

32 If after the manner of men I fought with beasts at Ephesus, what doth it profit me? If the dead are not raised let us eat and drink, for tomorrow we die.

33 Be not deceived: evil companionships corrupt good morals.

34 Awake to soberness righteously, and sin not; for some have no knowledge of God: I speak *this* to move you to shame.

29 Vs. 29 is one of the most difficult passages in the New Testament. Interpretations abound but no one has succeeded in giving an interpretation which is generally accepted. It is impossible to mention everything that has been written about this verse in the course of the years, nor do we pretend to offer an interpretation that overcomes every objection. A few observations, however, may perhaps give a measure of insight in the questions that are at stake here.

Else performs a special function here. After vs. 19 Paul had not continued to describe the condition which would obtain if Christ were not raised. But there is one more case which may serve to demonstrate how hopeless the state of man would be if Christ had remained in the grave. That is what *else* refers to. It means: if, as we assumed above for just a moment, there were no resurrection of the body.

What shall they do that are baptized or: have themselves baptized, for the dead? Paul implies that such a baptism is of no use to those who receive it, they will not benefit by it. They that *are baptized*, the present tense indicates that the action regularly occurs and is known to every Corinthian. *For the dead* may

371

mean: for the benefit of the dead. The objection that the apostle could not have meant anything like a baptism for the benefit of others is exegetically out of place. Moreover, Paul does not approve of that kind of baptism, he simply mentions that it occurs. On the other hand, if this type of baptism was actually practiced and if Paul had disapproved of it he probably would have written more about it than what this one reference contains. In any case the apostle could hardly derive an argument for the resurrection of the body from a practice of which he did not approve. The rendering "for the benefit of the dead" does not appear tenable.

The translation *for the dead* also meets with objections, especially since the apostle appeals to the baptism mentioned here to prove the truth of the resurrection of the body. To say that he who is baptized for the dead admits thereby the resurrection of the dead hardly suffices as an argument. For the *some* at Corinth did not deny the survival of deceased persons and he who believes in such a survival might conceivably be baptized for the dead and still deny the resurrection of the body. *The dead* in our context always represents the group of the dead as a whole, not individual dead persons. To be baptized for the dead would then mean that certain Corinthians (*they that are baptized*) were baptized not for certain dead persons but for the entire group of the deceased, which makes little sense. A second objection is that we have no information about any baptism for the dead. It is true that it is mentioned by Tertullian in *Adv. Marc.* V, 10. This church father himself, however, evidently knows nothing about the actual ceremony but deduces from our text that it must have been administered at Corinth (cf. also *De Resurr.* Carn. 48).[27] But early records are not extant. The difficulty could be removed if with

---

[27] Terullian, *Adv. Marc.,* V 10; qui vane pro mortuis baptizarentur. *De resurr. carnis* 48:si autem et baptizantur pro mortuis, videbimus an ratione. In this connection he also speaks of a vicarious baptism. Epiphanius, *Adv. Haer.,* I 28 speaks of a tradition that if heretics died unbaptized, others were baptized for them. And Chrysostom *ad loc.* reports that when a catechumen among the Marcionites died unbaptized, some one was hid under the bed of the deceased, and was asked whether he wished to be baptized himself and for the dead. It is possible, however, that such customs arose on the background of Paul's statement in I Cor. 15:29; so at any rate Chrysostom states with regard to the Marcionites.

Johannes Weiss we suppose that Paul, in referring to those who were baptized for the dead, thinks of those Corinthians who denied the resurrection. For those Christians there was no hope, they had themselves baptized for the dead. The subsequent words: *why do we also,* etc., would then follow quite normally. We must, however, question seriously whether the Corinthians could readily understand the words: *they that are baptized for the dead* of those who denied the resurrection.

We wish to mention two other interpretations. The first takes *for*[28] locally and translates it by *above.* This view implies that there were some at Corinth who had themselves baptized above the graves, namely of relatives who had died in Christ. This would then have been a way to express their unity and communion in Christ with the dead. It is interesting that by way of actual practice burials in churches and consequently baptisms above the dead have been practiced for many centuries. This custom might have sprung up from Rom. 6:3f. This view also allows one to construe "the dead" of the entire group. Such a baptism would be without any sense if there was not the belief that deceased bodies would come to life again. It is our doubt concerning this last point which makes us object to the interpretation in its entirety.

Another view is to take *for* in the sense of *beyond.* The words would then be used of the baptism by blood. The unbaptized who died during a persecution were reckoned as having been baptized in their death.[29] An argument in favor of this view is vs. 30. But the objections are: a) the church at Corinth enjoyed rest, there is no reference to persecution; b) we have no knowledge whether the idea of a baptism by blood, as it is derived from Mk. 10:38f. and Lk. 12:50[30] existed already in so ancient a time.

We are therefore compelled to conclude our remarks at this point with a *non liquet.* This much is clear, that Paul refers to a custom that clearly presupposed the resurrection of the dead. He

---

[28] ὑπέρ.

[29] See Origen, *Comm. Joh.,* VI, 43 (26), ed. Brooke, I, p. 161: εἰσὶ δέ καὶ αἵματός. Terullian, *De Bapt.,* 16; cf. Dölger, *Antike und Christentum* II, pp. 117-141.

[30] Cf. also the variant reading in Mt. 10:38f.

does not state explicitly whether he approved of that custom. Probably he did not disapprove of it.

30 Vs. 30 contains a thought related to 4:9f., but applied in a different way. Here it means that everything the apostles did would be in vain if there were no resurrection of the dead. The words: *why do we also* thus shift the attention from the Corinthians to Paul and his helpers and imply that their activities would not have any reason to exist without the resurrection. *We stand in jeopardy every hour*: the danger threatens the body in the first place (Rom. 8:36; II Cor. 4:11; 11:23f). If there is no resurrection the life may be saved but the body remains without glory. Its frequent heavy suffering is but in vain.

31 It may be that Paul fears that the Corinthians will not accept his argument. That accounts for the strong protestation followed by a striking example, possibly derived from a fact not unknown to the Corinthians. *I die daily*: the sense is not that Paul is every day in danger of life, for that had been said in vs. 30. Paul wishes to indicate that so far as he is concerned he abandons life daily; he knows that he may die and so he continually prepares himself for death. If he, in order to do his work, has to meet with mortal danger, he does not hesitate (Acts 25:11). That gives him the right to write: I die daily (cf. II Cor. 4:10f.) and that in very strong terms. *That glorying in you*: Paul's boasting in the Corinthians. The expression appears somewhat strange in view of the fact that at many points in this epistle the apostle has reprimanded the Corinthians because of their boasting (Your glorying is not good, 5:6; cf. 1:31). Still Paul boasts in the Corinthians (1:4) and the importance of this for Paul lies in the fact that it is both for himself and for the Corinthians a mark of his apostleship (9:1). That strengthens him in much suffering. The Corinthians are apparently convinced that Paul always boasts of them (*which I have* cf. Rom. 15:17). Paul glories not in himself but *in Christ Jesus our Lord*: all those names serve to point to the completeness of Christ's work and the glory He enjoys now as the ground of his boasting. By excluding himself Paul is able to assure the proud Corinthians, who accepted his boasting as something quite natural, of a truth which they did not think natural at all, namely that he was prepared to die every day. Nevertheless it is striking that Paul does not write simply: by the grace of Jesus Christ, or something like that, but: by that glorying . . . in Christ Jesus. To understand the expression better we should consider that Paul is able to boast of the Corinthians because Jesus Christ had blessed his apostolic work at Corinth. Thus Paul boasts in the results of his apostolic work, which is exactly that for which he dies daily.

32 Vs. 32 quotes a fact which was apparently known to the Corinthians but unknown to us. Paul once was in great danger. From early times on there has been a difference of opinion about the question whether "to fight with beasts" was to be taken in a proper or in a figurative sense. The latter appears to us most probable. First, it is almost impossible to fight with beasts and still escape with one's life. Secondly, there is no reference to such a fight in Acts, although Paul's stay at Ephesus is related very circumstantially. A rescue from a fight in the arena would have furthered the preaching of the gospel to such an extent that Luke, in keeping with the plan of his second book, could hardly have omitted reference to it. In I Cor. 11 where Paul speaks of his many experiences he does not mention any such conflict. Finally, a Roman citizen could not be condemned to the arena. If the Ephesian magistrates had condemned the apostle in spite of this fact, Paul would not have failed to appeal to his citizenship (Acts 22:25). For these reasons we take this fighting against beasts to refer to an extreme kind of opposition from which Paul escaped (cf. 16:9, where Ephesus is meant). The book of Acts records many attacks upon Paul's life during his third journey. One might think for a moment that the fighting against beasts would refer to the riot at Ephesus (Acts 19:23f.). But that is impossible for the apostle departed from Ephesus immediately after that riot (Acts 20:1), whereas Paul at the moment he writes I Corinthians intends to stay for some time at Ephesus (16:8). In fact, the whole riot could not have occurred if Paul had been sentenced to the arena. Therefore we understand this fighting with beasts of one or more events at Ephesus, during which Paul was engaged in a struggle with Jews or Gentiles and in which his life was in danger (cf. also II Cor. 1:8, 9; 11:23). This interpretation also clarifies the words: *after the manner of men*. Those words would be wholly superfluous if Paul had fought with beasts in the proper sense of the word. In 3:3 the

375

identical expression meant: as men who are nothing but men. That is also its sense in our text, namely, from a purely human point of view. In other words, Paul does not think of these experiences in terms of a fighting with beasts — his evaluation of the facts was a different one (cf. 9:8) — but according to human estimation what he did was a fighting against beasts. To Paul himself it was a part of his beautiful work. But Paul remains a man and suffers as a man.

The reason why Paul can do this difficult work is that he expects *profit*. But that profit exists only then if the dead are raised. Again the apostle writes: *if the dead are not raised,* which words are more difficult to explain here than in vs. 30 where they were only presupposed. If we could assume that some Corinthians denied immortality altogether, vs. 30 would have been easier to explain. But vss. 35f. deal very definitely with the resurrection of the body. The solution lies in the fact that Paul does not separate soul and body quite the same way as we are accustomed to do. In vs. 3 he writes: Christ died and Christ arose (not the body of Christ, but *Christ*). And in vs. 12 he speaks of the resurrection of the dead. Paul distinguishes between the dead and those that are fallen asleep. Not because man would be "dead" for one part and "fallen asleep" for another, but the two terms look at the deceased from two different sides. The deceased are "fallen asleep" in so far as they are no longer in this world but live as those who are Christ's (vs. 23). They are "dead" because they have ceased to live as "men." This implies that the "dead" are at the same time "fallen asleep" and that they will not become complete men again until Christ returns. If there were no resurrection of the body man would nevermore become a complete man, i. e., being man would end with this life. All that would then remain would be a corpse; there would be no hope. Under those conditions the best thing to do would be to live like a man, *after the manner of men,* during the short time of being "man." In other words *to eat and to drink* would then truly be the wisest maxim. The question of the immortality of the soul lies, as we notice, entirely outside of the scope of Paul's argument. Paul's point is that, if there is no resurrection, the dead cannot exist as men and that they consequently do not live in the full sense of the word. That same thought we find expressed in Ps. 115:17. Those who are "fallen asleep" exist, they are connected with Christ, their firstfruits, but as concerns their relation to the earth, they are dead corpses and they need to come to life (vs. 22; cf. Phil. 1:24; I Thess. 4:13f, "the dead in Christ"). There naturally remains a certain measure of obscurity here which is due to the fact that these things are outside of the limits of our earthly existence. But this much is clear, Paul sees in the resurrection a warrant of the restitution of human life in its fulness, after it has been broken by death.

The words themselves are a quotation from Is. 22:13 (LXX). They refer to a certain attitude toward life: if there is no resurrection, if everything must be had in this life, let us then eat and drink, let us enjoy life. In this way Paul shows the Corinthians the absurdity of their denial of the resurrection.

33 *Be not deceived*, i. e., do not err. This admonition follows by way of summary. First Paul demonstrated the absurdity of those who have themselves baptized for the dead and the uselessness of his own experiences, if the dead are not raised up. The warning not to err cannot mean that the Corinthians must discontinue to teach that there is no resurrection. The context does not speak of a deviation in doctrine but in life. Besides, the same warning against error is issued elsewhere (I Cor. 6:9; Gal. 6:7; Jas. 1:16). In all these cases it is possible to think of a deviation in doctrine but then a doctrine which has immediate implications for life. The phrase is apparently a standing expression which makes it necessary to interpret it the same way wherever it occurs. This causes us to think of a moral deviation rather than of the denial of the resurrection of the dead. Paul directs himself to the entire congregation whereas only some denied the resurrection of the body. Our assumption is, therefore, that there were some at Corinth who lived dissolutely, yea we know that some abused their Christian liberty. Perhaps they that denied the resurrection were among those practical antinomians since they did not suppose there was any hope for the body. That sheds new light on vs. 32, for Paul would then imply that he himself, if there were no resurrection, would adopt that wrong maxim as it was preached and practiced at Corinth. It also helps us to understand why Paul continues with a quotation from the pagan poet Menander. The proverb: *Evil com-*

panionships corrupt good morals is a line from a comedy of Menander, probably from the Thais. It may be that this is not a direct quotation from Menander but that this line had become generally known. If so, its value as a potent argument would be greatly increased for Paul would then be telling these Greek Christians, who had gone back to their former pagan customs, that their own proverb warned them against their evil conduct.

Be not deceived, present tense:[31] do not continue with your error, your propaganda. The latter consisted in the *evil companionships,* the corrupt conversations concerning the resurrection as well as concerning human conduct. The consequence of those sins is that also *the good morals of others are corrupted.*

34 Vs. 34 follows harmoniously after the preceding verse, since it contains an admonition to behave both in doctrine and in conduct as is demanded. *Awake to soberness righteously* (cf. Joel 1:5, LXX) implies that the Corinthians lived in a state of intoxication, inasmuch as they did not see things *righteously,* in the right way, and needed to come to true *soberness* (cf. I Thess. 5:6-8), or, as the text has it : *to awake.*[32]

The Corinthians should not continue to sin, they should arouse themselves from the evil condition into which they had fallen. From the preceding we can gather that the sins of the Corinthians consisted at least to a certain extent in erroneous doctrine and certainly in wrong conduct. There was also a wrong[33] *knowledge of God.* In 8:2 Paul referred already to this incorrect knowledge of the Corinthians. Here he lays a connection between the error concerning the resurrection of the body and that incorrect knowledge of God. That error does despite to God's omnipotence and to the fulness of the work of Christ. That must necessarily lead to sin for then the situation is like that in which the gentiles find themselves.

Knowledge must not be taken in a purely intellectual sense, it is knowledge that moves the heart. *To move:* to put the proud Corinthians to shame (cf. 4:14; 6:5).

---

[31] Greek: μὴ πλανᾶσθε.
[32] ἐκνήψατε, aor.; ἁμαρτάνετε, present.
[33] ἀγνωσία, non-knowledge.

THE RESURRECTION BODY

35 But someone will say, How are the dead raised? and with what manner of body do they come?

36 Thou foolish one, that which thou sowest is not quickened except it die:

37 and that which thou sowest, thou sowest not the body that shall be, but a bare grain, it may chance of wheat, or of some other kind;

38 but God giveth the body even as it pleased him, and to each seed a body of its own.

39 All flesh is not the same flesh: but there is one *flesh* of men, and another flesh of beasts, and another flesh of birds, and another of fishes.

40 There are also celestial bodies, and bodies terrestrial: but the glory of the celestial is one, and the *glory* of the terrestrial is another.

41 There is one glory of the sun, and another glory of the moon, and another glory of the stars; for one star differeth from another star in glory.

42 So also is the resurrection of the dead. It is sown in corruption; it is raised in incorruption:

43 it is sown in dishonor; it is raised in glory: it is sown in weakness; it is raised in power:

44 it is sown a natural body; it is raised a spiritual body. If there is a natural body, there is also a spiritual *body*.

45 So also it is written, The first man Adam became a living soul. The last Adam *became* a life-giving spirit.

46 Howbeit that is not first which is spiritual, but that which is natural; then that which is sprital.

47 The first man is of the earth, earthy: the second man is of heaven.

48 As is the earthy, such are they also that are earthy: and as is the heavenly, such are they also that are heavenly.

49 And as we have borne the image of the earthy, we shall also bear the image of the heavenly.

35 The preceding pericope was a kind of digression and ended with some general admonitions. But the real subject is not yet fully treated. And so the apostle returns to it in vs. 35. So far Paul has been zealous to point out the many inconsistencies which would be found in the life of the Corinthians as well as in his own if the dead would not rise. Fortunately, however, the Corinthians are not inclined to give up those inconsistencies, more particularly, they are not willing to abandon the resurrection of Christ. That proves that their premise is wrong. Paul also pointed out the danger of this error. And it is because of this danger that Paul approaches the question from another point of view, as he touches upon the manner of the resurrection. This proves that they who denied the resurrection of the body did so because they did not understand how it would be possible for dead flesh to arise. Here is a pagan influence. But the lack of a consistent system on the part of the erring Corinthians also appears: They did not understand how dead flesh could arise and nevertheless they continued to believe in Christ's resurrection. This inconsistency together with the fact that only some had gone astray, accounts for the calm tone of Paul's discussion, both here and in the entire epistle.

But some one will say: this sounds as if the apostle refutes an objection which he anticipates rather than a real one. On the other hand, *thou foolish one* in vs. 36 makes sense only if the thought of vs. 35 was actually expressed. The solution must lie in the consideration that the type of pagan, rationalistic reasoning, expressed in vs. 35, although not generally followed at Corinth, was nevertheless back of the denial of the resurrection.

How are the dead raised? The Corinthians inquired by what power and in what manner the resurrection was accomplished. In doing so they adopted, in principle, a wrong standpoint. The gospel is to be accepted in faith. But that point Paul does not discuss; he takes up these questions. *The dead*, a general designation but here to be taken of the dead in Christ, as appears from what follows. *With what manner of body*: a further development of the initial *how*. It was the body which caused the difficulty. Since the Corinthians saw bodies burned or buried in the grave to be wasted away, they could not understand how the dead could have a body. But they did not consider the great significance Christ's resurrection has for the dead. The relation between the dead and their bodies is a subject-object relationship, which confirms what we noticed at vs. 30. Christians are "dead" only in so far as they are in the state of death and lack a living body. Nothing is said about "them that are asleep" coming back with a body, neither do we know whether such a thing could be said at all. In any case, the dead, i.e. the deceased Christians, arise and require a body. What will the quality of such a body be? *They come*: at the general resurrection.

36 *Thou foolish one* (cf. Ps. 13:1, in the Hebrew 14:1): the rationalist who argues as was indicated in vs. 30, does not consider that what he deems impossible is an ordinary occurrence in nature. *Thou thyself*: mark what thou doest and learn from it. Paul does not imply that the grain of corn dies and is raised. That is, properly speaking, not the case. After the grain is sown the form in which it is sown perishes, to come to life again as an ear. There is an identity between what is sown and what sprouts out, and yet the grain does not come to life as it was sown. That is implied in *that which thou sowest*.

Is quickened, passive (cf. vs. 22), speaks of the resuscitating power of God. The great importance of this little trait is that it tells us that God will be able to do at the resurrection what He is already doing continuously. *Except*: introduces a necessary condition which is generally valid. Wherever the grain has been sown and dies, it comes to life.

37 Vs. 37 considers the question with what manner of body the dead shall come (vs. 35). A sower does not sow the fruit that will be, for then the sowing would be unnecessary. It is true that kernels of grain are sown and kernels of grain are reaped, but the difference between the ear that sprouts and the grain from which it arises is very pronounced. *A bare grain*: a grain of which nothing else can be said except that it is a grain. This figure of the grain and the ear illustrates to a certain extent that there may be "dead" who live and who nevertheless receive their full life through the resurrection (cf. vs. 20 f.). *It may chance* (cf. 14:10): the same thing happens every time,

381

whether it be wheat or something else. *Some other kind*: plants of the same nature as wheat (cf. also Jn. 12:24).

38 From the grain the stalk grows. But it is God and only He who does that (cf. 3:17 and also vs. 36: to quicken). Of necessary natural processes Paul knows nothing. God *gives a body* to every grain, i. e., its own material shape. A grain in the earth does not have a shape, for it does not appear on earth; God makes it grow into a body by giving it a body. That is not a natural process but an action of God, because not every grain sprouts out. The main point is that grain and sprout are the same. There is an identity; God once determined[34] that the plant should sprout from the grain and thus it happens every time. God fixed the rule of dying and rising and He carries it out. Upon that fact the following words are based. God gives continually to every grain its proper body.

39 Vs. 39 speaks of *"flesh,"* not of body. Flesh is the unorganized matter, body the organism.[35] The body is built of flesh. The connotation, "sinful flesh" which otherwise adheres to the word flesh is naturally absent from it in this context. The word designates the natural matter (cf. flesh of beasts, of birds, etc.). There is a large variety among the several kinds of flesh. Human beings and various animals have their own flesh; not only the form but also the material is different. How is it possible that every grain has its own body? Because there is a variety of flesh, a difference not of essence but of degree. All flesh remains flesh. This verse thus serves to explain the sense of the words: *a body of its own.*

40 Vs. 40 refers to bodies again, this time to stress a different kind of variety. *Celestial bodies*: not the heavenly bodies of human beings or of angels. There is no reference to angels in this context and the blessed in heaven are not introduced until vs. 42. Moreover, the glorified human body is not designated as "celestial" but rather as *spiritual* or *heavenly.* Thirdly, Paul writes about things which are already in existence. For those reasons we take *celestial*[36] bodies of the stars (cf. vs. 41).

---

[34] The Greek reads καθὼς ἠθέλησεν, not καθὼς ἐθέλει.
[35] G. Vos in PThR, XXVII (1929), p. 2.
[36] The Greek text has ἐπουράνιος; and οὐρανός may mean the visible heavens. Cf. Col. 1:23.

Bodies terrestrial: the bodies of everything that lives on earth. The contrast is greater than in vs. 39. Both are properly called bodies, but how great is the difference! *Glory*: this word is especially appropriate for the celestial bodies. The earthly things also have their glory but it is quite different from that of the stars.

41 Among the celestial bodies themselves also there is a difference of glory. Not only between the sun, the moon and the stars, but also between the various stars. This goes to prove that though there may be equality between the one body and the other, yet there is a great variety because of a difference in quality and in glory. Examples abound.[37]

42 Paul now applies the preceding remarks to the point under discussion. As happens often in parables, examples, etc., the transfer of thought is not exhaustive. Paul might have written: so it is also possible that in and through the resurrection bodies come into being which are different from what we know bodies to be but which are nevertheless genuine bodies. Instead we read only: *So also is the resurrection of the dead.* There is a transfer of thought on the following points: a) there may be life out of death through the power of God. b) it is possible that a new body is formed, which, though it be identical with the earthly body, is nevertheless distinguished from it. Paul makes this twofold application in the terms of the figure of speech used in vs. 36. The obvious reason for this is that, had the apostle openly written about the body being buried, the idea of a corpse would have been unavoidable and with a corpse the Corinthians associated something that was dead and remained dead. By using the simile of sowing the idea of burying is put in a different light and the possibility of life from death is indicated. The simile of sowing implies both the novelty of the new condition and the continuity and identity of the new with the old (cf. vs. 38). Paul does not go into details as to the manner in which this will happen. His adherence to the figure of speech prevents him from doing so.

---

[37] The comparison is confined to heavenly bodies; it is not between earthly and heavenly bodies, and so the differences in glory do not have in view the bodies of men.

The question might arise whether Paul, with his use of this simile, actually has the burial in view, since we noticed in vss. 30 and 32 that "corpse" or "dead" refers to the Christian in his deceased state in which he lives no longer on the earth. The answer is found in vs. 44 where *it is sown a natural body* compels us to take "to sow" of a burial (cf. also the figure of vs. 36). On the other hand, in writing about the manner of the resurrection, Paul goes on a step further than in the preceding pericope. There he had in view the resurrection of the dead as such, here he informs us that the resurrection implies a change of the body. Strictly speaking the subject of *it is sown* is not the dead body, or corpse, although the body is the subject of "is raised." Neither is the spiritual or heavenly body a part of that dead body; the living also have a spiritual body. The point is that Paul, in order to explain the resurrection of the dead, turns to another way of thinking. He does not have in view the whole man but only his body, and indicates thereby that the resurrection implies a change of body. At most we can say that the dead, or those who are asleep, have a body which is altered in a resurrection in a manner similar to what occurs in nature. In other words, the dead do not come to life the same way as they lie in the grave. But certain points must again remain unexplained, partly because Paul uses figurative language.

The principal thought is: to bury is to sow. *It is sown*: the indefiniteness of the expression serves to emphasize the words *"in corruption,"* just like *"it is raised"* stresses *"incorruption."* Both expressions indicate not the manner but the circumstances. The quality of the sowing is not one of corruption for then it would not be sowing, but the conditions of the sowing are those of corruption, i.e., death must come first. The whole process is marked by *corruption*, every sowing is marked by it (cf. vs. 36). The resurrection brings *incorruption*. The sowing belongs to this present time, the resurrection to the future (cf. vs. 23). The connection, rather the identity between the present and the future rests in the sowing.

43 Vs. 43 enumerates still other circumstances. First *dishonor* is contrasted with *glory*. When seed is sown there is dishonor because the grain is hidden in the dark earth. At a burial there is dishonor when the body of a man is hidden as a corpse. But when the ear sprouts from the earth there is *glory*, which is a figure of the glory of the resurrection.

There is also a relative *weakness* when the seed is sown, for the grain is weak when compared with the ear. Yet the grain also has some power, power to sprout out. This must serve to explain that the weakness which is so clearly apparent at the burial in view of the powerlessness of the dead body is followed by a resurrection which brings power for eternal life.

44 *It is sown*: the figure is probably continued because to speak of a burial would appear to abolish identity. *It is sown*: it is incorrect to say that the one body is buried, the other raised up. One and the same body is sown in one quality and raised in another. But all the same it remains the same body. For *natural* see on 2:24: it designates the bare idea of living. A *natural body* is a body that lives; it lives as life is possible on earth. The notion is contrasted with that of a corpse, a contrast similar to that of life and death. This natural body can be sown and is sown because it is subject to death. It should be kept in mind that I Cor. 15 deals only with the lot of the believers. Actually what is sown here is the body of God's children. As long as they were on the earth nothing happened to their bodies, the latter remained as they were in spite of the renewal of their spirits (souls). On the other hand, the body which is raised is spiritual, i.e., renewed and governed by the Spirit of the Lord (cf. 2:13). The resurrection means that the body will also share the fruits of Christ's work (cf. vss. 23f., 49; II Cor. 3:18; 4:16f.; Phil. 3:21). That resurrection is consequently the ushering in of complete glory.

Thus Paul has set forth the manner of the resurrection and the nature of the glorified body.

44b Paul continues with setting forth the difference between *the natural body* and the *spiritual body*. Giving a description of both the apostle indicates that the existence of a natural body presupposes the existence of a spiritual body. The one exists as certainly as the other. This presupposition is based on the assumption that the spirit cannot be inferior to the soul. If the existence of a natural body must be granted, no one can have doubts as to what Paul wrote concerning a spiritual body. Spirit and soul exist side by side and a body belongs to the one as well as to the other. Thus vs. 44b to a certain extent furnishes proof for what was said in vs. 44a.

45 The correctness of the preceding statement appears from the fact that vs. 45 does not intend to prove from the Scriptures that there is a natural body (*also*: this is an additional thought). Paul quotes Gen. 2:7 in the LXX, but he inserts *first* and *Adam* and the result of this insertion is that we must not think of man in general but of Adam only. Thus Paul leads up to what follows. This quotation is not meant to prove the existence of a natural body, it is introduced to remind us that Adam was created by God a *living soul,* and that he had a body belonging to that soul. *"Soul"* means here a living being. That which we call body *may* be reckoned to the soul.[39] The construction of the sentence would make it possible to take the words *the last Adam* etc. with the quotation, but we may assume that the Corinthians knew as well as we do that these words are not found in the Old Testament, but were added by Paul by way of supplement, possibly being derived from his preaching (cf. I Tim. 5:18). So we see again that Paul does not prove vs. 44b from the Scripture, for the Scripture does not mention the word "spirit." The argument is similar to that of vs. 44: As the one thing is true and is generally accepted on the basis of the Scriptures, so the other is true also. The words *the last Adam* needed no further elucidation since the Corinthians believed in Christ's work, including His resurrection. The expression is found nowhere else, although passages like Rom. 5:12f., 18f.; I Cor. 15:12 show that Paul is wont to compare Christ with Adam, especially in this respect that both acted in a representative fashion for those connected with them. This in itself is an indication that the last Adam is a designation for Christ. The context points in the same direction. The expression *first Adam* was suggested as an explanation of *man,* patterned after this expression is *the last Adam.* Still it is of a slightly different nature, as is implied in the absence of man. That indicates that

---

[39] We must take account of the fact that ASV translates ψυχικός by "natural," but ψυχή by "soul," and thus the relation between the two is somewhat obscured. ψυχικός is what has followed the natural order which has not changed. RSV in translating by "physical" easily leads to misunderstanding. ψυχικός is not φυσικός.

Christ's work is more important for others than that of Adam but also that no one of the same significance will arise after Him (last).

Spirit: the key to this word lies in the word *soul*. Although often the difference between spirit and soul is not very great, the word "soul" is never used with reference to Christ (cf. Mt. 26:38, *my* soul). The bare notion of life is never associated with Christ.[40] The Saviour is called *Spirit*, which stands for life that has direction and definiteness. *Spirit* is here not to be taken of the person of the Holy Spirit. Still there is a connection, for Christ gives that life of which Paul speaks here through the Holy Spirit (cf. Jn. 6:63, also II Cor. 3:17). Christ lives at this moment not just as Adam lived, He also gives life. Paul does not indicate the cause of this (see e.g. Jn. 5:21, 26). This being made alive by Christ finds its analogy in the natural growth (cf. vs. 38). In view of the fact that Paul speaks about the spiritual body which the believers receive at the resurrection, the term *life-giving* (unqualified) must be taken of the resurrection (cf. Rom. 8:11). An energy proceeds from Christ on the basis of His work, and that energy raises up bodies (Jn. 5:21; 6:33f.). *Became* can be said of Christ also. Paul does not imply that Christ became a life-giving Spirit by His resurrection. Probably he means that Christ became such a Spirit through His entire work as Mediator, although "firstfruits" (vs. 20) points particularly to the resurrection.

46 Vs. 46 first of all clarifies the *if* in vs. 44b. The *spiritual* i.e., in this context, the spiritual body, does not come into being except there be a natural body. That implies at the same time that the spiritual body, a fruit of Christ's resurrection, does not yet exist. *Howbeit*: though the spiritual body is more than the natural it is not *first*. Temporally the natural body that must be sown comes first. Perhaps the Corinthians thought that there was already a spiritual body. The sins of fornication, e.g., point in that direction. In any case, Paul preaches that the natural is first. "Spiritual" is used exclusively of that which is connected with the Holy Spirit (see on 2:13). This means that the spiritual follows the natural and that holds true of the body as well.

---

[40] Christ is called ἡ ζωή.

47 He now deals with the origin of Adam and of Christ. God formed Adam of the dust of the ground, which makes him *earthy*: he remains bound to the earth. Christ is called *the second man;* the Hebrew word *'adam* means "man" but in the Greek "Adam" is a proper name. In vs. 45 Paul introduced Adam's name with a lengthy explanatory clause and then he mentioned Christ. In our verse *man* is placed over against *man*, by which means the genuine humanity of both is indicated. The epithet *second* implies that *man* is used in a special sense, namely of those men whose actions had much significance for others. Paul contrasts the heavenly origin of Christ with Adam's earthly origin. The apostle does not deny that Christ had an earthly body (cf. Gal. 4:4), but Christ descends from heaven as the Son of God (Jn. 1:14). This makes it possible to distinguish Christ's origin as being *of the heaven* from Adam's origin as being *of the earth* (Jn. 3:31). We notice that the apostle, as appears from all the adjectives, does not discuss the question of substance but that of origin alone. Furthermore, it should be noted that Paul does not treat the preexistence of Christ but rather the incarnation of the Mediator especially as the latter revealed Him as the life-giving One after the resurrection.

48 Vs. 48 points to the similarity between the one who is *earthy* and all the others who are also earthy. This must not be taken of Adam and his descendants in particular but of a similarity which exists within one and the same kind, as appears from the emphasis on *as — such*. Paul's starting point is *the earthy*. The same kind of similarity exists within the kind of *the heavenly*.

49 Vs. 49 does not point to still another similarity for it compares *earthy* and *heavenly*. Besides, the verse makes a concrete application with the pronoun "we," which refers to believers. The conjunction *and* at the beginning of the verse does not add another new point to the preceding but introduces something of slightly different nature. The connection with vs. 48 is actually antithetical in nature. Vs. 48 distinguishes two groups, vs. 49 implies that the believers at the resurrection will go from the one group to the other, to bear the mark of their respective heads, first that of Adam, then that of Christ. This implies also that the resurrection is real since it brings new life. Paul does not deny that this life has its beginning in an earlier period; on the contrary, he recognizes that fact by speaking of *we* as a designation of the persons to whom all these things apply (cf. "we shall also bear"). But the apostle has in view here the fulness of that new life, as it can be obtained only through the resurrection of the body, which is the point under discussion. Thus seen, this verse is part of the answer to the question: "with what manner of body do they come?"

Image: Adam has his own image, we have his image, we are like him. There is a special reference here to the body, as the context bears out. The same thing holds true of the image of the *heavenly*, the glorified Christ (cf. vs. 22, also II Cor. 3:18; Phil. 3:21).[41] The Christians will receive a spiritual body to enjoy completely the glory of Christ. This pericope began with the assertion that there must be a spiritual body, it ends with the assurance that we will receive one.

---

[41] We read φορέσωμεν, not φορέσομεν, although the difference between the subj. aor. and the future is not great in the koine. Following the first aorist, Paul uses a second, and he thus thinks of the moment in which we also shall obtain our glorified body.

THE ASSURANCE OF VICTORY

15:50-58

50 Now this I say, brethren, that flesh and blood cannot inherit the kingdom of God; neither doth corruption inherit incorruption.

51 Behold, I tell you a mystery: We all shall not sleep, but we shall all be changed,

52 in a moment, in the twinkling of an eye, at the last trump: for the trumpet shall sound, and the dead shall be raised incorruptible, and we shall be changed.

53 For this corruptible must put on incorruption, and this mortal must put on immortality.

54 But when this corruptible shall have put on incorruption, and this mortal shall have put on immortality, then shall come to pass the saying that is written, Death is swallowed up in victory.

55 O death, where is thy victory? O death, where is thy sting?

56 The sting of death is sin; and the power of sin is the law:

57 but thanks be to God, who giveth us the victory through our Lord Jesus Christ.

58 Wherefore, my beloved brethren, be ye steadfast, unmovable, always abounding in the work of the Lord, forasmuch as ye know that your labor is not vain in the Lord.

50 In this new section of Paul's argument the apostle teaches us how we can obtain the benefits of which he has been writing and how they will fare who will still be living at the moment of Christ's return. At the same time this section contains an objective description of the circumstances of the resurrection of the dead and in that connection it sets forth the full fruit of Christ's work. Paul no longer engages in a refutation of error, but assuming that all Corinthians believe that the dead will rise up, he sets forth what the Christian can expect when that happens.

Now this I say, refers to vs. 49. The following summary is not directed against those who denied the resurrection but is meant as a further exposition of the glory of the church and of the means God chooses to realize it. Indirectly we thus receive a further insight into the possibility and the necessity of the resurrection of the flesh. *Flesh and blood*: a current phrase (Mt. 16:17; Gal. 1:16; Eph. 6:12; Heb. 2:14), which is to be taken figuratively, for in the proper sense of that word the flesh contains the blood. The expression designates man as material (not as sinful), man as he belongs to the earth and has a body that can be seen by others. But it also designates him as he is today in a world that has to bear the consequences of sin. This man whose only connection is with this earth *cannot inherit the kingdom of God.* To do the latter man has to be changed (Jn. 3:3, 6). For the kingdom of God is not of this earth, but of a heavenly order. To enter the kingdom of God means to break with this earth which is under God's curse. *Inherit*: to obtain in a secure way. *Kingdom of God* must be understood of the citizenship in that kingdom (cf. 6:10). When Christ will offer the kingdom to the Father, those who are only flesh and blood will not be citizens of that kingdom. *Cannot*: this verb implies that Paul does not think of what might happen at Christ's return in the future but of two things which are even now incompatible (cf. 2:14). Paul takes this statement as a starting point in the following verse. The Corinthians were convinced that flesh and blood could not inherit, i. e., durably obtain, the kingdom of God. Equally certain is it that *corruption* cannot inherit *incorruption.* For anyone to receive the spiritual body he has to be converted (cf. vs. 35 f.). *Corruption*: everything that is corrupt; it may have served to explain to the Greeks the Semitic notion of flesh and blood. Paul has in view man in general, not just the Christian.

51 Vs. 51 is not a simple continuation of vs. 50. What we should have expected, for instance, would be an exposition of the question why corruption cannot inherit incorruption and why that nevertheless happens. In a sense Paul has been giving us such an exposition, but things become too much for him. He interrupts himself with the words: *behold I tell you,* thereby abandoning his abstract type of argument and informing us what will happen to us Christians. *Mystery* in Paul's terminology refers to that part of God's decree which was hidden in former times but revealed now (Rom. 16:25, 26; Eph. 3:3f.). The contents of this mystery which Paul had not yet proclaimed follows immediately. The best translation is: *we shall all — although we may not sleep — we all shall be changed.*[42] *All* receives much emphasis. The subject *we* refers to the church as a whole: all believers. It is true, vs. 52 distinguishes between them that are yet alive at Christ's return and others that have died already, but that does not prevent the apostle from stressing *all*: all shall be changed. The argument here is exactly the reverse of that in I Thess. 4. There the question is: will the deceased at the moment of Christ's return receive the same benefits as they that are yet alive? In I Cor. 15 however, the point is: will they that are yet alive also enjoy the fruits of Christ's resurrection, since they have not been sown as those who are deceased. By emphasizing *all* the apostle implies that all the members of the congregation are a unity, and that all will receive the same blessings. Although some may not sleep, they will be changed, i. e., receive eternity.

52 Vs. 52 explains the preceding thought. The main point of the verse is in the second part in which are distinguished the two groups to be found at Christ's return. Paul does not explain the manner of the transformation; that remains a miracle. The apostle only speaks of the attendant circumstances, i. e., he reveals something more about this mystery than was strictly necessary in this context.

In a moment, in the twinkling of an eye: the change will only take a very short time. It is not a process which like the resurrection could be compared to the sprouting of seed. This change occurs outside of time. *At the last trump*: these words become clear in the light of what follows: *for the trumpet shall sound* (Mt. 24:31). Apparently this fact had not yet been revealed,[43] and so clarification was necessary. *The trumpet shall sound*: the apostle mentions one particular trumpet, the last one that will sound on earth; from vs. 23 it follows that that will be at Christ's return. *The dead*: The Christians who have died. *Incorruptible*, i. e., they will become imperishable at and through the resurrec-

---

[42] Note that πάντες οὐ is not the same as οὐ πάντες.

[43] One might recall I Thess. 4:16, but perhaps that Epistle was not yet known in Corinth.

tion. *And we shall be changed*: here we have again the distinction between the dead and those who are yet alive (cf. vs. 18f.; vs. 29f.). This means that the use of "we" here does not imply that they who are alive now will be alive also on the last day. Paul is not of the opinion that the Christians of his time will live to see the day of Christ's return; on the contrary, his starting point is that there will be some who will have fallen asleep in Christ (vs. 18, cf. also vs. 31). *We* designates the Christians, as they were living then and as they will live on the last day.

Note that vs. 51 spoke of all Christians as being changed, whereas vs. 52 refers only to those who are alive at Christ's return. This is no real difficulty, for in each case the change means the obtaining of incorruption, but with reference to the dead alone it may also be called resurrection.

53 *Must*: the change indicated in vs. 52 has its ground in something that the *corruptible* must do. The ability to fulfill that obligation is from God (vs. 57, cf. also the analogy of Rom. 8:30f.). *This corruptible*: the corruptible that is present now; *this mortal*, like the preceding. The same things which are now present will *put on incorruption*, immortality. The corruptible and the mortal will not continue to be what they are. God's glory demands that they put on the vestments of *incorruption* and of *immortality*. Paul does not imply that all men will obtain incorruption and immortality. The main point here is not one of quantity but of quality, as appears from the use of the abstract nouns "the corruptible" instead of the pronoun "we." In this context these things refer in the first place to those Christians who will be alive at Christ's return, for they are the ones last mentioned, but Paul's words cannot be restricted to them; they are too general for that. *To put on*: not in the sense that the incorruption would be put on over the corruptible, for that would do away with a complete change. The verb rather expresses identity along with a qualitative difference.

54 *When*: when these things have taken place, then what was prophesied in the Old Testament will be fulfilled. The quotation from Is. 25:8 is neither based on the LXX nor on the Hebrew text. This has given rise to the opinion that Paul is not quoting a text from the Old Testament but a word of the Lord. Be this as it may, the form in which this word is quoted agrees with the context of Is. 25, where the prophet speaks of the blessings God gives in the end. In the end *death* is abolished, it has made room for *immortality*. *In victory*: so that it is conquered (cf. II Tim. 1:10; Heb. 2:14f.; Rev. 20:14; 21:4).

55 A quotation from Hos. 13:14 again is not based on the Hebrew but adheres closely to the LXX, although the material difference is not great. Since death is conquered it can no longer conquer. *Sting*: death is as an insect that hurts or even kills with its sting. Once the sting is removed the power to conquer is gone. That will be so when *immortality* has been ushered in.

56 Paul gives an interpretation of this quotation. The *sting* with which death inflicts wounds is *sin*. The order is not sin — death as in Rom. 6:23 but rather death — sin. Death maintains itself in sin. Paul takes death in the most general sense; all things are in the power of death since our fall into sin. He who sins dies and experiences the power of death. Since man is under the power of death he must sin (Gal. 3:10). *The power of sin is the law*: not only death but *sin* also is described as a power that seeks to maintain itself. *Sin* uses the *law* which stimulates fallen man to sin (cf. Rom. 5:12; 7:7f.). Paul speaks of the ultimate victory; that victory is not present when some men are saved. but only after everything that had assumed dominion since Adam's sin has been abolished and after every God-opposing power has been annihilated.

57 Vs. 57 points in the same direction. Glory is due to God because of the great work He has done (cf. Rom. 8:31f.). In the Greek text the words *to God* come first and receive emphasis. The victory, hitherto held by death, is granted by God. Once death is swallowed up in victory, victory has come to believers. not through their own power but through the grace[44] of God. That is implied in: *through our Lord Jesus Christ*. who is the source of all grace. Our Lord rose from the dead, conquered death, and revealed Himself therein as Lord and Saviour (cf. Rom. 6:9f.; 8:11). The present tense *giveth* implies that God is even now giving us the victory. The latter is present in principle and will become ours more and more (Rom. 8:37).

Thus Paul, in speaking of incorruption and immortality, ar-

---

[44] The Greek word χαρις means "thanks" as well as "grace."

rives at the time when death and sin will be no more and the victory will be complete.

58   The admonition with which Paul concludes is not a summons to believe in the resurrection of the body, but in close connection with vs. 57, is of a more general nature. Thus it can serve also as the conclusion of the whole epistle: what follows in chapter 16 is of a different nature from the contents of the preceding chapters. This means that the admonition in vs. 58 applies to the preceding argument in its entirety, but its special sense is that Christians can have courage in all circumstances because God gives them the victory. Paul sets forth what the consequences of this fact are for the Christian life (*wherefore*).

My beloved brethren (cf. 4:14f.; also Phil. 4:1). *Be ye*, present tense; something of this is already present. Paul's admonition to be stedfast may well be because some adhered to false doctrine (vs. 12) and because the whole church was in danger of it (Gal. 1:6). In any case, to be reminded of the great benefits pictured by Paul should serve the Corinthians as a special admonition to persevere and to be faithful in order that they might obtain all those benefits. With the *abounding* grace of the Lord corresponds an *abounding in the work of the Lord*. This "work of the Lord" is to be taken not only of what we call work in the kingdom of God, but of good works in the broader sense of the word, for this admonition is put in general terms. *Forasmuch as ye know* is on a par with *abounding* :[45] both speak of the demeanor of the children of God. They must live in the knowledge that their assiduous *labor* is not *vain,* not without content, because it is done in the power of *the Lord.* This labor in the Lord must come first, before there can be the knowledge that it is not without significance. The life of Christians is a heavenly life.

Underlying this whole chapter is the certitude that because Christ rose from the dead there is a resurrection also for us. At the resurrection we receive such a body as Christ has now. That is very important for our life in this world.

---

[45] The Greek text has two participles: περισσεύοντες and εἰδότες.

CHAPTER XVI

FINAL ADMONITIONS AND COMMUNICATIONS

16:1-18

1 Now concerning the collection for the saints, as I gave order to the churches of Galatia, so also do ye.

2 Upon the first day of the week let each one of you lay by him in store, as he may prosper, that no collections be made when I come.

3 And when I arrive whomsoever ye shall approve, them will I send with letters to carry your bounty unto Jerusalem:

4 and if it be meet for me to go also, they shall go with me.

5 But I will come unto you, when I shall have passed through Macedonia; for I pass through Macedonia;

6 but with you it may be that I shall abide, or even winter, that ye may set me forward on my journey whithersoever I go.

7 For I do not wish to see you now by the way; for I hope to tarry a while with you, if the Lord permit.

8 But I will tarry at Ephesus until Pentecost:

9 for a great door and effectual is opened unto me, and there are many adversaries.

10 Now if Timothy come, see that he be with you without fear; for he worketh the work of the Lord: as I also do:

11 let no man therefore despise him. But set him forward on his journey in peace, that he may come unto me: for I expect him with the brethren.

12 But as touching Apollos the brother, I besought him much to come unto you with the brethren: and it was not at all *his* will to come now; but he will come when he shall have opportunity.

13 Watch ye, stand fast in the faith, quit you like men, be strong.

14 Let all that ye do be done in love.

15 Now I beseech you, brethren (Ye know the house of Stephanas, that it is the firstfruits of Achaia, and that they have set themselves to minister unto the saints),

16 that ye also be in subjection unto such, and to every one that helpeth in the work and laboreth.

17 And I rejoice at the coming of Stephanas and Fortunatus and Achaicus: for that which was lacking on your part they supplied.

18 For they refreshed my spirit and yours: acknowledge ye therefore them that are such.

1 The conclusion of our epistle contains various personal communications and salutations and among them a few independent admonitions.

Vss. 1-4 deal with *the collection for the saints*. Paul does not indicate which collection he has in view nor the saints for whom it is destined. The Corinthians were no doubt informed and did not need a further explanation, either because Paul had spoken about this during his stay at Corinth or because he had written about this collection in the epistle which is lost. In Acts 11:27f. we read of an expected famine and of the intention of the churches to gather money for the brethren in Judea and Jerusalem. According to Gal. 2:10 Paul promised at Jerusalem to take care of the poor (see also Rom. 15:26; II Cor. 8 and 9). It appears that the church at Jerusalem was very poor so that even the Macedonian churches, which were not rich themselves, had to collect money for Jerusalem. The reason for that poverty is not clear. Many expositors hold that when the fiery enthusiasm of which Acts 2:44, 45 and 4:34, 35 speak had calmed down, and when the people no longer prayed for the guidance of the Spirit, a normal care of the poor was not possible at Jerusalem. Nor must we forget the persecution of Stephen, which must have reduced the Jerusalem Christians to poverty. Furthermore, it should be kept in mind that a collection for the poor was not quite what our notion of it is today. It was also a collection for the maintenance of the church, for the care of the poor was an essential task the church had to perform. The church itself did not need much money, the poor needed much more (cf. Rom. 15:27; II Cor. 8:5; 9:12). Paul asks for money not for the *poor* at Jerusalem but for the poor *at Jerusalem*.

The Corinthians may have asked Paul to write something about this collection. The things Paul writes concerning it do not apply to the Corinthians only: he asks from them what he had asked from other churches too.

2 *Upon the first day*[1] i. e., on every Sunday. The reference is not to the church services but to a personal assignment which everyone had to perform. But the fact that Paul speaks of the first day of the week and calls that the day for the collection implies that Sunday was destined for the special service of the Lord. Paul trusts the Corinthians: he does not ask them to hand in their collection on a weekly basis, they are allowed to keep the collected money and thus little by little a sufficient amount will be saved up. Everybody is to give what he is able to give.[2] The giving must be voluntary (II Cor. 8:11, 12), and the church is permitted to fix the amount of its contribution itself. The main point is that there will be a fair amount when Paul arrives at Corinth.

3 Paul's wisdom in handling this matter again appears: he only asks the Corinthians to save the money until he *arrives* but he does not stipulate that the money shall be handed to him. The church may choose trustworthy men to take the money to Jerusalem. *With letters*: with credentials; Paul will authorize those men, he will identify them and assign them their task. By issuing such a letter to those emissaries Paul will be freed from his responsibility for he has kept his promise (Gal. 2:10). *Bounty*: the gift of the Corinthians is a token of their benevolence.

4 Vs. 4 does not mean: if the collection is large enough I myself shall go with the delegation, but rather: if circumstances are such that the mission work demands my journeying to Jerusalem *they shall go with me*. Then letters will not be needed.

5, 6 Paul discusses his plans (cf. 4:21), for the Corinthians must be informed about them in connection with this collection. *When*: the exact moment of the journey cannot yet be determined. When he has *passed* Macedonia he will travel to Corinth.

---

[1] κατὰ μίαν sc. ἡμέραν (τοῦ) σαββάτου. i.e. upon every first day of the week.

[2] εὐδῶται may be a present conjunctive, as well as perfect indicative, for the koine is not consistent in its use of augment and reduplication.

He will go from Ephesus through Macedonia to Corinth, for first he has to visit the Macedonian churches. Paul apparently assumes that his epistle together with Timothy's visit will have such a good result that it will not be necessary for him to travel hastily to Corinth. *I pass*: not at the moment that this letter is written, for that would be contrary to vs. 8, but: I shall pass.[3] A journey to Macedonia is necessary but Paul does not intend to stay there a long time. After that Paul does not yet know exactly how things will go, but he does want to go to Corinth perhaps to stay there a bit longer or to spend the next winter there. In vs. 8 Paul states that he will stay at Ephesus until Pentecost, i. e., he will not remain in Macedonia for a long time. Once winter is past and ships sail again (cf. Tit. 3:12), Paul can continue his journey. The winter season would thus compel Paul to sojourn at Corinth.[4] The Corinthians could then assist Paul in his trips to other churches not mentioned by name. In view of vss. 2 and 3 Paul cannot have meant to ask for money from the Corinthians (cf. also II Cor. 12:17). Their assistance could consist of the finding of reliable travel companions, a ship, etc.

7 Vs. 7 does not imply that Paul had previously paid a short visit to Corinth and that he did not intend to do so again. It means rather that Paul does not wish to visit the Corinthian church now in passing, but that he will wait till he finds an opportunity to stay a longer time. Perhaps Paul did consider the possibility of a brief visit, probably because the Corinthians invited him, but he preferred to send the letter and to await the result of Timothy's visit (cf. II Cor. 1:23). The apostle has something to do at Ephesus and in Macedonia and because of that he is not able to stay long at Corinth and so will not go to Corinth now. Paul uses many words to explain the matter lest the Corinthians should think that Paul did not care for them, or that he did not dare to come himself but preferred to send a letter and to dispatch Timothy, instead of making the journey

---

[3] The present tense of ἔρχομαι and other verbs that mean "to go" often has the sense of a future tense.

[4] Acts 19:22 gives us more definite information. I Corinthians must have been written before the plan of Acts 19:22 was made, or Paul did not want to inform the Corinthians fully since his plans were not yet fixed.

himself (cf. II Cor. 1:15f.; 10:10). Paul hopes to come as soon as the Lord will permit and the opportunity presents itself.

8, 9 Paul's work at Ephesus is not yet finished. He will stay there till Pentecost, because of the many opportunities in that city. *A great door is opened* (cf. Acts 14:27; II Cor. 2:12; Col. 4:3): Paul still sees many ways, means which he must use. We do not know the circumstances at Ephesus but they must have been very favorable for the preaching of the gospel. There are, however, also *many adversaries*, and therefore it is impossible for Paul to break off his work at Ephesus now. It is not known who these adversaries were, although Acts 19:9, 13f. seems to imply that they were both Jews and Gentiles. The first signs of the revolt of Demetrius may have shown themselves already.

10 In 4:17f Paul mentioned that he had sent Timothy to Corinth (cf. Acts 19:22). This mission may have resulted from what "those of Chloe" had told Paul. In any case, Paul's letter which is shipped by sea will arrive earlier at Corinth than Timothy who is traveling through Macedonia. That makes it possible to recommend Timothy in this letter. Timothy was known to the Corinthians for he had been in their midst with Paul. Timothy occupies a special place among the fellow-laborers of Paul. On the one hand, no one is so closely connected with Paul as Timothy, no one is so praised by Paul as Timothy, for of no one else Paul writes that *he worketh the work of the Lord as he himself also does.* But on the other hand, Timothy does not have the independence of Apollos or Titus, perhaps because he was young and somewhat timid (I Tim. 4:12); he was not energetic enough. When Paul sends special letters to Timothy they are filled with admonitions. That explains why Paul writes here: *without fear.* Paul feared that Timothy might meet with difficulties at Corinth. The reason why Paul does not send some one else is simply because there is no one who is better equipped, for again, Timothy works as Paul works (Rom. 16:21; Phil. 2:20f.). Moreover, Timothy's shyness might be an advantage in view of the boasting of the Corinthians.

11 *Therefore,* because he works as Paul works, let no one despise[5] him. In a city like Corinth, where even Paul was judged

---

[5] ἐξουθενήσῃ is a strong word. It indicates that Paul fears that the Corinthians might despise Timothy.

(9:3), this admonition does not appear superfluous. The Corinthians must create an easy situation and take care that Timothy can return to Paul. *Set him forward* (cf. vs. 6) : the Corinthians shall procure everything that is necessary for the journey. *In peace*: voluntarily. By acting thus the Corinthians will show that they rejoice in Timothy's visit; they will also show that there is not hard feeling between them and Paul. *I expect*: Paul intends to wait for Timothy at Ephesus, he will not depart before he has received tidings about the Corinthians (cf. II Cor. 2:13). This consideration must prompt the Corinthians to assist Timothy. *With the brethren*: each one of the various interpretations offered of this phrase leaves certain difficulties to be explained. The best view is perhaps to think of certain brethren of whom the Corinthians knew that they were with Paul. These may have been brethren which were to travel with Paul (or with Timothy) to Corinth.

12 The Corinthians may have asked Paul to send Apollos[6] who had good friends at Corinth (1:12). Apparently he was with Paul at Ephesus at the time the Corinthians wrote their letter to the apostle. Paul has granted the request of the Corinthians and he has invited Apollos to go to Corinth with Stephanas and his group who were to carry Paul's letter. The fact that Paul asks Apollos to travel to a church which Paul considered as one of his own implies that the relation between Paul and Apollos (*the brother*) was very good. But Apollos was no disciple of Paul, he made his plans independently and those plans did not call for a trip to Corinth just now. The words: *it was not at all his will* seem to imply that Apollos was no longer in Ephesus at the moment Paul wrote his letter. Neither does Paul convey the greetings of Apollos to the Corinthians. *He will come* some time. The request of the Corinthians had not moved Apollos.

13 The abrupt insertion of an admonition among a series of private communications occurs in more of Paul's letters (Rom. 16:17). The words remind us of 15:58, there is the same general tone and the same urging to a powerful spiritual life. *Watch ye*: this is a warning against a life that is not conscious. Watchfulness is necessary because a Christian is always menaced by many

---
[6] περὶ δὲ 'Απολλῶ may point to a question of the Corinthians (cf. 7:1 etc.).

dangers (Mt. 24:42; 25:13f). Christians must *stand fast*, i. e., they must not fall into sin, and this by the power of *faith*. Faith is mentioned rather infrequently in I Corinthians, but the passages where it occurs are significant (13:2, 13: 15:14, 17). Paul thus points to the central significance of faith. Faith is here to be understood of the act of faith.

14 Love must govern all of life (cf. ch. 13). That will restore every relationship. *In love*: in the sphere of love.

15 From this general admonition here inserted Paul derives the code of conduct which the Corinthians must follow with respect to Stephanas and the others with him. Stephanas was the messenger of the church but he had grounds for complaint and apparently he had poured out his heart to Paul. Probably the attitude of the Corinthians toward Stephanas had been the same as toward Paul: recognition without obedience. The Corinthians did *know the house of Stephanas*, but they did not treat it accordingly, although they had used him as their messenger.[7] Who Stephanas was we learn from the next clause: not only Stephanas but his house also was the *firstfruits* not just of Corinth but of *Achaia. House,* in Latin: *familia*: his slaves. Stephanas may have been converted at Athens (cf. *others with them;* Acts 17:34), although 1:16 points in another direction so that it appears better to assume that Stephanas was converted during Paul's first period at Corinth, when the gospel was preached to only a few (cf. Acts 18:5). In any case, the house of Stephanas was the first Christian family in the Roman province Achaia. This family deserved to be recognized as such, especially because they had been of assistance to the church, perhaps by hospitably opening their home. *To minister* cannot be taken of an official ministry in the church, because the subject of the verb is *they*, which refers to the whole family (Rom. 15:31). The actual content of the admonition with which vs. 15 begins follows in vs. 16.

16 *Ye also*: others apparently have subjected themselves. This subjection is due not only to the family of Stephanas but to all

---

[7] Perhaps because he was on his way to Ephesus for his own interest.

people like them (*such*). Other churches also had such prominent members and there the believers were in subjection to them. Those people were not ministers or elders, but co-laborers of Paul and thus they promoted the well-being of the churches to which they belonged (*everyone that helpeth*, etc.).

17 Vs. 17 also mentions something about Stephanas. Three Corinthians are with Paul at this moment and Paul *rejoices at their coming*. Though Paul does not say so, it is rather generally assumed that these three men brought the letter of the Corinthians to Paul. The words *that which was lacking on your part they supplied*, seem to point in that direction. These men may have functioned as messengers since they had of themselves conceived the plan of making a trip to Ephesus. Fortunatus and Achaicus are mentioned here for the first time. They may have been slaves of Stephanas. The reason for Paul's rejoicing is contained in the causal clause: Paul lacked something, not because the Corinthians had not done what they ought to do, but because Paul regretted that the Corinthians were not with him. That grief was taken away by the Corinthian delegation. That interpretation agrees with what we read in other parts of our epistle. There is no reference to any sorrow on the part of the haughty Corinthians because of Paul's absence. They may have asked for a visit on the part of the apostle (16:17) but they were content with sending a letter to which they expected a written answer. If there was something lacking at Corinth it was supplied by Paul's letter. But after hearing so many unfavorable reports about the Corinthians, the apostle had had no rest. How glad he was when the three messengers came to him with further news.

18 Vs. 18 explains how the messengers supplied what Paul was lacking. They *refreshed* the apostle, i. e., they put him to rest. The phrase: *my spirit and yours* is remarkable in view of the fact that the things Paul had heard about the Corinthians were far from favorable. But we must not forget that the Corinthians, in sending that letter to Paul and in asking him questions, had recognized his apostolic ministry. Moreover, Paul had also received encouraging information (1:4f.). For that reason, and in spite of everything that deserved rebuke, Paul is able to state that the messengers had *refreshed* his *spirit,* i. e., his person. But they refreshed also the *spirit* of the Corinthians because they carried out the latter's commission. For *acknowledge* see on vs. 16.

1-18   Vss. 1-18 give us an impression of the personal relations between Paul and the Corinthian church.

GREETINGS

16:19-24

19 The churches of Asia salute you. Aquila and Prisca salute you much in the Lord, with the church that is in their house.

20 All the brethren salute you. Salute one another with a holy kiss.

21 The salutation of me Paul with mine own hand.

22 If any man loveth not the Lord, let him be anathema. Maranatha.

23 The grace of the Lord Jesus Christ be with you.

24 My love be with you all in Christ Jesus. Amen.

19 *Asia*: the Roman province of Asia, where Paul sojourned and where he had preached. Some churches Paul had not visited personally (Laodicea, Colosse, Hierapolis, Col. 4:13), but he had connections with all of them and he could greet the Corinthians in the name of all of them. The Asian churches were interested in the churches in other countries. *Aquila* (here mentioned before his wife) *and Prisca* had provided a home for Paul at Corinth and their house had given shelter to the Corinthian church at the beginning (cf. Acts 18, also Rom. 16:5). Services had been held in their home of which Aquila probably was the leader. *In the Lord*: a Christian greeting, one which is demanded by Christ.

20 *All the brethren*: the brethren at Ephesus who were Paul's friends and of whom the Corinthians must have known many. *Holy kiss*: in eastern countries the kiss is used habitually as a greeting also among men. *Holy*: it was given in the name of the Lord in the public services (cf. *one another*). The holy kiss in the services is a token of unity. By kissing each other after having heard the reading of Paul's epistle, the Corinthians would indicate that they were united with one another and also with the churches in Asia.

21 A personal greeting of Paul. He writes it with *his own hand*, a kind of signature as a proof that the letter comes from

405

COMMENTARY ON FIRST CORINTHIANS

Paul (Gal. 6:11 et. al.). The Corinthians must have recognized Paul's writing. The signature is also a token of love.

22 This last admonition sums up everything that precedes. Paul has proclaimed that love is the great principle which should govern all actions. He who does not love the Lord walks on devious ways,[8] and is under God's judgment. *Anathema,* cf 12:3. *Let him be*: Paul addresses the whole congregation and announces God's judgment to everyone who does not love the Lord (cf. 3:17; Gal. 1:8). *Maranatha*: an Aramaic word which received a place in the Greek liturgy, of the early church.[9] Maranatha may mean: a) the Lord, or our Lord. has come, b) come O Lord, c) our Lord is a sign, d) thou art Lord. The second translation appears to be the best. It offers a parallel with Rev. 22:20. We can understand that the believers after the Lord's ascension were praying that He might return (I Thess. 1:10). There may have been a prayer formula in the Aramaic which was taken over by Greek speaking Christians (cf. Amen, Hosanna, Halleluja). A prayer of this kind also suits the context. After the many admonitions, after a passage like 15:23-28 and after the pronouncement of a curse on those who do not love the Lord, a prayer for the return of the Lord is a fitting climax. When He returns the battle will be finished and the judgment will come upon all who did not believe in Him.

23, 24 This is the usual blessing at the end. For *grace* see at 1:3. *My love*: love has such a large place in our letter that this assurance of the apostle's love should not surprise us. Christian love is founded on the work of Christ.

19-24 In these greetings Paul takes due account of the contents of the entire epistle. They reveal Paul's intense interest in the church at Corinth which he loved fervently in spite of all her sins.

---

[8] Paul's use of the verb φιλεῖν instead of ἀγαπᾶν is remarkable. The only other place where Paul uses φιλεῖν is Tit. 3:15. The question whether there is a real difference between these words is not settled. The verb may have been used here because of φίλημα which preceded. Or else Paul chose a weaker word to add emphasis to his pronouncement.

[9] Cf. *Did.* 10, 6. The word must have been in use in the oldest Aramaic speaking church

INDEX OF CHIEF SUBJECTS

INDEX OF SCRIPTURE REFERENCES
OLD TESTAMENT

NEW TESTAMENT